COMMUNITY PROGRAMS
TO PROMOTE
YOUTH
DEVELOPMENT

Committee on Community-Level Programs for Youth

Jacquelynne Eccles and Jennifer Appleton Gootman, *Editors*

Board on Children, Youth, and Families
Division of Behavioral and Social Sciences and Education

National Research Council
and
Institute of Medicine

NATIONAL ACADEMY PRESS
Washington, DC

NATIONAL ACADEMY PRESS   2101 Constitution Avenue, N.W.   Washington, D.C. 20418

NOTICE: The project that is the subject of this report was approved by the Governing Board of the National Research Council, whose members are drawn from the councils of the National Academy of Sciences, the National Academy of Engineering, and the Institute of Medicine. The members of the committee responsible for the report were chosen for their special competences and with regard for appropriate balance.

The study was supported by the Ford Foundation, the David and Lucile Packard Foundation, the William T. Grant Foundation, the Carnegie Corporation of New York, the Office of the Assistant Secretary of Planning and Evaluation of the U.S. Department of Health and Human Services, the U.S. Department of Housing and Urban Development, and the Office of Juvenile Justice and Delinquency Prevention of the U.S. Department of Justice. Any opinions, findings, conclusions, or recommendations expressed in this publication are those of the author(s) and do not necessarily reflect the view of the organizations or agencies that provided support for this project.

Suggested citation: National Research Council and Institute of Medicine (2002) *Community Programs to Promote Youth Development*. Committee on Community-Level Programs for Youth. Jacquelynne Eccles and Jennifer A. Gootman, eds. Board on Children, Youth, and Families, Division of Behavioral and Social Sciences and Education. Washington, DC: National Academy Press.

Library of Congress Cataloging-in-Publication Data

Community programs to promote youth development / Committee on Community-Level Programs for Youth ; Jacquelynne Eccles and Jennifer Appleton Gootman, editors ; Board on Children, Youth, and Families, Commission on Behavioral and Social Sciences and Education, National Research Council and Institute of Medicine.
    p. cm.
Includes bibliographical references and index.
  ISBN 0-309-07275-1 (hardcover)
  1. Youth—Services for—United States. 2. Teenagers—Services for—United States. I. Eccles, Jacquelynne S. II. Gootman, Jennifer Appleton. III. National Research Council (U.S.). Committee on Community-Level Programs for Youth. IV. National Research Council (U.S.). Board on Children, Youth, and Families. V. Institute of Medicine (U.S.)
  HV1431 .C657 2002
  362.7'083—dc21
                                    2001006226

Additional copies of this report are available for sale from National Academy Press, 2101 Constitution Avenue, N.W., Box 285, Washington, D.C. 20055. Call (800) 624-6242 or (202) 334-3313 (in the Washington metropolitan area).

This report is also available online at **http://www.nap.edu**

Printed in the United States of America

The photographs on the cover and used in this report are the work of young people from throughout the United States involved in a youth photography program. They are the work of Brittany Green, Lim Mom, Terrell Stewart, Shytise Taylor, and Lenna Vorn. The sponsor of the youth photography program was the EZ/EC Foundation Consortium, a partnership of 10 foundations formed to support implementation of the EZ/EC Initiative's 10-year effort to revitalize urban and rural areas of deep poverty, and to help document its lessons.

First Printing, February 2002
Second Printing, March 2003

THE NATIONAL ACADEMIES

National Academy of Sciences
National Academy of Engineering
Institute of Medicine
National Research Council

The **National Academy of Sciences** is a private, nonprofit, self-perpetuating society of distinguished scholars engaged in scientific and engineering research, dedicated to the furtherance of science and technology and to their use for the general welfare. Upon the authority of the charter granted to it by the Congress in 1863, the Academy has a mandate that requires it to advise the federal government on scientific and technical matters. Dr. Bruce M. Alberts is president of the National Academy of Sciences.

The **National Academy of Engineering** was established in 1964, under the charter of the National Academy of Sciences, as a parallel organization of outstanding engineers. It is autonomous in its administration and in the selection of its members, sharing with the National Academy of Sciences the responsibility for advising the federal government. The National Academy of Engineering also sponsors engineering programs aimed at meeting national needs, encourages education and research, and recognizes the superior achievements of engineers. Dr. Wm. A. Wulf is president of the National Academy of Engineering.

The **Institute of Medicine** was established in 1970 by the National Academy of Sciences to secure the services of eminent members of appropriate professions in the examination of policy matters pertaining to the health of the public. The Institute acts under the responsibility given to the National Academy of Sciences by its congressional charter to be an adviser to the federal government and, upon its own initiative, to identify issues of medical care, research, and education. Dr. Kenneth I. Shine is president of the Institute of Medicine.

The **National Research Council** was organized by the National Academy of Sciences in 1916 to associate the broad community of science and technology with the Academy's purposes of furthering knowledge and advising the federal government. Functioning in accordance with general policies determined by the Academy, the Council has become the principal operating agency of both the National Academy of Sciences and the National Academy of Engineering in providing services to the government, the public, and the scientific and engineering communities. The Council is administered jointly by both Academies and the Institute of Medicine. Dr. Bruce M. Alberts and Dr. Wm. A. Wulf are chairman and vice chairman, respectively, of the National Research Council.

COMMITTEE ON COMMUNITY-LEVEL PROGRAMS FOR YOUTH

JACQUELYNNE ECCLES (*Chair*), Institute for Social Research, University of Michigan
CHERYL ALEXANDER, School of Hygiene and Public Health, Johns Hopkins University
BRETT BROWN, Child Trends, Washington, DC
SARAH BROWN, National Campaign to Prevent Teen Pregnancy, Washington, DC
KENYON S. CHAN, Bellarmine College of Liberal Arts, Loyola Marymount University
ELIZABETH COLSON, Department of Anthropology, University of California, Berkeley
THOMAS COOK, Institute for Policy Research, Northwestern University
PETER EDELMAN, Georgetown University Law Center
CASWELL EVANS, National Institutes of Health, Bethesda, MD
RONALD FERGUSON, John F. Kennedy School of Government, Harvard University
ROBERT GRANGER, Manpower Demonstration Research Corporation, New York, NY*
TERESA LAFROMBOISE, School of Education, Stanford University
REED LARSON, Department of Human Development and Family Studies, University of Illinois, Urbana-Champaign
MILBREY McLAUGHLIN, School of Education, Stanford University
ROBERT PLOTNICK, Daniel J. Evans School of Public Affairs, University of Washington
ZENA STEIN, Mailman School of Public Health and the Sergievsky Center, Columbia University

ELENA O. NIGHTINGALE, *Scholar-in-Residence*

JENNIFER A. GOOTMAN, *Study Director*
AMY GAWAD, *Research Associate*
REBEKAH PINTO, *Senior Project Assistant*

---

*Member until March 2000.

FORUM ON ADOLESCENCE

DAVID A. HAMBURG (*Chair*), Carnegie Corporation of New York (President Emeritus)

HUDA AKIL, Mental Health Research Institute, University of Michigan, Ann Arbor

CHERYL ALEXANDER, Center for Adolescent Health, Johns Hopkins University

CLAIRE BRINDIS, Institute for Health Policy Studies, Division of Adolescent Medicine, University of California, San Francisco

GREG DUNCAN, Institute for Policy Research, Northwestern University

JACQUELYNNE ECCLES, Institute for Social Research, University of Michigan

ABIGAIL ENGLISH, Center for Adolescent Health & the Law, Chapel Hill, North Carolina

EUGENE GARCIA, School of Education, University of California, Berkeley

HELENE KAPLAN, Skadden, Arps, Slate, Meagher, and Flom, New York

IRIS F. LITT, Division of Adolescent Medicine, Stanford University

JOHN MERROW, The Merrow Report, New York

ANNE C. PETERSEN, W.K. Kellogg Foundation, Battle Creek, Michigan

KAREN PITTMAN, International Youth Foundation, Baltimore

ANNE PUSEY, Jane Goodall Institute's Center, University of Minnesota

MICHAEL RUTTER, Institute of Psychiatry, University of London

STEPHEN A. SMALL, Department of Child and Family Studies, University of Wisconsin, Madison

CAMILLE ZUBRINSKY CHARLES, Department of Sociology, University of Pennsylvania

BARUCH FISCHHOFF (*Liaison from the IOM Council*), Social and Decision Sciences, Carnegie Mellon University

ELEANOR E. MACCOBY (*Liaison from the Commission on Behavioral and Social Sciences and Education*), Department of Psychology Emerita, Stanford University

Acknowledgments

The Committee on Community-Level Programs for Youth is a project of the National Research Council (NRC) and the Institute of Medicine (IOM). This report is the product of a 2-year project during which a 15-member committee evaluated and integrated the current science of adolescent health and development with research and findings related to program design, implementation, and evaluation of community programs for youth. The funding for this project was provided by a diverse group of public and private sponsors: the Office of the Assistant Secretary for Planning and Evaluation in the U.S. Department of Health and Human Services; the Office of Juvenile Justice and Delinquency Prevention in the U.S. Department of Justice; the Office of Research, Evaluation, and Monitoring in the U.S. Department of Housing and Urban Development; the David and Lucile Packard Foundation; the William T. Grant Foundation; and the Ford Foundation. We are also grateful for the support provided to Jacquelynne Eccles, committee chair, by the John D. and Catherine T. MacArthur Foundation and the Center for Advanced Study in the Behavioral Sciences, during the time that she chaired this committee.

Beyond the expertise and hard work of the committee, we were fortunate to have many leaders in the field enthusiastically participate in this project. These individuals shared their knowledge and years of experience as researchers, evaluators, practitioners, policy makers, and funders of youth programs and interventions. We are thankful for their time and their intellectual insights.

During the planning and early working stages of this project, a small group of well-respected authorities in the area of youth development advised the staff and the committee. We wish to thank these individuals for sharing their wisdom and for their enduring commitment to issues affecting the health, development, and well-being of young people and the institutions that serve them: Peter L. Benson, Search Institute; Michele Cahill, Carnegie Corporation of New York; Jean Grossman, Public/Private Ventures; Richard Murphy, Academy for Educational Development; Karen Pittman, International Youth Foundation/Forum for Youth Investment; and Constancia Warren, Academy for Educational Development.

In October 1999 the committee convened a one-day Workshop on Opportunities to Promote Child and Adolescent Development During After-School Hours. Participants included leading researchers, policy makers, practitioners, and funders from the fields of education, research and evaluation, adolescent development, and program design and delivery: Michele Cahill, Carnegie Corporation of New York; Jennifer Davis, Office of the Mayor of Boston, Massachusetts; Joy Dryfoos, Hastings-on-Hudson, New York; Robert Halpern, Erikson Institute; Karen Hein, William T. Grant Foundation; Robin L. Jarrett, University of Illinois, Urbana-Champaign; Joan Lombardi, Bush Center in Child Development and Social Policy; Richard Negron, Children's Aid Society; Terry Peterson, U.S. Department of Education; Karen Pittman, International Youth Foundation/Forum for Youth Investment; Jane Quinn, DeWitt-Wallace Reader's Digest Fund; Elizabeth Reisner, Policy Studies Associates; Carla Sanger, LA's Best; Carter Savage, Boys and Girls Clubs of America; Constancia Warren, Academy for Educational Development; and Heather Weiss, Harvard Family Research Project.

In January 2000 the committee convened a second one-day Workshop on the Science of Youth Development Programs. Another set of leaders from diverse fields presented their work along with important insights about future directions and current needs: Dale Blyth, Center for

4-H Youth Development; Diane Chamberlain, Valley Community Clinic; Michelle Alberti Gambone, Gambone and Associates; Douglas Kirby, ETR Associates; David Milner, Community Impact! USA; Constancia Warren, Academy for Educational Development; Heather Weiss, Harvard Family Research Project; Kendra Wells, 4-H Youth Development; Gary Yates The California Wellness Foundation; and Hanh Cao Yu, Social Policy Research Associates.

In addition to formal workshops, a number of individuals were invited to make presentations and participate in discussions at the regularly scheduled meetings of the committee. In October 1999, we were fortunate to participate in a panel discussion about community programs and suggested future research directions with Ann Segal, Office of the Assistant Secretary for Planning and Evaluation of the U.S. Department of Health and Human Services; Pam Stevens, Edna McConnell Clark Foundation; and Xavier De Souza Briggs, Division of Research, Evaluation, and Monitoring of the U.S. Department of Housing and Urban Development. At the same meeting, Jodie Roth-Herbst, Center for Children and Families, Teachers College, Columbia University, and Jean Grossman, Public/Private Ventures, summarized research on preventing risk behaviors and promoting youth development. Lloyd Kolbe, Division of Adolescent and School Health at the Centers for Disease Control and Prevention, also discussed the threats to adolescent health and well-being.

In March 2000, several people described public and private supports that exist at the national, state, and local levels and ways in which intermediary organizations are organizing youth programming at the community level. Karen Pittman, International Youth Foundation/Forum for Youth Investment, provided an overview of major youth initiatives and organizations and suggested ways in which they fit together. Dale Blyth, Center for 4-H Youth Development, University of Minnesota, and Jeffrey Arnett, University of Maryland, provided their perspectives on positive youth development and suggested developmental milestones that mark or facilitate the end of adolescence and the transition to adulthood. Karen Reivich and Andrew Shatteé of the University of Pennsylvania summarized their research on the Penn Prevention Project. Michele Cahill, Carnegie Corporation of New York, described the array of activities that currently make up youth development programming. Jean Grossman, Public/Private Ventures, discussed measurement tools, indicators, and processes for youth programs. Finally, Richard Murphy and Constancia Warren of the Academy for Educational Development, discussed policy and system-level supports and barriers for youth development programs.

Two committee members spent a day with Richard Catalano at the University of Washington discussing the work he and his colleagues at the Social Development Research Group had done reviewing existing community-based programs for youth. Three other committee members and one staff person spent time with Bruce Saito and his staff at the Los Angeles Conservation Corps learning about their programs and talking with youth participants.

We also wish to acknowledge several consultants who either wrote or helped to write documents that were incorporated into this report: Jonathan Zaff, Child Trends, summarized the data on participation levels in youth programs and the measurement of positive youth outcomes; Naweko Dial, a graduate student at Stanford University, reviewed youth program opportunities on Indian reservations; Candice Jones, a law student at Georgetown University, collected information on youth development funding; Joanna Burton, a doctoral student at the University of Illinois-Champaign and an intern with the National Academies, helped review the research on community, school, and family influences on adolescent development; and Janice Templeton, a doctoral student at the University of Michigan, made an extraordinary commitment to reviewing and synthesizing the vast collection of evaluation research on community programs for youth and helped draft Chapters 6 and 7 of this report.

Dozens of scientists provided articles, papers, chapters, and books. We are most appreciative of the responses to our requests for information from Robert Blum, Center for Adolescent Health, University of Minnesota; James Connell, Institute for Research and Reform in Education; Delbert Elliot, Center for the Study and Prevention of Violence, University of Colorado, Boulder; Thaddeus Ferber, International Youth Foundation/Forum for Youth Investment; Michele Gambone, Gambone and Associates; Jean Grossman, Public/Private Ventures; Merita Irby, International Youth Foundation/Forum for Youth Investment; Douglas Kirby, ETR Associates; Bonnie Politz, Academy for Educational Development; and Gary Walker, Public/Private Ventures.

The photographs on the cover and used in this report are the work of young people from throughout the United States involved in a youth photography program. Professional photographer Steven Shames taught them to use cameras to capture positive community activities and community change. The photos represent young people engaged in community service, arts, music, recreation, and mentoring. They are the work of Brittany Green, Lim Mom, Terrell Stewart, Shytise Taylor, and Lenna Vorn. The sponsor of the youth photography program was the EZ/EC Foundation Consortium, a partnership of 10 foundations formed to support implementation of the EZ/EC Initiative's 10-year effort to revitalize urban and rural areas of deep poverty, and to help document its lessons.

This report has been reviewed in draft form by individuals chosen for their diverse perspectives and technical expertise, in accordance with procedures approved by the Report Review Committee of the NRC. The purpose of this independent review is to provide candid and critical comments that will assist the institution in making the published report as sound as possible and to ensure that the report meets institutional standards for objectivity, evidence, and responsiveness to the study charge. The review comments and draft manuscript remain confidential to protect the integrity of the deliberative process.

We thank the following individuals for their participation in the review of this report: Anthony Biglan, Oregon Research Institute, Eugene, OR; Angela Diaz, Community Medicine, Mt. Sinai Hospital, New York; Kenneth A. Dodge, Center for Child and Family Policy, Duke University; Greg J. Duncan, Institute for Policy Research/School of Education and Social Policy, Northwestern University; Paula Duncan, Agency for Human Services, State of Vermont; Lorraine V. Klerman, Maternal and Child Health Program, School of Public Health, University of Alabama; Jane Quinn, The Children's Aid Society, New York; Robert J. Sampson, Department of Sociology, University of Chicago; Shepherd Smith, Institute for Youth Development, Sterling, VA; Wendy Wheeler, National 4-H Council, Chevy Chase, MD; and Brian Wilcox, Center on Children, Families, and the Law, Lincoln, NE.

Although the reviewers listed above have provided many constructive comments and suggestions, they were not asked to endorse the conclusions or recommendations nor did they see the final draft of the report before its release. The review of this report was overseen by Beatrix Hamburg, Department of Psychiatry, Cornell University Medical College. Appointed by the National Research Council, she was responsible for making certain that an independent examination of this report was carried out in accordance with institutional procedures and that all review comments were carefully considered. Responsibility for the final content of this report rests entirely with the authoring panel and the institution.

The committee wishes to recognize the important contributions and support provided by several individuals connected to the NRC and the IOM. We thank the members of the Board on Children, Youth, and Families (BOCYF), under the leadership of Evan Charney, and the Forum on Adolescence, under the leadership of David Hamburg. We also thank Kenneth Shine, IOM president; Susanne Stoiber, IOM executive officer; Barbara Torrey, executive director of the NRC's Division of Behavioral and Social Sciences (DBASSE); Faith Mitchell, DBASSE deputy director; and Jane Ross, director of the Center for Economic and Social Sciences for their steadfast support of the project and their critical review of multiple drafts of the report.

It is because of the talent and hard work of Michele Kipke, director of the Board on Children, Youth, and Families, in developing this project and providing encouragement and leadership throughout, that this project was undertaken and completed. We are appreciative of the guidance and mentoring of Elena O. Nightingale, scholar-in-residence, who provided support during each phase of the committee's work. We are indebted to Eugenia Grohman, associate director for reports of DBASSE, who patiently worked with us through several revisions, and Christine McShane, who provided superb editorial assistance. Mary Graham, Maura Shea, and Michel Rosst of the BOCYF provided advice and assistance with report dissemination, as has Vanee Vines of the National Academies' Office of News and Public Information.

Finally, it is important to acknowledge the exceptional contributions of the National Academies staff who worked on this report. Amy Gawad, research associate, and Rebekah Pinto, senior project assistant, played an invaluable role in collecting, summarizing, and organizing background materials and managing the numerous and often complicated administrative and research responsibilities. Thanks are also due to Drusilla Barnes, senior project assistant, for handling primary administrative responsibilities during the first phase of the committee's work.

Jacquelynne Eccles, *Chair*
Jennifer A. Gootman, *Study Director*
Committee on Community-Level Programs for Youth

Contents

COMMUNITY
PROGRAMS
TO PROMOTE
YOUTH
DEVELOPMENT

Executive Summary

dolescence is the pivotal period between childhood and adulthood. It is the time when youth need to acquire the attitudes, competencies, values, and social skills that will carry them forward to successful adulthood. It is also the time when they need to avoid choices and behaviors that will limit their future potential. Parents and families play a crucial role in helping young people navigate this phase. In the past, schools, neighborhoods, and communities extended and enhanced positive development and supported young people. Indeed, an enduring image of American life is the participation of neighbors and community members watching out for children, taking responsibility for their safety and well-being, and helping to steer them in the right direction.

In recent decades, a number of social forces have changed both the landscape of family and community life and the expectations for young people. A combination of factors have weakened the informal community support once available to young people: high rates of family mobility; greater anonymity in neighborhoods, where more parents are at work and out of the home and neighborhood for long periods, and in schools, which have become larger and much more heterogeneous; extensive media exposure

1

to themes of violence and heavy use and abuse of drugs and alcohol; and, in some cases, the deterioration and disorganization of neighborhoods and schools as a result of crime, drugs, and poverty. At the same time, today's world has become increasingly complex, technical, and multicultural, placing new and challenging demands on young people in terms of education, training, and the social and emotional skills needed in a highly competitive environment. Finally, the length of adolescence has extended to the mid- to late twenties, and the pathways to adulthood have become less clear and more numerous.

Concerns about youth are at the center of many policy debates. The future well-being of the country depends on raising a generation of skilled, competent, and responsible adults. Yet at least 25 percent of adolescents in the United States are at serious risk of not achieving "productive adulthood" and face such risks as substance abuse, adolescent pregnancy, school failure, and involvement with the juvenile justice system. Depending on their circumstances and choices, they may carry those risks into their adult lives. Public investments in programs to counter such trends have grown significantly over the past decade or so. For the most part, these efforts have targeted specific problems and threats to young people. Substantial public health investments have also been made to prevent such problems as teen smoking, sexually transmitted diseases, unintended pregnancy, and alcohol and other drug use. Major funding has been allocated to the prevention and control of juvenile delinquency and youth crime.

These efforts have led to some successes. On one hand, adolescent well-being and behavior have shown substantial improvement in some areas since the late 1980s. Serious violent juvenile crime has declined, teen pregnancy has decreased, and more young people are graduating from high school and participating in volunteer and community service. On the other hand, cigarette smoking, HIV infection, school violence, and obesity have increased during this period, particularly among youth in high-risk urban neighborhoods and very poor rural communities. In addition, many youth are entering the labor market with inadequate knowledge skills, such as the ability to communicate effectively, resolve conflicts, and prepare for and succeed in a job interview.

Continued efforts to prevent and control these and other problems are clearly needed. An exclusive focus on problems, however, narrows the vision that society should have for all of its young people. Many who study adolescent development and work with young people have increasingly come to believe that being problem-free is not fully prepared. Beyond eliminating problems, one needs skills, knowledge, and a variety of other personal and social assets to function well during adolescence and adulthood. Thus a broader, more holistic view of helping youth to realize their full potential is gaining wider credence in the world of policy and practice.

This approach is not viewed as replacing the focus on preventing problems, but rather creating a larger framework that promotes positive outcomes for all young people. Public and private organizations are now engaged in a wide array of activities that fall within this framework. Such programs include mentoring, school-based community service programs and other volunteer activities, school-to-work transition programs, parenting skills, arts and recreation activities, among others. All are part of a new direction in public policy that places children and adolescents once again at the center of neighborhood and community life, where they can engage with caring adults inside and outside their families, develop a sense of security and personal identity, and learn rules of behavior, expectations, values, morals, and skills needed to move into healthy and productive adulthood.

Recent increases in funding from federal agencies, foundations, state and local governments, and the private sector have given impetus to these efforts and, at the same time, focused attention on the need to assess program effects and provide objective, reliable information to guide future investment. There is great diversity among the organizations that offer these programs, as well as the programs' emphases, curricula, and populations served. Organizations offering youth programs range from large national youth-serving agencies, such as 4-H, Boys and Girls Clubs, Girls, Inc., Boy Scouts, and Girl Scouts, to more local youth sports organizations, community centers, schools, libraries, faith-based institutions, museums, arts centers, service clubs, and numerous other grassroots organizations. Programs may target youth broadly or focus on a subset of them, defined by characteristics such as neighborhood, ethnic group, or special need. The focus of these programs may be general or specific (e.g., centered on sports, religion, or academic success).

This report focuses broadly on community-based programs for youth and examines what is known about their design, implementation, and evaluation. These are programs located in the communities in which the youth live. In the context of this report, communities may include neighborhoods, block groups, towns, and cities, as well as nongeographically defined communities based on family connections and shared interests or values.

THE COMMITTEE CHARGE

The Committee on Community-Level Programs for Youth was established by the Board on Children, Youth, and Families and the Committee on Adolescent Health and Development (formerly the Forum on Adolescence). The specific charge to the committee was:

- Review and synthesize available data on community interventions and programs to promote positive outcomes for adolescent development;
- Assess the strengths and limitations of data sources and indicators commonly used to characterize youth health, development, and well-being;
- Assess the strengths and limitations of methodologies and approaches used to evaluate these activities; and
- Identify gaps and central questions for the design of a unified conceptual framework and research agenda to promote the healthy development of youth.

To the extent feasible, the committee was asked to identify those programs with sufficiently strong evidence to suggest that they could serve as models for communities that are enhancing their youth programs.

Support for the committee's work came from private foundations and federal agencies. All those supporting this study share a common desire to understand more about how community programs for youth can be designed to promote the positive development of youth. Foundations seek guidance about wise investments in adolescent programming; policy makers seek guidance regarding effective prevention and youth development approaches; and program practitioners and managers seek assistance as they work to design and evaluate their programs.

The committee examined programs that target young people ages 10 to 18. While we made the decision to focus our review and analysis on programs promoting a "youth development" perspective, we rejected the often polarized view of youth programming as either "prevention/problem-centered" or " youth development" centered. Our view is that both approaches are valuable and necessary and that, in practice, the distinction between the two is often blurred.

The committee turned to multiple types and sources of information for this report—theory, practical experience, and qualitative and quantitative research and data—in order to gain as broad a perspective as possible on positive youth development. Based on its analysis of this information, the committee generated a set of conclusions and recommendations organized around two primary themes: (a) policy and practice; and (b) research, evaluation, and data collection.

In beginning its work, the committee agreed on a set of four core concepts that serve as a foundation for this report:

- Some youth are doing very well;
- Some youth are taking dangerous risks and doing poorly;
- All young people need a variety of experiences to develop to their full potential;
- Some young people have unmet needs and are particularly at risk of participating in problem behaviors (e.g., dropping out of school, participating in violent behavior). These include young people who often, but by no means always, live in high-risk neighborhoods, are poor, experience repeated racial and ethnic discrimination, and have a substantial amount of unsupervised time during nonschool hours. Other youth who are in special need of more programs include youth with disabilities of all kinds, youth from troubled family situations, and youth with special needs for places to find emotional support.

Although the committee stresses the importance of providing support for all youth regardless of economic status, we were also particularly interested in understanding community programs for young people who have the greatest need coupled with the fewest resources. We found very little research to talk specifically about the kinds of programs that would be particularly appropriate for these disadvantaged and underserved youth, including youth who are gay and lesbian, youth who are bullied at school, and youth who have experienced sexual and other forms of harassment.

POLICY AND PRACTICE

Promoting Adolescent Development at the Program Level

Understanding adolescent development and the factors contributing to the healthy development of all young people is critical to the design and implementation of community programs for youth. Consequently

---

BOX ES-1
Personal and Social Assets That Facilitate Positive
Youth Development

Physical development
- Good health habits
- Good health risk management skills

Intellectual development
- Knowledge of essential life skills
- Knowledge of essential vocational skills
- School success
- Rational habits of mind—critical thinking and reasoning skills
- In-depth knowledge of more than one culture
- Good decision-making skills
- Knowledge of skills needed to navigate through multiple cultural contexts

Psychological and emotional development
- Good mental health including positive self-regard
- Good emotional self-regulation skills
- Good coping skills

---

the committee began its work by identifying a set of personal and social assets that increase the healthy development and well-being of adolescents and facilitate a successful transition from childhood, through adolescence, and into adulthood. We grouped these assets into four broad developmental domains: physical, intellectual, psychological and emotional, and social development. Box ES-1 summarizes the four domains and specifies the assets within each.

Conclusions

❑ Individuals do not necessarily need the entire range of assets to thrive; in fact, various combinations of assets across domains reflect equally positive adolescent development.

- Good conflict resolution skills
- Mastery motivation and positive achievement motivation
- Confidence in one's personal efficacy
- "Planfulness"—planning for the future and future life events
- Sense of personal autonomy/responsibility for self
- Optimism coupled with realism
- Coherent and positive personal and social identity
- Prosocial and culturally sensitive values
- Spirituality or a sense of a "larger" purpose in life
- Strong moral character
- A commitment to good use of time

Social development
- Connectedness—perceived good relationships and trust with parents, peers, and some other adults
- Sense of social place/integration—being connected and valued by larger social networks
- Attachment to prosocial/conventional institutions, such as school, church, nonschool youth programs
- Ability to navigate in multiple cultural contexts
- Commitment to civic engagement

❑ Having more assets is better than having few. Although strong assets in one category can offset weak assets in another category, life is easier to manage if one has assets in all four domains.

❑ Continued exposure to positive experiences, settings, and people, as well as opportunities to gain and refine life skills, supports young people in the acquisition and growth of these assets.

Moving now from the individual to the environment, young people develop these positive personal and social assets in settings that have the following features.

- Physical and psychological safety and security;
- Structure that is developmentally appropriate, with clear expectations for behavior as well as increasing opportunities to make

decisions, to participate in governance and rule-making, and to take on leadership roles as one matures and gains more expertise;
- Emotional and moral support;
- Opportunities for adolescents to experience supportive adult relationships;
- Opportunities to learn how to form close, durable human relationships with peers that support and reinforce healthy behaviors;
- Opportunities to feel a sense of belonging and being valued;
- Opportunities to develop positive social values and norms;
- Opportunities for skill building and mastery;
- Opportunities to develop confidence in one's abilities to master one's environment (a sense of personal efficacy);
- Opportunities to make a contribution to one's community and to develop a sense of mattering; and
- Strong links between families, schools, and broader community resources.

Table ES-1 provides details on the features of positive developmental settings.

Conclusions

❑ Since these features typically work together in synergistic ways, programs with more features are likely to provide better supports for young people's positive development.

❑ Community programs can expand the opportunities for youth to acquire personal and social assets and to experience the broad range of features of positive developmental settings.

Among other things, community programs can incorporate opportunities for physical, cognitive, and social and emotional development; opportunities to address issues of ethnic identity, sexual identity, and intergroup relationships; opportunities for community involvement and service; and opportunities to interact with caring adults and a diversity of peers who hold positive social norms and have high life goals and expectations.

Recommendation 1—Community programs for youth should be based on a developmental framework that supports the acquisition of personal and social assets in an environment, and through activities, that

TABLE ES-1   Features of Positive Developmental Settings

	Descriptors	Opposite Poles
Physical and Psychological Safety	Safe and health-promoting facilities; practice that increases safe peer group interaction and decreases unsafe or confrontational peer interactions.	Physical and health dangers; fear; feeling of insecurity, sexual and physical harassment; and verbal abuse.
Appropriate Structure	Limit setting; clear and consistent rules and expectations; firm-enough control; continuity and predictability; clear boundaries; and age-appropriate monitoring.	Chaotic; disorganized; laissez-faire; rigid; overcontrolled; and autocratic.
Supportive Relationships	Warmth; closeness; connectedness; good communication; caring; support; guidance; secure attachment; and responsiveness.	Cold; distant; overcontrolling; ambiguous support; untrustworthy; focused on winning; inattentive; unresponsive; and rejecting.
Opportunities to Belong	Opportunities for meaningful inclusion, regardless of one's gender, ethnicity, sexual orientation, or disabilities; social inclusion, social engagement and integration; opportunities for socio-cultural identity formation; and support for cultural and bicultural competence.	Exclusion; marginalization; and intergroup conflict.
Positive Social Norms	Rules of behavior; expectations; injunctions; ways of doing things; values and morals; and obligations for service.	Normlessness; anomie; laissez-faire practices; antisocial and amoral norms; norms that encourage violence; reckless behavior; consumerism; poor health practices; and conformity.
Support for Efficacy and Mattering	Youth-based; empowerment practices that support autonomy; making a real difference in one's community; and being taken seriously. Practices that include enabling; responsibility granting; and meaningful challenge. Practices that focus on improvement rather than on relative current performance levels.	Unchallenging; overcontrolling; disempowering; and disabling. Practices that undermine motivation and desire to learn, such as excessive focus on current relativeperformance level rather than improvement.

continued

TABLE ES-1   *Continued*

	Descriptors	Opposite Poles
Opportunities for Skill Building	Opportunities to learn physical, intellectual, psychological, emotional, and social skills; exposure to intentional learning experiences; opportunities to learn cultural literacies, media literacy, communication skills, and good habits of mind; preparation for adult employment; and opportunities to develop social and cultural capital.	Practice that promotes bad physical habits and habits of mind; and practice that undermines school and learning.
Integration of Family, School, and Community Efforts	Concordance; coordination; and synergy among family, school, and community.	Discordance; lack of communication; and conflict.

promote both current adolescent well-being and future successful transitions to adulthood.

Serving Diverse Youth at the Community Level

Many different individual organizations provide community programs for youth; each has its own unique approach and activities. How communities organize youth policies, as well as support individual programs, also varies from community to community. For example, the organizing body might be the mayor's office, a local government agency, or a community foundation. A private intermediary organization or an individual charismatic leader, such as a minister or a rabbi, might also organize such efforts. However, it is often the case that there is no single person or group that is responsible for either monitoring the range and quality of community programs for youth or making sure that information about community programs is easily accessible to members of the community.

Conclusion

❑ Adolescents who spend time in communities that are rich in developmental opportunities for them experience less risk and show evidence of higher rates of positive development. A diversity of program opportunities in each community is more likely to support broad adolescent development and attract the interest of and meet the needs of a greater number of youth.

Community programs for youth differ in their objectives, design, approach, and focus, and some may choose to emphasize certain program features over others. Even with the best staff and best funding, no single program can necessarily serve all young people or incorporate all of the features of positive developmental settings. The complexities of adolescent development and the increasing diversity of the country make the heterogeneity of young people in communities both a norm and a challenge. Therefore, effective programs must be flexible enough to adapt to this diversity among the young people they serve and the communities in which they operate.

Recommendation 2—Communities should provide an ample array of program opportunities that appeal to and meet the needs of diverse youth, and should do so through local entities that can coordinate such work across the entire community. Particular attention should be placed on programs for disadvantaged and underserved youth.

Recommendation 3—To increase the likelihood that an ample array of program opportunities will be available, communities should put in place some locally appropriate mechanism for monitoring the availability, accessibility, and quality of programs for youth in their community.

Recommendation 4—Private and public funders should provide the resources needed at the community level to develop and support community-wide programming that is orderly, coordinated, and evaluated in reasonable ways. In addition to support at the community level, this is likely to involve support for intermediary organizations and collaborative teams that include researchers, practitioners, funders, and policy makers.

RESEARCH, EVALUATION, AND DATA COLLECTION

The multiple groups concerned about community programs for youth—policy makers, families, program developers and practitioners, program staff, and young people themselves—have in common the desire to know whether programs make a difference in the lives of young people, their families, and their communities. Some are interested in learning about the effectiveness of specific details in a program; some about the effects of a given program; some about the overall effect of a set of programs together; and others about the effects of related kinds of programs. Research, program evaluation, and social indicator data can help improve the design and delivery of programs, and in doing so can play a significant role in answering such questions and improving the well-being and future success of young people.

Research

The committee first reviewed research on both adolescent development and the features of positive developmental settings that support it. In both cases, the research base is just becoming comprehensive enough to allow for tentative conclusions about the individual assets that characterize positive development and features of settings that support it. The committee used a variety of criteria to suggest the tentative lists of both important individual-level assets and features of settings that support positive development outlined in Box ES-1 and Table ES-1. These suggestions are based on scientific evidence from short- and long-term experimental and observational studies, one-time large-scale survey studies, and longitudinal survey studies reviewed by the committee. However, much more comprehensive work is needed.

Conclusions

❑ More comprehensive longitudinal research, that either builds on current efforts or involves new efforts, is needed on a wider range of populations that follows children and adolescents well into adulthood in order to understand which assets are most important to adolescent development and which patterns of assets are linked to particular types of successful adult transitions in various cultural contexts.

❑ Despite its limitations, research in all settings in the lives of adolescents—families, schools, and communities—is yielding consistent evidence that there are specific features of settings that support positive youth development and that these features can be incorporated into community programs

❑ In the committee's judgment, current evidence supports the replication of a few specific integrated programs for positive youth development: the Teen Outreach Program, Big Brothers, Big Sisters, and Quantum Opportunities are three prime examples.

Very few integrated programs have received the kind of comprehensive experimental evaluation necessary to make a firm recommendation about replicating the program in its entirety across the country. However, there is sufficient evidence from a variety of sources to make recommendations about fundamental principles of supportive developmental settings and some specific aspects of programs that can be used to design community programs for youth. These are captured by the features of supportive settings outlined in Table ES-1.

Recommendation 5—Federal agencies that fund research on adolescent health, development, and well-being, such as the Department of Health and Human Services, the Department of Justice, and the Department of Education, should build into their portfolios new or more comprehensive longitudinal and experimental research on the personal and social assets needed to promote the healthy development and well-being of adolescents and to promote the successful transition from childhood through adolescence and into adulthood.

Recommendation 6—Public and private funders should support research on whether the features of positive developmental settings identified in this report are the most important features of community programs for youth. This research should encourage program design and implementation that meets the diverse needs of an increasingly heterogeneous population of youth.

Program Evaluation

Evaluation and ongoing program study can provide important insights to inform program design, selection, and modification. Program evaluation can also help funders and policy makers make informed choices about which programs to fund for which groups of youth. The desire to conduct high-quality evaluation can help program staff clarify their objectives and decide which types of evidence will be most useful in determining if these objectives have been met. Ongoing program study and evaluation can also be used by program staff, program participants, and funders to track program objectives; this is typically done by establishing a system for ongoing data collection that measures the extent to which various aspects of the programs are being delivered, how are they delivered, who is providing these services, and who is receiving these services. Such information can provide useful information to program staff to help them make changes to improve program effectiveness. Finally, program evaluation can test both new and very well developed program designs by assessing the immediate, observable results of the program outcomes and benefits associated with participation in the program.

Such summative evaluation can be done in conjunction with strong theory-based evaluation or as a more preliminary assessment of the potential usefulness of novel programs and quite complex social experiments in which there is no well-specified theory of change. In other words, program evaluation and study can help foster accountability, determine whether programs make a difference, and provide staff with the information they need to improve service delivery.

Clearly there are many purposes for evaluation. Not surprisingly then, there are different opinions among service practitioners, researchers, policy makers, and funders about the most appropriate and useful methods for evaluating community programs for youth. In part, these disagreements reflect different goals and different questions about youth programs. They also reflect philosophical differences about the purposes of evaluation and nature of program development. Program practitioners, policy makers, program evaluators, and others studying programs should decide exactly which questions they want answered before deciding on the most appropriate methods. The most comprehensive experimental evaluation, which involves assessment of the quality of implementation as well as outcomes, is quite expensive and involves a variety of methods. It also provides the most comprehensive information regarding both the effectiveness of specific programs and the reasons for their effectiveness.

Conclusions

❑ Very few high-quality comprehensive experimental evaluations of community programs for youth have adequately assessed the impact of the programs on adolescents.

❑ Some high-quality experimental and quasi-experimental evaluations show positive effects on a variety of outcomes, including both increases in the psychological and social assets of youth and decreases in the incidence of such problem behaviors as early pregnancy, drug use, and delinquency.

❑ Experimental designs are still the best method for estimating the impact of a program on its participants and should be used when this is the goal of the evaluation.

Comprehensive program evaluation is an even better way to gather complete information about programs. It requires asking a number of questions through various methods. The committee identified six fundamental questions that should be considered in comprehensive evaluations:

- Is the theory of the program that is being evaluated explicit and plausible?
- How well has the program theory been implemented in the sites studied?
- In general, is the program effective and, in particular, is it effective with specific subpopulations of young people?
- Whether it is or is not effective, why is this the case?
- What is the value of the program?
- What recommendations about action should be made?

All six questions may not be answered well in one study; several evaluative studies may be needed to address these questions. Thus comprehensive experimental evaluation can be quite expensive and time-consuming—but provides the most information about program design, as well as fundamental questions about human development. Thus, it is particularly useful to both the policy and research communities, as well as the practice community.

In order to generate the kind of information about community programs for youth needed to justify large-scale expenditures on programs and to further fundamental understanding of the role of community programs in youth development, comprehensive experimental program evaluations should be used when:

- the object of study is a program component that repeatedly occurs across many of the organizations currently providing community services to youth;
- an established national organization provides the program being evaluated through many local affiliates; and
- theoretically sound ideas for a new demonstration program or project emerge, and pilot work indicates that these ideas can be implemented in other contexts.

Comprehensive experimental evaluations are not appropriate for newer, less established programs or programs that lack a well-articulated theory of change underlying the program design. A variety of non-experimental methods, such as interviewing, case studies, and observational techniques, and more focused experimental and quasi-experimental studies are ways to understand and assess these types of community programs for youth. Although the nonexperimental methods tell us less about the effectiveness of particular community programs than experimental program evaluations, they can, when carefully implemented, provide information about the strengths and weakness in program implementation and can be used to identify patterns of effective practice. They are also quite helpful in generating hypotheses about why programs fail.

Programs that meet the following criteria should be studied through nonexperimental or more focused experimental and quasi-experimental methods, depending on the goals of the evaluation:

- An organization, program, project, or program element that has not matured sufficiently in terms of its philosophy and implementation;
- The evaluation has to be conducted by the staff of the program under evaluation;
- The major questions of interest pertain to the quality of the program theory, the implementation of that theory, or to the nature of its participants, staff, or surrounding context;
- The program is quite broad, involving multiple agencies in the same community; and
- The program or organization is interested in reflective practice and continuing improvement.

Whether experimental or nonexperimental methods are used, high-quality, comprehensive evaluation is important to the future development and success of community programs for youth and should be used by all programs and youth-serving organizations.

Recommendation 7—All community programs for youth should undergo evaluation—possibly multiple evaluations—to improve design and implementation, to create accountability, and to assess outcomes and impacts. For any given evaluation, the scope and the rigor should be appropriately calibrated to the attributes of the program, the available resources, and the goals of the evaluation.

Recommendation 8—Funders should provide the necessary funds for evaluation. In many cases, this will involve support for collaborative teams of researchers, evaluators, theoreticians, policy makers, and practitioners to ensure that programs are well designed initially and then evaluated in the most appropriate way.

Data Collection and Social Indicators

Over the past decade, social indicator data and technical assistance resources have become increasingly important tools that community programs can employ to support every aspect of their work—from initial planning and design, to tracking goals, program accountability, targeting services, reflection, and improvement. There are now significant data and related technical assistance resources to aid in understanding the young people involved in these programs. Community programs for youth benefit from ready access to high-quality data that allow them to assess and monitor the well-being of youth in their community, the well-being of youth they directly serve, and the elements of their programs that are intended to support those youth. They also benefit from information and training to help them use these data tools wisely and effectively.

Conclusion

❏ **Even when exploited to their full potential, administrative, vital statistics, and related data sources can cover only limited geographic areas and only some components of a youth development framework. Adding local survey data in diverse communities, as has been done in a number of states and individual communities, can help create a more complete picture.**

Community programs for youth are interested in building their capacity to assess the quality of their programs. To produce useful process evaluations, performance monitoring, and self-assessment, however, program practitioners need valid, reliable indicators and measures of the developmental quality of the experiences they provide. Such information would also facilitate the ability of communities to monitor change over time as new program initiatives are introduced into the community. If communities know how their youth are doing on a variety of indicators for an extended period of time both before and after a new program is introduced, they can use this information as preliminary evidence that their program is effective. Such inferences are strengthened if information on the same indicators is available in comparable communities that did not introduce that program at the same time. Research is needed to determine whether appropriate indicators vary depending on the characteristics of the specific youth population served by a program and as understanding of the determinants of positive youth development improves, these indicators should be periodically revisited and, if necessary, revised.

Many community programs also lack staff knowledge and the funds to take full advantage of social indicators as tools to aid in planning, monitoring, assessing, and improving program activities. Individual programs and communities would benefit from opportunities to improve their capacity to collect and use social indicator data.

Recommendation 9—Public and private funders should support the fielding of youth development surveys in more states and communities around the country; the development, testing, and fielding of new youth development measures that work well across diverse population subgroups; and greater coordination between measures used in community surveys and national longitudinal surveys.

Recommendation 10—Public and private funders should support collaboration between researchers and the practice community to develop social indicator data that build understanding of how programs are implemented and improve the ability to monitor programs. Collaborative efforts would further the understanding of the relationship between program features and positive developmental outcomes among young people.

Recommendation 11—Public and private funders should provide opportunities for individual programs and communities to increase their capacity to collect and use social indicator data. This requires better training for program staff and more support for national and regional intermediaries that provide technical assistance in a variety of ways, including Internet-based systems.

CHAPTER 1

Setting the Stage

A ll adolescents, in all economic and social circumstances, need generous amounts of help, instruction, discipline, support, and caring as they make their way from childhood through adolescence and into adulthood. Such assistance comes from many sources: solid families, good schools, supportive and safe neighborhoods, and a surrounding culture that emphasizes constructive lives and respectful relationships.

Community programs for youth, found in many neighborhoods in America, provide these sources of support. They exist in many forms: special clubs and service programs, sports leagues, community service organizations, faith-based youth groups, academic enrichment programs, music lessons, and many others. They are identified by a vast array of terms—after-school programs, youth clubs, youth development programs, or programs during non-school hours or out-of-school time.

Many such groups have been around for decades. They range from well-known national organizations with long histories—for example, Little League, Boy Scouts and Girl Scouts, Campfire U.S.A., YMCAs and YWCAs, and 4-H Clubs—to countless smaller groups and organizations that may be only a few years old and whose names are known only to the teens and families who participate in them—for example, programs that teach swimming and lifesaving run by a neighborhood community center, a series of studio art classes offered by a local museum for talented young artists, and math and computer enrichment programs for middle school youth sponsored by a local business.

GROWING SUPPORT FOR PROGRAMS

Increased funding from diverse federal agencies, foundations, state and local governments, and the private sector has expanded the availability of such programs. For example, in 2000 Congress appropriated $453 million (an amount that increased to $846 million in 2001) to enable schools and school districts to provide after-school programs designated as 21st Century Learning Centers. Private philanthropic foundations have also rapidly expanded their support of community programs for youth. At the same time, a variety of youth-serving organizations, research institutions, technical assistance organizations, and funders have been working, both together and independently, to create frameworks for thinking about positive youth development (e.g., Public/Private Ventures, Chapin Hall Center for Children, the Academy for Educational Development, the National Collaboration for Youth, the National Youth Development Information Center, and the International Youth Foundation). Others have developed studies and frameworks for understanding how much of adolescents' time is unstructured and potentially available for programmatic activities (Pittman et al., 2000c). However, exactly what should fill that time is still being debated. Some would like to see it used primarily for educational remediation and skill acquisition; others would like to see it used primarily for prevention-focused activities; others argue that it should be used to promote positive development in the fullest sense; and still others express concern that children and adolescents need this time to relax and do the things they want to do with minimal adult-structured activities. Many programs have been designed and implemented across the country—only some of which are being evaluated. Efforts have been made to develop a more integrated, systematic perspective on how best to provide learning and growth-promoting activities for children and youth.

At the same time, there is evidence of increasing public conviction that organized programs during after-school hours can prevent problem behavior in children and adolescents as well as promote their health, development, and well-being. Polls of parents, educators, other adults in the community, and young people themselves indicate increasing endorsement for improving the supply, quality, and access to after-school programs:

- In one survey of the voting public, 93 percent of respondents favored making safe daily enrichment programs available to all children; 86 percent thought that organized after-school activities were a necessity; only 11 percent thought they were not necessary (Charles Stewart Mott Foundation, 1998b);
- In a second survey, 84 percent of elementary school principals responded that there was a need for supervision both before and after school in their communities. The teachers surveyed singled out the need for after-school programs as critical to helping students with difficulties (Metropolitan Life, 1994);
- In a third survey, children and adolescents reported that they want constructive activities outside school, safe places to go where they can prepare for their future, learn and practice new skills, and spend quality time with caring adults and other children and adolescents (Quinn, 1999).

ADOLESCENT DEVELOPMENT

Perhaps more important than the increased interest in and funding of community youth organizations, however, has been the focus of community programs on goals related to positive youth development, as well as the prevention and reduction of problem behavior. In the early 1990s, a couple of seminal reports on adolescent development and the role of youth organizations attracted the attention of policy makers, youth service practitioners, researchers, educators, and families. The *Forgotten Half,* published by the William T. Grant Foundation, urged Americans to recognize that young people's experiences at home, at school, in the community, and at work are strongly interconnected and argued that all young people need more constructive contact with adults; opportunities to participate in valued community activities; special help with difficult problems; and initial jobs that offer a path to accomplishment (William T. Grant Commission on Work, Family and Citizenship, 2000). This report also stressed the fact that poor children and children not headed for college were being severely underserved in terms of programs and opportunities that could support positive development and preparation for adulthood.

This was followed in 1992 by *A Matter of Time*, a Carnegie Council on Adolescent Development report that observed that individuals develop through connection with a variety of people and systems. The report underscored the broad theoretical and empirical support for the essential role of community programs in promoting young people's healthy development (Carnegie Corporation of New York, 1992). It also stressed: (1) the growing need for such programs, given the complexity of life in the United States and the growing ambiguity about how best to prepare for a rapidly changing adult landscape, and (2) the paucity of high-quality community programs, especially for youth living in high-risk neighborhoods.

Numerous other reports and books have stressed the growing complexity of adolescent development. Not that long ago, adolescence ended somewhere between 18 and 22—at which point young adults moved into the labor market, married, and began their families. As recently as the 1960s, the transition into adulthood in most Western industrialized countries (particularly in the United States and Canada) was well defined for most social class groups. Adolescents finished high school and either went to college or into the labor market or the military. People generally married and began families in their early 20s. People were thus usually launched into adulthood by their early 20s, and there were only a limited number of fairly well-defined pathways from adolescence into adulthood (Arnett, 2000b).

This is no longer the case (Brown and Corbett, in press; Arnett, 2000b; Mortimer and Larson, 2002). Rapid demographic, sociocultural, and labor market changes have extended adolescence well into the 20s. The median age for marriage and childbearing has moved up to the late 20s. Both the length of time and numbers of youth involved in some form of postsecondary education have increased dramatically. Finally, the heterogeneity of passage through this period of life has exploded. There is no longer a small, easily understood set of patterns for the transition to adulthood. The future job market is unclear because it is changing so rapidly; youth are being advised to expect as many as four quite different occupational careers. The likelihood of today's youth moving into jobs similar to those held by their parents or other adult mentors has decreased substantially over the last 50 years, as has the likelihood that they will live in the same communities in which they grew up, and the likelihood that they will form a permanent intimate partnership with one other person and raise a family with that person (Elder and Conger, 2000; Giddens, 1990, 1992; Gleick, 1999; Larson, in press).

In the United States, the level of challenge for adolescents is especially high for noncollege-bound youth and for members of several ethnic minority groups, particularly blacks and Hispanics, for at least two reasons: (1) unlike many European and Asian industrialized countries, there is very little institutional support for the transition from secondary school to work in the United States, creating what the W.T. Grant Foundation labeled a "floundering" period (W.T. Grant Commission on Work, Family and Citizenship, 2000; see also Rosenbaum et al., 1992) and (2) stereotypes about the competence of blacks and Hispanics, coupled with lower levels of "soft skills" (e.g., the ability to communicate effectively, resolve conflicts, and prepare for and succeed in a job interview) (Murnane and Levy, 1996) and the loss of employment options in many inner-city communities (Wilson, 1987), have made employment for these youth (particularly males) quite problematic.

Coupled with these changes in the complexity of the adult world into which today's youth will be moving are the widespread risks confronting them. In the United States, the use of and access to drugs and alcohol has increased. Nearly 90 percent of 10th graders and 75 percent of 8th graders think that alcohol is either "fairly easy" or "very easy" to get (National Institute on Drug Abuse, 1996). "Rave drugs," such as the synthetic psychoactive drug called ecstasy, have become popular at nightclubs, rock concerts, and late-night parties, particularly in urban and suburban neighborhoods and among white middle-class young adults. Ecstasy has become the most frequently mentioned drug in telephone calls to the Poison Control Center (Partnership for Family Involvement, 2000). A review of top-selling popular songs found alcohol mentioned in 47 percent of rap music lyrics (Roberts et al., 1999). In recent television programs, 9 out of 10 drinkers of alcohol are portrayed as either experiencing no effects at all or only positive personal and social outcomes from their alcohol consumption (Gerbner, 1996).

Adolescents are surrounded by a culture of violence. In America, young people are being exposed to increasing amounts of media violence, especially in television, movies, video games, and youth-oriented music. By age 18, the average young person will have viewed an estimated 200,000 acts of violence on television alone (Huston et al., 1992). Youth gangs have grown considerably in the last two decades. The incidence of gangs in schools has almost doubled from 1989 to 1995 (Howell and Lynch, 2000). This presence of gangs in schools has been linked with increased gun possession among adolescents; students reported knowing a classmate who has brought a gun to school at a higher percentage (25 percent) when gangs were present in the schools than when gangs are not present (8 percent) (Howell and Lynch, 2000). According to a recent report issued by the U.S. Department of Education, over 6,000 students were expelled in the 1996-1997 school year for bringing guns to their public school (American Bar Association, 2000).

Programs for young people to combat these negative trends may be helpful. The idea of "positive youth development programs" has emerged over time as common shorthand for a philosophy asserting that "problem-free is not fully prepared," that remediation and prevention services alone are not enough, and that schools have to be supported and complemented by broader options in the community (Pittman and Irby, 1996; Pittman et al., 2000b).

COMMITTEE CHARGE

Stimulated by the growing national interest in the link between positive adolescent development and community programs, the National Academies formed the Committee on Community-Level Programs for Youth with support from a consortium of federal agencies and private foundations. The committee is an interdisciplinary group of individuals with expertise in a range of relevant fields, including child and adolescent development, maternal and child health, sociology, psychology, anthropology, economics, public policy, statistics, evaluation research, youth service programs, urban planning, and community development. The committee was asked to summarize the rapidly expanding body of research on community interventions and programs designed to promote positive outcomes for adolescent development. It was asked to assess the strengths and limitations of data sources and indicators commonly used to characterize youth health, development, and well-being, as well as to assess the strengths and limitations of methodologies and approaches used to evaluate these activities. The committee was asked to identify gaps and central questions for the design of a unified conceptual framework and research agenda to promote the healthy development of youth. And the committee was asked to identify, to the extent feasible, programs with sufficiently strong evidence to suggest that they could serve as models for communities that are expanding their youth programs.

YOUTH IN THE UNITED STATES: A MIXED PICTURE

The committee began its work by looking closely at the behaviors, needs, and circumstances of adolescents in the United States. We recognized from the beginning that the health and well-being of young people across the country is uneven. Some are doing quite well; others are doing very poorly.

Some Good News

The current cohort of adolescents presents a confusing mix of good and bad news. The good news is very good indeed—many measures of adolescent well-being and behavior have shown significant progress over the past 20 years.

More youth than ever are graduating from high school, and a large number are enrolled in some form of higher education (Ekston et al., 1987). High school dropout rates, although still unacceptably large for some population subgroups, are at all-time lows (National Campaign to Prevent Teen Pregnancy, 2001; Ekston et al., 1987).

In 1998, the rate for serious violent crimes committed by juveniles had dropped by more than half since 1993 and was the lowest it had been since the first data collection efforts in 1973 (U.S. Department of Health and Human Services, 1999). From 1991 to 1997 the percentage of students in grades 9 through 12 who reported carrying a weapon at least once in the past month declined from 26 to 18 percent (U.S. Department of Health and Human Services, 1999).

Between 40 and 50 percent of high school seniors report having participated in a volunteer or community-based service program at least a few times in the previous year (Institute for Social Research, 1999).

In 1999, 70 percent of high school students reported engaging in vigorous physical activity in the previous week, and over half of all high school students were enrolled in high school physical education classes (Centers for Disease Control and Prevention, 2000b). The use of illicit drugs by youth ages 12 to 17 has declined over the past three years, from a high of 11 percent in 1997 to 9 percent in 1999 (U.S. Department of Health and Human Services, 1999). Sexual activity has, on average, declined among teens and contraceptive use has increased (National Campaign to Prevent Teen Pregnancy, 2001). Furthermore, the overall rate of babies born to adolescents dropped by a third between 1991 and 1998, and in 1998 the birth rate for 15- to 17-year-olds was the lowest it has been in over 40 years (U.S. Department of Health and Human Services, 1999).

Continuing Problems

Nonetheless, some social indicators suggest continuing problems for many young people, particularly some specific subsets of them.

Academic Failure

Although the gap between white and black students' achievement on the National Assessment of Educational Progress tests has narrowed somewhat since 1973, there are still substantial racial and ethnic group differences in performance on these tests. In addition, youth from poor inner-city and rural areas are doing substantially worse on these tests than youth from more affluent school districts (Campbell et al., 2000; Jencks and Phillips, 1998). Youth in poor inner-city areas lose a substantial portion of their school-year academic achievement gains over the summer months—perhaps due to fewer learning opportunities, less support for learning in the home, and limited quality and quantity of parent interaction—leaving them farther behind their more affluent peers at the start of each new school year than they were at the end of the previous one (Entwisle and Alexander, 1992). The proportion of young people dropping out without completing high school increases with age and is particularly high among Hispanic youth and adolescents living in poor communities (National Center for Health Statistics, 2000). Finally, in the most recent comparative international academic achievement tests, U.S. youth scored substantially lower on tests of both mathematical and scientific knowledge than youth in most other industrialized countries (National Center for Education Statistics, 1995).

Poor Physical and Mental Health

Some teens are still becoming sexually active quite young: 8 percent of students reported having had sex before age 13—a disturbing 15 percent increase between 1988 and 1995 (National Center for Health Statistics, 2000; National Center for Chronic Disease Prevention and Health Promotion, 1999). The rates of sexual activity were particularly high among black youth living in poor communities (Blum et al., 2000; National Center for Health Statistics, 2000). And although most teens (88 percent) said they thought it was important to use contraception each and every time they had sex, 30 percent of girls reported having been completely unprotected the last time they had sex, and between 30 and 38 percent of teens who used contraception did so inconsistently (National Campaign to Prevent Teen Pregnancy, 2000). Furthermore, rates of sexually transmitted diseases and both HIV and AIDS were alarmingly high among adolescents in general, and particularly high among black and American Indian youth living in poor communities (National Center for Health Statistics, 2000). In fact, half of all new HIV infections occurred among people under the age of 25, and one-quarter of new infections occurred among people between the ages of 13 and 21 (Kirby, 1998).

Smoking among teens in 2000 had declined since its peak in 1996, following a dramatic 50 percent increase since 1991. However, smoking is still quite high among youth. Nearly 63 percent of adolescents have tried cigarettes by the 12th grade, and 31 percent are currently frequent smokers (Federal Interagency Forum on Child and Family Statistics, 2000). Smoking rates among white and Hispanic young people are also notably higher than among black youth (Centers for Disease Control and Prevention, 2000b). Binge drinking is also quite high, particularly among white and Hispanic youth (National Center for Health Statistics, 2000; Blum et al., 2000).

The daily participation of adolescents in high school physical education classes dropped from 42 percent in 1991 to 27 percent in 1997 (Centers for Disease Control and Prevention, 2000b). The overall prevalence of obesity among adolescent 12- to 19-year-olds in the United States more than doubled in 34 years—increasing from 5 percent in 1965 to 14 percent in 1999 (National Center for Health Statistics, 1999). And, from 1988 to 1994, approximately 11 percent of 12- to 17-year-olds were seriously overweight (National Center for Health Statistics, 2000). Of the youth surveyed in the National Longitudinal Study of Adolescent Health (called Add Health), 13 percent (representing 2.5 million U.S. youth) reported having had suicidal thoughts or had attempted suicide in the previous 12 months. White, Hispanic, female, and poor youth were the most likely to report these thoughts and behaviors (Blum et al., 2000; National Center for Health Statistics, 2000).

Violent Behavior

In 1997, homicide was the second leading cause of death for young people ages 15 to 24; it was the leading cause of death among black youth and the second leading cause of death for Hispanic youth (National Center for Injury Prevention and Control, 2000). Of the youth surveyed in the most recent wave of the Add Health study, 26 percent reported having been involved in weapon-related violence in the past 12 months. Black and Hispanic youth living in poor communities were the most likely to report these experiences (Blum et al., 2000). Between July 1992 and June 1994, 105 violent deaths occurred on or near school grounds or at school-related events. Firearms were used in 77 percent of these deaths (National Center for Injury Prevention and Control, 2000). There was an increasing number of highly publicized incidences of gun violence on school campuses in 2000 and 2001, in places such as Jonesboro, Arkansas; Columbine, Colorado; and Santee, California.

Poor Economic and Family Circumstances

An ever-increasing proportion of teenagers were living some or all of their adolescent years in single-parent homes. Since 1980 the percentage of young people living in single-parent households rose from 7 percent in 1980 to 27 percent in 1999. Despite the recent booming economy, 18 percent of youth under 18 lived in households below the poverty level in 1998. Among minority adolescents, the picture is even bleaker. When poverty is combined with living in a single-parent household, minority youth are at particular risk for all of the problems outlined in this section (Federal Interagency Forum on Child and Family Statistics, 2000).

Adolescent Use of Time

There is evidence that how young people spend their out-of-school time influences their health and well-being.

Compared with young people in both Europe and Asia, teens in the United States have more discretionary time—only about 20 percent of adolescents' hours are spent in school. They spend limited time on schoolwork; much of their discretionary time is spent watching television (especially by young adolescents, boys, youth from low socioeconomic environments, and black youth) or "hanging out" with friends (Larson and Verma, 1999; Zill et al., 1995). In addition, there are approximately 8 million children, ranging from ages 5 to 14 who spend time without any kind of supervision during nonschool hours. And their numbers increase as children get older. Unsupervised time can account for approximately 20-25 hours per week (National Institute on Out-of-

School Time, 2001a). A variety of factors, including rising child care costs, increased work hours, welfare reform, and the limited availability of good programs may account for the large number of children left alone during nonschool hours.

Being alone during nonschool hours invites problems. This is not a new thought: recall the adage: "idle hands are the devil's workshop." Filling empty hours, of course, can be overdone, and there is merit in offering young people unhurried blocks of time to think, play, have fun, talk to parents and friends, and even read for pleasure. However, there is evidence that teens left alone during nonschool hours are more likely to engage in sexual intercourse, alcohol or drug abuse, smoking, violence, and gang-related behavior (Zill et al., 1995). Others simply use this unstructured time to play video games. Some experience fear and anxiety when left at home by themselves.

A study of 5,000 8th grade students in the San Diego and Los Angeles areas found that children left home alone, regardless of race, sex, or economic status, are more likely to drink alcohol or take drugs than children who are supervised by a parent or another adult. And the more hours they were left by themselves, the greater their risk (Richardson et al., 1989). Similar results have been reported by Marshall et al. (1997) and the YMCA (2001).

There is also evidence that participation in "constructive learning activities" during nonschool hours may predict success or failure in school. Reginald Clark's work (1983, 1988) suggests that participating in such activities as leisure reading and writing, music, chores, homework, or problem-solving games creates opportunities for young people to enhance their cognitive skills and extend their learning. In contrast, young people who do not have the opportunity to participate in these kinds of activities or who engage in excessive hours of unstructured activities (e.g., television, video games, hanging out with friends) tend to underachieve in school.

Participation in Community Programs

What these data mean in the context of this report is that a significant number of young people—particularly those who are poor and live in high-risk neighborhoods—are in particular need of support. Such youth are disproportionately likely to be members of racial and ethnic minority groups. Community programs for youth are being looked on as one way to redress the social inequities that currently confront America.

Studies indicate that participation in voluntary structured activities during nonschool time is associated with development of positive identity, increased initiative, and positive relationships with diverse peers and adults, better school achievement, reduced rates of dropping out of school, reduced delinquency, and more positive outcomes in adulthood (Barber et al., in press; Clark, 1988; Eccles and Barber, 1999; Larson, 2000; Vandell and Posner, 1999). For example, in the National Longitudinal Survey of Youth, students who reported spending no time in some kind of school-sponsored activity (versus those spending 1 to 4 hours per week in such activities) were 57 percent more likely to have dropped out before they reached the 12th grade. Also, students with high levels of participation in school activities were less likely than nonparticipants to engage in problem behavior, such as being arrested, taking drugs, engaging in teen sex, smoking, and drinking (Zill et al., 1995).

In recent community-based surveys conducted by the Search Institute (Benson, 1997; Scales and Leffert, 1999) and by Sipe and colleagues for Public/Private Ventures (Sipe et al., 1998), a substantial number of young people were not involved in programs during their out-of-school time. For example, less than 25 percent of youth in low-income communities in Austin, Texas, St. Petersburg, Florida, and Savannah, Georgia, reported having been involved in any formal leadership activities in the previous year (Sipe et al., 1998; Scales and Leffert, 1999). The communities included in this survey were chosen to represent communities with high crime rates, low rates of school performance, and high unemployment. In another survey, with a more representative sample from across the United States, similar results were found; only 50 percent of the youth in public and alternative schools, surveyed from over 213 different towns and cities across the United States by the Search Institute, spent even 3 hours per week in constructive out-of-school activities (Scales and Leffert, 1999). Finally, according to an analysis of national survey data collected for the committee by the Urban Institute and Child Trends, 60 percent of youth did not participate in any kind of community-based youth activity. Of the few that were involved, about 20 percent participated less than an hour a day, leaving about half of the youth between 12 and 14 years of age not taking part in any kind of extra-curricular class or lesson. Research from the National Longitudinal Survey of Youth (U.S. Department of Labor, 1997) echoes these findings, with only about a fifth of teenagers in the United States in the late 1980s and 1990s having participated in some kind of structured out-of-school activity.

The prevailing problem regarding participation in after-school community programs seems to be one of unmet need. The number of youth left without some kind of after-school programming now exceeds 11 million (Newman et al., 2000). While not all young people want or need such programs, this number is probably some indication of unmet need. And, adolescents from low- to moderate-income working families are the least likely to have access to programs because of financial and transportation constraints (Newman et al., 2000). Among grantees of the federally funded 21st Century Learning Centers, 40 percent report that they have long waiting lists for youth to get into programs (U.S. Department of Education, 2000). The U.S. General Accounting Office estimated that in the year 2002, the current number of school-age child care programs will meet as little as 25 percent of the demand in some urban areas (U.S. General Accounting Office, 1997). Over half of the teens polled by the YMCA (2001) said they wished there were more after-school programs in their community. More than half (54 percent) said they would not watch so much television or play video games if they had other things to do after school.

Nevertheless, it is clear that community programs for young people cannot bear the full weight and responsibility for producing healthy, robust future generations. They may help, but no program can fully compensate for a dysfunctional family, poor schools, chaotic neighborhoods, poor medical care, environmental toxins, and stress-filled early lives, particularly given that many, perhaps most community programs for youth are small and fragile, with unstable funding and questionable futures. Expectations should not therefore be excessive or naive, even for the best and strongest model programs.

SCOPE OF THE STUDY

Program Characteristics

One hurdle faced by the committee was developing a common understanding of what constitutes a community program for youth. The characterization of these programs is complicated, and the landscape is vast. They may be called after-school programs, youth programs, youth activities, youth development programs, community programs, extracurricular activities, or programs during out-of-school time or nonschool hours. In addition, we debated whether school programs should be included, since schools in the United States are, for the most part, locally controlled. We also debated what constitutes a community.

Rather than thinking of such programs in certain categories—such as those that focus on sports or academics or those that are faith-based or school-based or recreational center-based— we decided that it would be more useful to see programs as arrayed along a continuum and to be generous in our definition of community. At one end are small, informal, and unaffiliated programs, typically only marginally funded by public dollars, that touch the lives of relatively few teenagers. At the other end are the large, often national programs that may have many state and local-level franchises, enroll sometimes millions of young people, have large and relatively stable budgets (often including substantial public dollars), and involve many adults in various capacities ranging from membership on a national board to service as volunteers in a particular program. In the context of this report, communities include neighborhoods, block groups, towns, and cities as well as nongeographically defined communities based on family connections and shared interests or values.

The committee also decided to look at programs and the organizations operating them in terms of the developmental needs the program is attempting to fill, rather than the particular structural form they have taken. This perspective stems from our view that young people have a number of fundamental needs—including, for example, the need for affiliation, friendship, and belonging to a group and the need to feel competent, efficacious, respected, and significant—and that they will seek ways to meet these needs in a variety of places and situations. Some of the possible places and situations can increase the likelihood of developmental pathways that include antisocial behaviors, such as joining a gang; others can increase the likelihood of developmental pathways rich in positive social (prosocial) and health-promoting behaviors, such as joining a community service group or a prosocial peer network. Community programs are therefore best seen and described from the perspective of how they are addressing what teenagers need and how these needs may change over the years of adolescence. In developing this report, we began by discussing what current research, theory, and practice show that young people require from their immediate environments as they grow toward young adulthood (see especially Chapters 2, 3, and 4). We then looked at individual programs and their evaluations through this lens (see especially Chapters 5 and 6).

Equally important is the question of what role these programs play in the lives of young people. Are they extensions of school? Are they merely luxuries for some families, or are they essential for healthy development for all adolescents? Are they simply efforts to fill empty hours while parents are at work—even serving as a kind of babysitter? Our answer to these questions is that community programs should be purposeful, voluntary activities designed to offer concrete benefits to all the young people enrolled in them. Although they may indeed keep young people occupied while their parents are at work, their goal is not to simply fill up time but rather to support positive development during adolescence in specific ways that also help prepare youth for adulthood. As such, these programs and organizations should, and do, complement and support the primary nurturing and teaching roles of the family and the academic mission of the schools. Many of the best-regarded programs craft explicit links with both home and school. Some of the programs we reviewed even take place during the normal school hours in the school building itself.

Moreover, there is no question that some programs are organized to provide a modest counterweight to popular youth culture, which some see as toxic and damaging to young people. For example, some, seeing the current youth culture as misogynistic, organize programs for young men to encourage them to be respectful of young women and programs for young women to understand how current popular culture demeans them. Others offer both young women and men programs that teach them techniques to resist cultural pressures to become sexually active at an early age, to use illicit drugs, and to join gang activities. And still others include "media literacy" training that attempts to teach young people to become critical, discerning consumers of media. Thus, in such instances, community programs are not so much filling gaps left by families and schools, but rather trying to counteract broader cultural influences perceived to be harmful.

Discussion of whether or not to include school-based programs occupied a significant portion of the committee's early deliberations. Although there are often fundamental structural, budgetary, and organizational differences between school-based and other programs, the function and potential impact of these programs are more similar than they are different. In our view, the examination of youth programs operating in schools and taking a positive youth development approach yet are independent of the schools' instructional activities is necessary in order to provide a complete picture of community programs for youth. This is particularly true given the increased movement toward housing community programs for youth in schools and creating collaborations between schools and community-based organizations.

Population Characteristics

The committee made the decision to focus on programs and policies for young people between ages 10 and 18; we refer to this target population throughout the report by multiple terms: young people, youth, adolescents, and teens. We recognize that among practitioners, researchers, and policy makers, different age brackets often define adolescence. Some community programs and policies for youth target children as young as 8 years old and as old as 21; others identify a subset within this larger range, such as 12 to 15 or 16 to 18. The committee chose the 10 to 18 age range because in our view it covers the most critical years of adolescent development and coincides more or less with the years of secondary school. However, this age range did not constrain the committee's work and some deviation occurred when examining programs and policies. Furthermore, we recognize that the principles of adolescent development and the program features identified in this report have useful implications for the programming for younger children and older adolescents and young adults.

There are countless subpopulations of adolescents defined by a great variety of characteristics—such as youth of a particular race or ethnic group; youth with disabilities; gay and lesbian youth; gifted and talented youth; youth with special physical or emotional needs; incarcerated youth; runaway youth; and youth in foster care. The committee made the decision to look broadly at adolescents and not explicitly identify features of programs aimed at adolescents who fall within a particular subpopulation, while recognizing that some adolescents may, in fact, have special needs or interests and that programs may need to be adapted to accommodate them.

Finally, there are various individuals and groups interested in community programs for youth. This report was written in great part with an eye toward these various interests—service practitioners, policy makers, researchers, and the young people and their families participating in the programs. We defined service practitioners as the staff and managers who provide direct services to young people. We defined policy makers broadly, as elected officials and bureaucrats, as well as public- and private-sector staff at the community and national levels, who develop, implement, build the capacity of, provide technical assistance to, and fund these programs. Members of the research community include evaluators of local, state, and national initiatives, developmental researchers, and professionals who consult on the theory, design, and implementation of community programs for youth.

Program Approaches

For those who design, study, fund, and work in the field of community programs for youth, there can be a tension in approach. Two major program orientations are often identified: on one side are "prevention" or "problem-centered" programs; on the other are "positive youth development" programs. Programs focused on prevention or problems are often stereotyped by advocates of a positive youth development perspective as identifying teenagers as collections of specific problems in place or about to happen—drug use, early and inappropriate sexual activity, violent behavior, school failure, etc. Such programs often emphasize preventing problem behavior (e.g., reducing teenage drug use) and are often centered on a single problem, even though problems may be closely related (e.g., a program may concentrate on preventing teenage pregnancy but give minimal attention to preventing sexually transmitted diseases). In contrast, people linked to the positive youth development orientation define themselves as being interested in young people as collections of assets and opportunities, rather than problems (Pittman and Irby, 1996; Roth and Brooks-Gunn, 2000). Programs designed from this orientation emphasize positive growth and development and are not usually designed to address specific individual problems. Broad skills are typically fostered and taught rather than strategies for preventing or managing single problematic behaviors.

From the outset, the committee rejected this polarized view of youth programming. Although our charge stresses the importance of programs designed to promote positive adolescent development, we decided that both prevention and promotion approaches are needed and have great value. Clearly, all young people need multiple opportunities to grow in positive, healthy ways. They need adults who teach and encourage them, who help them set challenging and meaningful goals for the future, and who nurture an array of skills and values. But young people often also need specific, focused help in steering clear of specific obstacles that current popular culture places in their paths, such as the lure of drugs and alcohol and inappropriate and early sexual activity. Although an emphasis on overall positive youth development can help in addressing specific problems and challenges, more targeted, problem-centered interventions are often needed as well.

But even more important, this distinction is often blurred when one examines the content and nature of individual programs. In fact, many programs that are broad in nature and clearly designed to promote positive youth development in fact devote significant time to efforts designed to prevent specific problems from emerging. Similarly, many programs that call themselves prevention programs include activities linked to community service, mentoring, and other activities associated with positive development approaches. We suspect that much of the tension between these two perspectives derives from competition for funding and the changing trends in public rhetoric and policy. It is not rooted in irreconcilable differences in program design or theory. Consequently, we looked at both types of programs.

The committee concluded that the quest for the perfect program is quixotic. We are unlikely to ever define a single all-time-winner program that should be replicated in cookie-cutter fashion in all American communities. There are several reasons for this cautionary note. First, the diversity of young people, their particular needs, and their surrounding environments argue against the notion that a single program will fit all situations. Second, the funding needed to evaluate all possible models, thereby closing in on the perfect intervention, is simply not available and unlikely to become so. Third and perhaps most important, there is a certain aspect to the challenge of working with young people that is an art, not a science, as any parent or teacher can tell you. Yes, we can describe broad aspects of programs for youth that seem especially useful, such as the widely recognized value of having youth themselves play an active role in the design and tone of individual programs, but in the end, success often hinges on such intangibles as the quality of the relationship between an individual young person and the program leader, or the interpersonal chemistry of a particular group of teenagers (McLaughlin, 2000).

Underlying Values and Perspectives

Conducting the study that produced this report raised numerous questions of values, which are not scientific matters and can spark vehement disagreement. First, although the government has a long history of investing in schools and supporting universal access to education, there is less consensus about whether it should invest in young people's nonschool hours. For that reason, persuasive evidence that community programs for youth improve their lives cannot be expected to lead automatically to increased public investment in such programs.

One reason cited for the increasing interest in after-school and youth development programs is that the growing presence of women in the workforce has led to greater demands for activities that, among other things, provide youth with supervision during nonschool hours. Discussion of these programs often reveals widely varying views about the role of women (or, in this case, mothers) in the workforce and the extent to which their changing roles underlie community programs for young people.

Any attempt to understand the role of community programs in the lives and development of young people necessarily incorporates some basic judgments about the attributes we hope that young people develop (see Chapter 3). The committee acknowledges up front that cataloguing the personal characteristics that young people need to possess invariably includes subjective judgment. Other groups might come up with a different set of desirable attributes. But we also decided that it is important for community programs to have explicit goals regarding what assets or characteristics they would like to promote. Such goals are important because they should be used to design and then evaluate the program activities. Having explicit goals makes both evaluation and accountability much easier. The committee expanded its charge to include a scientific assessment of what such goals might be.

This report does not take on directly the question of the appropriate relationship between schools and community programs. Rather, as noted earlier, we concentrate on discussing what young people need for healthy growth and development, recognizing that, in some communities, families, schools, and existing community organizations may well provide most, if not all of the structures, conditions, and experiences necessary to meet the needs of young people—making additional government-funded community programs relatively marginal. In other areas, the need for community programs may be acute because existing institutions, including the schools, are not able to meet the needs of all adolescents. What this logic suggests is that communities as a whole should regularly review what is available for their young people and then make judgments about which institutions—schools, community programs, and others—can and should fill the gaps. Invariably, communities will answer this challenge differently and come to varying views about the precise responsibilities of home, school, and community programs.

Finally, we do not pretend that this report offers the definitive or final blueprint for positive youth development. Young people are influenced by a large array of factors, ranging from their family to the complicated world of the Internet and the forces of popular culture. In truth, all such forces can and should be enlisted to bolster the development of the next generation. But the work of this committee and its report are confined to one small part of the puzzle: community programs for youth. We have not outlined a plan to overhaul adolescence in America, but only to consider one small part of the enterprise.

Core Concepts

There is a set of core concepts around which the committee based its work and that serve as a foundation for this report:

- Some youth are doing very well;
- Some youth are taking dangerous risks and doing poorly;
- All young people need a variety of experiences to develop to their full potential; and
- Some young people have unmet needs and are particularly at risk of participating in problem behaviors (e.g., dropping out of school, participating in violent behavior). These include young people who often, but by no means always, live in high-risk neighborhoods, are poor, experience repeated racial and ethnic discrimination, and have a substantial amount of free, unsupervised time during nonschool hours. Other youth who are in special need of more programs include youth with disabilities of all kinds, youth from troubled family situations, and youth with special needs for places to find emotional support.

GUIDE TO THE REPORT

This report has four parts. Part I, which includes Chapters 2, 3, and 4, provides a framework for promoting adolescent development. Chapter 2 is an overview of adolescent development with attention to developmental issues for youth of different ages. Chapter 3 discusses what constitutes evidence of positive youth development, drawing on empirical studies of well-being and positive developmental outcomes, as well as practical wisdom from leaders in this field about the core human needs and attributes that young people need to develop. This chapter presents a list of personal and social assets that predict current and future well-being. Chapter 4 reviews what is known about the features of the settings in adolescents' daily life that facilitate the development of these assets. Evidence from both theoretical and practical field-based observations is included.

Part II, which includes Chapters 5 and 6, reviews what the committee found out about community programs themselves. Chapter 5 examines the ways in which programs incorporate features of positive developmental settings and provide opportunities for young people to acquire the personal and social assets characteristic of positive youth development. To do this, we map the features of positive developmental settings against a variety of programs that have been studied with nonexperimental evaluation methods and then draw conclusions about the program practices that are linked empirically to positive indicators of adolescent development. Chapter 6 reviews the evidence of effective program practices from experimental evaluations of community programs for youth. We end this chapter by mapping what we learned from experimental program evaluations onto the features of positive developmental settings outlined in Chapter 4.

Part III, which includes Chapters 7 and 8, examines the role for evaluation and social indicator data in thinking about community programs for youth in the future. Chapter 7 discusses the various methods and tools available to evaluate youth programs and generate new information about them. Chapter 8 explores existing social indicators and data instruments that help elucidate the attributes of program participants. We also suggest other information and tools needed in order to better understand young people and evaluate these programs.

Finally, Part IV examines the intersection among research, policy, and practice for community programs for youth. In Chapter 9 we examine existing and anticipated policy and system-level supports and barriers. In the final chapter, Chapter 10, we summarize the committee's conclusions and recommendations that span the areas of practice and policy and evaluation, research, and data collection.

PART I

Promoting Adolescent Development

Adolescence is a pivotal period for youth to acquire the attitudes, competencies, values, and social connections that will help carry them forward to successful adulthood. As described in Chapter 1, some young people do very well during this time; others experience gaps in their lives that lead to risky and harmful behaviors. Understanding how to characterize positive adolescent development was a fundamental aspect of the committee's work.

This section has three goals: Chapter 2 provides an overview of adolescent development; Chapter 3 summarizes what is known about the personal and social assets that are likely to be linked to both well-being during adolescence and the transition into adulthood; and Chapter 4 explores what the daily settings and experiences of adolescents need to include in order to promote the acquisition of these assets and function as a positive developmental setting. In our view, a good understanding of these topics is important in the design and evaluation of community programs for youth. These programs are intended to both support positive development and prevent involvement in problematic behaviors likely to mortgage a youth's future. To accomplish these aspirations, program designers and evaluators need to be guided by what is known about development during adolescence as well as about resilience more generally. They also need to be guided by what is known about the kinds of social experiences that facilitate positive development.

Scientists and program providers have suggested a number of core human needs, attributes, and both personal and social assets that can facilitate adolescents' present well-being, reduce their risk-taking, and increase the likelihood of their successful future transitions. Development occurs over time, with experiences in the present being critical for both current well-being and future success. From research in this area, the committee developed a set of core concepts:

- The acquisition of personal and social assets—in the domains of physical, intellectual, psychological and emotional, and social development—leads to positive adolescent development.
- Adolescents with more personal and social assets in each of these areas have a greater chance of both current well-being and future success.
- Personal and social assets are enhanced by positive developmental settings.

What do the daily settings and experiences of adolescents need to include in order to promote the acquisition of these assets and function as a positive developmental setting? Based on theories of positive development and empirical research on features of settings, the committee developed a list of eight features of settings that promote adolescent development: physical and psychological safety; appropriate structure; supportive relationships; opportunities to belong; positive social norms; support for efficacy and mattering; opportunities for skill building; and opportunities for integration among family, schools, and community efforts. Research shows that the more settings that adolescents experience reflecting these features, the more likely they are to acquire the personal and social assets linked to both current and future well-being.

There are a variety of settings in which adolescents' can experience the opportunities needed for positive development. Young people need continuous exposure to positive experiences, settings, and people, as well as abundant opportunities to refine their life skills so that they have the means to move into productive jobs and other roles that build fulfilling relationships. Some youth live in families and neighborhoods that ensure these experiences; others live in environments in which community programs are necessary to ensure them.

CHAPTER 2

Adolescent Development

hat do you think of when you imagine an adolescent? Although some people picture a helpful, well-functioning young person, others envision a gangly, awkward, brooding, and troublesome individual. Even parents and teachers sometimes bemoan the changes that occur as their children move into and through adolescence. Elementary school-age children are seen as cute, cooperative, and ready to learn. In contrast, adolescents are often seen as problems waiting to happen. Until recently, researchers shared this view. Historically, this period of life was labeled by developmental scientists as a time of storm and stress (Arnett, 1999). Although we now know that most young people pass into and through adolescence with few major problems, some find this a very difficult period of life (Arnett, 1999; Carnegie Corporation of New York, 1989; Eccles et al., 1993; Moffitt, 1993; Rutter and Smith, 1995).

Many developmental scientists, policy makers, and practitioners working with youth believe that enhancing the lives of adolescents with positive opportunities and experiences could reduce the likelihood and magnitude of these problems (e.g., Carnegie Corporation of New York, 1989; Charles Stewart Mott Foundation, 1998a; Dryfoos,

1996; Eccles et al., 1993; Jessor, 1993, 1998; Larson, 1994, 2000; Lerner and Galambos, 1998; Lerner et al., 2000; Lipsitz, et al., 1997; Metropolitan Life, 1994; Pittman et al., 2000b; Roth, 1996; Quinn, 1999). In this chapter, we provide an overview of what is known about development during the years from 10 to 18 so that individuals interested in community programs for youth have an accurate understanding of whom adolescents are and what they need as they design, fund, operate, and evaluate programs.

What is adolescent development really like? There is no doubt that it is a time of great change on many levels. Probably most dramatic are the biological changes associated with puberty, which include shifts in the shape of the body, increases in gonadol hormones, emergence of cyclical patterns of gonadol and related hormonal systems in females, onset of fertility, and changes in brain architecture and the receptivity of neurons to a variety of chemicals (Brooks-Gunn and Reiter, 1990; Buchanan et al., 1992; Gubba et al., 2000; Herbert and Martinez, 2001). These biological transitions are linked to changes in sexual interest, as well as to changes in both cognitive and physical capacities and emotional well-being. There are also major social changes associated with both school transitions and shifts in the roles that adolescents are expected to assume as they mature. Finally, there are major psychological changes linked to increasing social and cognitive maturity. In fact, few developmental periods are characterized by so many changes at so many different levels.

Adolescence is also a time when individuals in most Western and postindustrialized cultures make many choices and experiment with a wide variety of behaviors and experiences that can influence the rest of their lives (Brown and Corbett, forthcoming; Mortimer and Larson, 2002). For example, adolescents select which peer groups to join and how to spend their after-school hours. Adolescents make future educational and occupational plans and then pursue them through secondary school course work and out-of-school vocational and volunteer activities. Finally, some youth experiment with risky behaviors, such as tobacco use, alcohol and other drug use, and unprotected nonmarital sexual intercourse. For some of these youth, the experimentation has few or no long-term consequences; for others, this experimentation seriously compromises their future (Carnegie Corporation of New York, 1989; National Research Council, 1999c; Cairns and Cairns, 1994; Cicchetti and Toth, 1996; Elder and Conger, 2000; Jessor et al., 1991; Moffitt, 1993; Steinberg and Morris, 2001). Given the influence that these choices and behaviors can have over future life options, it is critical to understand

what influences whether young people stay on healthy, productive pathways or move onto more problematic, and potentially destructive ones
as they pass through this important life stage.

DEVELOPMENTAL CHALLENGES, OPPORTUNITIES, AND RISKS

Many theorists have proposed systematic ways to think about the
developmental challenges, opportunities, and risks of this period of life.
Historically, most prominent among these was Eric Erikson (1968). Integrating adolescence into his more general life-span model of development (see Appendix A), he suggested that the specific challenges for children between ages 10 and 18 are: developing a sense of mastery, identity,
and intimacy. Others have expanded these challenges to include autonomy, sexuality, and achievement (e.g., Carnegie Corporation of New
York, 1989; Havinghurst, 1972). In many cultural groups, these challenges translate into the following more specific tasks: (1) changing the
nature of the relationship between young people and their parents so
youth can take on a more mature role in the social fabric of their community (among white Americans this change often takes the form of
greater independence from parents and greater decision-making power
over one's own current and future behavior; in other cultures, this change
can take the form of greater responsibility for family support and increased participation in family decision making; in all cultures this change
typically results in starting one's own family and becoming integrated
into the mainstream adult community); (2) exploring new personal,
social, and sexual roles and identities; (3) transforming peer relationships into deeper friendships and intimate partnerships; and (4) participating in a series of experiences and choices that facilitate future economic independence and interdependence.

As made clear by many scientists interested in adolescence, each of
these tasks is played out in an increasingly complex set of social settings
and in both cultural and historical settings (e.g., Bronfenbrenner and
Morris, 1998; Cairns and Cairns, 1994; Eccles et al., 1993; Elder, 1998;
Elder and Conger, 2000; Elliott, et al., 1996; Erikson, 1968; Jessor and
Jessor, 1977; Lerner and Galambos, 1998; Moffitt, 1993; Rutter and
Smith, 1995; Steinberg and Morris, 2001). Optimal progress on each of
these tasks depends on the psychosocial, physical, and cognitive assets of
the individual, the social supports available to the individual, and the

developmental appropriateness of the each of the social settings encountered by young people as they pass through adolescence.

With rapid change of course comes a heightened potential for both positive and negative outcomes. Although most individuals pass through this developmental period without excessively high levels of storm and stress, a substantial number do experience difficulty (see Chapter 1). Involvement with criminal and antisocial behavior accelerates dramatically between the ages of 10 and 15, as does drug and alcohol use and sexual interactions (see Cicchetti and Toth, 1996; Eccles et al., 1996a; Moffitt, 1993; Steinberg and Morris, 2001). The incidence of mental health problems and more general alienation also increases, particularly in modern, postindustrialized societies (Giddens, 1990; Eccles et al., 1996a; Rutter and Smith, 1995). Finally, rates of school disengagement and school failure in the United States increase (see Eccles et al., 1998, for a review). Many of these changes begin during the earliest years of adolescent development—between the ages of 10 and 14. In turn, these early changes set in motion problems that can culminate in subsequent school failure, high school dropout, incarceration, and teen pregnancy— any one of which can have serious consequences for young people's future (Jessor et al., 1991; Sampson and Laub, 1995).

With specific regard to the developmental tasks of adolescence outlined above, there are several concrete risks. First, renegotiation of the relationship with one's parents can be so turbulent that a permanent rift and alienation between youth and their families emerges. Second, adolescents can get so caught up with a deviant peer group and its behaviors and values that they get involved in behaviors and circumstances that seriously endanger their ability to make a successful transition into mainstream adulthood. Third, adolescents can fail to make social connections with the kinds of adults and social institution that can help them make the transition into mainstream adulthood. Fourth, educational opportunities can be so limited that some adolescents fail to acquire the intellectual and soft skills needed to move successfully into the labor market. Fifth, experiences with civic engagement and social institutions can be so minimal or so poorly designed that some adolescents fail to develop either the will or the skills necessary to participate fully as adult community members. Finally, experiences of racism, prejudice, and cultural intolerance can so alienate some adolescents that they withdraw from or rebel against, mainstream society and conventional social institutions.

Community programs for youth have the potential to play a critical role during this developmental period. Evidence from several sources supports the conclusion that participation in constructive and supportive programs during out-of-school hours both encourages positive development in many areas and reduces the likelihood of engagement in problematic behaviors. These programs can remediate deficiencies in skills already evident by early adolescence, teach new intellectual and soft skills critical for high school success and movement into jobs that provide sufficient income to support a family, provide intellectually challenging experiences to foster continued cognitive development, support continued positive socioemotional development, help establish strong social connections between the kinds of individuals and social institutions that help youth both to be conventionally successful during their adolescence and to make a successful transition into adulthood, provide a place to meet peers with positive social values and a positive vision of their futures, and provide a place where adolescents can feel accepted and can explore both their personal and social identities without having to continually confront racism and cultural intolerance (e.g., Barber et al., in press; Blum et al., 2000; Larson, 2000; Vandell and Posner, 1999; Eccles and Barber, 1999; Furstenberg et al., 1999; Elder and Conger, 2000; see Chapters 4, 5, and 6 for more details).

But such programs need to be developmentally, as well as culturally, appropriate to achieve these goals. As we discuss in more detail in the following sections, youth of different ages are likely to benefit from different experiences. During the years between 10 and 14, they are experiencing the most dramatic biological changes and are most susceptible to peer influence. During this time they also typically experience the transition from elementary school to secondary school, and conflicts with parents peak. Finally, they are just beginning to have the cognitive capacity to engage in formal reasoning. Programs for this age group need to take these characteristics into account. Developmental theory and the empirical evidence reviewed in Chapters 3 and 4 suggest the following kinds of programmatic needs for this age group:

- Educational programs that:
  —Help young adolescents and their parents understand the biological changes they are experiencing;
  —Make sure young adolescents have the academic skills necessary to take and succeed in college preparatory secondary school courses; and
  —Provide sufficient intellectual challenge that young adolescents can learn to use formal reasoning skills effectively.

- Social and communication skill training programs that:
  —Help them learn to resist negative peer pressures and to communicate better with their parents about such issues as sexuality, negative peer pressures, and the health risks of drug and alcohol use.

- Career planning activities that:
  —Expose young adolescents to a wide range of possible careers, help them to develop high expectations for themselves about their future, and provide them with the information needed to begin to make appropriate educational choices that will help them achieve their future aspirations.

- Practices that:
  —Respect young adolescents' growing maturity by providing opportunities for meaningful inputs into program development and governance.

Evidence reviewed later in this report suggests that, as youth get older, the family conflicts common to the early adolescent years decrease, susceptibility to peer influence decreases, and both personal and social identity concerns increase, particularly those related to occupational, sexual, and ethnic identities. In addition, the biological systems stabilize, cognitive skills increase, and expertise in a variety of areas grows. Programs for older youth need to change in ways that reflect their growing maturity and expertise, the new courses they are taking in high school, their increasing cognitive capacities, their increased concerns about identity issues, and their movement toward the transition into adulthood. Again, developmental theory and empirical evidence suggest the following kinds of programs for older youth:

- Educational programs that:
  —Provide tutoring for college preparatory courses;
  —Teach about multiple cultures; and
  —Help youth learn skills needed to navigate across multiple cultural settings.

- Opportunities to:
  —Play an increasing role as mentors of younger adolescents and to be leaders in an organization.

- Career-related experiences in a variety of occupational settings
  and career planning activities that:
  —Help them begin to focus their educational and career goals in
  ways more directly related to their emerging personal identities.

We say more about the issue of developmentally appropriate programming in Chapters 3 and 4. We now turn to a more specific discussion of developmental changes during the adolescent years.

Biological Changes

A complete review of the biological changes associated with puberty
is beyond the scope of this report, but, given the centrality of these
changes, it is important to provide a brief overview (see Adams et al.,
1989; Brooks-Gunn and Reiter, 1990; Brooks-Gunn et al., 1994;
Buchanan et al., 1992; Caspi et al., 1993; National Research Council,
1999a). As a result of the activation of the hormones controlling pubertal development, most children undergo a growth spurt, develop primary
and secondary sex characteristics, become fertile, and experience increased sexual libido during early adolescence. Recently researchers have
studied exactly how the hormonal changes occurring at early adolescence (ages 9 to 13) relate to changes in behavior (e.g., see Buchanan et
al., 1992; Petersen and Taylor, 1980). There is some evidence for direct
effects of hormones on such behaviors as aggression, heightened sexual
feelings, and mood swings (e.g., Albert et al., 1993; Brooks-Gunn et al.,
1994; Buchanan et al., 1992; Caspi and Moffitt, 1991; Olweus et al.,
1988; Sussman et al., 1987; Udry et al., 1986). However, these relations
are quite complex, with hormones and other biological systems interacting in complex ways with both social behavior and genetic predisposi-
tions to influence behaviors; the direct effects of hormones are often over-
ridden by social experiences (e.g., see Kendler and Karkowski-Shuman,
1997; Haggerty et al., 1994a; Robins and Robertson, 1998; Silberg et
al., in press). To make matters even more complex, behaviors and experience, in turn, influence the hormonal systems in quite complex ways,
including even the timing of the onset of menarche (Goodyer, 1997;
Graber et al., 1995).

Because the hormonal changes are most dramatic and more irregular
during the early adolescent period, some developmental scientists have
suggested that young adolescents are particularly susceptible to these

biological influences (Carnegie Corporation of New York, 1989). The actual evidence for this suggestion is minimal due to paucity of relevant research (see Buchanan et al., 1992). But this suggestion is consistent with evidence that many of the mood and behavioral changes most often hypothesized to be related to the hormonal changes associated with puberty are most marked during the early adolescent years (Carnegie Corporation of New York, 1989; Moffitt, 1993).

Equally critical for this report is the issue of individual and group differences in both the rates and types of changes in these hormonal systems and individual differences in the reactions to these changes. Both current and previous life events and genetically linked vulnerabilities and propensities affect adolescents' reactions to the hormonal changes occurring particularly during early and middle adolescence (Caspi and Moffitt, 1991; Graber and Brooks-Gunn, in press; Gubba et al., 2000; Rutter et al., 1997; Silberg et al., in press). The nature of these interactions suggests that early adolescents living in high-risk settings may be more prone to the problematic effects of changes in the gonadol and adrenal hormone systems associated with late childhood and early adolescence.

There are, of course, also sex differences in the nature of pubertal change. The hormonal changes associated with puberty are different for girls and boys: levels of testosterone increase more in boys, while levels of estrogen and progesterone increase more in girls. In addition, girls develop a monthly cycle of gonadol hormones; for the most part, boys do not. It has been suggested that the sex differences associated with the emergence of depression, eating disorders, and aggression may be linked to these differences in patterns of hormonal changes associated with pubertal development. But evidence suggests that the origins of both sex differences and individual differences more generally in these mood and behaviors patterns lie in complex interactions between experience, life events, intensified gender role socialization, genetically linked vulnerabilities, and changes in hormonal systems (Buchanan et al., 1992; Goodyer, 1995; Graber and Brooks-Gunn, in press b; Keel et al., 1997; Kendler and Karkowski-Shuman, 1997; Kessler et al., 1993; Petersen et al., 1991; Rutter et al., 1997; Silberg et al., in press; Wichstrom, 1999; Zahn-Waxler et al., in press). Each of these authors stresses that we are just beginning to understand the nature of these interactions and therefore encourages cautious interpretation of simplistic models of the role of hormones in accounting for sex differences in moods or behaviors.

There are also sex and ethnic group differences in the timing of puberty. In general, pubertal changes begin 12 to 18 months earlier for girls than for boys—a fact that is likely to affect social interactions between males and females of the same age, particularly during the early years of adolescence. In addition, pubertal changes begin about 15 months earlier in black females than in white females (Herman-Giddens et al., 1997; National Research Council and Institute of Medicine, 1999a). As a result, anyone working with 6th graders will immediately notice major differences in the physical maturity between girls and boys, as well as among groups of girls. Many females at this age look and act like fully mature young women. In contrast, most of the males still look and act like boys. The impact of these differences on the development of early adolescents is likely to vary by cultural group, depending on beliefs and norms about appropriate roles for physically mature individuals, appropriate sexual activities, and ideals related to female and male beauty. Such differences also have implications for the design of developmentally appropriate experiences for early adolescent girls and boys of different racial or ethnic groups in community programs. Girls will need educational programs related to puberty and fertility change earlier than boys. Girls are also likely to need places in which to discuss family interactions and concerns about their changing bodies at a younger age than boys are, and black girls are likely to need these experiences at a younger age than white girls.

There are also major individual differences in the timing of puberty within each sex and racial/ethnic group—some children begin their pubertal changes earlier than others (Stattin and Magnusson, 1990). The timing of pubertal development has major implications for many aspects of life. Once again, cultural beliefs and norms are likely to influence the meaning of early maturation for both girls and boys, so the implications of pubertal timing for youth programming will differ across groups. For example, among white populations, early maturation tends to be advantageous for boys, particularly with respect to their participation in sports activities and social standing in school. In contrast, early maturation is often problematic for white girls—being linked to increased rates of eating disorders, depression, and involvement in a variety of problematic behaviors (Caspi and Moffitt, 1991; Flannery et al., 1993; Ge X et al., 1996b; Graber and Brooks-Gunn, in press; Silbereisen et al., 1989; Simmons and Blyth, 1987; Stattin and Magnusson, 1990). Interestingly, these problematic correlates of early puberty are not as evident in black populations (Michaels and Eccles, 2001; Simmons and Blyth, 1987). We do not know about the strength of association for other racial/ethnic groups. Although we do not yet understand the origins of these ethnic group differences, it has been suggested that early pubertal maturation may be particularly problematic for white American girls, because the kinds of physical changes girls experience with puberty (such as gaining weight) are not highly valued by many white Americans, who seem instead to value the slim, androgynous female body characteristic of white fashion models (see Petersen, 1998; Simmons and Blyth, 1987). In fact, early-maturing white females have lower self-esteem and more difficulty adjusting to school transitions, particularly the transition from elementary to junior high school than later-maturing white girls, white boys in general, and both black girls and boys (e.g., Eccles et al., 1996b; Simmons and Blyth, 1987). These results suggest that youth-serving organizations should be especially sensitive of the need to design programs that will support self-esteem and prevent depression and eating disorders for early-developing white adolescents.

Early maturation can also lead to increased sexual attention from boys and men, which can be quite difficult for adolescent girls to handle. Programs designed to help girls deal with these pressures would be especially useful during the early adolescent years. The need for such programs is made even more salient by the work of Magnusson and Stattin (Magnusson, 1988; Stattin and Magnusson, 1990).

Magnusson and Stattin traced the long-term consequences of early maturation in a population of Swedish females. The early-maturing girls in this study obtained less education and married earlier than their later-maturing female peers. These researchers attributed this difference to the fact that the early-maturing females were more likely to be recruited into older peer groups and to begin dating older males; in turn, as these girls got older, they were more likely to drop out of school and get married, perhaps because school achievement was not valued by their peer social network, while early entry into the job market and early marriage were (Magnusson, 1988; Stattin and Magnusson, 1990).

Although this study focused on Swedish youth, it clearly illustrates the fact that pubertal changes influence individual development as much through their impact on social roles and social interactions as through their direct impact on the mind and body of the individual. Because these girls looked more mature, they were recruited into an older peer group. In turn, participating in older peer groups created a particular set of experiences that had long-term consequences for individual development.

Similar processes are now being studied in other groups. For example, there is growing concern about the ways in which adults change their interaction style with black boys as these boys' bodies mature. Teachers and adults on the street react with more fear and avoidance of black boys as they begin to look more like men (Spencer, 1995; Spencer et al., 1998). Similarly, the body changes associated with puberty may lead to increased pressure to join gangs in communities in which gangs are a major form of peer interaction. As discussed throughout this report, community programs have the potential to provide alternative settings that reduce such pressures and negative experiences. Such programs are particularly important during the early adolescent years, when young people do not have the social and emotional maturity to cope well with these kinds of pressures.

Directly linked to the biological changes associated with puberty are the changes in both body architecture and emotions related to sexuality. Puberty is all about the emergence of sexuality. The physical changes of puberty both increase the individual's own interest in sex and others' perception of them as sexual objects. Both of these changes can have a profound impact on development. Sexual behavior increases dramatically during early to middle adolescence: the most recent report from the National Longitudinal Study of Adolescent Health (Blum et al., 2000) indicates that rates of sexual intercourse rise from 16 percent among 7th to 8th graders to 60 percent among 11th and 12th graders.

Accompanying these age-related increases are increases in pregnancy and sexually transmitted diseases. The rate of age-related increases in sexual intercourse is particularly high among blacks and adolescents living in poor and single-parent households. The rate of age-related increase in sexual intercourse is also especially high among adolescents who are involved in an extended romantic relationship and who perceive the benefits of sexual relations as high and the cost of sexual relations (including the cost of becoming pregnant) as low. Rates are particularly low among adolescents who want to avoid becoming pregnant so that they can fulfill their educational and occupational aspirations (Blum et al., 2000; see also Kirby and Coyle, 1997).

Some interventions designed to help adolescents form and maintain high educational and occupational aspirations and to reduce their early involvement in romantic relationships have been effective at lowering rates of unprotected sexual activity and unplanned pregnancies (Kirby and Coyle, 1997; Nicholson and Postrado, 1992; Weiss, 1995). Community programs have the potential to support these aspirations as well as provide adolescents with constructive activities that help them resist peer pressure for involvement in unprotected sexual behavior. Programs that help girls and boys deal with sexual feelings and support positive communications with parents would be especially useful for early adolescents. Programs that stress future life planning and support high educational goals would be especially useful as the boys and girls mature into middle and late adolescence.

Interesting new research on the development of the brain during adolescence also points to the important biological changes youth undergo. Based on a series of brain scans, neuroscientists have documented that the development of the brain continues beyond the early years into adolescence. In fact, the frontal lobes of the brain, responsible for functions such as self-control, judgment, emotional regulation, organization, and planning, may undergo the greatest change between puberty and young adulthood (Begley, 2000). This work points to the importance of opportunities to develop and practice these skills during the early and middle adolescent years. We discuss this need in more detail in the next section.

Changes in Cognition

The most important cognitive changes during this period of life relate to the increasing ability of youth to think abstractly, consider the hypothetical as well as the real, process information in a more sophisticated and elaborate way, consider multiple dimensions of a problem at once, and reflect on oneself and on complicated problems (see Keating, 1990). Indeed, such abstract and hypothetical thinking is the hallmark of Piaget's formal operations stage, assumed to begin during adolescence (e.g., Piaget and Inhelder, 1973). Although there is still considerable debate about when exactly these kinds of cognitive processes emerge and whether their emergence reflects global stage-like changes in thinking skills as described by Piaget, most researchers are now convinced by evidence that these kinds of thought processes are more characteristic of adolescents' than of younger children's cognition. The emergence of these skills, however, is a gradual process that takes place over the entire adolescent period and depends on having extensive experience in learning how to use these skills and then practicing them repeatedly and applying them to novel and increasingly complex problems (Clark, 1988; Keating, 1990). Too often, however, such opportunities are not provided in secondary schools, particularly in high-risk and poor neighborhoods (Coleman et al., 1966; Coleman and Hoffer, 1987). Out-of-school community programs may help fill this gap.

Many cognitive theorists have also assessed how more specific information-processing skills (topic-specific thinking and problem-solving skills), cognitive learning strategies (strategies consciously used by people to learn new information), and metacognitive skills (skills related to the conscious monitoring of one's own learning and problem-solving activities) change over development (e.g., Bjorklund, 1989; Siegler, 1986; Zimmerman, 1989). There is a steady increase in children's information-processing skills and learning strategies, their knowledge of a variety of different topics and subject areas, their ability to apply their knowledge to new learning situations, and their awareness of their strengths and weaknesses as learners. Although one would think that these types of cognitive changes ought to allow adolescents to be more efficient, sophisticated learners, ready to cope with relatively advanced topics in many different subject areas, Keating (1990) has argued that these changes do not necessarily make adolescents better thinkers, particularly during the early adolescent years. They need a lot of experience exercising these skills before they can use them efficiently (see also Clark, 1988). Community programs may provide adolescents the opportunity to practice these skills and take advantage of increasing competence by allowing them to play significant roles in program design and implementation. Enlisting adolescents as peer tutors for younger children, for example, is an excellent example of both of these opportunities. Tutoring experiences are also likely to help adolescents: (1) consolidate earlier learning related to the fundamental skills needed for college preparatory high school courses; (2) learn to analyze learning as they try to teach someone else new skills (which in turn can help them become better learners themselves); (3) feel valued and respected by adults; and (4) improve their skill at taking the perspective of others.

Along with their implications for children's learning, these cognitive changes also affect individuals' self-concept, thoughts about their future, and understanding of others. Theorists from Erikson (1963) to Harter (1990), Eccles (Eccles and Barber, 1999), Youniss (Youniss, 1980; Yates and Youniss, 1998), and Sullivan (1953) have suggested that the adolescent years are a time of change in self-concept, as young people consider what possibilities are available to them and try to come to a deeper understanding of themselves in the social and cultural settings in which they live. In a culture that stresses personal choice in life planning, these concerns and interests set the stage for personal and social identity formation focused on life planning toward educational, occupational, recreational, and marital choices. These sorts of self-reflections require the kinds of higher-order cognitive processes just discussed. Community programs have the potential to provide the opportunity for youth to use these new cognitive skills to form positive, realistic views of themselves and then to make well-informed future plans.

During adolescence, individuals also become much more interested in understanding others' internal psychological characteristics, and friendships come to be based more on perceived similarity in these characteristics (see Selman, 1980). Again, these sorts of changes reflect the broader changes in cognition that occur at this time. Community programs have the potential to provide a safe setting in which adolescents can explore themselves in relation to a wide range of activities and people. Such experiences are likely to help adolescents deal with issues related to social identity formation, as well as both tolerance and respect for cultural diversity. This should be especially true for adolescents during their high school years.

Social-Contextual Changes

Changes related to social context associated with adolescence in the United States need to be taken into consideration in designing community programs for youth. These include friendships and peer groups, changes in family relations, and school transitions.

Friendships and Peer Groups

Probably the most controversial changes during adolescence are those linked to peer relationships. One major change in this area is the general increase in peer focus and involvement in peer-related social, sports, and other extracurricular activities; the other major change is the increase in the importance of romance and sexuality in peer relationships. We discussed this second aspect of adolescent peer relationships earlier. Here we focus on the first aspect of change in peer relationships.

Many adolescents attach great importance to the activities they do with their peers—substantially more importance than they attach to academic activities (Wigfield et al., 1991). Indeed, often to the chagrin of parents and teachers, activities with peers, peer acceptance, and appearance take precedence over school activities, particularly during early adolescence. Furthermore, early adolescents' confidence in their physical appearance and social acceptance is often a more important predictor of self-esteem than confidence in their cognitive or academic competence

(Harter, 1990; Lord et al., 1994). The strength of these relationships declines as adolescents get older and more confident of their abilities, their social standing, and their own goals and values.

In part because of the importance of social acceptance during adolescence, friendship networks during this period often are organized into relatively rigid cliques that differ in social status within school and community settings (see Brown, 1990). The existence of these cliques probably reflects adolescents' need to establish a sense of identity; belonging to a group is one way to answer the question: Who am I? Several theorists have argued that the peer group is a powerful place for identity formation and consolidation (Eccles and Barber, 1999; Mead, 1935; Sullivan, 1953; Youniss, 1980; Youniss et al., 1997). Vygotsky (1978) argued that peer interactions are also particularly important for the kinds of advances in cognitive reasoning associated with adolescence precisely because these interactions are more egalitarian than adult-child interactions.

Also, in part because of the importance of social acceptance, children's conformity to their peers and susceptibility to negative peer influence peaks during early adolescence (Brown, 1990; Ruben et al., 1998). Much has been written about how this peer conformity can create problems for adolescents, and about how "good" children often are corrupted by the negative influences of peers, particularly by adolescent gangs (Harris, 1995; Steinberg, 1997; Steinberg and Morris, 2001). In fact, many of the prevention programs discussed in Chapter 6 were specifically designed to counter negative peer influences. However, although pressure from peers to engage in misconduct does increase during adolescence (see Brown, 1990; Ruben et al., 1998), most researchers do not accept the simplistic view that peer groups are primarily a bad influence during adolescence. More often than not, adolescents agree more with their parents' views than their peer groups' views on major issues, such as morality, the importance of education, politics, and religion (Ruben et al., 1998; Smetana, 1995; Smetana et al., 1991). Peers have more influence on such things as dress and clothing styles, music, and activity choice. In addition, adolescents tend to hang around with peers who hold similar views as their parents on the major issues listed above. Finally, adolescents usually seek out similar peers; this means that those involved in sports will have other athletes as friends; those serious about school will seek those kinds of friends.

These changes in the nature of peer relationships provide an excellent rationale for the availability of high-quality community programs.

By their very nature, these programs create and support peer groups. By providing a setting in which youth in peer groups can be actively and regularly involved in social, productive activities, these programs likely can increase the positive and decrease the negative influence that peers can have in each other's development. Such experiences are likely to be especially important during the early and middle adolescent years, when there are such dramatic increases in involvement in delinquent and antisocial behaviors (Moffitt, 1993) and when susceptibility to negative peer influences is at its peak. Later in adolescence, community programs can provide opportunities for middle and late adolescents to both work with and supervise younger adolescents and be mentored by older adolescents and young adults. Such experiences both provide the older adolescents with a feeling of being respected and making an important contribution to the organization, as well as the opportunity to see concrete examples of successful transitions into adulthood.

Youth-serving organizations do have to be careful about one thing: programs that enroll or attract a disproportionately large number of adolescents who have antisocial values and are already involved in criminal, aggressive, and otherwise problematic behaviors. Work by Tom Dishion and his colleagues have shown that one can get increases in problem behavior when programs specifically target youth already involved in problematic behaviors (Dishion and Andrews, 1995; Dishion et al., 1999a). This is particularly likely if such youth are the majority of program participants.

Changes in Family Relations

Although the extent of actual disruption in parent-adolescent relations is not as great as one might expect given stereotypes about this period of life, there is little question that parent-child relations do change during adolescence (e.g., Buchanan et al., 1992; Collins, 1990; Paikoff and Brooks-Gunn, 1991; Petersen, 1988). As adolescents mature, they often seek more independence and autonomy and may begin to question family rules and roles, leading to conflicts particularly around issues like dress and appearance, chores, and dating, particularly during the early adolescent years (see Collins, 1990; Smetana, 1995; Smetana et al., 1991). However, despite these conflicts over day-to-day issues, parents and adolescents agree more than they disagree regarding core values linked to education, politics, and spirituality.

With the onset of adolescence, parents and their children in some cultural groups show a decrease in the time they spend interacting with each other and in the number of activities they do together outside the home. These declines are quite common in white middle-class families in America (Larson and Richards, 1991; Steinberg, 1990). We know much less about how typical these declines are in other cultural groups. Steinberg (1990) argues that this "distancing" in relations between adolescents and parents is a natural part of adolescent development, citing evidence from nonhuman primates that puberty is the time at which parents and offspring often go their separate ways. Because parents and adolescents in American culture usually continue to live together for a long time after puberty, distancing rather than complete separation may be the evolutionary vestige in humans. Although he did not take an evolutionary perspective, Collins (1990) also concluded that the distancing in parent-adolescent relations has great functional value for adolescents, in that it fosters their individualization from their parents, allows them to try more things on their own, and develops their own competence and efficacy. It should be noted, however, that this distancing is not universal. It occurs less frequently and less extremely in many non-Western cultures and in both Hispanic and Asian communities in the United States (Larson and Verma, 1999; Mortimer and Larson, 2002).

These changes in family relationships have two important implications for community programs for youth. First, community programs, particularly for early adolescents, can help support good communications and relationships between youth and their parents. Programs such as those developed by Girls, Inc. (2000a) for preventing adolescent pregnancy have specifically focused on facilitating parent-youth communication about issues of sexuality and resisting peer pressure. Community programs can provide a setting outside the family in which adolescents can explore their growing independence and autonomy from their parents in well-supervised, safe, and constructive environments. These programs have the potential to provide the opportunity for youth to form close supportive relationships with both familial and nonfamilial adults. These relationships in turn can provide a way for youth to discuss and explore issues of identity and morality as well as future life options. These relationships also have the potential to provide them with important social connections that can help them as they navigate adolescence and the transition into adulthood.

School Transitions

In most American communities, youth experience at least one major school transition—the transition into high school—and often two major school transitions—an additional transition into either middle or junior high school—during the years from 10 to 18. Several scholars and policy makers have suggested a link between these school transitions and the declines in academic success experienced by many early adolescents. For example, Simmons and Blyth (1987) compared the developmental outcomes for youth in two different school configurations: a traditional K-6, 7-9, 10-12 grade configuration versus a K-8, 9-12 school configuration. They found a greater decline in school grades for those adolescents who moved from an elementary school into a junior high school at the end of 6th grade than for those who remained in a K-8 school. Furthermore, because this decline in grades was predictive of subsequent school failure and dropping out, the youth who experienced the junior high school transition were at greater risk of subsequent school failure and dropping out than those who remained in the K-8 schools. Roderick (1993) provided similar evidence of an association between the drop in grades over the junior high school transition and high school dropout. Simmons and Blyth (1987) also documented a greater decline in females' self-esteem and a greater increase in males' sense of being victimized for young people who experienced the junior high school transition than for those in the K-8, 9-12 grade configuration. Both Eccles and her colleagues (Eccles et al., 1993) and the Carnegie task force on middle grades education concluded that the junior high school transition also contributes to declines in interest in school, intrinsic motivation, self-concepts and self-perceptions, and confidence in one's intellectual abilities, especially following failure (see Carnegie, 1995; Eccles et al., 1993, for evidence that these declines are especially marked for youth living in poor communities and for youth who are already having academic or other difficulties before the school transition).

Drawing on person-environment fit theory, Eccles and Midgley (1989) proposed that the negative motivational and behavioral changes associated with these school transitions result from the fact that many junior and senior high schools do not provide appropriate educational environments for youth in early and middle adolescence. According to this theory, behavior, motivation, and mental health are influenced by the fit between the characteristics that individuals bring to their social environments and the characteristics of the environments themselves.

Individuals are not likely to do very well or be very motivated if they are in social environments that do not fit their psychological needs. If the social environments in the typical junior high schools and middle schools do not fit very well with the psychological needs of adolescents, this theory predicts a decline in their motivation, interest, performance, and behavior.

Evidence from a variety of sources supports this hypothesis (see Eccles et al., 1998). Both of these early adolescent school transitions often involve the following types of contextual changes: (a) a shift from a smaller to a larger school; (b) a shift from a less to a more bureaucratic, more controlling, and more heterogeneous social system; (c) a shift to a social setting with less personal contact with adults and less opportunity to be engaged in school activities and responsible school roles; (d) a shift to a more rigid, socially comparative grading system; and (e) a shift to a more rigid curriculum tracking system focused on different life trajectories (e.g., the vocational educational track versus the college-bound educational track). Along with these changes, evidence from classroom-based studies suggest that teachers in junior high schools and large middle schools feel less able to teach all of their students the more challenging academic material and are more likely to use exclusionary and harsh discipline strategies that can effectively drive low-achieving and problematic students away from school (see Eccles and Midgley, 1989; Fine, 1991).

Research in a variety of areas has documented the impact on motivation and school engagement of such changes in classroom and school environments. For example, the big school/small school literature has demonstrated the motivational advantages of small secondary schools, especially for marginal students (Barker and Gump, 1964; Elder and Conger, 2000). Similarly, the teacher efficacy literature has documented the positive consequences of high teacher efficacy on student motivation (Ashton, 1985; Brookover et al., 1979). The list of such influences could go on. The point is that the motivational problems seen at early adolescence may be a consequence of the type of school environment changes these students are forced to adapt to rather than the characteristics of the developmental period per se.

Eccles and her colleagues stress the fact that these school changes are particularly problematic for early adolescents—in fact they label this phenomenon stage-environment misfit. Evidence suggests that early adolescent development is characterized by increases in the desire for autonomy, peer orientation, self-focus and self-consciousness, salience of identity issues, concern over heterosexual relationships, and capacity for abstract cognitive activity (see Brown, 1990; Eccles et al., 1998; Harter, 1990; Keating, 1990; Simmons and Blyth, 1987). Simmons and Blyth (1987) argue that young adolescents need safe, intellectually challenging environments to adapt to these shifts. In light of these needs, the environmental changes associated with the transition to junior high school seem especially harmful, in that they emphasize competition, social comparison, and ability self-assessment at a time of heightened self-focus; they decrease decision making and choice at a time when the desire for control is growing; they emphasize lower-level cognitive strategies at a time when the ability to use higher-level strategies is increasing; and they disrupt social networks at a time when adolescents are especially concerned with peer relationships and may be in special need of close adult relationships outside the home. Consequently, the nature of these environmental changes, coupled with the normal course of individual development, is likely to result in a poor fit between early adolescents and their classroom environment, increasing the risk of negative motivational outcomes, especially for low-achieving adolescents.

Youth-serving organizations can use this information to design more developmentally appropriate activities and settings for early adolescents. By so doing they may be able to counteract the experiences in many schools that undermine early adolescents' academic motivation and school engagement, through activities such as tutoring younger children and having a real voice in program decision making.

SUMMARY

In this chapter, we have provided a general overview of adolescent development and summarized the major changes associated with adolescent development. We stressed the fact that adolescence itself is not a static stage of life. Early adolescents (between ages 10 and 14) are much different from older adolescents (between ages 15 and 18). In many ways, early adolescence is likely to be the most stressful. It is during this period that youth are dealing with the most dramatic changes on all levels—from the biological changes associated with puberty to the social changes linked to the onset of roles and norms linked to adolescent culture. Many also have to deal with major transitions at school. During this period we see the most dramatic increases in problematic behaviors and decreases in school engagement, the most evidence of family conflict, and the most evidence of negative peer influences. By middle adolescence, some of this turmoil has settled down, but the long-term consequences of some of these changes begin to emerge—consequences such as inadequate academic skills needed to take college preparatory courses, teen parenthood, dependence on drugs and alcohol, and alienation from conventional social institutions. By middle adolescence, there are also growing needs for help with more intellectually challenging courses and support in dealing with identity issues, cultural heterogeneity, career planning, and romantic relationships. By late adolescence, occupational and postsecondary educational issues are particularly salient.

It is critical that community programs for youth take these developmental changes and needs into account. First and foremost, program designers need to make sure programs are developmentally appropriate by providing the opportunity for increasing autonomy, participation in program decision making, leadership, and exposure to intellectually challenging material as participating youth mature. Second, program designers need to design the specific content of their programs to the changing developmental needs of the young people attending their programs.

CHAPTER 3

Personal and Social Assets That Promote Well-Being

Having laid out the major developmental changes and challenges associated with adolescence, we now turn to a discussion of the personal and social assets likely to facilitate both successful passage through this period of life and optimal transition into the next phase of life—adulthood.[1] What assets during adolescence facilitate both current well-being and successful future transitions? The answer to this question is fundamental to both the design and the evaluation of community programs for youth. Without such a blueprint, funders will be unable to decide which programs to support, program developers will be hard pressed to design programs since they will not know what they should

---

[1]We use the terms *successful, optimal, positive,* and *healthy* with great caution. We debated the meaning of these terms several times. These debates made it clear that different disciplines and different groups of individuals attach different connotative meaning to each of these terms. We have chosen to use all of them interchangeably to describe the condition of positive development. We are using these terms to convey the idea of appropriately positive development that reflects the individual's capabilities, limitations, and cultural milieu. We do not mean better than most other individuals or much better than normal or average levels of development. Instead we mean development that is headed along a positive trajectory toward finding a meaningful and productive place in one's cultural milieu.

66

be trying to facilitate, and evaluators will have little basis for deciding what outcomes to measure.[2]

HOW TO MEASURE WELL-BEING

Many scientists and practitioners have offered suggestions. Most importantly, there is wide consensus that being problem-free is not sufficient. "Adolescents who are merely problem-free are not fully prepared for their future" (Pittman, 1991). As noted in Chapter 1 (and described in Chapter 6), this view goes well beyond a prevention focus. It emphasizes that programs aimed primarily at reducing the odds of adolescents becoming involved in problem behaviors are not sufficient. Interestingly, as noted in Chapter 1 many successful "prevention" programs do more than just prevent problem behavior. They also provide experiences aimed at preparing youth for the future. But deciding what constitutes either fully prepared or positive youth development more generally is quite complex. Although many characteristics have been suggested, determining the value of each is not a simple matter. It involves value judgments regarding what is good as well as comprehensive longitudinal research on the links between youth characteristics and adult outcomes. In this chapter, we provide an overview of the many positive assets suggested by both scientists and practitioners and then summarize the empirical foundation supporting these suggestions.

We begin with a brief discussion of the issue of universality versus cultural specificity. Is it possible to come up with a set of indicators that is universal? Or is cultural specificity the norm? The committee debated this issue extensively. There is no question that cultural groups vary in the characteristics they value most for both their youth and adults. A very good example of this is the contrast between groups who value individuality, autonomy, and self-focused achievement and groups who value cooperation and group-focused achievement efforts (Garcia Coll and Magnuson, 2000; Shweder et al., 1998). Specific indicators of well-being are likely to be somewhat different in these two groups. However, it is also likely that there are some universal human needs that manifest themselves in specific characteristics or assets as indicators of the individuals' well-being. Even so, it is likely that the exact manifestations

---

[2]We use the term "outcomes" cautiously since most of the indicators we discuss are not final outcomes per se but rather indicators of progress along a successful life path.

vary depending on the cultural context. For example, both theory and empirical research suggest that a sense of competence is key to positive human development. However, the exact domains in which one "should" feel competent are likely to be quite culturally specific; that is, a positive sense of competence will depend on competence in those areas valued by the cultural group of which one is a member (Ogbu, 1994; Shweder et al., 1998).

The committee concluded that this debate could be reconciled to some extent by carefully considering the level of analysis. On one hand, we agreed that there are some universals at the most abstract level of consideration—universals such as the need to feel competent, to be socially connected, to feel valued and respected, to actually be making a difference in one's social group, to feel that one has some control over one's own behaviors and experiences, and to have one's physical and emotional needs met. We also agreed that the failure to have these needs met has a negative effect on development (see evidence later in this and the next chapter). On the other hand, we agreed that there would be extensive cultural specificity when one moves to a more specific level of analysis. What this means is that one must take the local cultural context into account as programs are designed and evaluated.

The committee also spent a great deal of time discussing how to select a list of indicators of well-being, particularly given the cultural issues just outlined. We decided to rely on three sources: theory, practical wisdom, and empirical research. Within the theory category, we drew on developmental theories from psychology, anthropology, and sociology. Within the category of empirical research, we reviewed three types of evidence: (1) evidence that particular characteristics are either positively related concurrently to other indicators of well-being or negatively related concurrently to indicators of problematic development; (2) evidence that particular characteristics predict positive indicators of adult well-being and of a "successful"[3] transition to normative adult statuses; and (3) evidence that the experimental manipulation or training of particular characteristics produces changes on other indicators of either

---

[3]Again we use the term "successful" cautiously, since what is a successful transition to adulthood is likely to be culturally specific and hotly contested across groups. There is clearly no single way to be a successful adult, and the range of normative variations has increased dramatically in the United States in the past 25 years (Arnett, 2000b).

current well-being and adequate functioning or a successful transition into adulthood. Finally, we included practical wisdom as a source, because practitioners in both the prevention and youth development communities have done considerable work over the past 20 to 30 years that merits inclusion. In addition, cultures have developed theories of well-being over centuries of experience. We agreed that these sources of wisdom should not be overlooked.

We found substantial convergence across these three sources of information. However, it is important to note that such convergence does not necessarily mean that we have found "the truth." Only true experiments (the third type of empirical study) provide unequivocal evidence of a causal relation between the characteristic being studied and other indicators. There are few such studies and they are often very difficult to conduct, given the nature of the characteristics being studied. In addition, in order to run carefully controlled experimental studies, scientists often have to simplify the proposed relations between hypothesized causes and effects. Some developmental scientists have questioned the impact of such simplifications on the generalizability and ecological validity of the findings (see Cook and Campbell, 1979; Damon and Lerner, 1998). Consequently, they have turned to longitudinal studies as one way to study these associations over time in the complexity of the real world. However, although longitudinal studies provide information about hypothesized causal relations, obtained relations may reflect the impact of variables not measured in the study (for example, see Damon and Lerner, 1998; Robins and Robertson, 1998; Rutter, 2000, for discussions of this issue). Cook and his colleagues (see Cook and Campbell, 1979; Damon and Lerner, 1998), as well as others, have provided a variety of alternative methods for investigating causal inferences; more studies using these methods are badly needed.

In the meantime, the convergence of theory, practical wisdom, and empirical research does provide us with strong hints regarding likely important personal and social assets. It should be noted that manipulating program and participant characteristics is exactly what we are asking the community programs to do. Careful evaluation of these programs will not only tell us about the program's effectiveness, but it will also provide experimentally based evidence for the hypothesized causal relations underlying the program's design. Developmental scientists need to pay more attention to these programs as laboratories for studying fundamental questions about human development.

THEORETICAL PERSPECTIVES

Developmental theoreticians have speculated on the core human needs and how their fulfillment relates to well-being. Perhaps the most fully elaborated developmental model of this link was proposed by Eric Erikson (see Appendix A). We provided details on his theoretical framework in Chapter 2. For our current purposes, what is most important about Erikson's framework is the specific assets he outlined as critical to healthy development: trust (which he linked to a positive emotional relationships with caring adults), a strong sense of self-sufficiency, the ability to exercise initiative, a strong sense of industry (confidence in one's ability to master the demands of one's world), a well-formed sense of personal identity, and the ability to experience and express true intimacy. Interestingly, quite similar assets have been proposed by many other developmental theorists (e.g., Bowlby, 1969,1973; Harter, 1998; Bandura, 1994; Deci and Ryan, 1985; Connell and Wellborn, 1991; Lerner and Galambos, 1998; Lerner et al., 2000; Rutter and Garmezy, 1983). Their lists include: confidence in one's ability to influence the world and achieve one's goals (a sense of personal efficacy), a strong internal desire to engage in important activities (intrinsic motivation), a desire to master the learning tasks one is confronted with in life (mastery motivation), a strong desire to be socially connected, the ability to control and regulate one's emotions (good emotional coping skills), a sense of optimism, and an attachment to at least one or two conventional prosocial institutions, such as schools, faith-based institutions, families, and community organizations.

Recently, Murnane and Levy (1996) stressed the importance a set of skills like the ones just listed, for successful entry into the adult labor market. Together these theorists suggest the following characteristics as core assets for both current and future well-being:

- A sense of safety and having one's basic physical needs met;
- A sense of social security and attachment—confidence that one's emotional needs will be met (social connectedness);
- A sense of competence and mastery (a sense of personal efficacy and mastery motivation);
- A desire to learn and curiosity about one's world (intrinsic motivation);
- A sense of identity and meaning in one's life (personal and social identities);

- Positive self-regard and general mental health; and
- A positive sense of attachment to social institutions.

PRACTICAL WISDOM

Over the past 20 or so years, many lists of assets have been proposed by foundations, youth-serving organizations, and practitioners—for example, Connell et al., (2000); the Center for Youth Development and Policy Research (1999); the Search Institute (Scales and Leffert, 1999); Carnegie Corporation of New York (1989); Dryfoos (1990); Lerner et al. (2000); Lipsitz et al. (1997); Pittman et al. (2000b); and Roth and Brooks-Gunn (2000). The Search Institute has provided the most extensive list of personal and social assets, along with a comprehensive review of supporting empirical research (Scales and Leffert, 1999). Their set falls into six general areas: commitment to learning, positive values; social competencies (including planning skills and both interpersonal and cultural competence); positive personal identity; commitment to positive use of time; and a sense of autonomy and "mattering." Others have added good physical health, cultural knowledge and skills, the ability to navigate across multiple cultural contexts and groups, creativity, the skills needed to get and keep a job, and strong institutional attachments. Finally, in one of the most parsimonious lists, Connell, Gambone, and Smith (2000) proposed three critical assets: the ability to be productive, the ability to connect, and the ability to navigate.

In a recent consensus meeting (see Roth and Brooks-Gunn, 2000), youth development advocates and youth development researchers met and agreed on the following set:

- Caring and compassion;
- Character;
- Competence in academic, social, and vocational arenas;
- Confidence; and
- Connection.

Consistent with our general notion that one can have both universals and culturally specific assets, each of these five assets can be broken down into subcomponents that reflect cultural specificity. These five are very consistent with the set of assets growing out of developmental theory. As we show in the next section, there is also growing evidence to support the importance of each of these five general characteristics.

EMPIRICAL RESEARCH

There has been substantial research over the past 50 years aimed at identifying the key characteristics associated with success in American society. Much of this work has grown out of an effort to understand resilience and well-being. By and large, these suggestions coincide quite closely with the suggestions made by both practitioners and theorists.

For example, in a classic longitudinal study of development of poor children and their families on Kauai, Hawaii, Emmy Werner and her colleagues (1982, 1992) concluded that the following characteristics are key for resilience: good cognitive skills; good social skills and an engaging personality; self-confidence, self-esteem, and a sense of personal efficacy; good self-regulation skills; good coping and adaptation skills; good health; strong social connections to family; strong social connections to prosocial organizations and networks, such as schools, faith-based institutions, community organizations, and service-related clubs and organizations; and spirituality or a sense of meaningfulness. Clausen (1993) and Elder (1974) reached similar conclusions based on their classic longitudinal work done on the Berkeley and Oakland Growth Studies. Clausen (1993) added "planfulness" (i.e., planning for the future and future life events) to the list.

In each of these studies (as well as many others), the presence of these assets predicted better current and subsequent well-being. Furthermore, in each of these studies, having more assets predicted better outcomes than having fewer assets. The benefits of these assets, on the average, appear to accumulate both over time and over the number of assets one has.[4] Recent reviews of both the prevention and resiliency literatures suggest quite a similar list of characteristics as protective factors against getting involved in a variety of problematic behaviors (e.g., Catalano et al., 2000).

---

[4]This does not mean that an individual cannot do quite well with a limited number of assets. Many people lead quite successful and productive lives with only a limited number of assets. Some of our greatest "geniuses" have excelled despite physical and social disabilities. What these data do mean is that well-being on the average is easier to achieve when one has more rather than fewer assets.

PERSONAL AND SOCIAL ASSETS

Based upon the committee's review of theory, practical wisdom, and empirical research, as well as related studies of resilience and adolescent development, we have organized our list of key assets around four general categories: physical health, cognitive development, psychological and emotional development, and social development. The key indicators associated with each of these categories are listed in Box 3-1. The subcomponents of our list closely match the characteristics already discussed. Our final list differs only in the addition of good physical and mental health and in the elaboration of the general categories.

The existing literature suggests three major conclusions: (1) it is beneficial to have assets in each of the four general categories; (2) within each general category, one can do quite well with only a subset of the many characteristics listed; and (3) in general, having more assets is predictive of better current and future well-being than having only a few. However, as noted earlier, these inferences are based largely on correlational designs (both time-limited and longitudinal). More experimental studies are needed to confirm these hypotheses.

Physical Health

Despite the importance of physical health for youth well-being and development, much of the empirical research focuses on poor health outcomes, such as obesity, chronic illnesses (e.g., asthma), and acute conditions (e.g., sexually transmitted diseases) rather than indicators of good health. This emphasis on physical health risks rather than positive health status is driven in part by evidence linking specific behaviors in childhood and adolescence to the development of chronic diseases in adulthood. There is, however, a growing body of research suggesting that some behaviors have direct health benefits for adolescents in addition to reducing risks of illness and death in the adult years. Two behaviors—physical activity and healthy eating—have strong support for their beneficial health effects for young people.

Regular physical activity has been shown to improve the aerobic endurance and muscle strength of children and youth (Dotson and Ross, 1985; Treuth et al., 1998; Baranowski et al., 1992). It has been associated with decreases in blood pressure (Strazzullo et al., 1988), higher HDL cholesterol levels, lower triglycerides (Armstrong and Simon-Morton, 1994), and favorable glucose and insulin levels (Voors et al.,

---

BOX 3-1
Personal and Social Assets That Facilitate Positive
Youth Development

Physical development
- Good health habits
- Good health risk management skills

Intellectual development
- Knowledge of essential life skills
- Knowledge of essential vocational skills
- School success
- Rational habits of mind—critical thinking and reasoning skills
- In-depth knowledge of more than one culture
- Good decision-making skills
- Knowledge of skills needed to navigate through multiple cultural contexts

Psychological and emotional development
- Good mental health including positive self-regard
- Good emotional self-regulation skills
- Good coping skills

1982), particularly among young people at risk for cardiovascular disease. In addition, there is some evidence that regular physical activity bolsters self-esteem and self-confidence, important determinants of psychological and social functioning (Jaffee and Manzer,1992; Brown and Harrison,1986).

In the United States, overnourishment, not undernourishment, is a major health issue, and much of the research on diet has focused on obesity. Once viewed as a primary risk factor for adult cardiovascular disease, cancer, and diabetes, there is some recent evidence to suggest that excess weight carries with it more immediate health consequences for young people. In particular, recent increases in the prevalence of Type 2 diabetes, generally an adult disorder, has been associated with rising obesity rates for children and youth (Libman and Arslanian, 1999; Falkner and Michel, 1999; Rosenbloom et al., 1999). On the deficit

- Good conflict resolution skills
- Mastery motivation and positive achievement motivation
- Confidence in one's personal efficacy
- "Planfulness"—planning for the future and future life events
- Sense of personal autonomy/responsibility for self
- Optimism coupled with realism
- Coherent and positive personal and social identity
- Prosocial and culturally sensitive values
- Spirituality or a sense of a "larger" purpose in life
- Strong moral character
- A commitment to good use of time

Social development

- Connectedness—perceived good relationships and trust with parents, peers, and some other adults
- Sense of social place/integration—being connected and valued by larger social networks
- Attachment to prosocial/conventional institutions, such as school, church, nonschool youth programs
- Ability to navigate in multiple cultural contexts
- Commitment to civic engagement

side, failure to consume adequate amounts of essential nutrients has been linked with poor school performance (Meyers et al., 1991) and general deficits in cognitive functioning (Kretchner et al., 1996).

Not all youth are equally affected. Minority and poor adolescents are disproportionately represented among the obese (Troiano et al., 1995; Winkleby, 1994) and dietary-related deficits in cognitive functioning have been found among poor schoolchildren (Meyers et al., 1991). Families who live in poor communities are constrained by both the cost and ready availability of healthful foods required for a balanced diet.

Most interventions to promote healthy diets and physical activity for youth have been conducted in schools (Resnicow et al., 1996). There is less empirical work that assesses the effectiveness of community programs to improve their diet and physical activity (Pate et al., 2000). The Active Winners, an after-school and summer physical activity program targeting black 5th grade students in rural South Carolina (Pate et al., 1997) and the Minnesota Heart Health Program, one site of three in a large-scale cardiovascular risk reduction study (Keldner et al., 1993) are two community-based studies demonstrating promising trends in dietary choices (Keldner et al., 1993) and physical activity (Keldner et al., 1993; Pate et al., 1997) but no significant changes in behaviors at this point in the study. New programs focused jointly on diet and exercise have been developed by such organizations as Boys and Girls Clubs of America (e.g., their Body Works program) and Girls, Inc. (e.g., their Peer Coaches, Steppingstones, and Bridges programs) and are currently moving beyond successful pilot tests to more comprehensive evaluations. Given the paucity of community-based studies, it is premature to discount the potential effectiveness of programs to promote healthy eating and physical activity delivered in such community settings as recreation centers, churches, and schools. There is a need to better understand how community health promotion programs work with school-based and family interventions to foster optimal physical health.

Intellectual Development

There is quite strong support for the importance of life skills, academic success in school, "planfulness," and good decision-making skills for positive development. Academic success is, without a doubt, one of the most powerful predictors of both present and future well-being, including mental health, school completion and ultimate educational attainment, ultimate occupational attainment, prosocial values and behaviors, good relations with parents and prosocial friends, high levels of volunteerism, and low levels of involvement in such problematic behaviors as risky sexual behavior, drug and alcohol abuse, and involvement in criminal activities (e.g., Alexander et al., 1993, 1994; Clausen, 1993; Elder, 1998; Elder and Conger, 2000; Entwisle and Alexander, 1993; Entwisle et al., 1987; Jessor et al., 1991; Scales and Leffert, 1999; Schweinhart et al., 1993; Werner and Smith, 1982, 1992).

Interestingly, the link of academic success in school to mental health and self-esteem is much weaker for blacks and for females (Eccles et al., 1999). As a group of individuals (such as blacks or females) learns that they are not expected to do well in school (or in math and physical science for females) and in fact do not do as well as other groups, they often, according to Claude Steele (Steele, 1992; Steele and Aronson, 1995), come to place less importance on doing well in school (or math and physical science for females). By less "importance," Steele means the importance of the domain for the individual's self-esteem and self-evaluation; specifically, he predicted that both success and failure in devalued domains would come to mean less to the person's sense of self than success or failure in more valued domains of life. By lowering the value attached to doing well in school (or in particular subjects like math and science), individuals in particular groups can protect their self-esteem from the experience of failure and discrimination in those settings.

Steele labeled this phenomenon "deidentification" (see also Fordham and Ogbu, 1986). It is critical to note here that deidentification occurs because of the social conditions that groups of people experience in school or other institutional settings. Consequently, the processes associated with deidentification are quite amenable to intervention and policy changes, and Steele and his colleagues have developed and tested model programs for such interventions (see work by Stelle and Aronson, 1995). Such programs consist of experiences designed to prepare the early adolescent for the stereotypes they are likely to confront about their ability to do well in school, provide them with alternative explanations for their academic difficulties, provide them with experiences of success in mastering these academic tasks, and provide them with tutoring to bolster their basic skills.

The issues addressed by Steele and Ogbu need to be researched for other populations. It seems likely that any personal or cultural characteristic that lowers the value attached to academic achievement will serve to both reduce the connection between academic success and subsequent mental health and lessen adolescents' commitment to working hard to do well in school. Furthermore, it is likely that cultural norms and values that stress adult outcomes not linked to education and competitive occupational pursuits will also reduce the value attached to school-based academic achievement during the adolescent years. Finally, school practices that stress behaviors and values at odds with local cultural norms and values (such as a school's valuing of competition and individual success more highly than the cooperative success and joint problem solving valued in some cultural communities) are likely to reduce the value that members of the local cultural group place on academic school achievement.

The research on girl-friendly math and science instruction is an excellent example of this last point. Years of research (see Eccles et al., 1998) have documented the fact that many girls and boys are turned off to math by competitive motivational strategies and individualistic work activities (rather than cooperative motivational strategies and group-oriented work activities). Changing these teaching practices has a substantial impact on both girls' and boys' interest and performance in math and science courses. More work is needed to determine if similar processes and interventions would work to support school achievement in those cultural groups that currently are not doing as well in school as white middle-class populations. Educational programs reviewed in later chapters suggest that such interventions can work in community programs. The Family Math and Family Computer Literacy programs developed at the Lawrence Hall of Science, University of California, provide excellent models of such interventions (University of California, Berkeley, 2001). But more experimental evaluation studies of such interventions are needed.

Interestingly, many intervention studies have used school academic success as the outcome and have attempted to change psychological and social characteristics in an effort to raise academic achievement. Some of these efforts have been quite successful in limited experimental settings (e.g., Felner et al., 1997; Schunk, 1994; Schweinhart and Weikart, 1997). Efforts to expand such interventions to scale have yielded more mixed results (see Eccles et al., 1998). In addition, more work is needed to see if these interventions can be adapted for use in programs in out-of-school hours. Finally, although several studies have documented the importance of life skills training for positive development, we know little about which particular life skills and competencies are most important for youth in different cultural, ethnic, gender, and social class settings.

Most of the work on "habits of mind" has been done by educational researchers. They define habits of mind in terms of approaching challenging intellectual tasks and new learning opportunities with active reasoning and "deep" and recurring inquiry and questioning, experimentation, continual monitoring of one's learning, continual attempts to apply new learning to novel situations, and being intellectually curious about one's world. Both correlational studies and experimental interventions have demonstrated that these cognitive approaches facilitate new learning, persistence in the face of failure, and generalization of what one has learned to new situations (National Research Council, 1999; DeLoache et al., 1998; Jackson and Davis, 2000; Pintrich and Schunk, 1996 for reviews).

The work on the importance of knowledge of multiple cultures for well-being is also very limited because it is so new. This work has focused primarily on how the knowledge of multiple cultural scripts and norms is advantageous to minority youth who have to navigate in both their own culture and the majority white culture (see Banks, 1995; Castro et al., 2000; Phelan et al., 1992; Phelan and Davidson, 1993; Spencer and Markstrom-Adams, 1990; Markstrom-Adams and Spencer, 1994). Other work has documented the role of multiple cultural knowledge and friendships in facilitating interethnic relations (Banks, 1995; Hawley and Jackson, 1995). Much more work is needed on whether knowledge of multiple cultures is an asset for white middle-class youth.

Psychological and Emotional Development

There is quite strong longitudinal and cross-sectional support for the importance of mental health, good self-regulation skills of all kinds, a sense of autonomy and self-control, confidence in one's self-efficacy and in one's competence in valued domains (such as sports, music, school subjects, and getting along with others), optimism, and "planfulness" (Bandura, 1994; Clausen, 1993; Compas et al., 1986; Connell and Wellborn, 1991; Deci and Ryan, 1985; Dweck, 1999; Elder and Conger, 2000; Jessor et al., 1991; Lord et al., 1994; Luthar and Zigler, 1992; Mac Iver et al., 1991; Skinner, 1995; Pintrich et al., 1993; Werner and Smith, 1992; Zimmerman, et al., 1992; Zimmerman, 2000; see Eccles et al., 1998, and Scales and Leffert, 1999, for additional references). The relations appear to be equally strong among all groups studied. However, little research has been conducted on American Indian youth, recent immigrant populations, or Hispanics. Finally, intervention efforts to change some of these assets have shown positive consequences for other indicators of positive development, such as school success, positive transitions into the labor market, and both avoidance of and reduction in problem behaviors.

Most often, however, the studies (both correlational and experimental) have included only one or two psychological characteristics and only one or two outcomes, so little is known about the relative importance of these various psychological characteristics for different outcomes. What we do know is that the associations are particularly strong when there is close correspondence between the characteristic being trained and the outcome being studied. For example, training in resistance skills is quite effective at increasing both confidence in one's ability to resist peer pressure and actual ability to resist peer pressure; similarly, conflict management training is effective at producing declines in aggressive behaviors and conduct disorder (Bandura, 1994; Donahue, 1987; Ellickson and

Hayes, 1990, 1991; Johnson and Johnson, 1996; Miller et al., 1998; see also Scales and Leffert, 1999). These patterns of findings suggest that programs should be careful in selecting evaluation indicators that closely match the characteristics targeted for support and training.

Consistent findings among a limited number of high-quality correlational (both concurrent—data collected only at one point in time—and longitudinal—data collected over a period of time) studies are emerging to support the predictive importance of such characteristics as prosocial values, spirituality and a sense of purpose, moral character (e.g., Benson and Donahue, 1989; Benson et al., 1997; Eisenberg and Fabes, 1998; Hanson and Ginsburg, 1987; Kirby et al., 1994; Litchfield et al., 1997; Wentzel, 1991; Werner and Smith, 1992), a strong sense of personal responsibility (Elder and Conger, 1999), a strong sense of mattering and meaning in life (DuRant et al., 1995; Elder and Conger, 2000; Werner and Smith, 1992), and a positive and coherent personal identity (Abramowitz et al., 1984; Erikson, 1968; Marcia, 1980; Waterman, 1982). However, many of these studies have been correlational, short term, and have included only one or two assets. Consequently, little is known about the relative predictive importance of these assets. We also know very little about how to influence these characteristics and whether increases in them will actually produce changes in other characteristics in the short term as well as in successful transition into adulthood over the long term.

Similarly, good support is emerging for the potential importance of positive and coherent social identities (identities related to one's membership in a social group, such as male or female, black, Hispanic, Jewish, Catholic, Irish, etc.). A few recent studies have found that having a strong positive ethnic identity is associated with having high self-esteem, a strong commitment to doing well in school, a strong sense of purpose in life, great confidence in one's own personal efficacy, and high academic achievement (e.g., Beauvais, 2000; Boykin, 1986; Cross, 1991, 1995; Ford and Harris, 1996; Phelan and Davidson, 1993; Phinney, 1990, 1990; Fisher et al., 1998; Spencer, 1995; Tatum, 1997). Researchers studying the importance of ethnic identities stress the importance of adolescents of non-European ethnic heritage having the opportunity to explore their ethnic identities and other's ethnicity without fear of being stereotyped, harassed, or rejected (Fine et al., 1997; Tatum, 1997). Community programs may provide such opportunities.

Interestingly, these same studies indicate that discriminatory racial experiences have a less negative association with subsequent psychological and emotional development for black adolescents with strong African American identities. The data suggest that these youth respond to the experiences of racial discrimination with an increased commitment to doing well in school and to equipping themselves with all of the social and intellectual skills needed to succeed in mainstream society (Wong and Taylor, 1998).

More comprehensive long-term longitudinal work and more work focused on actually changing these assets and then assessing the effect of such changes on well-being are urgently needed. In addition, little is known about the importance of these characteristics across cultural, ethnic, social class, and gender groups. The little available evidence suggests that most of these characteristics are important in all cultural groups (see Scales and Leffert, 1999). However, this work is still in its infancy.

Social Development

There is very strong concurrent and longitudinal correlational evidence of the predictive importance of connectedness, being valued by the larger society, and institutional attachments for positive youth development. These social assets predict school success, mastery of all types of "taught" skills, long-term educational and occupational attainment, good mental health, positive personal and social identities, confidence in one's efficacy, optimism, and good self-regulation skills of all kinds. These social assets also predict both the avoidance of involvement in problem behaviors and a relatively smooth transition into such key adult roles as intimate partner, spouse, parent, worker, and active community member (e.g., Cairns and Cairns, 1994; Connell et al., 1995; Conger and Elder, 2000; Furstenberg et al., 1999; Wentzel, 1991; Werner and Smith, 1992). These relations hold for all groups studied. However, there have been very few experimental studies focused on assessing whether changes in these social assets are causally related to changes in either current well-being or future successful transition into adulthood.

The need to belong has been suggested to be one of the strongest human motivational needs (Bowlby, 1969, 1988; Rossi and Rossi, 1990). As a result, individuals act as though they are highly motivated to become a part of a larger social group, even if such associations are not always good for them in the long run. Becoming integrated into a group usually entails adopting the group's social norms, behaviors, and values. As identification with the group becomes stronger and more long-lived, the individual is likely to internalize these values and norms. It is this internalization of values and norms that is likely to underlie the impact of social group membership on specific behaviors (Deci and Ryan, 1985). Under optimal conditions, these processes lead to the internalization of prosocial and moral values and goals. It is important to note, however, that individuals can form quite strong connections with antisocial or problematic groups or individuals. This is very likely to happen when connections with more prosocial groups and organizations do not form because the individual either fails in these healthier environments or is excluded or pushed out by the prosocial groups themselves (Cairns and Cairns, 1994; Fine, 1991; Sampson and Laub, 1993). Community programs provide an excellent venue for providing the opportunity to become socially attached to positive social institutions and peer groups with positive social values.

There is less evidence for the importance of either the ability and desire to participate in multiple cultural settings or a commitment to civic engagement and service—not because the evidence is negative but because there have been so few studies focusing on these social developmental characteristics. The few existing studies provide preliminary support (e.g., Phalen et al., 1992; Yates and Youniss, 1998, 1999), but more research is needed, particularly given the strong theoretical reasons to believe that these two characteristics should be important in a multicultural society.

Conclusions

We have reviewed what is known about the relation of a set of personal and social assets widely acknowledged as important for development to both adolescent well-being and functioning and the successful transition into adulthood. We used three types of empirical studies in this review: studies linking the personal and social assets listed in Box 3-1 to indicators of positive current development, studies linking these characteristics to indicators of future positive adult development, and experimental studies designed to change the asset under study. The indicators of current well-being include good mental health, good school performance, good peer relations, good problem-solving skills, and very low levels (or the absence) of involvement in a variety of problem behaviors, such as gang membership, drug and alcohol use, school failure, school dropout, delinquency, and early pregnancy. Indicators of positive development during late adolescence and adulthood include completing high school, completing higher education, adequate transition into the labor market (obtaining and keeping a job that pays at least a living wage), staying out of prison, avoiding drug and alcohol abuse, and entering a stable and supportive intimate relationship (often through marriage). Some recent studies also include involvement in civic and community activities as indicators of positive adult development.

We found strong correlational support for the relation of most of the assets listed in Box 3-1 with indicators of both positive development during adolescents and the successful transition into adulthood. Because of the recency of interest in the role of cultural understanding and tolerance and social identities, few studies document the association of these assets to well-being. The strongest experimental evidence of a causal relation between personal assets and other indicators of positive development exists for intellectual and social or life skills.

Limitations of the Research Base

Most of the studies reviewed used only a small subset of these indicators of positive development—often only one. Too many of the studies relied on data collected only at one point in time (called concurrent studies). Findings from such studies are difficult to interpret because the causal directions underlying the relations are unclear. In addition, the majority of the concurrent studies focused on white middle-class populations. In contrast, several ongoing longitudinal studies have included a wide range of populations in many types of environments. The findings of these studies suggest that the findings from the concurrent studies are likely to also be true of groups other than white middle-class populations. Together the concurrent and longitudinal studies provide a growing body of consistent evidence supporting the predictive importance of the set of characteristics we have identified. Nevertheless, more comprehensive longitudinal studies that follow children and youth into and through the young adult years are urgently needed. This need is particularly true for populations that are neither white, middle class, nor suburban. Work on American Indian and recent immigrant populations is particularly sparse.

The issue of causal direction of influence is quite complex and is equally problematic for both concurrent and longitudinal research. It is likely that many of these assets are reciprocally related to each other—making the search for causal order in naturalistic studies difficult. Some researchers argue that such a search is actually counterproductive, precisely because of the complex and reciprocal nature of the relations among the constructs discussed in this chapter and the next. But intervention programs have to consider whether changing particular characteristics or assets, such as self-esteem or a sense of personal efficacy, will lead to changes in other indicators of well-being, such as school achievement or avoidance of problem behaviors. Controlled intervention studies are needed to address this issue; some were discussed in this chapter; more are discussed in later chapters. We have indicated when such studies provide support for the importance of particular characteristics. More research involving active efforts to change assets and then measure the effect of such changes on other assets and on future indicators of well-being is urgently needed.

SUMMARY

The period of adolescence is complicated: it is full of opportunities and risks. Adolescents have the potential to develop into mature, strong, creative, and smart adults. But, some take, or are exposed to, unhealthy and unsafe risks that can endanger both their present health and well-being and their future adult opportunities. In this chapter, we provide a summary of what is known about the personal and social assets likely to facilitate positive development during this period of life. We suggested ways in which this information is relevant to the development of community programs for youth. This information, in conjunction with the material discussed in the next chapter, can help program developers design programs, funders decide what kinds of programs to fund, and evaluators to design or select appropriate implementation and outcome measures.

Based on the material summarized in this chapter, the committee identified a set of personal and social assets that both represent healthy development and well-being during adolescence and facilitate a successful transition from childhood, through adolescence, and into adulthood. The committee grouped these assets into four broad developmental domains: physical, intellectual, psychological and emotional, and social development. One does not need necessarily need the entire range of assets listed in this chapter to have a good life. For instance, studies that include more than one of these assets have found that youth can do quite well with various combinations of the studied assets. Nevertheless, having more assets is better than having a few and having positive assets in each of the four broad categories is beneficial. Although strong assets in one category may be able to offset weak assets in another category, life is easier to manage if one has assets in all four categories.

Although the body of evidence supporting the assets listed in this chapter is growing, much more comprehensive longitudinal and experimental research on a wider range of populations that follows children and adolescents well into adulthood is needed in order to understand which assets are most important to adolescent development and which patterns of assets are linked to particular types of successful adult transitions in various cultural settings. There is a pressing need for longitudinal studies to illuminate:

- How these assets work together (this means more comprehensive studies of both assets and outcomes) and
- How these various assets are manifested and valued in different cultural groups.

There is also a pressing need for more field-based experimental studies to confirm the hypothesized causal relations in complex settings.

In conclusion, it is also important to note that these personal and social assets do not exist in a vacuum. Evidence suggests that these assets influence life chances because they both (1) facilitate the engagement of youth in positive social settings that support continued positive development and (2) protect them against the adverse effects of negative life events, difficult social situations, pressure to engage in risky behaviors, and academic failures. So on one hand, the personal and social assets discussed in this chapter can increase life chances. On the other hand, excessive and prolonged exposure to negative life events, dangerous settings, and inadequate schooling are likely to undermine young people's life chances despite their assets. Young people need continued exposure to positive experiences, settings, and people as well as abundant opportunities to gain and refine their life skills in order to support the acquisition and growth of these assets.

CHAPTER 4

Features of Positive Developmental Settings

Picture a diverse group of American adolescents: girls and boys; rural, urban, suburban; affluent and disadvantaged; youth living with one parent, two parents, a foster parent, a grandparent, or on their own; adolescents with and without physical disabilities; adolescents who are lesbian and gay; youth who are introverted and extroverted; youth with parents who are Chinese immigrants, Mexican migrant laborers, Laotian, Dakotan, Salvadoran, African American, European American.

Now picture each of them walking through the front door of a community program. How do we make sure that this program engages all these youth and supports their development? What can a program do to give each person who walks in the door the best chance possible of growing up to be a healthy adult and have the personal assets described in the last chapter? Having described assets of positive development in Chapter 3, this chapter summarizes what is known about the daily settings and experiences that promote this development in young people.

Before starting, we need to recognize that even with the best staff and best funding, no single program is going to succeed in helping every participant. Adolescents have many other, often more powerful influences in their lives;

some will be more ready for change and growth than others. In addition, any given program will work better for some teens than for others. Finally, we need to recognize that there is very little research that directly specifies what programs can do to facilitate development, let alone how to tailor it to the needs of individual adolescents and diverse cultural groups. Few studies have applied the critical standards of science to evaluate which features of community programs influence development.

Despite these limitations, there is a broad base of knowledge about how development occurs that can and should be drawn on. Research demonstrates that certain features of the settings that adolescents experience make a tremendous difference, for good or for ill, in their lives. For example, research on families and classrooms shows that the presence or absence of caring relationships affects whether an adolescent thrives or has problems. We think it is valid to hypothesize that this will be true in community programs as well.

This chapter employs this wider base of knowledge from developmental science to generate a list of features of adolescents' daily settings and experiences that are known to promote positive youth development. We suggest that these eight features should be seen as a provisional list—subject to further study—of the processes or "active ingredients" that community programs could use in designing programs likely to facilitate positive youth development. We stress that the implementation of these features needs to vary across programs precisely because they have diverse clientele and different constraints, resources, and goals.

There are numerous theories in developmental psychology, sociology, public health, anthropology, and other fields that direct attention to a panorama of individual, community, and cultural processes that are related to positive development. Appendix B is a review of the theories of human development that highlight ways of seeing the full framework within which development takes place for different youth. It describes how development includes multiple processes: an adolescent's active creativity, thoughtful mentoring and management by others, acquisition of social capital, and socialization into a culture. The opportunities an adolescent has for development are shaped by numerous personal, institutional, and cultural factors (see Damon, 1997; Feldman and Elliott, 1990; Grotevant, 1998; Steinberg, 2000; Steinberg and Morris, 2001). The major implications of these theories of human development for community programs for youth include the importance of good developmental, cultural, and personal fit; the important role that community organizations can play in helping adolescents build the social capital and life skills necessary to successfully manage their lives in a very complex social system; and the importance of community programs being interconnected with each other, with families, and with other youth-serving institutions and programs in the community.

FEATURES THAT MAXIMIZE POSITIVE DEVELOPMENT

In this section we present a provisional list of eight features of daily settings that are important for adolescent development. This list is based partly on theories of positive developmental processes and partly on empirical research on the many types of settings that youth experience—families, schools, neighborhoods, and community programs. We have also drawn on lists of features created by other scholars and practitioners (e.g., American Youth Policy Forum, 1997; Benson, 1997; Connell et al., 2000; Dryfoos, 1990; Gambone and Arbreton, 1997; Lipsitz, 1980; McLaughlin, 2000; Merry, 2000; Roth and Brooks-Gunn, 2000; Zeldin et al., 1995). Table 4-1 is a summary of the eight features. In assessing the evidence for these eight characteristics, we relied on the most recent peer-reviewed literature reviews (e.g., those published in the 1998 *Handbook of Child Psychology*, edited by William Damon, 1997; the recent *Annual Reviews* for psychology, sociology, and anthropology; the major review journals in each of these fields as well as recent articles published in the major peer-reviewed journals in these fields). Instead of a lengthy list of citations following each conclusion, we cite representative articles and reviews.

Two qualifications need to be kept in mind. First, we emphasize that this list is provisional: it is based on the current research base, thus it is likely to have omitted features important to various cultural groups. Second, the boundaries between features are often quite blurred. This list, then, is only a step on the path toward formulating a more comprehensive framework; more research needs to be done. Although we describe these as features of settings, this is really shorthand for saying that they are features of the person's *interaction with* the setting. Bronfenbrenner and Morris (1998) have decried a recent tendency for scholars to discuss the setting without the child and to discuss the child without the setting. We want to avoid encouraging these shortcomings. It is the experience of the adolescent-in-setting—the *processes* of interaction—that is critical to development. When adolescents walk in the door, it is not what they see that is important, but rather it is how they become engaged.

Physical and Psychological Safety

At the most basic level, safety is essential for positive development. Safety is both a physical and a psychological phenomenon. Starting with the physical side, positive settings must be free from violence and unsafe health conditions because of their direct impact on physical health and survival. Childhood sexual abuse appears again and again as a causal factor in numerous adult psychological disorders (Finkelhor, 1990; Briere and Runtz, 1991); it is a profound breach to the trusting relationships that attachment and object relations theorists see as critical to positive development. Both school health professionals (Institute of Medicine, 1997b) and professionals working in the area of youth development programming design, implementation, and evaluation (Pittman et al., 2000b) have articulated a variety of other safety issues, including freedom from exposure to environmental hazards, infectious agents, and both unintentional and intentional injuries. The corollary is that adults in charge of youth need to do more than just mouth the importance of safety; they need to take extra steps to instill practices that reduce the probability of unforeseen threats. Having guns in the home, for example, increases the likelihood of their use by adolescents (Blum and Rinehart, 1997). Similarly, fears of physical hazards and violence have made parents wary of their children's schools and community centers.

The psychological side of safety is also of great importance. The experience, witnessing, or even the threat of violence sends psychological ripples through a community of adolescents that can be severe and long-lasting. Youth who are victims of violence, as well as those who witness violence, show continuing symptoms of posttraumatic stress disorder, including depression, dissociative reactions, helplessness, emotional disregulation, aggression, intrusive thoughts, and flashbacks (Dubrow and Garbarino, 1989; Martinez and Richters, 1993). Experience of violence and harassment in school (being picked on, hit, or talked about unkindly) are related to skipping school, more negative attitudes toward school, lower achievement levels, and fewer friendships (Jackson and Davis, 2000; Scales and Leffert, 1999). Finally, biological research shows that prolonged stress, such as that from experience with the threat of violence, is associated with suppression of immune response and deleterious effects on the brain, with likely effects on the capacity to learn (Cynader and Frost, 1999).

There are also community-level effects of violence. Violence tends to breed more violence. When youth are victimized by others, they often

TABLE 4-1   Features of Positive Developmental Settings

	Descriptors	Opposite Poles
Physical and Psychological Safety	Safe and health-promoting facilities; and practices that increase safe peer group interaction and decrease unsafe or confrontational peer interactions.	Physical and health dangers; fear; feeling of insecurity; sexual and physical harassment; and verbal abuse.
Appropriate Structure	Limit setting; clear and consistent rules and expectations; firm-enough control; continuity and predictability; clear boundaries; and age-appropriate monitoring.	Chaotic; disorganized; laissez-faire; rigid; overcontrolled; and autocratic.
Supportive Relationships	Warmth; closeness; connectedness; good communication; caring; support; guidance; secure attachment; and responsiveness.	Cold; distant; overcontrolling; ambiguous support; untrustworthy; focused on winning; inattentive; unresponsive; and rejecting.
Opportunities to Belong	Opportunities for meaningful inclusion, regardless of one's gender, ethnicity, sexual orientation, or disabilities; social inclusion, social engagement, and integration; opportunities for sociocultural identity formation; and support for cultural and bicultural competence.	Exclusion; marginalization; and intergroup conflict.
Positive Social Norms	Rules of behavior; expectations; injunctions; ways of doing things; values and morals; and obligations for service.	Normlessness; anomie; laissez-faire practices; antisocial and amoral norms; norms that encourage violence; reckless behavior; consumerism; poor health practices; and conformity.
Support for Efficacy and Mattering	Youth-based; empowerment practices that support autonomy; making a real difference in one's community; and being taken seriously. Practice that includes enabling, responsibility granting, and meaningful challenge. Practices that focus on improvement rather than on relative current performance levels.	Unchallenging; overcontrolling; disempowering, and disabling. Practices that undermine motivation and desire to learn, such as excessive focus on current relativeperformance level rather than improvement.

TABLE 4-1   Continued

	Descriptors	Opposite Poles
Opportunities for Skill Building	Opportunities to learn physical, intellectual, psychological, emotional, and social skills; exposure to intentional learning experiences; opportunities to learn cultural literacies, media literacy, communication skills, and good habits of mind; preparation for adult employment; and opportunities to develop social and cultural capital.	Practices that promote bad physical habits and habits of mind; and practices that undermine school and learning.
Integration of Family, School, and Community Efforts	Concordance; coordination; and synergy among family, school, and community.	Discordance; lack of communication; and conflict.

react with retributive violence, and gang formation or membership is often not far behind (Prothrow-Stith and Weissman, 1991). A high prevalence of violence changes the social norms of a community. Even when a community program is safe, getting to and from it without risk is critical.

In conclusion, physical and psychological safety are prerequisites to all the categories of positive development we described in the last chapter. In addition to the direct effects of harm on physical well-being and development, violence or the threat of violence interferes with the allocation of attention to intellectual, psychological, emotional, and social development. They create psychological trauma that requires adolescents to cope in maladaptive ways, psychologically, emotionally, and behaviorally.

Clear and Consistent Structure and Appropriate Adult Supervision

One of the first things a new participant experiences in a community program for youth is whether the environment is structured or chaotic. According to theories and empirical research, development requires that a child experience a stable, predictable reality. Cognitive theories (Piaget, 1964, 1971; Piaget and Inhelder, 1973) stress the need for a stable environment to which children can assimilate and accommodate their emerging cognitive structures; object relations theorists also stress the predictability of caretakers as essential to the development of trust and confidence (Mahler et al., 1975; Winnicott, 1975). Similarly, applied researchers have shown that, in all settings studied, adolescents benefit from experiencing clear rules, discipline, and consistently enforced limits on their behavior (Connell and Wellborn, 1991; Dryfoos, 1990; Jackson and Davis, 2000; Lipsitz, 1980; Roth and Brooks-Gunn, 2000). More classroom and school discipline is a major cause of poor academic achievement and psychological disengagement from school.

Structure is a critical feature of all settings. On one hand, research on families shows that firm parenting and clear behavioral expectations, when coupled with warmth and emotional support, are associated with more positive developmental outcomes than lax parenting (Steinberg et al., 1992; Steinberg, 2000). Evidence is also emerging that the best adolescent outcomes are associated with parents gradually reducing their control over their adolescents and providing them with increasing opportunities to help establish family rules and participate in family decision making. Adolescents desire both consistency and structure and increasing opportunity to manage their own behavior. They appear to do better in families that over time provide both of these experiences (see Eccles et al., 1993, for a review).

Similarly in classrooms, maintenance of discipline, control, and organization by the teacher is related to student satisfaction, growth, and achievement. Once again, however, as they grow older, students desire increasing opportunity to have input into classroom and school governance and rules. Evidence suggests that their motivation is optimized when they experience this type of change in classroom and school management over time (Epstein and McPartland, 1979; Jackson and Davis, 2000; Lipsitz et al., 1997; Maehr and Midgley, 1996; see Eccles et al., 1998, for a review).

On the other hand, research on peer relations shows that the amount of time adolescents spend with peers in unstructured activities, like driving around in cars, predicts increases in involvement in problem behaviors (Osgood et al., 1996). One important study found that participation in community programs that lacked structure predicted greater involvement in problem behaviors both in the present and 20 years later (Mahoney et al., in press).

A critical element of structure is consistent monitoring and enforcement of rules and expectations. Across settings, there is more positive development and fewer problem behaviors with consistent monitoring by parents (Grotevant, 1998; Pettit et al., 1999; Steinberg, 2000), teachers (Eccles et al., 1993; Maehr and Midgley, 1996), and community members (Fisher et al., 1998; Scales and Leffert, 1999). In sports-based community programs, for example, a distinctive feature of effective coaches is that they repeatedly emphasized adherence to the rules of the game (Heath, 1994). Finally, a key characteristic of successful community programs is that they have clear rules about expected behavior when in the program, and the staff are regularly involved in monitoring participants' behavior, even when youth are elsewhere (Dryfoos, 1990; Heath, 1999; McLaughlin, 2000; Merry, 2000; Roth et al., 1998a).

As with all eight features, it is critical that structure be developmentally, ecologically, and culturally appropriate. With regard to age, as individuals' mature, they need less external structure and control to support their well-being. In most cases, they become increasingly able to create their own structure and to provide adequate self-control over their behavior. Consequently, the exact extent of structure and adult supervision needed to support positive behavior and development will change as children and adolescents grow older. Younger youth need more structure than older youth; older youth may balk at leadership that is too rigid, overcontrolling, or authoritarian. Consequently, structure must permit age-appropriate levels of autonomy. The way this shows up in studies is as a curvilinear relation between structure and outcomes: both too little and too much adult-imposed structure is related to poorer outcomes than moderate levels of adult-imposed structure. The exact optimal point in the curve moves toward less adult-imposed structure as the population being studied gets older (see Eccles et al., 1993, for an example of this dynamic relation in classroom research).

Both neighborhood conditions and culture also influence what is the most optimal level of structure and adult control. Greater limits on behavior may also be necessary in dangerous neighborhoods, where the costs of stepping outside the bounds of authority are higher (Steinberg et al., 1992; Sampson and Morenoff, 1997, cited by Roth and Brooks-Gunn, 2000). We should also recognize that cultures differ in their expectations regarding appropriate levels of structure. For example, in India, a more hierarchical culture than that of the United States, Cub Scout troops define obedience to leaders as a fundamental obligation; in contrast, in the United States, the Cub Scout pledge focuses on "obeying the law of the Pack."

Much evidence indicates that appropriate structure is a necessary condition to positive development. Without stability and order, adolescents cannot engage in physical, cognitive, emotional, or social growth, and they are at risk for the development of negative behavioral patterns. It is notable that Csikszentmihalyi (1975, 1990) found structure to be a prerequisite to engagement itself. To become psychologically engaged in an activity, people need structure and predictability. But too much adult control can drive older youth away. Youth participation is increased when opportunities are provided for them to take on more active roles in governance, rule setting, and leadership as they get older and more experienced in the setting (McLaughlin, 2000; Merry, 2000; we discuss this more in Chapter 5). Nonetheless, without sufficient structure, all the other features of good environments become irrelevant.

Supportive Relationships

Whether you ask a researcher, a theorist, a practitioner, or an adolescent, the quality of relationships with adults comes up again and again as a critical feature of any developmental setting. Researchers speak of the importance of warmth, connectedness, good communication, and support (Blum and Rinehart, 1997; Brooks-Gunn and Paikoff, 1993; Dryfoos, 1990; Eccles et al., 1998; Ford and Harris, 1996; Grotevant, 1998; Lipsitz, 1980; Roth and Brooks-Gunn, 2000). Theorists talk about adults who provide secure attachments, are good mentors and managers, and provide scaffolding for learning (Bowlby, 1969; Furstenburg et al., 1999; Vygotsky, 1978). Practitioners talk about caring and competent adults. Adolescents themselves may use more evocative terms to describe positive adults—like being loving or just "cool" (McLaughlin, 2000).

As a whole, these descriptions suggest a family of related qualities that make for good relationships with adults. They include interrelated qualities of emotional support (e.g., being caring and responsive) and qualities of instrumental support (e.g., providing guidance that is useful to young people). On the surface these appear to be objective qualities, but research suggests that these qualities reside less in the adult than in the adolescent's *perception* of the adult and in the adolescent's *experience of interactions* with the adult (Clark, 1983; Eccles et al., 1992; Noller and Callan, 1986). This is an important point, because it suggests that there is not one perfect type of adult for all adolescents and all settings (i.e., there is no single template of a good parent, teacher, or leader) but rather that different adolescents are likely to respond to different elements within this family of desirable qualities. This point is also important because it suggests that, inasmuch as there is an underlying essential element here, it consists of attentiveness and responsiveness to adolescents' subjective worlds.

The largest body of research on relationships with adults focuses on the qualities of parents that are associated with positive development. Longitudinal studies consistently show that parental support is associated with positive school motivation (Clark, 1983; Eccles et al., 1992; Epstein and Dauber, 1991; Eccles and Harold, 1996; Henderson and Berla, 1994; Booth and Dunn, 1996; Marjoribanks, 1979), better mental health, and lower rates of drinking, drug use, delinquency, and school misconduct (Furstenberg et al., 1999; Grotevant, 1998; Steinberg, 2000). Similar findings are suggested for feeling connected to a parent or parents (Blum and Rinehart, 1997) and having good communication (Brooks-Gunn and Paikoff, 1993; Steinberg, 2000). Parental support provides a buffer against the effects of negative racial stereotypes, and parental guidance promotes cultural pride (Comer, 1988; Fisher et al., 1998; Ford and Harris, 1996; Romo and Falbo, 1996). On the negative side, ambiguous and insecure relationships with parents (e.g., when there is fear of rejection as well as substantial disruptions in parenting relationships) are associated with adolescent involvement in problem behaviors.

Similar findings show the importance of supportive relationships with adults in other settings. In the classroom, positive support from teachers is related to greater educational success, and when teachers have positive expectations for students, they do better (Comer, 1988; Eccles et al., 1998; Ford, 1996; Ferguson, 1998; Jackson and Davis, 2000; Lee and Smith, 1993; Rosenthal and Jacobson, 1968). In addition, when students care about what teachers think and expect of them, they do better both academically and socially and care more about doing well in school (Jackson and Davis, 2000). The importance of one caring adult at school has also been documented by studies of resilience and of the role of school advisors (Masten, 1994; Galassi et al., 1997). In sports programs, youth develop greater self-esteem and lower anxiety when coaches focus on the development of skills rather than winning (Seefeldt et al., 1995; Roberts and Treasure, 1992). For example, Smoll et al. (1993) found that a three-hour intervention that trained coaches to be emotionally supportive was effective in increasing the self-esteem of their Little League players. Similarly, an evaluation of the Big Brothers, Big Sisters program, in which a relationship with an adult is the heart of the program, showed that adolescent outcomes were especially positive for mentors who developed "youth-centered" relationships with adolescent mentees, rather than more controlling relationships (Grossman and

Rhodes, in press). Research in other settings reinforces the finding that adult overcontrol is related to less positive outcomes (Eccles et al., 1993; Grolnick and Ryan, 1987, 1989; Hauser et al., 1991; Roth and Brooks-Gunn, 2000). Grossman and Rhodes also found that longer-term relationships were associated with better youth outcomes (indeed, relationships that were terminated quickly were associated with decrements in several indicators of functioning). These findings underscore the importance of qualities of communication, respect, and long-term stability.

We stress again that these qualities have to be fit to the adolescent; this is implicit in the notion of responsiveness. Different cultural groups have different models of adult-adolescent relationships, and hence support needs to fit with the cultural model of the adolescent's social group. For some, this will involve more deference to authority (e.g., Doi, 1990); for others, it will involve the granting of autonomy in conjunction with strong emotional support (LaFromboise and Graff Low, 1998). Appropriate types of mentoring may vary by the gender, age, or previous experiences of the adolescent. In general, adolescents need less direct guidance and minute-to-minute support as they grow older and become better able to regulate their own emotions and behavior (Rogoff et al., 1995).

In summary, supportive relationships are critical "mediums" of development. They provide an environment of reinforcement, good modeling, and constructive feedback for physical, intellectual, psychological, and social growth. Parental support strengthens a child's ability to take on challenge (Csikszentmihalyi and Rathunde, 1998). In Vygotsky's theoretical view (Vygotsky, 1978), the attentive, caring, and wise voice of a supportive adult gets internalized and becomes part of the youth's own voice.

Opportunities to Belong

Research across settings substantiates the importance of opportunities to develop a sense of belonging. Families that provide multiple opportunities for the children to be actively involved in family decision making and activities have adolescents who are less antisocial and who exhibit better self-regulation and social responsibility (Grotevant, 1998). Similarly, teachers who provide opportunities for all students to participate and feel valued have students who do better on a wide range of academic outcomes (Goodenow, 1993; Ford and Harris, 1996; Eccles et al., 1996b, 1998; Maehr and Midgley, 1996). Adolescents who feel connected to their schools report lower levels of emotional stress, violent behavior, and substance abuse and are more likely to delay initiation of sexual intercourse (Blum and Rinehart, 1997). Conversely, students who feel alienated and left out or rejected by their teachers and schools are more likely to drop out of school (Fine, 1991; Roderick, 1991, 1993). Adolescents who perceive peers as prejudiced report higher levels of emotional stress than those who do not (Blum and Rinehart, 1997). Research with American Indians has found that bicultural school curricula that bridge Indian and European cultures had a positive influence (LaFromboise et al., 1993). Gambone and Arbreton (1997) concluded that settings that provide a sense of membership and belonging to a group and allow for adolescents to be recognized and valued decrease the likelihood that they will become involved in high-risk behaviors, increase their sense of responsibility, and improve self-competence, school attitude, and performance. Finally, similar though incomplete findings suggest the value of opportunities to belong in community programs. Programming strategies for positive bonding have proven effective for adolescents at risk for antisocial behavior (Catalano et al., 1999; Dryfoos, 1990; Lipsitz, 1980; Merry, 2000).

In a multicultural society like ours, the issue of belonging is especially important. One of the first issues for an adolescent walking through the door or even thinking about trying a community program is whether he or she can belong to this group of people: "Will I fit in, will I be comfortable?" The adolescent may ask, not only is my ethnic group welcome, but also will the people here accept someone of my gender, sexual orientation, disability status, or the peer crowd that people think I belong to (e.g., jock, nerd)? Research suggests that these considerations can be significant barriers that keep adolescents from joining youth activities (Larson, 1994). Beyond the issue of interpersonal comfort, we also discuss here the constructive role that community programs can play in helping adolescents address underlying developmental issues related to sociocultural belonging. Whether one is a member of a minority group, the dominant culture, or has not decided, there are important issues to be faced about how one fits into the diverse and sometimes conflicting marketplace of cultural messages and identities. Along with schools, community programs provide a particularly valuable setting for youth to work on these important developmental tasks (Merry, 2000; National Research Council and Institute of Medicine, 2000a).

The theoretical foundation for this feature lies in a number of cultural theories: anthropologists' emphasis on intrinsic links between person and culture (LeVine et al., 1988), sociologists' insights into integration versus alienation (Durkheim, 1951), educational psychologists' emphasis on the importance of belonging for school engagement (Goodenow, 1993), and Erikson's descriptions of identity development as a process of situating oneself within a sociocultural milieu (Erikson, 1968). Cultures provide meaning, and meaning is fundamental to well-being. Research shows that youth with stronger ethnic identity have more positive self-esteem, stronger ego identity, and greater school involvement (Phinney et al., 1997a; Wong et al., submitted), and they are less likely to engage in violence (National Research Council and Institute of Medicine, 1999c). But a sense of belonging to a group becomes a two-edged sword if it means exclusion or hostility in relation to others. LaFromboise, Coleman, and Gerton (1993) suggest that the desirable developmental outcome is "bicultural competence," which involves development of abilities to function and be comfortable in multiple cultural settings (see also Phinney et al., 1997b). Although issues of ethnic identity are found to be least salient for European American adolescents (Roberts et al., 1999), awareness of intergroup processes is important for them, too. The ability of other youth to achieve and enjoy bicultural competence is dependent on whether people in the majority culture are sensitive to and knowledgeable about other cultures and aware of the ways in which their privilege is experienced by others.

Interestingly, some of the best evidence for the importance of belonging comes from studies of programs designed to be welcoming to adolescents often ignored by mainstream programs. A study of a drop-in center for lesbian, gay, and bisexual youth in Chicago, for example, found that the opportunity to be connected to a community of similar youth and adults made a great difference in the well-being of these youth and helped them adjust to their sexual minority status (Herdt and Boxer, 1993). Another study found that community programs that were sensitive to the special needs of youth with disabilities had positive benefits for the youth, their families, and other participants (Fink, 1997).

Other good evidence comes from programs designed to be welcoming to adolescents from multiple cultural groups. For example, black adolescents living in predominantly white neighborhoods and participating in Jack and Jill, a program for black youth, reported that this program facilitated their adjustment to the challenges of the situation (Nicholson, 1999). Similar evidence of the negative consequences of feeling devalued by one's teachers and school peers because of one's cultural background, language, ethnicity, and religion provides more support for the importance of belonging for a wide variety of positive outcomes (Fisher et al., 1998; Jackson and Davis, 2000).

How is inclusiveness across cultural groups achieved? Simply bringing different groups into contact with each other does not necessarily lead to mutual understanding and respect; the conditions of contact are critical (Merry, 2000; National Research Council and Institute of Medicine, 2000b). Experimental studies introducing multiethnic cooperative learning groups have demonstrated that such experiences increase cross-ethnic group friendships and, in turn, increase a sense of belonging in the school and the classroom (Slavin, 1995). The following elements were identified by a recent gathering of scholars as critical to cultivating positive intergroup relationships through inclusiveness (National Research Council and Institute of Medicine, 2000b: 15):

- Interactions between different groups must be on a level of equal status;
- Activities must be cooperative rather than competitive, involving pursuit of a shared goal;
- There must be individualized contact between members of groups;
- Institutions and authority figures must support the goal of intergroup understanding; "institutional silence," an atmosphere in which race is never mentioned, can lead to unspoken perceptions of discrimination and intergroup tensions; group differences must be acknowledged; and
- Adults have an important roles, as "role models, pathfinders, arbitrators, peacemakers, interpreters, mentors, promoters of civic ethics, and administrators."

As with all other features, issues of person-environment fit are important here (see Appendix B for more details). Adolescents have different attitudes, past experiences, and levels of readiness. For example, research suggests that issues of ethnic identity become more salient with age (National Research Council and Institute of Medicine, 2000b), and thus younger adolescents may have different concerns from older ones. In addition, stage theories of ethnic identity formation suggest that some youth from nonmajority cultures may need intense periods of immersion in their own culture as a step toward being able to function in a multicultural environment (Phinney, 1990). Similar issues can be important for male and female youth and for youth with different sexual orientations.

Positive Social Norms

Every group of people that has sustained interaction develops a set of habits, norms, and expectations that govern their behavior (Berger and Luckmann, 1966; Coleman, 1990; Shweder et al., 1998). Whether we are talking about a family, a peer group, a classroom, or a community program for youth, the group develops a way of doing things and not doing things; deviations from these group norms are often strongly sanctioned. The group "culture" includes not only the formal organizational culture but also the informal habits and expectations that arise from daily interactions; these informal norms may diverge from the official organizational norms and expectations. Research across multiple settings suggests that adolescents' perceptions of these kinds of social norms have immediate and lasting effects on their behavior. For example, when adolescent girls perceive that their parents disapprove of sexual activity, they are less likely to become pregnant (Blum and Rinehart, 1997). In discussing opportunities to belong, we stressed the role of the group culture in relation to identity and meaning. Here we stress its role in shaping behavior.

The impact of peer norms on adolescent behavior has often been discussed under the rubric of "peer influence." While adults often demonize the negative effects of peer pressure, research suggests that peer influence is typically more subtle and multidimensional. Rather than being pressured, adolescents often perceive certain behaviors to be normative and so come to view them as appropriate ways of acting (Brown, 1990). Research also shows that peer influence toward *positive* behavior (finishing school, excelling at something, not using drugs) is much more common than influence toward deviant behaviors (Brown, 1990; Scales and Leffert, 1999; Steinberg, 2000). For example, peer modeling is an important motivating force for participation in service activities (Stukas et al., 1999). Nevertheless, for a subset of teens, peers are an important influence on use of substances, delinquent behavior, and sexual activity (Brown, 1990; Scales and Leffert, 1999). Most of the research is based on adolescents' perceptions of their peers' behavior, and their *perceptions* of peer norms often do not correspond very closely with the actual behaviors of their peers. For example, adolescents who take up smoking or initiate sexual intercourse often overestimate the prevalence of these behaviors by their peers (Scales and Leffert, 1999). But whether accurate or inaccurate, perceptions of peer norms do have a lasting influence on behavior (Guerra et al., 1994), and interventions designed to change students' perceptions about peer norms regarding problem behaviors do reduce their incidence (Cook et al., 1993).

Although not a social group itself, the media is also an important source of adolescents' views about social norms. Youth and adults who watch more television believe the world is a more violent and dangerous place than do those who watch less television, and they are more likely to believe that violence is an appropriate problem-solving strategy. They also score higher on a scale of sexism and have more distorted views of the world of work (Gerbner et al., 1994). On the positive side, health education programs that incorporate mass media intervention as a way of changing perceived social norms are more effective at reducing adolescent smoking than health education programs without media (Elster and Kuznets, 1994). In addition to their effect on perceived social norms, the media must be recognized as an important competing influence on adolescents' internalization of the prosocial norms advocated by schools, families, and other traditional socializing institutions, such as faith-based institutions.

Research on community programs also indicates that social norms are critical. On the positive side, Cook et al. (1993) reported that acquiring conventionally positive social norms did a better job of explaining the results of one prevention program than did social skills training. Smoking prevention programs that taught both how to resist peer pressure and support heath behavior changes are among the more effective youth health promotion programs (Sallis, 1993). Efforts at teaching social norms against early steady dating and against sexual intercourse were also related to reductions in dating and pregnancy in three studies of the Girls, Inc., Preventing Adolescent Pregnancy Project (Nicholson and Postrado, 1992; Postrado et al., 1997). A more rigorous evaluation of these programs in now under way.

Promotion of certain types of positive social norms may be particularly strong in faith-based youth settings: religiosity is positively associated with what developmental psychologists call prosocial values and behavior (see Eisenberg and Fabes, 1998) and negatively related to substance abuse, premature sexual involvement, and delinquency (Benson et al., 1997; Catalano et al., 1999; Elder and Conger, 2000; Jessor et al., 1991; Werner and Smith, 1992).

On the more controversial side, two in-depth observational studies have documented the reinforcement and reproduction of gender stereotypes in sports and extracurricular activities; for example, both studies found that sports promoted masculine aggressive and competitive norms

(Eder and Parker, 1987; Fine, 1987). And on the more negative side, participation in sports is associated with lower rates of altruism (Kleiber and Roberts, 1981).

Finally, Dishion and his colleagues have shown that adolescents who are grouped together for an intervention with a large proportion of peers demonstrating problem behaviors often show increases in a variety of problem behaviors as a consequence of participating in the intervention (Dishion et al., 1999a). This negative impact has been explained by pointing to the impact of the antisocial norms created by the large number of youth heavily involved in problem behaviors. The bottom line is that, whether they are intentionally cultivated or not, community programs have an internal culture of social norms that shapes youths' perception of appropriate behavior for good or ill, depending on the social norms that emerge. Program personnel need to carefully consider exactly what social norms are being created and reinforced in their programs.

As with all our features, it is critical to consider how the influence of social norms varies across cultural groups and individuals. Cultures and subcultures, of course, are an important source of social norms, and groups differ in the norms they hold most highly. Many cultures share fundamental moral values (for example, against murder and harm to others), but they vary in norms related to conventions, and these norms often carry moral weight during adolescence, when group belonging is so important (Turiel, 1983). Leaders of community programs need to be sensitive to how congruent the norms of their organization are with norms of the culture of their participants.

Such cultural variations also make it difficult to identify a single set of positive social norms that should be supported in all community programs for youth. Communities will differ in the norms they hold most dear. We include this feature of settings not so much to outline a particular set of social norms as universally critical but more to highlight the significance of social norms for development in settings such as community programs for youth.

Before leaving this section, it is important to note two additional important considerations about social norms. First, research suggests that the strength of different sources of influence may vary across cultural groups. Landrine and colleagues (1994) found that peers had a stronger influence on smoking for white youth than for Hispanic and Asian youth, and peers had no influence on smoking among black youth.

Second, individual differences are also important. Susceptibility to peer influence is a critical mediator of the effect of peer norms on behavior (Fuligni and Eccles, 1993), and susceptibility to peer pressure is higher among younger adolescents and those with less confidence in their social skills (Brown, 1990). People with low self-esteem, low self-confidence, low autonomy, and an external locus of control are more likely to be influenced by social norms (Cook et al., 1993). Susceptibility to peer influence also varies across youth from different family structures and parenting styles (Brown, 1990). Children who are more integrated into cohesive families or peer groups are more resistant to the influence of media (Gerbner et al., 1994) and are likely to be more resistant to negative peer influences as well.

How do norms influence development? Both sociologists and psychologists describe a process in which observation of, and participation in, behavior becomes internalized to form values, morals, and "cognitive schemata" (Berger and Luckmann, 1966; Coleman, 1990; Huesmann and Guerra, 1997). This process begins earlier in life, through interactions with family and peers. Huesmann and Guerra (1997) concluded that normative beliefs about aggression get formed in childhood and become more difficult to change as children move into adolescence. Once internalized, Guerra et al. (1994) suggested, behavioral patterns become automatic (i.e., they are followed without reflection or evaluation). The experience of positive social norms is therefore important to the development of good habits in all areas of positive development. We think norms are particularly important to social, psychological, and emotional development because they shape morals, present ways of relating to others, and provide templates of self-control.

Support for Efficacy and Mattering

A critical contribution of psychological theories, such as those of Piaget and Erikson, is the recognition that positive development is not something adults do to young people, but rather something that young people do for themselves with a lot of help from parents and others. They are the agents of their own development. To foster development, then, it follows that settings need to be youth centered, providing youth—both individually and in groups—the opportunity to be efficacious and to make a difference in their social worlds—we refer to this opportunity as "mattering." We combine under this feature multiple elements drawn from other researchers and practitioners: the importance of actually having the opportunity to do things that make a real difference in one's community, the idea of empowerment, and support for increasingly autonomous self-regulation that is appropriate to the maturing individuals' developmental level and cultural background. After some discussion, we added the opportunity to experience meaningful challenge to this feature, because success at such experiences is critical to developing a sense of personal efficacy (Bandura, 1994). Efficacy results not just from turning power over to youth, but from seeing that they are challenged to stretch themselves in demanding, novel, and creative activities (Bandura, 1994; Gambone and Arbreton, 1997). It must be emphasized that "opportunity" is not experienced as "challenge" unless youth identify with it: adolescents need to be engaged by opportunities for efficacy and mattering that are meaningful to them.

Evidence for the importance of this feature comes from research on multiple settings. Research on families shows that when parents support their adolescent children's autonomy by allowing them to express their point of view and to have serious input into family decisions, they develop more positive motivation, engage in more identity exploration, and show higher ego development (Deci and Ryan, 1985; Grolnick and Ryan, 1987, 1989; Grotevant, 1998; Hauser et al., 1991; Steinberg, 2000). Conversely, overcontrolling and restrictive parenting are associated with constricted development of ego functions and greater likelihood of internalizing problems (Baumrind, 1971; Epstein and McPartland, 1979; Steinberg, 2000). Challenge and the demandingness of parents are a part of this. There is a well-established link between the educational expectations of parents and a child's self-esteem, locus of control, sense of personal efficacy, academic motivation and performance (Eccles et al., 1992; Marjoribanks, 1979), and some protection from emotional distress (Blum and Rinehart, 1997). Parents' encouragement and acceptance of their adolescent children's desire to take some risks, learn new skills, and take responsibility, combined with consistent parental support, careful monitoring, and good communication, are predictive of growing competence and motivation in adolescents (Csikszentmihalyi and Rathunde, 1998).

Support for efficacy and mastery is also important in school and adolescent work settings. Mastery-oriented classrooms that focus on self-improvement rather than social comparison foster higher motivation and perceptions of oneself as more capable; in contrast, overly controlling classrooms that do not provide opportunities for autonomy undermine motivation, self-concepts, expectations, and direction and induce learned helplessness in response to difficult tasks (National Research Council, 1999; Eccles et al., 1998; Jackson and Davis, 2000; Maehr and Midgley, 1996; Newmann and Associates, 1966; Eccles et al., 1996b;

Wehlage et al., 1996; Wiggins and McTighe, 1998). A poignant example is the finding that low teacher expectations for academic performance of ethnic minority children conveyed in teacher-student interactions in elementary schools lead to alienation from learning experiences and underachievement (Jackson and Davis, 2000; Fisher et al., 1998; Romo and Falbo, 1996). In the workplace, adolescents in jobs that use their skills show more positive outcomes than those in unchallenging jobs (Mortimer et al., 1999).

Although less likely to involve longitudinal designs, research with community programs suggests similar relations. Participation in decision making is correlated with positive developmental outcomes, such as a sense of sharing and respect for others (Dryfoos, 1990; Gambone and Arbreton, 1997; Lipsitz, 1980; Merry, 2000; McLaughlin, 2000). In school settings, the opportunity to participate in making and enforcing school rules leads to an increase in students' willingness to follow the rules and in their attachment to the school (Darling-Hammond, 1997). Adolescents in youth-centered activities develop new cognitive skills that increase their confidence and ability to make positive decisions (Heath, 1999; McLaughlin et al., 1994). For example, a group of adolescents who planned alcohol-free activities showed less subsequent alcohol use (Scales and Leffert, 1999). Similarly, the experience of challenging activities predicts greater likelihood of participating in a community program for youth and less high-risk behavior (Dryfoos, 1991; Gambone and Arbreton, 1997; Merry, 2000). A description of what it means for a community program to be youth centered is provided in Chapter 5 (see also McLaughlin, 2000). Finally, both longitudinal survey-type studies and experimentally evaluated small-scale intervention studies have shown the positive consequences of participating in a wide variety of well-designed community service activities (Dryfoos, 1991; Merry, 2000; Lipsitz, 1980; Scales, 1999; Youniss, 1997; Yates and Youniss, 1999).

The notion that this feature must fit with the adolescents being served is particularly important here. For a setting to support efficacy and the sense that one is making a useful contribution, it must be developmentally and culturally appropriate. Most young adolescents are not cognitively or emotionally ready to take full responsibility for a community program. Empowerment involves gradually increasing freedoms and responsibilities as young people mature (McLaughlin, 2000; Scales and Leffert, 1999). Culturally, a setting must be attuned to the level and modes of efficacy and mattering that are normative in the adolescents' larger cultural system. As we noted earlier, people differ in the amount of value they place on autonomy. Many American Indian tribes, such as the Navajo, place high value on letting children make their own decisions (LaFromboise and Graff Low, 1998), whereas other ethnic minority groups in this country do not (Fisher et al., 1998). People also differ in the degree to which they conceptualize efficacy as individualized action rather than a collective process. Programs need to take these characteristics into account.

The challenges must also fit with the adolescents' level of competence. Research in classrooms shows that students are more motivated to learn when material is appropriate for their current levels of competence (Maehr and Midgley, 1996). Challenges that are too high or two low for a given person will undermine sustained engagement (Csikszentmihalyi, 1990). Vygotsky, too, theorized that growth is most likely when people are challenged at a level somewhat above but not too far beyond their skills. In community programs, it appears that the availability of a variety of novel and interesting activities increases youth's active participation (Gambone and Arbreton, 1997; McLaughlin, 2000). Culture is important here, too, because it determines what will make for a personally meaningful challenge.

Like structure, support for efficacy and mattering are *necessary* features for development in any setting. If adolescents do not experience personal engagement and a sense of mattering, they are not likely to grow personally. These features, then, are prerequisite to all types of development described in Chapter 2, but they have a particular relevance to psychological, emotional, and social development. Theory suggests that it is through acting, taking on challenges, and making meaningful contributions that a person's sense of self and identity develops.

Opportunities for Skill Building

Good settings provide opportunities to acquire knowledge and learn both new skills and new habits of mind. We include here cognitive, physical, psychological, social, and cultural skills. Of course, some community programs specialize in promoting the development of specific skills, such as athletic or artistic abilities. But good programs encourage learning in other areas as well. They can encourage the development of good habits and a wide range of competences and life skills, from media literacy to acquiring job skills through the use of an "embedded curriculum" and a curriculum that systematically cycles through planning, practice, and performance (McLaughlin, 2000). The specific skills promoted should vary across cultural groups, depending on the outcomes different groups see as most important. For individuals who are or who will be participants in multiple cultures—as is increasingly the case across America—skill training should involve learning how to function in several different cultural systems (LaFromboise et al., 1993; Phelan and Davidson, 1993). Involvement in activities with embedded curricula leads to gains in both social and cultural capital (Clark, 1988; McLaughlin, 2000).

Research on how curricula function in community programs is found in diffuse literatures, employs diverse paradigms, and is generally underdeveloped. Some studies show that sports programs develop athletic skills and music programs develop music skills. More important is newer research showing that programs that teach basic life skills, such as coping, assertiveness, and problem solving, predict improved emotional well-being, better school performance, and reduced risk behaviors (Compas, 1993; LaFromboise and Howard-Pitney, 1994). More research is needed on how these opportunities to learn basic life skills can be effectively woven into activities of community programs.

On a more positive note, studies of schools and nonschool community-based programs show consistent evidence of the importance of learning new cognitive and life skills (Coleman et al., 1966; Clark, 1983, 1988; Comer, 1980, 1988; Murnane and Levy, 1996, see also Chapter 2 for evidence of the importance of good academic outcomes). McLaughlin (2000) concluded that having an intentional learning environment was one of the critical characteristics of the successful community-based programs she and her colleagues studied. Similarly, Merry (2000), in her Chapin Hall report, concluded that educational supports and career exploration programs are characteristics of community-based programs with positive outcomes for their participants. A similar conclusion was reached 10 years ago by Dryfoos (1990) and more recently by the Carnegie Corporation in its report *A Matter of Time*. Schinke and his colleagues provided additional evidence of the positive impact of well-designed educational enhancement programs in Boys and Girls Clubs in a public housing development on both school outcomes and reductions in drug-related activities (Schinke et al., 1993). The reports by Dryfoos and Merry also stressed the positive linkage between programs designed to teach adolescents peer-pressure resistance skills, such as those taught in the Girls, Inc. Will Power Program. We discuss some of these programs in more detail in Chapter 5.

Abundant research now exists for educational settings on how to best teach new skills, new knowledge, new understandings, and new habits of mind (see, for example, Ames, 1992; Bransford et al., 1999; Darling-Hammond, 1997; Eccles et al., 1998; Jackson and Davis, 2000; MacIver et al., 1995; Meece, 1994; Newmann and Associates, 1996; Pintrich and Schunk, 1996; Wehlage et al., 1996; Wiggins and McTighe, 1998; Zemelman et al., 1998). A full review is beyond the scope of this report, but there is growing consensus that the following teaching strategies and techniques are important:

Authentic Instruction

- Active construction of knowledge in which students are asked to construct or produce knowledge rather than just reproducing or repeating facts and views expressed by teachers and textbooks;
- Disciplined inquiry in which students are encouraged to engage in deep cognitive work "that requires them to rely on a field of knowledge, search for understanding, and communicate in 'elaborated forms' their ideas and findings" (Jackson and Davis, 2000: 69). This characteristic also includes active instruction in the meta-cognitive skills needed to monitor one's own learning and progress;
- Relevance of material being studied to the student and his or her community culture. The work that students are doing in school should be valued and recognized as important beyond the school and classroom;
- Regular feedback on progress so that students understand what they know and what they still need to learn and master. The feedback needs to focus on progress and on new learning needs, rather than one's current performance level compared with others in the class or learning group;
- Abundant opportunities to rethink one's work and understanding;
- Ongoing reflective practices by teachers and instructors that involve a careful examination of "what kinds of knowledge, skills, habits of mind, and attitudes are prerequisites for successful final performance, then deciding what instructional activities will give all students the chance to be successful, while engaging their interest and allowing for exploration" (Wiggins and McTighe, 1998: 124);
- Differentiated instruction that recognizes the individual differences in levels of current knowledge, interests, and learning styles

and provides multiple ways of learning new material and demonstrating that learning; and

- Cooperative and highly interactive learning activities that allow students to work with and tutor each other and allow instructors to work with them in designing learning activities that provide the kinds of experiences listed above.

Practices that support positive motivation

- Grading practices that stress improvement rather than social comparison;
- Teaching practices that stress mastery and improvement rather than current levels of knowledge;
- Practices that reflect high teacher expectations for all students' performance;
- Practices that make sure all students are expected to participate fully in the learning activities of the classroom; and
- Practices that involve hands-on activities (like laboratory exercises and field-based data collection efforts).

Perhaps the most striking research findings concern ways in which athletic community programs can fall short in establishing skills and habits that would seem to follow naturally from physical activity. Findings regarding the association of participating in organized sports as a youth and physical activity as an adult are conflicting. A number of reports show an association; others find no significant relations (Elster and Kuznets, 1994). On one hand, many sports teams do not prepare adolescence for life-long physical activity and can lead to excessive exercise and eating habits or the use of steroids (Sallis, 1993). On the other hand, adolescent physical activity is associated with higher short-term levels of fitness, greater resistance to cigarette and alcohol use, and possibly enhanced academics and cognition (Institute of Medicine, 1997a; Seefeldt et al., 1995). In a national survey, female athletes were less likely to get pregnant than nonathletes, irrespective of ethnicity. They were more likely to be virgins, to have later onset of intercourse, to have sex less often and with fewer partners, and to use condoms (Sabo et al., 1998). In other studies, participation in sports in high school was linked to better educational and occupational outcomes in early adulthood (Barber et al., in press; Eccles and Barber, 1999). Finally, one of the coaches discussed by McLaughlin (2000) integrated mathematics, economics, and history into his sports program by having the participants do a series of intellectual activities directly related to the sport. The basic point, however, is that participating in an activity does not mean that adolescents are acquiring the habits of and dispositions for the activity in the future. Programs need to be explicitly designed to teach these habits as well as other critical life skills.

Integration of Family, School, and Community Efforts

In Bronfenbrenner's and various other models, adolescent development is facilitated when there is meaningful communication and synergy among the different settings of adolescents' lives and among the adults who oversee these settings. Optimal conditions for development exist when there is cohesion and information flow between systems—for example, when parents know what is going on at school and with peers and when principals, community leaders, and parents are in touch and have a shared perception of community standards for behavior. This communication facilitates acquiring social capital, and it increases the likelihood of adequate structure in the setting. It also adds to the fund of developmental resources that adolescents can draw on. Communication and integration also facilitate the processes of management described by the family management perspective (Furstenburg et al., 1999). When it is lacking, when different parts of adolescents' worlds are out of touch and on different wavelengths, there is increased likelihood that developmental opportunities will be missed, that adolescents will be confused about adult expectations, and that deviant behavior and values will take root.

Research substantiates the importance of this integration between the settings and institutions in adolescents' lives. This is evident, first, in the links between home and school. When young adolescents receive reassurance, assistance, and support from their parents, they are more likely to believe that their in-school effort will pay off (Eccles et al., 1992; Feagans and Bartsch, 1993; Marjoribanks, 1979). Parent involvement and interest in children's school activities are related to better school motivation and performance as well as more successful school transitions (Baker and Stevenson, 1986; Comer, 1980, 1988; Eccles and Harold, 1996; Epstein and Dauber, 1991; Henderson and Berla, 1994; Booth and Dunn, 1996; Jackson and Davis, 2000; Romo and Falbo, 1996; Stevenson and Baker, 1987). We also see it in the links between family and community. Rural adolescents whose parents were actively involved in the community showed higher academic and peer success (Elder and Conger, 2000; Grotevant, 1998). Darling and Steinberg (1997) found similar results in a study of six communities in the San Francisco Bay area: they found that positive development was clearer in communities that had strong shared prosocial norms.

We also see it in the links between schools and communities. School programs that included one or more community program components have longer-lasting and larger effects on adolescent drug use and smoking than school programs alone (Dryfoos, 2000). Health messages that are reinforced through multiple settings, such as school, home, and health care facility, have greater effects than those delivered by only one source (Elster and Kuznets, 1994).

The opposite side of the coin is research showing that lack of integration among these settings is associated with more problem behavior in adolescents. Lack of communication and conflict between parent and school values are related to lower school achievement (Comer, 1988; Fisher et al., 1998; Peshkin, 1997; Romo and Falbo, 1996). Conflict between family values and community values is related to more adolescent problem behavior (Schwartz, 1987; Romo and Falbo, 1996). Part of the reason is that it is harder for parents to play a management role when they are out of touch with the other parts of adolescents' lives. Among a Southeast Asian immigrant population in Minnesota, Detzner found that parents had difficulty asserting themselves with their adolescents in a social setting they did not understand. This appeared to be related to increases in delinquency, juvenile arrests, and gang activity among adolescents in the community (Grotevant, 1998; Hughes and Chen, 1999).

The potential for communication and integration varies widely across communities. Those that are small, are culturally homogeneous, and have more resources are likely to find it easier to maintain integration. It is a common observation that a sense of community is harder to achieve given the fast-paced, anonymous, culturally diverse, urban lifestyle that has taken over much of the United States. However, pessimism and passivity are not warranted. There are numerous examples of contemporary communities that have come together to establish communication, bridge differences, and find common ground for facilitating adolescent development (Benson, 1997; Damon, 1997; Dryfoos, 2000; Merry, 2000). Even when there are intransigent problems, parents can make a difference. Parents of middle-class black children often engage in deliberate strategies of "racial socialization" to help protect their children from the effects of racism (Stevenson, 1995). Parents with more limited resources often face fewer choices and more constraints in managing their children's experiences, yet Jarrett's (1997) research shows that effective parents in disadvantaged neighborhoods are active in monitoring their children, seeking resources, and developing in-home learning strategies (see Furstenburg et al., 1999).

There has been limited conceptual work and systematic research that examines integration across community programs; however, given past research in other settings, there is every reason to believe that community programs will be more effective when they coordinate their activities with parents, schools, and communities. Exciting efforts in this direction are emerging and are discussed in more detail in Chapters 5 and 6.

ESSENTIAL INGREDIENTS OF GOOD PROGRAMS

In concluding this chapter, we consider what developmental science suggests about the essential components of community programs in terms of three points of view: the program perspective, the individual participant perspective, and the perspective of the community in which programs reside.

Perspective of the Program

The evidence, although incomplete, suggests that the more of the eight positive features described in this chapter that a community program has, the greater the contribution it will make to the positive development of youth (Dryfoos, 1991, 2001; Merry, 2000; McLaughlin, 2000). Although each feature is related to positive processes of development, they also work together in important ways. For example, adolescents' experience of attachment to adult leaders is likely to magnify the influence of the social norms and organizational culture of the program. Likewise, not experiencing one of these features or experiencing the negative aspects of one of the features is likely to undermine the effects of other features. Programs cannot focus only on promoting the positive; they need to be attuned to limiting the negative. Empowering young people is not enough to keep them from abusing drugs; one needs to communicate the message that drugs are harmful and actively cultivate social norms that discourage their use.

Programs, of course, differ in their objectives. Some may choose to give more emphasis to particular features and the processes of development that follow from them. Nonetheless, we consider all of the features to be highly desirable. Adequate structure and safety, for example, are necessary to any community programs for youth. Little development can occur in an environment that is chaotic or where adolescents fear harm. Positive social norms and messages about relations between diverse groups (belonging) are going to exist in all youth environments; the question is whether they will promote positive behavior and group relationships. Supportive relationships with adults and integration of the program with other institutions in the community are highly desirable, but they may not happen in all instances. Sometimes youth persevere even if they do not like the leader, and sometimes organizations cannot work well with each other. Likewise, the specific skills that youth learn will vary across community programs: sports programs focus on physical skills, chess clubs on intellectual skills. However all community programs need to be attuned to the social, psychological, and emotional skills they are imparting.

We are not suggesting here that all youth programs and youth-serving organizations must have a wide variety of different activities. A program or organization can be quite focused on one activity, such as sports or tutoring or music instruction, and still have all eight of the features discussed in this chapter. Both McLaughlin (2000) and Merry (2000) provide many examples of both comprehensive and focused programs that provide structure, close relationships with caring adults, opportunities to learn new skills, opportunities to develop feelings of efficacy and mattering, opportunities to belong, exposure to positive social norms, and strong connections to either school or family.

A point we have stressed throughout is that these features also need to fit well with the individual participants' needs and characteristics. They are features of a youth's *interaction with* the setting; they do not exist independently of the individual. Two adolescents walking in the door at the same time may have very different experiences of the same community program. One may find it friendly, whereas the other finds it hostile. One may find it empowering, whereas the other finds it stifling. Within their capability, community programs need to be sensitive and adapt according to gender, age, developmental readiness, sexual orientation, and culture, so they can provide these eight features for as many youth as possible. Research in nontraditional classrooms shows that students are more motivated, develop more autonomy, have better self-concepts, and capitalize better on their strength and preferences when they can choose among activities according to their ability level (see

Eccles et al., 1998, for a review). Likewise, a mismatch between an adolescent's needs and the characteristics of the school may be causally related to reduced self-esteem and academic achievement (see Eccles et al., 1998; Feagans and Bartsch, 1993). Any program that is not sensitive to the participants' culture is not likely to succeed (Ford and Harris, 1996; LaFromboise and Howard-Pitney, 1994; Romo and Falbo, 1996; Goldenberg and Gallimore, 1995).

Individual Adolescent's Perspective

If our ultimate goal is fostering positive development in youth, then it is critical to think about how community programs fit into the rest of the adolescents' lives, into the vulnerabilities and developmental assets that exist across all the settings in which they spend their days. Research suggests that adolescents with more developmental assets have greater positive development (Benson, 1997). This finding suggests that the more settings adolescents experience that have more of the eight features, the better off they will be. Redundancy of features is good; for example, adolescents who experience two settings with similar positive social norms are more likely to internalize the norms than someone who experiences conflicting norms across settings. In addition, experiencing a positive feature in one setting may be able to compensate for its absence in other settings. For example, research shows that having one warm and supportive relationship with a nonfamily member, like a leader or a coach, can make a big difference in compensating for the absence of such a relationship at home (Werner and Smith, 1982). Finally, adolescents who do not experience these features on a regular basis are likely to have more developmental problems than adolescents who do experience these features in some settings. The adolescent who does not experience any of the eight features *anywhere* in his or her daily life is at great risk for developmental delays or for heading down a negative developmental pathway.

The reality is that there are many gaps in adolescents' experience of these eight features. Many settings fall short of providing all of them. For example, schools often provide adolescents the experience of challenge but without engaged motivation (Larson, 2000). Families often provide warmth without challenge (Csikszentmihalyi and Rathunde, 1998). And some adolescents do not experience one or more of these features anywhere. Youth in disadvantaged neighborhoods may experience chaotic environments at home, at school, and on the streets. Across social classes, there are youth who do not have any adult with whom they experience a caring relationship. The growing obesity of the population speaks to the lack of opportunity for physical development.

Community programs are important because they can provide features that are missing or in short supply in other settings. They can fill gaps. Across adolescents' daily settings, community programs are unique in consistently providing the experience of engaging challenges (Larson, 2000). They often entail connection to a group that can provide opportunities to address underlying issues of ethnic identity and intergroup relationships (National Research Council and Institute of Medicine, 2000b). They can provide unique opportunities for youth to be involved in volunteer service activities that cultivate and internalize prosocial norms and values. They can provide opportunities for physical development, artistic development, and socioemotional development that are missing in other parts of adolescents' lives.

Advocates of community programs have promoted this abundance of developmental opportunities for more than 100 years. What struck us as researchers was the paucity of empirical evidence on how often and when adolescents actually experience conditions for positive development in community programs, much less across the whole array of settings in which they participate over time. There is a critical need for survey data that examine how often each of the eight features is experienced, which types of community programs most often provide these experiences, and how these experiences differ by age, gender, socioeconomic status, ethnicity, sexual orientation, and community. Research is needed on the role community programs play in filling gaps in adolescents' total array of experience and what gaps remain, as well as on specific groups of adolescents who are consistently underserved by the options that exist.

Community Perspective

It is unrealistic and unwise to expect that every community program will be able to provide all eight features to all youth. To begin with, many adolescents may simply not be interested in the activities offered by specific programs. Furthermore, no single community program can be all things to all people. With limited resources, they may not be able to provide programming across all ages and developmental levels. Specific programs may have particular strengths that lead them to focus on more limited experiences. Intervention provided at one stage of life should not be assumed to work at another (Compas, 1993). Communities need to think about the full set of programs they provide and how adequately they supply opportunities for all their youth. Communities need a menu or portfolio of programs that allows adolescents and their families to select out the experiences most needed or desired.

The importance of the community as a unit of analysis for youth development is becoming increasingly popular. For example, this perspective is being encouraged by the research of the Search Institute in Minneapolis, which shows, first, that communities differ substantially in the number of psychological and social supports they have for youth and, second, that youth are healthier in communities that have more of these supports. This relation goes beyond the predictive power of the number of assets experienced by an individual youth: when a community is rich in supports, even at-risk youth seem to be doing better than in communities without such supports and opportunities (Benson, 1997; Blyth and Leffert, 1995). This perspective is also central to the work by Hawkins and Catalano (Hawkins, Catalano, and Associates, 1992; Development Research and Programs, Inc., 2000) on Communities that Care and by Public/Private Ventures on community-wide initiatives for youth (Gambone, 1997). Both of these programs are discussed in more detail in Chapter 5. Finally, the community perspective is gaining prominence in prevention work, in which more and more efforts are being made to design and evaluate community-wide interventions (see work by Biglan and colleagues as one such example [Biglan et al., 2000]).

What has not been researched systematically is how community programs fit into this picture of community supports and whether they can actually cause changes in the prevalence of both positive and risky youth outcomes. The associations undercovered by Benson and his colleagues at the Search Institute could result from characteristics of the communities that were unmeasured and influenced both the communities' ability to generate and support multiple supports for their youth and the resilience of the youth themselves. Community-wide experiments are just beginning to be reported. For the most part, these experiments do not vary the number of supports but rather the commitment of the community to change and the provision of financial and person-power resources for a change initiative. In addition, there is not yet a model for how a community can assess whether its set of community programs provides good coverage for all youth, or whether there are major gaps. In general, we know that the availability of youth development focused institutions and programs vary with neighborhood socioeconomic status. Fewer community programs are available in poorer neighborhoods (Halpern-Fisher et al., 1997). Access is also lower for minority youth and in rural areas (Carnegie Corporation of New York, 1992). Clearly more research is needed that takes the community as its focus.

There are lessons here for communities as well. They should not just sit back and assume that their youth are being taken care of. They need to actively assess whether there are opportunities for all youth and whether their range of programs provides good coverage of the eight features. This means they need to have someone or some agency that attends to the community menu of programs, who has responsibility for oversight and coordination, and perhaps even helps youth get connected to community programs that suit their needs and abilities.

SUMMARY

Research demonstrates that certain features of the settings that adolescents experiences help facilitate positive development. Research on the settings of the family, schools, and the community supports the conclusion that daily settings are more likely to promote positive developmental assets if they provide:

- Structure and limits that are developmentally appropriate and that recognize adolescents' increasing social maturity and expertise;
- Physical and psychological safety and security;
- Opportunities to experience supportive relationships and to have good emotional and moral support;
- Opportunities to feel a sense of belonging;
- Opportunities to be exposed to positive morals, values, and positive social norms;
- Opportunities to be efficacious, to do things that make a real difference and to play an active role in the organizations themselves;
- Opportunities for skill building, including learning how to form close, durable human relations with peers that support and reinforce healthy behaviors, as well as to acquire the skills necessary for school success and successful transition into adulthood; and
- Strong links between families, schools, and broader community resources.

Although there is limited research that specifies what community programs for youth can do to facilitate positive adolescent development, the list identified in this chapter is a step toward formulating a framework for features of community programs that support the acquisition of assets of personal and social development and, in turn, support positive adolescent development.

As was summarized in Chapter 3, there is evidence that adolescents with more personal and social assets have greater positive development. Since program features typically work together in synergistic ways, programs with more features are likely to provide better supports for young people's positive development.

We need to reemphasize the limits of the research used in this chapter. First, the chapter has drawn primarily on studies of such settings as families and schools and then extrapolated the findings to community programs. Research focusing directly on these features in community program settings would increase our understanding of how community programs for youth could incorporate these features into program design and implementation.

Second, we have stressed that our configuration of these features into a list of eight is provisional. The boundaries between features are indistinct, and the titles given to them tentative. It is unlikely that another group of scholars would come up with the exact same list, although the underlying content is likely to be very similar. Research is needed that further sharpens the conceptualization of these features and does so in the context of community programs. It is also possible that new research will find features that we have not included.

Finally, there is evidence that adolescents in communities that are rich in developmental opportunities for them experience reduced risk and show higher rates of positive development. This suggests that communities need a menu or portfolio of programs that provides a fit for every adolescent. Communities need models for how they can assess whether its set of community programs provides good coverage for all youth or whether there are major gaps in who they are serving. Research focusing directly on these features in community programs for youth is essential—research that sharpens the conceptualization of these features in community program settings.

PART II

The Role of Community Programs for Youth

As summarized in the Part I, evidence suggests that the more positive features a setting has, the greater contribution it will make to young people's positive development. The list of features of positive developmental settings we have presented was generated primarily from evidence about families, schools, and neighborhoods. Given that the focus of this report is on community programs for youth, we turn now to a review of the ways in which these programs incorporate features of positive developmental settings and provide opportunities for young people to acquire personal and social assets and promote their positive development.

What can community programs for youth do to give each person who walks in the door the best chance possible of acquiring the assets described in Part I of this report? How do we make sure that programs engage all youth and support their development?

In this part we provide examples of community programs that promote adolescent development. There is great diversity in the structure, focus, and size of these programs. Funding mechanisms, staff training, and management styles also vary. Programs differ in their objectives and the emphasis they place on particular program features. But all programs can strive toward incorporating developmental opportunities while working to meet the needs of individual participants.

This part of the report reviews studies and evaluations that detail how programs incorporate features of positive developmental settings and their impact on the outcomes for adolescents. Chapter 5 considers findings from a number of nonexperimental studies using various methods to collect information; Chapter 6 looks at findings from a set of comprehensive experimental evaluations.

CHAPTER 5

The Landscape of Community Programs for Youth

group of 20 young people meets twice a week for three hours after school with their school dance teacher and a professional dancer from the city's local dance troupe. They spend one hour doing their homework and receiving tutoring assistance from the staff. Then they participate in an hour of rigorous stretching and calisthenics. Exhausted but exhilarated, they spend the remainder of their afternoon rehearsing for their upcoming dance performance at a school talent show.

A half-dozen teenagers meet at their local community centers with adult city council members to share the results of a survey they conducted to help the city council understand adolescent needs and how to serve young people more effectively. They leave the meeting with plans to meet again the following week with two city council members to plan a community service event for young people and their families.

Hundreds of young people in uniforms fan out to various neighborhoods across the city in one of the country's largest urban areas. Working in teams, they participate in various community service tasks, such as tutoring children, landscaping, and cleaning a park. Between community service projects, these youth receive tutoring and assistance in preparing for a high school equivalency exam.

These examples of community programs for youth represent just a few of the many diverse programs operating throughout the United States. There are various efforts at both the individual organization level and the broader community level to promote adolescent development through community programs. While many youth organizations, foundations, and citywide initiatives support youth development concepts and practices, there is little agreement on what specifically constitutes a youth development program and little systematic information on the breadth and diversity of efforts to provide these kinds of opportunities.

Community programs for youth vary in many significant ways. A program represents a number of elements and decisions that together constitute a program setting. Some of these dimensions represent choices made, such as the program focus, curriculum, and membership; others are not choices but the consequences of structural arrangements, organizational affiliations, local community issues, geographic location, funding, and political climate.

This chapter creates a bridge between the framework for adolescent development and program design and implementation by providing examples of ways in which community programs for youth incorporate the features of positive developmental settings described in Chapter 4. Committee members observed a variety of community programs for youth and reviewed literature describing these programs. We also drew heavily on the findings from studies that used various nonexperimental methods to describe the design, implementation, and management of a number of community programs for youth that appear to work at the community level.

INSIGHTS FROM NONEXPERIMENTAL STUDIES

Nonexperimental studies provide valuable insight about these programs because they generally go beyond traditional evaluation input factors, such as size, funding, activity focus, and participants served and help elucidate the realities of program practices and consequences. Although these studies cannot draw conclusions about the impact of program design characteristics on adolescent outcomes, they can help program planners and program staff build internal knowledge and skills and can highlight theoretical issues about the developmental qualities of programs. Nonexperimental studies can also help develop a solid understanding about program operations, components, and relationships in order to inform the design of future experimental evaluations.

The illustrations used throughout this chapter represent only a small sample of the many innovative community programs for youth. The extent to which and methods by which these programs have been systematically studied varies. Consequently, they cannot be said to represent "model programs" in a formal sense; instead, they illustrate the application of youth development concepts to program design dimensions. In Chapter 6 we examine findings from another set of evaluations on community programs for youth—those that use experimental methods—and consider the additional insight gained from these evaluation methods.

The committee examined in detail two studies of specific programs—Community Impact! (Association for the Study and Development of Community, 2000) and Save the Children (Terao et al., 2000)—and one study of a set of programs—Community Counts (McLaughlin, 2000). These studies used a variety of field-based and ethnographic methods to address youth development questions. They embrace an array of study purposes, employ various strategies to enhance the validity and reliability of the research, and provide important contributions to both knowledge and research. These three illustrations are summarized in Boxes 5-1, 5-2, and 5-3. Our discussion of programs in this chapter, however, is not exclusive to these three program illustrations. The programs identified throughout this chapter are based on various sources of information, including program materials, site visits, and field observations by committee members.

A WIDE RANGE OF PROGRAMS

In order to understand how community programs for youth may incorporate features of settings, it is first useful to understand the diverse nature of these programs. The characterization of community programs for youth is complicated. The landscape of programs is vast. And the variety of terms used to describe the programs varies. At the most basic level, "programs are semi-structured processes, most often led by adults and designed to address specific goals and youth outcomes. This category incorporates a range of programs from those that are highly structured, often in the form of curriculum with step-by-step guidelines, to those that may have a looser structure" (Benson and Saito, 2000: 126). They may be called after-school programs, youth programs, youth activities, community programs, extracurricular activities, or programs during out-of-school time or nonschool hours.

BOX 5-1
Community Counts

An exploratory study that aimed to identify elements of community organizations that youth judged effective and the accomplishments of the youth participants, Community Counts (McLaughlin, 2000) included exploratory research aimed at better understanding the organizational settings youth found supportive and inviting—settings that reflected many of the features of settings presented in Chapter 4. The sample was purposely biased to include "effective" programs; youth steered researchers toward organizations they identified as good places to spend their time—places where they felt valued, respected, and challenged in positive ways. The organizations and activities studied were a diverse lot—Boys and Girls Clubs, dance troupes, YMCA/YWCAs, basketball teams, and improvisational theater. More than 1,000 youth participated in these groups; all were poor, and the majority were members of minority groups.

During the first phase of the study, research associates living in each of the communities carried out primary data collection. These researchers spent full time for three years getting to know the communities, the youth, and their organizations. They and the principal investigators conducted interviews, observations, and focus groups with youth, community-based organizations, and community leaders over a three-year period. The study developed a strategy to engage youth in data collection and interpretation. Approximately five young people from the organizations in each of the three communities were recruited and trained to serve as ethnographers. These youth were responsible for interviews with youth and adults in their organization and neighborhood and for providing field notes from activities that researchers could not attend. Phase 2 of the research continued these data collection strategies, employing "traveling" research associates instead of community-based researchers. Phase 2 also included a survey that asked a subset of questions from the National Education Longitudinal Survey of Youth (NELS:88) instrument in order to "locate" the characteristics and accomplishments of participating youth in terms of representative American youth.

BOX 5-2
Community Impact!

Community Impact! was founded in 1990 to help low-income neighborhoods across Washington, DC, invest in their youth through neighborhood-based programs focused on youth development, entrepreneurship, and academic enrichment. The Association for the Study and Development of Community and Community IMPACT! (CI!) used a "utilization-focus" with three interdependent studies to evaluate CI! efforts, to examine research and practice as it relates to CI! strategies, and to assess CI!'s organizational capacity (Association for the Study and Development of Community, 2000).

The first study included personal interviews, archival data review, and evaluator observations. Data collection focused on nine domains of interest: (1) community climate, cooperation, and participation; (2) leadership; (3) program legitimacy; (4) community awareness; (5) steering committee membership; (6) committee activities and empowerment; (7) resources and technical assistance/training; (8) financial and partnership management; and (9) financial resources.

The second study focused on providing knowledge and a new understanding of what "community" means to community members (adults and youth) and how youth leadership affects a community and its members. They conducted both adult and youth focus groups, administered a youth survey, and conducted a literature review.

The third study involved a questionnaire that asked program staff to evaluate the following six dimensions of their organizational structure: culture, leadership, systems and structures, communication of information, teams, and evaluation.

The institutional structure of programs can fundamentally affect the degree to which they address adolescent development, respond to local conditions, and provide appealing and safe settings. The Carnegie Council on Adolescent Development described youth programs through various categories (Carnegie Corporation of New York, 1992):

- Private, nonprofit national youth organizations: There are a number of large national youth-serving organizations that have local franchises throughout the United States, and often internationally.

BOX 5-3
Save the Children (U.S. Programs)

Since 1997, Save the Children has been running an initiative called Web of Support to promote quality programs for young people ages 5 to 18 during out-of-school time. Community organizations across the country, identified by Save the Children as Rural Community Partners or Urban Collaboratives, serve children and youth sponsored by Save the Children. The evaluation, conducted by the Aguirre Group, reports on the accomplishments and outcomes of 43 Rural Community Partners (Partners) and 7 Urban Collaboratives (Collaboratives) from October 1998 through September 1999 (Terao et al., 2000).

The evaluation was based on a participatory/empowerment model. This study documents the positive outcomes associated with children and youth, partners and collaboratives, regional and Home Office staff, and the Save the Children national network. The evaluation included a variety of data collection methods including content analysis of evaluation reports developed by each participating partner and collaborative; conducting pre-post surveys of youth interns and new partners (through written surveys and through focus groups); conducting post surveys of youth-intern supervisors, pilot and first-year partners, and collaboratives facilitators; conducting telephone interviews with collaboratives members, and regional and home office staff; conducting observations during site visits and training; conducting pre-post adult surveys (staff, teacher, and/or parent); conducting parent interviews; developing and using observation checklists; and reviewing a collection of existing records (e.g., grades and test scores).

Although these organizations share many common aspects, each has unique components within the structure of its program. For instance, the program content may vary and the demographics of the service populations may vary, depending on the local community.

- Grassroots youth development organizations: These autonomous community-based organizations are fundamentally independent from other organizations or institutions. While they generally do not operate in isolation, their work with youth does not depend on the acceptance or support of any single institution.

- Religious youth organizations: These organizations may vary in their particular program activities and focus, but they generally share the common objective of fostering moral and faith development.
- Private community groups (i.e., adult service clubs, sports organizations, senior citizens groups, and museums): These organizations sponsor a broad range of youth programs; although their primary mission is not to provide youth programming, they engage youth in various activities.
- Public-sector institutions (i.e., public libraries, parks and recreation departments): These institutions often serve as a gathering point for adolescents and may offer activities and services specifically to promote adolescent development.

In addition to these categories, the committee also recognized that institutional collaborations, such as school-based programs being run by community-based organizations, offer many programs for youth.

There is great diversity in the specific focus and character of community programs for youth. Community Counts, for example, examined 120 community organizations that differed in nearly every objective way possible (McLaughlin, 2000). The Younger Americans Act (discussed in Chapter 9), introduced in the Senate in September 2000 and the House in January 2001, included a useful list of youth program activities:

- Character development and ethical enrichment activities;
- Mentoring activities, including one-to-one relationship building and tutoring;
- Community youth centers and clubs;
- Nonschool hours, weekend, and summer programs and camps;
- Sports, recreation, and other activities promoting physical fitness and teamwork;
- Services that promote health and healthy development and behavior on the part of youth, including risk avoidance programs;
- Academic enrichment, peer counseling and teaching, and literacy;
- Camping and environmental education;
- Cultural enrichment, including music, fine, and performing arts;
- Workforce preparation, youth entrepreneurship, and technological and vocational skill building, including computer skills;
- Opportunities for community service;
- Opportunities that engage youth in civic participation and as part-

ners in decision making;
- Special-interest groups or courses, including video production, cooking, gardening, pet care, photography, and other youth-identified interests; and
- Public and private youth-led programs, including ones provided by youth-serving or youth development organizations.

To this list, the committee added program activities associated with such developmental passage rituals as bat and bar mitzvahs, American Indian rite of passage rituals, and Christian first communion and confirmation ceremonies.

There is little comprehensive information on the prevalence and distribution of the various community programs for youth in this country. The Carnegie Council on Adolescent Development's 1992 report, *A Matter of Time,* provided the most comprehensive summary of basic national statistics on the pervasiveness of youth programs (Carnegie Corporation of New York, 1992). Based on data from the National Center for Charitable Statistics, this study concluded that there were 17,000 active youth organizations in the United States in 1990. No other national studies as comprehensive as this have been undertaken in the past decade, a period when there has been considerable increases in funding and opportunity for these programs. A variety of independent efforts to compile information about a particular set of youth programs have been conducted, but they are neither comprehensive nor national in their scope (National Collaboration for Youth, 1997).

FEATURES OF COMMUNITY PROGRAMS FOR YOUTH

The committee mapped the features of settings developed in the Chapter 4 against various program illustrations and drew some conclusions about effective strategies to incorporating features of positive developmental settings. While there are fairly obvious links between some program dimensions and features of settings, there is also a great deal of overlap. For instance, programs that develop clear and consistent rules of behavior demonstrate appropriate structure; at the same time, these rules may help nurture an environment that promotes physical and psychological safety.

Physical and Psychological Safety

Physical and psychological safety is fundamental to attract young people to programs and to keep them coming back. This requires both creating an environment that is safe, as well as handling conflicts among participants as they arise.

The objective of some programs is to enable youth to just participate in safe environments free from pressures associated with violence and substance abuse. In many cases, accessibility makes a difference to safety, which in turn often affects participation. Some programs or facilities are too far for youth to get to conveniently, requiring a bus ride or long walk through uncertain neighborhoods. Other clubs or programs may be only a few blocks from a young person's home but require navigating hostile gang territory. Hours of operation matter, too. Programs unavailable until after six in the evening, for example, have difficulty attracting youth at all (Cahill et al., 1993). Programs operating only one evening a week or that are closed on weekends also seem insufficient to sustain youth interest. Most appealing from youth's perspective were organizations that provided reliable access to adults and safe space to meet daily and on weekends (McLaughlin, 2000).

Sometimes maintaining an atmosphere of safety requires denying some young people participation. Directors describe the process as a sort of triage, in which difficult decisions are sometimes made to deny needy and deserving youth a place in the organization for the sake of the whole. For example, the director of HOME in Alameda, California, pays close attention to school records and will not accept (or continue to involve) youth with consistent records of failure. These youth, she feels, could erode the spirit of entrepreneurship and responsibility that is the group's signature. The director of East Oakland's Youth Development Center has more pragmatic concerns—the safety of the young people who come through the door every afternoon. The director explained that they could not serve everyone and still have an environment that is safe and supportive for everyone.[1] This means that the most needy youth—youth of most concern to society—are sometimes excluded. It also means that youth who could benefit from and contribute to the organization may be denied a space simply because the program is full.

Several prevention studies have also documented a negative effect of programs that focus exclusively on adolescents already engaged in risky

---

[1]From field notes collected by committee member Milbrey McLaughlin.

behaviors, as described more in Chapter 6. For example, programs that put together a group of young people who are all already involved in problem behaviors often produce increases in the very behaviors the programs were designed to reduce (Dishion et al., 1999). These negative effects have been interpreted as the consequence of participation in a peer group comprised primarily of adolescents already actively involved in troubling behaviors.

Clear and Consistent Structure Appropriate Levels of Adult Supervision

Appropriate structure in community programs for youth includes developing clear and consistent rules and expectations, setting limits, and being clear about behavioral expectations. Settings with appropriate structure have predictability and consistency. The staff develop clear boundaries that take into consideration the age and developmental maturity of the youth involved.

Appropriate structure is often based on the rules maintained by a program. Rules of membership, such as bans on gang colors, weapons, drugs, and alcohol, are an essential set of agreements and understandings; also important are rules about members treating each other and the adult leaders with honesty, and teamwork. Youth report that these guidelines for behavior are elemental to their own feelings of safety and comfort—especially as the program environment provides a safe haven in their neighborhood (McLaughlin et al., 1994).

Appropriate structure is also based on the focus of the program and its underlying curriculum. Many community programs for youth attract young people of varying ages. Programs may explicitly seek to make the curriculum and program activities also reflect different developmental needs.

Supportive Relationships

Programs that focus on supportive relationships provide settings in which youth feel a strong sense of warmth, closeness, caring, support, and guidance from the adult leaders in the program.

Community programs for youth provide opportunities to expose young people to caring adults who challenge them, encourage them to participate in positive experiences, and respect their opinions. Youth respondents to the Community Impact! survey indicated that they desire and require guidance from adults (Association for the Study and Development of Community, 2000). This may be one of the most important characteristics of highly valued programs (McLaughlin, 2000).

Programs vary in terms of the characteristics of the staff they employ—by age, race, previous experience, and educational attainment. Some programs are staffed by full-time or part-time staff; others rely heavily on community or family volunteers. Adult leaders—both paid and volunteer—came from various personal and professional backgrounds in the programs reviewed in *Community Counts*. Some had been in military services; others had been teachers; many had worked in church groups or athletic teams all of their lives (McLaughlin, 2000). Save the Children programs involve paid and volunteer adults and teens, youth interns, teachers, and community elders (Terao et al., 2000). Participants in the Community Impact! survey place value on adults leaders who were getting or had gotten an education (Association for the Study and Development of Community, 2000).

From the perspective of young people, supportive relationships are based less on the professional qualifications of the staff and more on the staff's attitudes toward them (McLaughlin, 2000). Some community programs are led by adults deeply committed to young people and their futures. The staff that run these programs have an opportunity to influence a young person's sense of belonging, their sense of empowerment, and their connectedness to the program.

For some youth, the strength of relationships may be heightened by interaction with adults of their own ethnicity or experience as role models, coaches, and program administrators. Staff who are members of the same community from which the young people come may provide particularly strong support. A participant explained, "The [program] really taught me how to survive on the street. Most of the staff members here grew up just like I did on the street and stuff like that so they really taught me how to stay out of trouble and protect myself."[2]

Most important to developing connectedness and providing support and guidance is staff who are committed to a program and its young participants, who are consistent in the messages they teach, and who communicate warmth and caring while setting clear boundaries and consistent rules and expectations (McLaughlin, 2000). These staff attitudes matter more than do questions of race, age, or ethnicity. Youth see staff who they perceive are their allies and who are committed and trustworthy.

---

[2]From field notes collected by committee member Milbrey McLaughlin.

Opportunities to Belong

Promoting a sense of belonging is fundamental to attracting and retaining the participation of young people, as well as helping them develop confidence and a personal identity. Young people need to feel included, regardless of their gender, ethnicity, sexual orientation, personality, or physical, intellectual, or social limitations.

A program's curriculum and strategy describe what it does and how it carries out its mission and goals. A number of things about the nature of a program's curriculum and strategy matter for youth involvement, the benefits youth derive from participation, and the sense of belonging that is nurtured. One is the quality of program content; another is the extent to which activities embed various learning goals. At the most basic level, a sense of belonging and inclusion requires that the program strategy attract and interest young people. "Activities for youth need to be attractive to the youth audience. This means having fun, fresh, and interactive things to do" (Morley and Rossman, 1997). Youth want challenging, age-appropriate programming.

A program's size and membership may also fundamentally shape its design and operation and its ability to adequately offer opportunities that promote meaningful inclusion. Membership matters not only to its approach to youth development but also to how it organizes itself to facilitate opportunities for youth. The target membership for a program may be broad or it may focus on a particular ethnic or religious group. It may be only for boys or only for girls. It may be restricted to a particular age group. Some programs reach out to disenfranchised or at-risk youth; others limit participation to young people who have maintained a certain grade point average or have applied or auditioned to participate in the program. Many programs seek a heterogeneous set of participants to build understanding and tolerance among young people. Many of the national organizations, such as Big Brothers/Big Sisters, focus their activities on a large, diverse group of community participants. Some other programs are targeted toward homogeneous groups in order to offer specific support, cultural awareness, a sense of belonging, and pride to a particular subgroup of youth.

Both the Center for Young Women's Development (CYWD) and the Lavender Youth Recreation and Information Center (LYRIC), for example, are organizations that nurture belonging among youth with particular histories and experiences. They are committed to offering supports and opportunities to socially marginalized youth—in the case of CYWD to young female prostitutes in San Francisco, and in the case of

LYRIC, to transgender, bisexual, lesbian, and gay youth (McDonald et al., 2001).

Community programs for youth may engage a set of youth in communities that are particularly isolated and where youth have less access to social integration. For adolescents living in rural communities, where the proportion of parents working outside the home is the largest in the country, community programs for youth can nurture engagement and create a strong sense of belonging (Charles Stewart Mott Foundation, 1998a). An after-school program in rural Kentucky (the Clinton County School District), for example, offers an academic summer camp to 100 youth. These young people participate in sports activities, dancing and music, hunter education courses, computer skills training, communications skills activities, and public speaking. Given the isolated nature of this Kentucky community, opportunities for special field trips or exposure to diverse skills training are more limited than in urban areas. For these reasons, the on-site program is complemented with a Spanish course taught on-line by a teacher 90 minutes away, and young people take electronic field trips by way of the Internet (Charles Stewart Mott Foundation, 1998a).

Positive Social Norms

Some community programs for youth are designed as drop-in activities, where young people can come and go and participate in rotating activities of their choice. Other programs require youth to make a commitment to the program and as a result have high expectations for their involvement. These programs support prosocial norms by teaching youth responsibility to uphold certain rules of behavior, to be accountable to the program and its expectations, and to agree to live up to a set of morals and values.

Participants in the East Oakland Youth Development Center, which offers a range of activities for young people and their families, are required to make a commitment to the program through membership in one of the program's teams, dance troupes, or clubs. And to become a member of one of these groups, participants have to agree to the programs' values, which encourage self-respect and respect among peers and adults. At all costs, the center enforces these established rules and expectations of respect. The objective is to help young people integrate these norms into their character and their behavior in other parts of their lives (McLaughlin et al., 2001).

Support for Efficacy and Mattering

Many community programs for youth incorporate multiple opportunities to build efficacy. Programs may vary in the extent to which they allow youth to participate in the leadership of the program. However, many programs believe that youth can play a variety of roles in designing, delivering, and evaluating activities. Youth participants may help identify needs and set goals; help design the structure, activities, and supports that will be attractive and accessible to youth; help staff understand what youth need and how to relate to them; help identify community and family issues that may be barriers for youth participation; and help create an environment for youth to positively contribute to their community. Some programs develop youth councils to systematically generate youth involvement. Others involve youth in responsible leadership positions around program activities, such as tutors, peer counselors, and event organizers (Burt, 1998).

Community programs for youth that incorporate opportunities for efficacy may, in fact, be youth-centered or run entirely by adults. In practice, what often matters from the adolescent's perspective is the stance about youth communicated by program goals and philosophy. Are program goals focused on youth as resources or as problems? Do youth see programs as resources to help them grow or succeed, rather than as efforts to "fix" them? They are likely to avoid or leave programs that seem punitive or deficit-based and instead choose ones that acknowledge their assets and help them to develop their strengths. Youth-centered programs provide rich opportunities to support youth efficacy—for youth to experience leadership, assume responsibility, and develop problem-solving skills.

Faced with declining enrollment of youth over 13 years of age, Louisiana 4-H developed a survey to ensure that their curriculum and program strategy were designed around ideas that teens themselves indicated were of interest. They found that the topics of interest changed as young people got older. At higher grade levels, for instance, they were much more interested in jobs, careers, and options after high school. They also discovered that the traditional 4-H program topics of health, safety, and nutrition had to be packaged in terms of fitness or sports in order to attract adolescent interest. Although the youth did not want to discuss personal grooming, they were eager to participate in activities about fashion (Acosta and Holt, 1991). This program granted youth responsibility and supported efficacy by involving them in deciding the nature of the program activities.

There are programs that have explored including young people as evaluators of their programs. The Department of Children, Youth and Their Families in the City of San Francisco launched a comprehensive effort to promote leadership development among San Francisco youth. The city's efforts included a youth-led evaluation program that trains 12-15 youth in research, planning, and evaluation. This component of the city's work was designed both to create new leadership among young people and to improve the effectiveness of the organizations being funded, from a youth perspective (Department of Children, Youth and Their Families, 2001).

Opportunities for Skill Building

At the heart of many community programs for youth are opportunities for skill building. Programs can use a wide variety of activities, such as community service, adventure and outdoor activities, art, drama, music, religious instruction, sports, cultural awareness, academic improvement, and career preparation, to support positive youth development and to meet the program-specific objectives. The exact content or focus (e.g., sports, music, community service) may be designed to attract adolescents to the program, while the curriculum may focus more on developmental skills (e.g., cooperation, creativity, communication). Save the Children programs, for example, include activities to promote cognitive ability and intellectual growth, as well as social and emotional growth, through a range of activities, including tutoring, computer training, recreation activities, team-building programs, and youth leadership activities (Terao et al., 2000).

Programs focusing on a specific activity can support skill building in a number of different areas. An arts program, for example, may involve youth in researching their cultural history and painting community murals to reflect what they learn. A sports program may focus not only on skills development, but also on teamwork and problem solving (McLaughlin, 2000). Library-based programs encouraging teens to read can provide a variety of educational, recreational, and cultural opportunities that help the participants improve academic performance, develop social skills, learn new hobbies, and build self-esteem. Through reading opportunities, these programs focus on critical thinking, communication skills, social skills, and creativity (American Library Association, 2000).

Examples of skills that are incorporated into programs are plentiful. Volunteers of Campfire Boys and Girls provide youth with assistance, guidance, and direction in a myriad of programs, including citizenship and community leadership, health and safety, food and nutrition, energy, economics, jobs and careers, natural resources, sciences, and plant and animal production (Campfire Boys and Girls, 2000). "Always on Saturday," a teen pregnancy program for black boys in Hartford, Connecticut, focuses on teaching life skills. The program curriculum incorporates general decision-making, problem-solving, planning, and goal-setting techniques taught through life examples that both the director and the youth provide (Ferguson, 1994:74).

Programs that address a number of developmental outcomes with each activity offer what is referred to as an *embedded curriculum* (McLaughlin, 2000). Embedded within an organization's programs are activities that build a number of competencies and life skills. For example, YO!, a Northern California youth-run newspaper, provides jobs for youth, training in reporting, writing, and production, and experience in the business side of newspaper production. An after-school dance program for youth integrates cultural history into the dance lessons and gives them responsibility for program planning, advertising, and marketing. A championship inner-city basketball team begins each after-game briefing with an assessment of teamwork and sportsmanship. Programs such as these teach skills—writing, dance, and basketball—but they also build skills around responsibility, leadership, persistence, and connection to the family, schools, and the community.

Integration of Family, School, and Community Efforts

Community programs for youth offer many opportunities for the integration of families, schools, and the broader community. Thus far we have described the specific ways in which individual organizations design and operate programs. But youth development depends not only on the independent efforts of programs, but also on these efforts in collaboration with the community as a whole.

Peter L. Benson, president of the Search Institute, describes a community by three characteristics: (1) a shared commitment, in which adults, organizations, and community institutions unite to affirm their responsibility to youth and their ability to make a difference and take action; (2) daily opportunities for individuals to acknowledge, encourage, and support youth; (3) intentional involvement of organizations, institutions, and systems—including schools, congregations, youth organizations, businesses, health care providers, and foundations—in programs and activities that provide youth with positive experiences (Benson, 1996).

Given the focus of this report, the committee was particularly interested in highlighting strategies through which community programs for youth integrate their activities with the broader community. Many programs in fact do target the community more broadly, seeking to reach and influence young people, their families, and other community members, organizations, and businesses. HOME, for example, is a community-based youth membership organization where young people throughout the city of Alameda, California, collaborate with each other and adults to create important projects and innovative businesses. The achievements made through these youth-initiated projects pave the way for adults to embrace youth as contributing members of the community and for youth to learn the skills they need to be effective, enterprising citizens.

As well, many programs that are focused on individual-level outcomes also influence community-level outcomes. Community programs for youth may, in fact, focus beyond individual-level outcomes to strengthen community capacity. Where youth live, what their communities are like, and what the general climate is like in their neighborhood—factors of safety, schools, and economic stability, for example—have significant impacts on individual development (National Governors' Association's Center for Best Practices, 1999). Youth participants in the Community Impact! survey, for example, specifically reported that they perceived a supportive community as one with adequate resources, including such activities as community programs for youth (Association for the Study and Development of Community, 2000).

Most young people grow up in families, spend much of their time in schools, and are surrounded by communities, so incorporating opportunities for developmental outcomes into their lives demands coordinated efforts among these stakeholders. "Youth development requires collaboration. No single community organization can provide the range of developmental, preventive, and intervention programs and services required to give young people the experiences they need to mature into successful adults. Rather, creation of such programs requires collaborative planning by a community's youth-serving agencies, other social services and educational institutions, policy makers, community leaders, and young people" (National Clearinghouse on Families and Youth, 1996).

Agreeing on what communities want for all young people is an important factor in supporting youth development. Youth service providers, in conjunction with youth, parents, and community members, need to develop a shared understanding of the needs of the young people in their community. They must decide what youth need to develop into healthy, self-sufficient, and involved adults and how the community can best meet those needs. Through that collaborative process, they can begin discussing a youth development framework and how it might translate into a vision for young people in their community.

The committee explored in more depth a few particular strategies to integrate community programs for youth with broader community priorities.

Community-Wide Initiatives

Over the past 10 years, there has been growing interest in community-wide programming initiatives for youth. Consistent with the importance we place on the interconnections across the various social settings in which adolescents live, these community-wide initiatives have sought to take a broader view of the developmental needs of youth. Also growing out of a community development perspective, these initiatives have focused on a coordinated effort to increase the services and programs for youth across the community. Communities That Care in Pennsylvania, based on a curriculum developed by Hawkins, Catalano, and Associates (1992; Development Research and Programs, Inc., 2000) and Public/Private Ventures Community Change for Youth Development (Gambone, 1997) are two prime examples of these efforts.

These types of initiatives are particularly noteworthy, since they seek to provide a coordinated approach to meeting the needs for positive youth development. Such initiatives also offer the possibility of implementing a monitoring and self-evaluation system that regularly assesses the needs of youth and matches them against the range of services and programs provided by the community. Such a coordinated approach appears to have a good chance of actually ensuring the adequacy of community-wide services for youth.

Communities That Care. The Communities That Care approach, developed by David Hawkins and Richard Catalano, is an operating system for prevention. It helps states and communities assess and prioritize needs, choose the best approaches to promote youth development and prevent problem behaviors based on those needs, and evaluate the effectiveness of policies, programs, and actions that have been implemented in their communities.

The scientific knowledge base underlying this approach includes understanding the root causes of both positive and problem behaviors. These root causes include risk factors for adolescent problem behaviors—those factors associated with an increased likelihood of such behaviors. Root causes also include protective factors—those factors that appear to buffer the effects of risk and promote positive youth development even in the presence of risk. The approach is designed to reduce risk in ways that enhance protective factors. The knowledge base also includes identification of programs, policies, and actions that have demonstrated their ability to reduce risk and enhance protection.

The model began with a field test in 1988 in Washington State with 25 communities, then in 1989 in Oregon with 39 communities. It has now been adopted by the U.S. Department of Justice's Office of Juvenile Justice and Delinquency Prevention as the prevention component of their comprehensive strategy and is offered as training to assist communities to spend Title V funds. The states of Colorado, Illinois, Kansas, Louisiana, Maine, Michigan, New York, North Carolina, Oregon, Pennsylvania, Utah, and Washington have adopted this approach state-wide in a single agency or in multiple youth-serving agencies. It has allowed them to take the lead in prevention, get funds transferred, and helped to educate citizens and practitioners about this effective approach to prevention.

The state of Pennsylvania (in collaboration with federal funding sources) serves as one example of the use of this model. The state made a commitment to help communities put together a coordinated effort around prevention. Communities were encouraged to combine the processes and skills of community building and community development with the evidence emerging from the field of prevention science in order to evaluate community needs and resources; design a more comprehensive, coordinated set of services and programs for children, youth, and families; implement their design; and put in place an extensive evaluation component to monitor progress and improve design. Communities applied for planning and training grant funds. At present, the state plans to provide training for up to 20 new communities per year until the demand for this program is met. The evaluation of this effort, based on a quasi-experimental design, is just beginning. Initial results focus only on implementation in a limited number of communities. Reports over the next

PROCESS →	IMPLEMENTATION →	SHORT-TERM →	LONG-TERM
Community	Increased number and	YOUTH	YOUTH
mobilization	quality of activities and	OUTCOMES	OUTCOMES
	opportunities in core	Increased developmental	Positive
	concept areas in	supports/experiences	achievements
	community	in core concept areas	by community's
		in youth's daily lives	youth

FIGURE 5-1   Theory of Change. Source: Gambone (1997).

several years will reveal a great deal about this effort (Hawkins, Catalano, and Associates, 1992; Development Research and Programs, Inc., 2000).

Community Change for Youth Development. The Community Change for Youth Development demonstration, initiated by Public/Private Ventures, involved selecting three communities (St. Petersburg, Florida; Savannah, Georgia; and Austin, Texas) and working with them to develop and implement an integrated set of activities for youth ages 12 to 20 (Gambone, 1997). Public/Private Ventures approached communities with a very well-articulated theory of change (see Figure 5-1) and offered technical assistance during a 6-month planning period, followed by partial support of the implementation phase.

The three communities with the most comprehensive plan that was consistent with the goals and developmental perspective were selected. Unlike the Communities That Care initiative, this project involved little state funding. Instead, the communities received some support and were required to identify and recruit other sources of funding.

Two things are very exciting about this community effort. First, the core concepts identified were based on solid research and fit with the positive developmental features of settings outlined in Chapter 4. Second, initial studies of the planning and implementation phases suggest that communities can come together to increase the range of opportunities available to their youth (Gambone, 1997). Nonexperimental evaluations of this effort are ongoing, and a great deal will be learned from these studies.

School-Based Community Centers. Schools often serve as a gathering spot for community activity focused on the development of its youth. Two schools in New York City, I.S. 218 and P.S. 5, decided to extend the use of their existing facilities to include a multiservice center providing services to neighborhood children and families, through the aid and guidance of the Children's Aid Society and other partners. A survey of parents indicated concern about homework patterns, so the program began as a homework tutorial. Gradually it has expanded to include computer labs, dance classes, arts programs, and career readiness support. Resources are also available through the program to parents and the community (U.S. Department of Education, 2001). Other similar models now exist across the country.

Intermediary Organizations

Closely related to these community-wide initiatives are a wide variety of capacity-building intermediary organizations that have emerged over the past decade. These organizations have grown out of a need to advance the vision of comprehensive promotion and implementation of youth development. These organizations are helping to chart, support, implement, and sustain multiple changes for multiple stakeholders, such as youth development providers, funders, and researchers (Academy for Educational Development, 1999).

The Community Network for Youth Development (CNYD), an example of an intermediary organization located in San Francisco, California, has been instrumental in promoting a youth development approach and supporting youth workers and directors. Through its Learning Network, directors and youth workers become familiar with best practices that support youth to build relationships with other youth and adults, participate in decision-making and leadership roles, become involved in the larger community, and develop skills and knowledge through their participation in challenging and interesting learning opportunities. In addition, the Learning Network provides a shared space in which directors and youth workers throughout the Bay area can jointly reflect on youth development practices and learn from one another regarding what works in practice. There are a number of other such capacity-building intermediaries across the country, such as Youth Net in Greater Kansas City, Missouri, the Hampton Coalition for Youth in Hampton, Virginia, B. BRAVO for Youth in Baltimore, Maryland, and the Chicago Youth Agency Partnership. Intermediary organizations are discussed more in Chapter 9.

There are a number of other efforts to coordinate learning among individuals and organizations involved in identifying and developing youth development research and policies. The Harvard Family Research Project, for instance, developed the idea of learning communities as one way to institutionalize continual and coordinated self-examination. The Forum for Youth Investment (formerly the International Youth Foundation) is also involved in such efforts to help community programs flourish.

Faith-Based Organizations

Faith-based organizations have long been important providers of services to young people and the broader community, creating links between youth, families, and the community. Research on faith-based institutions and the role of religious organizations, such as churches and synagogues, suggests that they can contribute to community-wide efforts to promote youth development in several key areas, helping to reduce risky behaviors, building a value base from which young people make decisions, and involving a variety of people across the life span. While schools and social service agencies reach only targeted populations, congregations often touch a cross-section of the population. Nearly 40 percent of Americans say they attend some form of worship regularly and 65 percent are members of a church or synagogue (Saito and Blyth, 1992).

These institutions may attract increased attention with President George W. Bush's focus on faith-based initiatives. President Bush has proposed to allow religious groups to compete on an equal basis with secular organizations for federal grants and to create a nationwide faith-based initiative. This has taken the form of the White House Office of Faith-Based and Community Initiatives, which plans on using government subsidies to prompt religious and community organizations' role in combating such problems as juvenile delinquency and drug abuse.

Catholic Charities is a good example of a faith-based national organization that stimulates local affiliates to undertake new activities, offers training and technical assistance in their ongoing work, assists with fund raising, and coordinates public policy advocacy. Two current examples of initiatives emanating from the national office of Catholic Charities are illustrative. Catholic Charities has been encouraging affiliates to get involved in restorative justice for young people who have gotten into trouble with the law. For example, Project Payback in Newark, New Jersey, is a program that allows young people to avoid incarceration by working in the community on service projects that help victims of crime.

Catholic Charities also encourages local affiliates to get involved in delivering treatment services that are a key part of the drug court model now being replicated in many communities (Catholic Charities USA, 2000). Leaders of Tomorrow in Cleveland, for example, helps young people convicted of selling drugs to find and keep jobs and stay in school. Catholic Charities uses convening people, e-mail, and publications to let its affiliates know about new activities it encourages them to undertake (Catholic Charities USA, 2000).

Another example of the ways in which the juvenile justice system has become involved in forming a partnership with faith-based community organizations is the Boston Ten-Point Coalition. Responding to escalating violence, black clergy joined with the Boston police force to create a coalition, aimed at reaching out to at-risk youth and gang members through "adoption" of gangs, patrolling neighborhoods, counseling, and using the church as a community center. The coalition, working with law enforcement and social service officials, has been successful in reducing gun violence and formulating future plans for a program that will help create entrepreneurial businesses run by former gang members, who in turn, will employ other former gang members (Congress of National Black Churches, 2001).

Project SPIRIT (Strength, Perseverance, Imagination, Responsibility, Integrity, and Talent) is an after-school, church-based curriculum program for students ages 6-12. The program, run by the Congress of National Black Churches, is built on the idea that church is a major institution in the lives of many black families. By joining together parents, pastors, community and business leaders, and politicians, the program aims to provide youth with a safe haven for teaching and learning. Youth participants engage in a variety of activities, including life skills enhancement programs, after-school tutorials, and Saturday School. Project SPIRIT, which has spread to at least eight states, also provides parents with education, pastoral counseling, and training (Congress of National Black Churches, 2001).

Community-Based Ceremonies for Youth Development

As we have described, public and private organizations often provide communities with programs to support young people. However, communities themselves also often initiate and maintain vital programs to nurture their young members—particularly through unique programs rooted in the communities' own cultural traditions.

Among many Jewish communities in America, perhaps the single most important rite is the celebration of puberty, the bar mitzvah (for males) and bat mitzvah (for females) (Neuser, 1994). The bar/bat mitzvah[3] (Diamant and Cooper, 1991) celebrates the coming of age of young men and women, after which the community regards them as adults, obligated to fulfill Judaism's religious commandments. While the rite varies among congregations, three elements are ubiquitous: the young person reads from the Torah (Old Testament) before the community, gives a speech, and holds a celebration (Diamant and Cooper, 1991). The ceremony represents the social order of the Jewish community and affirms the place of the youth and their family in that order (Liebman, 1990). Family and community members begin preparing the young man or woman at least one year before the ceremony and are deeply involved throughout. Community members teach the youth to read and speak the Hebrew language, instruct them on the ceremonies of the bar/bat mitzvah, direct their study of the particular passage of Torah to be read, and tutor them as they prepare their speech. The bar/bat mitzvah and the preparations for it incorporate the support of relatives and the larger community.

Navajo communities hold a coming-of-age ceremony for young women, called kinaalda. Navajo communities have maintained kinaalda, part of the larger Navajo Blessing Way, and it is now a most anticipated Navajo ceremony. Shortly after a girl announces the beginning of her first menstrual cycle, relatives and community members begin the formal ceremony, which lasts two to four days. With the assistance of family and community elders, kinaalda instills young girls with a pride in their cultural traditions, identity, and community, as well as signifying their coming life (Roessel, 1993; see also, Ryan, 1998). Kinaalda mobilizes family and community support around a young woman's growth and integration into the Navajo social order. Community programs that support youth, such as the bar/bat mitzvah and the kinaalda, exist in many different communities—Catholic first communion and confirmation, Mexican and Mexican American quinciñera ceremonies for young women, Afrocentric coming-of-age programs, religious missions among

---

[3]One author posits, "The differences between bar and bat mitzvah have been steadily diminishing to the point that today, in many congregations, they are virtually indistinguishable," thus, we refer to the bar mitzvah and the bat mitzvah as "bar/bat mitzvah" (Diamant, 1991).

Latter-Day Saints, debutante balls, and the culture and language schools found among such ethnic communities as Chinese Americans and Japanese Americans. Research has only begun to explore the similarities, connections, and benefits of such community efforts to youth development.

SUMMARY

Program providers, program administrators, community leaders, and policy makers face a variety of choices in developing, implementing, supporting, and sustaining successful community programs for youth. The committee draws several conclusions from a review of illustrative community programs for youth and the ways in which these programs incorporate features of positive developmental settings into their design and implementation.

Community programs have the potential to provide opportunities for youth to acquire personal and social assets and experience features of positive developmental settings. Among other things, these programs can incorporate opportunities for physical, cognitive, and social/emotional development; opportunities that address underlying issues of ethnic identity and intergroup relationships; opportunities for community involvement and service; and opportunities to interact with caring adults and a diversity of peers.

There is great diversity in the design, approach, and focus of community programs for youth. Priorities vary among the diverse programs and therefore may emphasize different program features. Mentoring programs, for example, may focus on creating supportive relationships and developing a sense of belonging and inclusion. Programs that emphasize sports activities, for example, may place greater priority of developing team building and physical skill building. Priorities vary, and consequently program features vary.

No single program can necessarily serve all young people or incorporate all of the features of positive developmental settings. Diverse opportunities are more likely to support broad adolescent development and outcomes for a greater number of youth. As noted in Chapter 4, communities that are rich in opportunities reduce adolescent risk and increase positive development for a greater number of young people. This further supports the conclusion that communities need to offer multiple opportunities to experience positive developmental settings. Community-wide approaches to developing and implementing community programs for youth are more likely to meet the needs of the diverse population of adolescents. Programs for youth offered by more than one organization—in schools, community centers, or both—focusing on different areas of interest and through different kinds of curricula provide the greatest opportunity for young people to acquire personal and social assets.

Finally, collaboration among researchers, providers, funders, and policy makers is important in order to develop and support community-wide approaches and implement a coordinated approach to designing, delivering, and evaluating community programs for youth.

CHAPTER 6

Lessons from Experimental Evaluations

F indings from nonexperimental and small scale quasi-experimental studies of community programs for youth provided the foundation for the descriptions in Chapter 5 of programs considered to be effective by participants, evaluators, observers, and qualitative researchers. In this chapter we summarize the committee's review of findings from experimental and large-scale quasi-experimental evaluations of community programs for youth. The committee examined several meta-analyses and review articles that summarize the findings from many different studies of community programs for youth and considered in more detail three specific program evaluations.

This examination had four primary objectives. First, we were interested in whether there is evidence from the most rigorous evaluations available that community programs for youth make a difference in the lives of their participants. Second, we wanted to know whether the programs that had received these types of rigorous evaluations included either the program features outlined in Chapter 4 as potentially important components of community programs for youth or the personal and social assets outlined in Chapter 3 as potentially important targets for these programs. Third, when this information was available, we wanted to know whether the program features hypothesized to be important in Chapter 4 were indeed important in both facilitating positive youth development and preventing the emergence of serious problems. Finally, as a lead-in to the next chapter, we also wanted to assess the quality of these evaluations. We include in this chapter comments on whether the evaluations selected for inclusion in this chapter meet the most rigorous methods of evaluation—described in Chapter 7—that can be used with community programs for youth.

REVIEWS AND META-ANALYSES OF EVALUATIONS

The committee reviewed seven reputable reviews and meta-analyses of prevention and promotion programs for youth from the fields of mental health, violence prevention, teenage pregnancy prevention, and youth development.[1] We considered reviews that included both programs for youth with a primary focus on prevention and programs explicitly focused on a youth development framework since, as explained previously, the committee found the distinction between prevention and positive youth development not very clear in practice. Programs with prevention goals, for example, often included components common to programs with youth development goals. Details of the programs included in the meta-analyses reviewed are summarized in Table 6-1.

As noted, the primary objective of reviewing these meta-analyses was to provide our best assessment of the extent to which community programs have beneficial effects for youth. Our secondary objective was to determine the extent to which these programs incorporate the features of positive developmental settings developed in Part I and whether there is evidence of links between these program features and positive youth outcomes. Since none of the programs were designed with these specific assets and features in mind, we often had to make assumptions about likely features from the descriptions of the programs included in the various reviews. Through this review, we also identified the strengths and limitations of these evaluations.

---

[1]We included reviews and meta-analyses published between 1997 and 2000 that appeared in either published, professionally reviewed journals, or selected government documents. In the latter category, only government documents using rigorous methods of review were included in order to reduce the potential biases associated with reviews conducted by groups with high stakes in positive or negative conclusions.

We begin with meta-analyses focused nominally on mental health promotion and mental illness/problem behavior prevention programs because these have the most rigorous evaluations. There are several reasons for this: first, there is a long tradition of both mental health promotion and mental illness/problem behavior prevention work; consequently, these programs have had time to develop and to have comprehensive rigorous evaluations completed. Second, many of these programs are being conducted in school buildings during the official school day. These two characteristics make it much easier to conduct a successful randomized trial design evaluation because the participants are drawn from a "captive" population. Conducting such evaluations in community programs is much more difficult precisely because participation is voluntary. We say more about this later in this chapter and in Chapter 7. We then move onto the meta-analyses and summative reviews of largely out-of-school time community programs.

Mental Health Programs

Durlak and Wells

Durlak and Wells (1997, 1998) conducted two meta-analytical reviews of primary and secondary prevention mental health programs operating prior to 1992 for youth under the age of 19. (Primary prevention programs intervene with normal populations to prevent problems from developing. Secondary prevention programs target individuals already at risk or exhibiting problems). Both meta-analyses included only programs with a control group of some type (e.g., a group that is not participating in the program or a group that is on a waiting list to participate in the program). Randomized designs were used in 61 percent of the primary prevention program evaluations and 71 percent of the secondary prevention program evaluations. The primary prevention review (Durlak and Wells, 1997) included 177 programs; the secondary prevention review (Durlak and Wells, 1998) included 130 evaluations. Finally, most of these programs took place in schools (a likely reason that these studies had such low attrition rates of young people leaving the program before completion and final testing).

In general, the results suggest that preventive mental health programs can be effective across a variety of psychological outcome measures for periods of up to two years following the intervention exposure. They are particularly effective at increasing such personal competencies as

TABLE 6-1 Community Programs to Promote Adolescent Development

Program Name/Age, Grade Evaluated	Program Description	Outcomes	Personal and Social Assets	Features of Positive Developmental Settings
Across Ages [a,b] **Grade:** 6th	**Location:** Family, school, community **Sessions:** Mentoring (2 hrs/wk), community service (1 hr every other week), social problems solving (26 1 hr sessions) over school year **Content:** mentoring by older adults, classroom-based life skills training, community service activities, workshops for parents	↑ Positive attitudes toward school, the future, older people, knowledge of elders, and community service ↓ School absence	Intellectual psychological emotional social	Emotional and instrumental support; belonging; positive social norms; opportunity for efficacy; opportunities for skill building; integration with family, schools, and community
Adolescent Transitions Project [a,d] **Age:** 10-14 **Grade:** 6th-8th	**Location:** Family, school, community **Sessions:** 12 over 18 hrs **Content:** Youth self-regulation skills training (teen focus group), parent management skills training (parent focus group), consultant to improve parent-youth communication (teen/parent focus group)	↑ Social learning ↓ Negative engagement with family, conflict, negative family events, youth aggression (increased school behavior problems for teen focus group at one year follow-up)	Psychological emotional social	Emotional and instrumental support; belonging; positive social norms; opportunities for skill building; integration with family, schools, and community

Bicultural Competence Skills [a] **Age:** 11-12	**Location:** Community **Sessions:** 10 **Content:** Skills training to promote competence and positive identity based on bicultural fluency	↑ Self-control, assertiveness, healthy coping, substance abuse knowledge ↓ Alcohol, tobacco, and other drug use	Psychological emotional physical	Belonging; positive social norms; opportunities for skill building
Big Brothers Big Sisters [a,b,c,d] **Age:** 10-16	**Location:** Community **Sessions:** 9-12 hrs/mon for one year **Content:** Activities with mentor	↑ Grade point average, parental trust ↓ Hitting behavior, likelihood of initiating alcohol and drug use, skipping school, lying to parents	Intellectual psychological emotional social physical	Emotional and instrumental support; belonging; positive social norms; physical and psychological safety; opportunity for efficacy; opportunities for skill building
Brainpower Program [f] **Age:** 10-12 (indicated)	**Location:** School **Sessions:** 12 lessons (60-90 minutes each) **Content:** Social competency: focus on improving the accuracy of children's perceptions and interpretations of others' actions	↓ Aggressive behavior following the intervention	Social	Belonging; opportunities for skill building

Continued

TABLE 6-1 Continued

Program Name/Age, Grade Evaluated	Program Description	Outcomes	Personal and Social Assets	Features of Positive Developmental Settings
Bullying Prevention Program [c,d] **Grade:** 4th-7th Norway; 5th-8th U.S. equivalent (universal)	**Location:** School **Sessions:** 9-12 hrs/mon for one year **Content:** 32-page booklet included information on the scope, cause, and effects of school bullying and detailed suggestions for reducing and preventing it. Abbreviated bullying info to families with school-age children. A 25-minute video with vignettes of bullying situations. Students completed a brief questionnaire related to bullying to increase awareness and promote discussion of the problem	↓ 50 percent or more in bully/victim problems for boys and girls across all grades (4-9), with more marked effects after 2 years than after 1 year (sleeper effects)	Psychological emotional social	Positive social norms; physical and psychological safety; opportunities for skill building

Program	Location / Sessions / Content	Outcomes	Developmental domains	Assets
The Child Development Project [a] Age: 11-12 Grade: 3rd-6th	Location: Family and school Sessions: Integrated curriculum over school year Content: Cooperative learning, reading and language arts, developmental discipline, school community building, home activities	↑ Peer social acceptance ↓ Alcohol and tobacco use, loneliness and social anxiety; marijuana use, carrying weapons, vehicle theft (high implementation subgroup)	Intellectual psychological emotional social physical	Belonging; positive social norms; opportunities for skill building; integration with family, schools, and community
Coping and Support Training [d] Grade: 9th-12th (indicated)	Location: School Sessions: 12-sessions Content: Group life skills training	↑ Self-control, problem-solving abilities, and perceived family support ↓ Suicide risk behaviors and anger problems	Intellectual psychological emotional social physical	Emotional and instrumental support; belonging; positive social norms; physical and psychological safety
Coping with Stress Course [d] Grade: 9th-10th (indicated)	Location: After school Sessions: 15, 45 min each Content: Cognitive intervention to encourage adaptive coping (cognitive restructuring, identify and challenge negative or irrational thoughts)	No significant differences at the end of the intervention, but ↓ cases of "major depressive disorder" or dysthymia (milder depressive disorder) at 12 months postintervention.	Intellectual psychological emotional	Opportunities for skill building
Counselor-CARE [d] Grade: 9th-12th (indicated)	Location: School Sessions: 1, 3.5-4 hrs Content: Brief assessment and resource identification program using computer program and counselor	↑ Self-esteem ↓ Suicide risk behaviors and anger problems, reports of depression	Psychological emotional	Emotional and instrumental support

Continued

TABLE 6-1 Continued

Program Name/Age, Grade Evaluated	Program Description	Outcomes	Personal and Social Assets	Features of Positive Developmental Settings
Creating Lasting Connections [a,b] Age: 12-14	Location: Family, church, community Sessions: Youth (15 hrs); parents (55 hrs); volunteer service (18 hrs); follow-up and consultation support (1 yr) Content: Church community mobilization, parent and youth strategies to promote communication and self-management skills, follow-up case management service	↑ Youth use of community services, related action tendencies, perceived helpfulness ↓ Onset of substance abuse delayed as parents changed their substance use beliefs and knowledge	Psychological emotional social physical	Emotional and instrumental support; belonging; positive social norms; opportunities for skill building; integration with family, schools, and community
ENABL [e] Age: 12-13 Grade: 7th-8th	Location: School classroom, community organization Sessions: 5, 1 hr each Content: Social influence theory; help youth understand social and peer pressures to have sex, develop and apply resistance skills, emphasis on postponing sexual involvement.	↑ Pregnancies in teen-led groups, otherwise no effects ↓	Psychological emotional social physical	Positive social norms; opportunities for skill building; integration with family, schools, and community

Friendly PEERsuasion [b] **Age:** 11-14 (indicated)	**Location:** Girls, Inc. **Sessions:** 14, 1 hr each **Content:** Hands-on, inter-active activities teach about the short- and long-term effects of substance abuse; healthy ways to manage stress; how to recognize media and peer pressure to use drugs; skills to make responsible decisions about drug use. As peer leaders, youth plan and implement substance abuse prevention activities for 6- to 10-yr-olds	↓ Drinking and delayed onset of drinking	Intellectual psychological emotional social physical	Emotional and instrumental support; belonging; positive social norms; opportunity for efficacy; opportunities for skill building
Functional Family Therapy [c] **Age:** 11-18 (indicated)	**Location:** Family **Sessions:** 8-12 hrs, 26 hrs max. **Content:** Behavioral systems family therapy; flexible delivery of service: 1-2 person teams to clients in-home, clinic, juvenile court, and at time of reentry from institutional placement	↓ Rates of offending, foster care or institutional placement reduced at least 25 percent	Intellectual psychological emotional social	Positive social norms; opportunities for skill building; integration with family, schools, and community

Continued

TABLE 6-1 *Continued*

Program Name/Age, Grade Evaluated	Program Description	Outcomes	Personal and Social Assets	Features of Positive Developmental Settings
Growing Healthy [a] **Grade:** 4th–7th	**Location:** School **Sessions:** 43-56 lessons over 1 or 2 yrs **Content:** Health competence promotion	↑ Positive knowledge and attitudes toward health, development and personal responsibility ↓ Smoking and intention to smoke	Psychological emotional physical	Positive social norms; physical and psychological safety
Improving Social Awareness–Social Problem Solving (**ISA-SPS**) **Grade:** 5th	**Location:** School **Sessions:** 2 yrs **Content:** Individual skill-building to promote social competence, decision making, group participation and social awareness; targets transition to middle school	↑ Coping with stressors related to middle school transition ↓ Teacher reports of problem behavior, psychopathology at six-year follow-up; boys: ↓ Alcohol use, violent behavior toward others, self-destructive/identity problems; girls: ↓ rates of cigarette smoking, chewing tobacco, and vandalism	Psychological emotional social physical	Belonging; positive social norms; opportunities for skill building
Know Your Body [a] **Grade:** 4th–9th	**Location:** School **Sessions:** 2 hrs/wk for 6 yrs **Content:** Health promotion	↑ Healthy dietary patterns ↓ Smoking initiation	Physical	Positive social norms

Life Skills Training [a,c] **Grade:** 7th-9th	**Location:** School **Sessions:** 2 sessions/wk for 15 wks (Y1); 10 booster sessions (Y2); 5 booster sessions (Y3) **Content:** Competence promotion and resistance training	↑ Interpersonal skills, knowledge of smoking and substance abuse consequences ↓ Cigarette and marijuana smoking, alcohol intoxication and polydrug use	Intellectual physical	Positive social norms; opportunities for skill building
Louisiana State Youth Opportunities [b] **Age:** 14-16	**Location:** School, community **Sessions:** Summer, 8 weeks **Content:** Live on campus, half-day in math and reading classes, half-day working at on-campus sites earning minimum wage, required to open saving account, other services provided: counseling, study skills training, health care, recreation, field trips and speakers	↑ Standardized math test scores, intention to stay in school, career maturity ↓ In reading skills, but less so than control group	Intellectual psychological emotional social	Positive social norms; physical and psychological safety; opportunity for efficacy; opportunities for skill building

Continued

TABLE 6-1 Continued

Program Name/Age, Grade Evaluated	Program Description	Outcomes	Personal and Social Assets	Features of Positive Developmental Settings
Midwestern Prevention Project [a,b,c] **Grade:** 6th–7th	**Location:** Family, school, community **Sessions:** School program (10 hrs), homework activities with parents (10 hrs) **Content:** Parent education about parent-child communication skills, resistance skills training for youth, community organization, mass media coverage	↓ Monthly, weekly and heavy use of cigarettes, marijuana and alcohol	Intellectual social physical	Positive social norms; opportunities for skill building; integration with family, schools, and community
Multisystemic Therapy (MST) (indicated)	**Location:** Family, community **Sessions:** 60 hrs over 4 months **Content:** Family ecological systems approach; home-based services delivery	↓ Criminal activity, drug-related arrests, violent offenses and incarceration	Psychological emotional social	Emotional and instrumental support; belonging; positive social norms; physical and psychological safety

| **Penn Prevention Project** [a]
Age: 10-13
(selected) | **Location:** After school
Sessions: 1.5 hrs/week for 12 wks
Content: Cognitive behavioral; taught coping strategies to counteract cognitive distortions, specific focus on explanatory style | ↑ Parents reported improvements in children's home behavior at follow-up, but not posttreatment (sleeper effects)
↓ Depressive symptoms immediately posttreatment and at a 6-month follow-up period mediated by changes in the children's explanatory styles | Intellectual
psychological
emotional | Positive social norms; opportunities for skill building |
| **Positive Youth Development Program**
Age: 11-14 | **Location:** School
Sessions: 20
Content: Social/emotional cognitive skill-building; curriculum to promote general social competence and refusal skills for alcohol and drugs | ↑ Coping skills, ability to generate alternative responses to hypothetical situations, teacher reports of social adjustment including conflict resolution with peers, impulse control, and popularity
No significant effects on measures related to drugs, cigarettes or wine, and only marginal effects related to alcohol | Intellectual
psychological
emotional
social
physical | Positive social norms; opportunities for skill building |

Continued

TABLE 6-1 Continued

Program Name/Age, Grade Evaluated	Program Description	Outcomes	Personal and Social Assets	Features of Positive Developmental Settings
Project ALERT [a] **Grade:** 7th-8th	**Location:** School **Sessions:** 10 (7th), 3 booster (8th) **Content:** Competence promotion and refusal/ resistance training	↑ Self-efficacy, cigarette and marijuana knowledge and positive attitude, beliefs about immediate and negative social consequences of drugs ↓ Smoking cigarettes and marijuana, expectations of using	Intellectual psychological emotional social physical	Positive social norms; opportunities for skill building
Project Northland [a] **Grade:** 6th-8th	**Location:** Family, school, community **Sessions:** Weekly activities and/or training over 3 yrs **Content:** Youth skills and parent competence training, community organization	↑ Parent-youth communication, knowledge and attitudes for resisting peer influence, self-efficacy ↓ Alcohol use, cigarettes and marijuana for subgroups by previous risk level; alcohol for full sample	Intellectual psychological emotional social physical	Positive social norms; opportunities for skill building

Program	Description	Outcomes	Developmental areas	Features
Quantum Opportunities [a,b] **Grade:** 9th-12th	**Location:** School, community, work **Sessions:** Education-related activities (250 hrs), development activities (250hrs), service activities (250hrs) each year for 4 yrs **Content:** Education activities, peer tutoring, community service activities, mentoring, life and family skills, incentives: hourly stipends and bonuses for completing program components	↑ High school graduation rates, college or post-secondary school attendance, honors and awards, positive attitudes and opinions about life and future, volunteer community service work ↓ Trouble with police, high school drop out, number of children	Intellectual psychological emotional social physical	Emotional and instrumental support; belonging; positive social norms; physical and psychological safety; opportunity for efficacy; opportunities for skill building; integration with family, schools, and community
Reducing the Risk [a,c] **Grade:** 10th	**Location:** Health education classes **Sessions:** 15 **Content:** Cognitive-behavioral, teacher and peer role modeling, parent involvement, emphasis on avoiding unprotected sex either by abstinence or using protection	↑ Knowledge and communication with parents about contraception and abstinence, changes in normative beliefs; increased contraceptive use for females, lower-risk and sexually inexperienced at pretest ↓ Rates of initiation of intercourse	Intellectual psychological emotional social physical	Positive social norms; opportunities for skill building

Continued

TABLE 6-1 *Continued*

Program Name/Age, Grade Evaluated	Program Description	Outcomes	Personal and Social Assets	Features of Positive Developmental Settings
Responding in Peaceful and Positive Ways [a] **Grade:** 6th	**Location:** Family, school, community **Sessions:** 25 over school yr **Content:** Social/cognitive skill-building to promote nonviolent conflict resolution and positive communication; activities included team building and small group work, role playing, and relaxation techniques	↑ Decision-making knowledge and use of peer mediation (not found on student self-reports of behavior however) ↓ Weapon carrying, in-school suspensions	Intellectual social physical	Positive social norms; opportunities for skill building
School Transitional Environment Project **Grade:** 6th-7th (universal)	**Location:** School, family **Sessions:** Transition to middle school yr **Content:** Students placed in cohort, homeroom teacher becomes adviser to cohort and liaison among student, family, and school. Homeroom teacher meets with other teachers to identify students needing counseling or support	↑ Better adjustment on measures of anxiety, depression, self-esteem and delinquent behavior; better teacher ratings of classroom behavioral adjustment; grades and attendance patterns ↓ Levels of school transitional stress	Social	Emotional and instrumental support; belonging; integration with schools

Program	Location/Sessions/Content	Outcomes	Domains	Assets
Social Competence Program for Young Adolescents [a] **Grade:** 5th–8th	**Location:** Family and school **Sessions:** 16, 45 min each over 12 weeks; teacher and aide training, consultation and coaching **Content:** Social competence promotion, family involvement	↑ Peer involvement, social acceptance, problem solving, use of conflict resolution strategies, positive solutions → Aggressive and passive solutions	Psychological emotional social physical	Positive social norms; opportunities for skill building
Summer Training and Education Program (STEP) [b] **Age:** 14–15	**Location:** School, community **Sessions:** 6–8 weeks during summer; half-time jobs (90 hours), half-day academic classes (90 hours), 2 mornings/wk in life skills training **Content:** Employment and academic classes, life-skills training, part for classroom time as well as work time	↑ Reading and math test scores, knowledge tests of responsible social and sexual behavior (summer effects only; no effect for school year or long-term)	Intellectual physical	Positive social norms; opportunity for efficacy; opportunities for skill building
Teen Incentives Program [c] **Grade:** 9th	**Location:** After school program **Sessions:** 14 weeks **Content:** Small group sessions focused on self-esteem, decision making, communication, relationships, sexuality topics; career mentorship program with professional in health care (6wks); extensive role playing	↑ Contraceptive use by females inexperienced at pretest, consistent use by experienced males at pretest ↓ Initiation of intercourse for males	Intellectual psychological emotional social physical	Belonging; positive social norms; opportunity for efficacy; opportunities for skill building

Continued

TABLE 6-1 *Continued*

Program Name/Age, Grade Evaluated	Program Description	Outcomes	Personal and Social Assets	Features of Positive Developmental Settings
Teen Outreach Program (TOP) [a,b,c] **Grade:** 10th	**Location:** School and community **Sessions:** (school year) 45 hrs volunteer service, weekly classroom discussions and activities **Content:** Small group classroom discussions of values, decision making, communication skills, parenting, life options and volunteer experiences; volunteer service in school or community	↓ School failure and suspension, school suspension and teen pregnancy	Intellectual psychological emotional social physical	Emotional and instrumental support; belonging; positive social norms; physical and psychological safety; opportunity for efficacy; opportunities for skill building
Valued Youth Partnership [a] **Age:** 12	**Location:** family, school, community **Sessions:** 30 over school yr, 4 hrs of tutoring/week **Content:** peer tutoring, stipends, leadership training, parent and business community involvement	↑ Reading grades, positive self-concept, positive attitudes toward school ↓ School dropout rates	Intellectual psychological emotional social	Positive norms; opportunity for efficacy; opportunities for skill building

			Intellectual psychological emotional social	Emotional and instrumental support; belonging; positive social norms; opportunities for skill building; integration with family, schools, and community
Woodrock Youth Development Project [a,b] **Age:** 6-14	**Location:** Family, school, community **Sessions:** Weekly classes and activities, daily mentoring, home visits and contacts **Content:** Social competence promotion, life skills, human relations classes to develop resiliency skills, peer tutors, homework assistance, extra-curricular activities (weekend retreats, after-school clubs, crisis intervention, summer program), parent training and involvement	↑ Positive race relations, school attendance ↓ Drug use for past year (younger subgroup) and past month (older and younger subgroups) Wrong direction outcome on attitudes toward drug use in older subgroup		

[a]Catalano et al., 1999.
[b]Roth and Brooks-Gunn, 2000.
[c]Elliot and Tolan, 1999.
[d]Greenberg et al..
[e]Kirby, 1997.

assertiveness, communication skills, feelings of self-confidence, and skill performance, assets consistent with the committee's framework. More specifically, the meta-analysis of the primary prevention programs (Durlak and Wells, 1997) revealed that most programs significantly reduced problems (e.g., anxiety, behavior problems, and depressive symptoms) and increased competencies.

Durlak and Wells (1997, 1998) also compared the effects of environment-centered versus person-centered approaches. Person-centered programs worked directly with individuals using techniques based on social learning theory (either modeling appropriate behaviors or reinforcing appropriate behaviors) and other direct instructional approaches focused on educational and interpersonal problem solving. Environment-centered programs tried to change either the home setting (through parent education about child development and changing parental attitudes and childrearing techniques when appropriate) or the school setting (often through teacher training in interactive instructional techniques and classroom management skills). Parent education was often used as a general descriptor, but all of the person-centered programs were effective for some outcomes, particularly for increasing competencies. Of the environment-centered approaches, only school-based programs were effective, and these were more effective at increasing competencies than reducing problems. Most of the school-based environment-centered programs focused on changing the psychological and social aspects of the classroom environment through increasing either interactive instructional techniques or effective classroom management techniques.

In their secondary prevention meta-analysis, Durlak and Wells (1998) compared the effectiveness of behavioral, cognitive-behavioral, and nonbehavioral treatments.[2] In general, all three treatments were effective at both problem reduction and competency enhancement. In addition, cognitive-behavior treatment was more effective than either behavioral treatment or nonbehavioral treatment at reducing mental health problems, and the behavioral treatments were more effective than the nonbehavioral treatment at improving children's competencies.

---

[2]Reinforcement, modeling, and desensitization procedures were the behavioral treatments used in these interventions. The cognitive-behavior treatments emphasized self-instructional training and other ways of using cognitive processes to modify behavior. The nonbehavioral treatments mostly used classic talking analytic techniques (the classic situation in which a client talks with a therapist about his or her problems or concerns) for older children and activity-oriented play therapy for younger children.

Because these programs are based on well-established clinical theories, they have a strong theory of change.[3] Little information about these theories, however, was included in the information provided by the programs, and very little information was provided about the quality of the services actually provided. Such information is critical if these programs are to be implemented in other settings and programs by staff members who are not clinical psychologists or social workers. Certainly the primary prevention efforts should be replicable in after school community-based programs. But more information will be needed about the specifics of the programs before this is possible.

Greenberg and Colleagues

Greenberg and colleagues (1999) reviewed 130 universal, selective, or indicated mental illness prevention programs for children and adolescents. The universal prevention programs targeted whole populations of youth. The selective programs targeted individuals or subgroups identified as at risk for developing mental disorders. The indicated prevention programs targeted individuals identified as having early warning signs of mental disorders but not yet meeting diagnostic criteria. Out of 130 total programs, researchers selected 34 using the following criteria: a randomized experimental design or quasi-experimental design with a comparison group; pretest and posttest measures; a written manual specifying the theory and procedures used in the program intervention; a clearly defined sample, with adequate information about their behavior and social characteristics; and some evidence of positive mental health outcomes. Follow-up assessments were preferred but not required. This review focused less on the personal and social assets identified in the committee's framework and more on the features of the programs themselves and on prevention of problem behaviors. In general, the researchers concluded:

1. Multiyear preventive programs produce longer-lasting effects than short-term programs.

---

[3] "Theory of change" is described as a clear, substantive theory that explicitly states the process by which change should occur. Ideally, this theory should be the driving force in program development and should guide the decision of what to measure and how. See Chapter 7 for elaboration.

2. Preventive program interventions should be directed at risk and protective factors[4] rather than at categorical problem behaviors, such as school dropout, delinquency, substance abuse, and teenage pregnancy.

3. The few studies with follow-up data suggest possible "sleeper effects" in program benefits (that is, some programs showed a greater effect at a time somewhat distant from the end of the treatment than immediately following the intervention). If this is true, programs that do not collect follow-up data may underestimate the impact of their program.

4. Prevention programs targeting multiple domains (i.e., individual, school, and community) are more effective than programs targeting one domain.

We looked more closely at whether these conclusions held true for the 10 programs targeting 10- to 18-year-olds (see Table 6-1 for details). Do short-term programs produce time-limited benefits? This was difficult to determine for this subset of programs because half of the eight short-term program evaluations (less than one year) did not do follow-up testing. Of the three programs that did follow-up testing, two found mixed results and one found positive follow-up effects. These three programs are summarized below.

The Adolescent Transition Project randomly assigned participants to one of four groups: teen focus, parent focus, teen-parent focus, and a self-directed control group. The teen focus group received training in self-regulation development along with skill development exercises. The parent focus curriculum provided training for parents in parent management skills in areas such as setting appropriate limits and problem solving with teens. The combined parent-teen group used peer consultants to open discussions between teens and parents on issues of self-regulation, parent-child interaction, and communication patterns and life skills. In the comparison group, the teens were provided with self-directed instructional materials focused on self-regulation and life skills development. After 12 weekly 90-minute sessions, the parents and adolescents in all three treatment groups reported significantly less home-based problem behavior than at the pretest; in contrast, however, there was an in-

---

[4]Risk factors, such as academic failure or poverty, are variables associated with a greater likelihood of negative or undesirable outcomes. Protective factors, such as warm, nurturing adult relationships, and the personal and social assets outlined in Chapter 3, reduce the likelihood of problem behavior in the presence of risk.

crease in teacher reports of school problem behavior for the adolescents in the teen-focused treatment group at the one year follow-up. No explanations were provided for these patterns of results or for why school problem behavior may have increased in the teen-focused treatment group.

In the Coping with Stress Course, a subset of targeted adolescents with elevated self-reported depressive symptomatology were randomly assigned to 15 group clinical counseling sessions of 45 minutes each. The "treated" adolescents' reports of depressive symptomatology declined more that the control adolescents from pretest to posttest, but this difference had disappeared by the 12-month follow-up. In contrast, however, there were fewer cases of major depressive disorder and dysthymia (a milder form of depression) in the treatment group than in the control group at the follow-up testing.

Only the Penn Prevention Project found unambiguous evidence of both follow-up and sleeper effects. This selected intervention program targeted children ages 10 to 13 at risk due to elevated depressive symptoms or family conflict. The randomly selected intervention groups met once each week for 12 weeks after school for 1.5 hours. Postintervention data showed fewer depressive symptoms, better classroom behavior, and reduced likelihood of attributing negative events to stable enduring causes for the treatment group compared with the "untreated" control group. While levels of both the experimental and control groups' depressive symptomatology increased over the 24-month follow-up period in the Penn Prevention Project, this increase was larger in the control group than in the treatment group. Also, even though there were no significant differences at the posttest, parents of the intervention group reported more improvements in the children's home behavior at the 24-month follow-up than parents of the control group. Effects were maintained at the 12-, 18-, and 24-month follow-ups. Interestingly, although this program is considered short-term, it was the only program of the six in this review focused on adolescents with follow-up data suggesting a possible sleeper effect in program benefits. This calls into question the claim that long-term interventions are needed for long-lasting effects.

What is most interesting about the Penn Prevention Project is that it has been implemented in a variety of in-school and out-of-school settings, including community-based organizations. It has also been evaluated repeatedly and has had good success at replication. The program consists primarily of training in self-management skills and social interpretative skills. The adolescents are taught new ways to cope with interpersonal conflict as well as new ways to interpret other people's behaviors so that they do not misinterpret social interactions as more hostile or demeaning than they actually are. These skills in turn are assumed to help the adolescent cope better with interpersonal interactions likely to reinforce depression and conflict. The Penn Prevention Project has extensive program materials and training manuals to help organizations implement the program based on its principles (Shatté and Reivich, no date).

Do multiyear programs foster more enduring benefits than short-term program interventions? Four programs involving adolescents come close to meeting the multiyear criteria, but only two, the Improving Social Awareness-Social Problem Solving (ISA-SPS) and the Bullying Prevention Program, actually extended beyond one year. The ISA-SPS two-year program targeted the transition to middle school by focusing on changing the school culture. The social problem-solving curriculum in ISA-SPS has three phases. The readiness phase emphasized teaching self-control, group participation, and social awareness. In the instructional phase, teachers teach social decision-making and problem-solving strategies. In the final application phase, teachers extend the curriculum to real-life conflicts in which the students are helped to use problem-solving skills to solve their conflicts through modeling, direct instruction, and group discussion. In the evaluation reviewed, positive gains in the youth's interpersonal behaviors (see Table 6-1 for details) were maintained for six years after exposure to the intervention.

The Bullying Prevention Program, part of a national campaign against bullying in Norway, lasted two years. It is a school-based universal prevention program focused on reducing bullying problems by increasing awareness and knowledge of the problem, involving teachers and parents together with adolescents in discussing these problems, establishing clear rules against bullying behavior, and providing support and protection for bullying victims. In the evaluation of this program reviewed by Greenberg, there were decreases in bullying for the "treated" adolescents. The positive effects of this program were maintained at least through the 20-month follow-up assessment.

The other two programs, Big Brothers Big Sisters and the School Transition Environmental Project, were 9 to 12 months in length. Mentors in the Big Brothers Big Sisters program (described in more detail later in this chapter) met with their assigned child three times per month for three to four hours for at least one year. Treatment effects were found across multiple outcome measures ranging from hitting behavior to academic performance (see Table 6-1 for details). Follow-up data have not been collected.

The School Transitional Environmental Project focused on changing the school social climate to assist in the transition to middle school in large school systems with many feeder schools. Homeroom teachers were assigned to smaller cohorts to function as a liaison and guidance counselor. The effects of the program intervention were positive (see Table 6-1 for details), but no follow-up data were collected, so we know nothing about the stability of the effects over time.

So, do the programs targeting adolescents, warrant the same conclusions reached by Greenberg and colleagues for the full array of programs included in the review? First, do multiyear preventive programs produce longer-term effects than short-term program interventions? Many positive long-term effects were found in the two programs lasting longer than one year; however, with only two programs as examples, it would be unfair to conclude that multiyear programs contribute to longer-lasting effects than short-term programs, especially given the evidence of sustained effects from two of the short-term programs discussed earlier.

Second, are programs targeting multiple levels and settings (i.e., individual, school, community) more effective than programs targeting one domain? The programs most relevant to our age group give mixed support for this conclusion. On one hand, the eight programs concentrating on individual change achieved positive postintervention effects. The two programs with follow-up data, the Penn Prevention Project and the Coping with Stress Course, also showed evidence of sustained effects at follow-up assessments. Thus, programs targeting the individual can be effective. However, it is quite likely that these programs also indirectly create changes in other domains, such as the family or school. On the other hand, the four programs targeting multiple levels also yielded positive postintervention effects, and the three programs with follow-up data showed long-term effectiveness as well.

In summary, from the 12 programs targeting youth ages 10 to 18, we can draw several conclusions. Short-term programs can be just as effective as programs lasting nine months to two years. Program interventions concentrating on individual change can be as effective as those focusing on multiple domains. One program, a selected intervention, demonstrated evidence of a sleeper effect. The possibility of sleeper effects underlines the importance of collecting follow-up data to ensure that effective programs are not being underestimated in their impact and to capture potential effects of programs yielding initial null results. Based

on these evaluations, it appears that mental disorder prevention programs can be designed to support positive psychological and emotional
development. By and large, the effective programs used skill-building
instruction and extensive opportunities to practice these new skills at the
individual level, and both social support and social norm-building strategies at the school and program level. Future evaluation research in this
domain should focus on the causal links between program interventions
and outcomes and on the extent to which these programs can be implemented in community settings beyond the school and the school day. Some
clearly were. Nonetheless, these results do suggest that life skill-building
and positive norm-setting programs can be effective when done well.

Summary

By and large, the program interventions designed to prevent mental
illness can be quite effective and, when assessed, appear to have long-
term positive consequences. Programs based on clinical theories of behavior change and sound instructional practices are effective at both reducing problem behaviors and increasing a wide range of social and
emotional competencies. In addition, interventions in the field of mental
health promotion use high evaluation standards. All evaluations included
in both reviews used control group comparisons, and the majority used
random assignment. The high level of evaluation rigor obtained was
understandably facilitated by the short-term nature of the programs, the
integration of these programs into the school day, and the fact that program participation was more likely to be seen by participants as required
rather than voluntary. Consequently, generalizabilty of the findings to
nonschool settings is problematic. Nevertheless, there is sufficient evidence to conclude that programs such as the ones reviewed, which target
the prevention of mental disorders, can be effective in both reducing
problems and increasing social and emotional competencies. These programs are appropriate for consideration in many types of community-
based programs and organizations.

Violence Prevention Programs

The Center for the Study and Prevention of Violence at the University of Colorado at Boulder published a series of Blueprints (Center for
the Study and Prevention of Violence, 2000) describing program interventions effective in preventing violence. The Blueprints series was de-

veloped to give practical information to communities to help them select a program intervention that best matched their needs and resources. Of the 450 delinquency, drug, and violence prevention programs the center reviewed, 10 met most of the following criteria: an experimental design with random assignment or a strong quasi-experimental design; evidence of a statistically significant deterrent (or marginal deterrent) effect on delinquency, drug use, and/or violent behavior; at least one additional site replication with experimental design and demonstrated effects; and evidence that the deterrent effect was sustained for at least one year following treatment.

Of the 10 model programs, 6 included youth ages 10 to 18 in their target population: Big Brothers Big Sisters, Quantum Opportunities, the Midwestern Prevention Project, Life Skills Training, Multisystemic Therapy, and the Bullying Prevention Program. The first three are described in detail later in this chapter; the Bullying Prevention Program was described earlier. The remaining two—Life Skills Training and Multisystemic Therapy (see Table 6-1 for more details)—are described below.

The Life Skills Training program is a school-based universal prevention program designed to prevent drug use. The program intervention is a curriculum to teach general life skills and social resistance skills training.

The Multisystemic Therapy Program uses a family ecological systems approach to help serious violent or substance-abusing juvenile offenders. The therapy focuses on getting families involved in changing those aspects of the youth's setting (i.e., peers, school, family, and community) that contribute to the problem behavior. The primary method is teaching effective parenting skills and helping parents overcome such barriers to effective parenting as drug abuse and lack of a social support network in the community.

In an effort to understand the source of change across the 10 violence prevention programs reviewed, Elliot and Tolan (1999) looked for evidence that change in risk or protective factors mediated change in violent behavior. However, the program evaluations either had not collected the necessary data to analyze the causal processes or had not reported on the analysis. Likewise, because the studies evaluated whole program packages rather than specific program components, it was not possible to determine exactly what worked in any given program. Nevertheless, these 10 programs do provide models of what can be done in communities to decrease rates of violence. Interestingly, most of the programs involved the kinds of experiences and settings outlined in Chapter 4 as critical for promoting positive youth development. Teaching life skills and providing better adult social supports were common across all of the effective programs. Consequently, these programs are also good models for what can be done to promote positive development as well. Most actually gathered data relevant to this goal (see Table 6-1 for details) and were effective at promoting some aspects of positive development as well.

Teen Pregnancy Prevention Programs

Kirby (1998) reviewed evaluations of primary prevention programs designed to reduce sexual risk-taking and teen pregnancy. These programs met the following criteria: published in 1980 or later; experimental or quasi-experimental in design; a minimum sample size of 100 in combined experimental and control groups; targeted 12- to 18-year-olds; conducted in the United States or Canada; and measures of program impact on sexual or contraceptive behavior or pregnancy or birth rates.

Kirby divided programs into three groups based on whether they focused primarily on sexual antecedents (i.e., age, gender, pubertal timing), on nonsexual antecedents (i.e., poverty, parental education, parental support, drug and alcohol use), or on a combination of sexual and nonsexual antecedents. We focused on the latter two groups because of their fit with our youth development framework. Youth development programs were further categorized as service-learning, vocational education and employment, and other. All three categories focused on improving education and life options as the means to reduce pregnancy and birth rates.

Service-learning programs consisted of unpaid service time in the community as well as structured time for training, preparation, and reflection. The results for such programs were equivocal. On one hand, Teen Outreach Program participants reported lower rates of pregnancy and school failure than the controls during the school year in which they participated in the program intervention. Similarly, a health education curriculum combined with service learning was effective at reducing reported sexual activity. On the other hand, although a quasi-experimental evaluation of service-learning programs showed a short-term trend in reduced pregnancy rates, the result was not statistically significant and the trend disappeared one year later.

Vocational education and employment programs included academic education and either vocational education or actual jobs. Again the results were equivocal. On one hand, the Youth Incentive Entitlement Pilot Projects was effective at reducing birth rates and increasing both teen employment and school enrollment. This program guaranteed part-time employment to youth during the school year and full-time employment during the summer if they remained in high school. On the other hand, four very rigorously evaluated employment and education programs were not effective in reducing pregnancies or birth rates. This evidence suggests that vocational and employment programs are not effective in decreasing pregnancy or birth rates.

In summary, the strongest evidence for program effectiveness using a youth development framework comes from the Teen Outreach Program. Why was this service-learning program effective while the others were not? We do not have an answer for this question because causal links in the interventions were not evaluated. Therefore, we do not know whether to attribute its success to the service-learning component or to other characteristics of the program, such as strong bonds with adults. Nevertheless, the program evaluations do offer promise that a youth development approach may provide opportunities that reduce the risk of teenage pregnancy.

Furthermore, Kirby summarized the strengths and limitations of each evaluation based on the following methodological principles: sampling, random assignment, sample size, long-term follow-up, measurement of behavior (sexual and contraceptive behaviors), statistical analyses, publication of results, replication, and independent evaluation. Kirby concluded that few studies abided by high standards for each principle, thus limiting generalizations about which specific programs or types of programs reduce sexual risk-taking and teen pregnancy.

Positive Youth Development Programs

Catalano and Colleagues

The most comprehensive review of positive youth development program evaluations was funded by the Department of Health and Human Services and compiled by Catalano, Berglund, Ryan, Lonczak, and Hawkins (1999). This report examined evaluations of positive youth development programs solicited from a wide variety of sources. The authors reviewed 77 program evaluations and chose 25 for their report (see Table 6-1 for details). Only research designs using a control or strong comparison group with measures of youth behavioral outcomes were included. Programs had to have at least one significant effect.[5] The programs selected had to include at least one of the following objectives identified by the authors as important for positive youth development: promotes bonding; fosters resilience; promotes social, emotional, cognitive, behavioral, and moral competence; fosters self-determination, spirituality, self-efficacy, a clear and positive identity, belief in the future, and/or prosocial norms; or provides recognition for positive behavior and/or opportunities for prosocial involvement. In general, these characteristics and strategies of effective positive youth development programs closely match the personal and social assets and features of positive developmental settings identified in Part I as important for healthy adolescent development.

Catalano et al. concluded that the most effective programs sought to strengthen social, emotional, cognitive, and behavioral competencies, self-efficacy, and family and community social norms for healthy social and individual behavior. To achieve these goals, the effective programs targeted a combination of social settings (family, school, church, community, and work). Of the social settings mentioned, 88 percent had a school component, 60 percent had a family component, and 48 percent had a community component.

Many of the positive youth development principles identified by Catalano et al. are closely linked to the assets and social settings identified by the committee. Opportunities to develop competence and self-efficacy, as well as the inclusion of prosocial norms (positive social norms in our language) were present in all 25 programs. Opportunities for prosocial involvement and recognition of positive behavior were provided in 88 percent of the programs. Social bonding was promoted in 76 percent of the programs. Explicit opportunities to develop the other five target assets (positive identity, self-determination, belief in the future, resiliency, and spirituality) were a focus for fewer than half of the programs.

---

[5]Although some may feel that the researchers erred in including only programs with significant results, the state of evaluation in this area is still such that it is virtually impossible to draw conclusions from nonsignificant results. Nonsignificant results could reflect poor program implementation, weak measures of outcomes, inadequate specification of what outcomes should be effected, program attrition, etc. All of these design problems make it very difficult to reach any conclusion about what does not work. Given this state of affairs, we agree with Catalano et al.'s decision not to include programs with nonsignificant effects in their review, and we have also chosen not to report on programs that do not work.

Catalano et al. (1999) concluded that two general program strategies were evident in the most effective programs: skill building and environmental/organizational change. A focus on social or cognitive behavioral skills occurred in 96 percent of the programs; decision-making and self-management skills in 73 percent; coping skills in 62 percent; and refusal-resistance skills in 50 percent. Effective environmental or organizational change programs focused on influencing teacher classroom practices and peer social norms.

This review of youth programs was very comprehensive. Catalano et al. concluded that positive youth development approaches could, when implemented well, increase positive youth behavior outcomes and decrease youth problem behaviors. In 19 of the programs reviewed, positive changes in youth behavior included significant improvements in interpersonal skills, quality of peer and adult relationships, self-control, problem solving, cognition, self-efficacy, commitment to schooling, and academic achievement. Of the programs reviewed, 24 showed significant reduction in problem behaviors, including drug and alcohol use, school misbehavior, aggressive behavior, violence, truancy, high-risk sexual behavior, and smoking.

However, Catalano et al. also noted that many of the evaluations themselves had limitations. Of the 25 programs meeting the inclusion criteria, only 64 percent used experimental designs with randomization and only half gathered any follow-up data. None included comprehensive information about the program, the implementation process, the youth development constructs being addressed, or the relation between the implementation information and outcomes. Also, assessment measures were rarely adequate to track positive youth development over time, and problem behaviors were measured much more frequently than positive behaviors. Consequently, much more research is needed before one can be confident about which programs and which aspects of these programs actually impact youth development. Nonetheless, the findings are promising enough that they can be used to inform future program design and to make decisions about which programs are ready for more rigorous evaluation.

Roth and Colleagues

Roth et al. (1998a) reviewed over 60 evaluations of prevention and intervention programs for adolescents that incorporated positive youth development program objectives. Of the 60 programs reviewed, 15 were selected for inclusion in the review (see Table 6-1 for details). These 15 shared the following characteristics: a positive youth development focus, an experimental or quasi-experimental design, and a focus on youth not currently demonstrating problem behaviors. The programs were grouped into three categories (listed in order of how closely they matched a youth development framework): (a) programs focused on increasing positive behaviors and competencies (asset-focused programs); (b) programs focused on both reducing problem behaviors and increasing competencies and assets (problem-behavior and asset-focused programs); and (c) prevention programs focused on resistance skills.

The authors concluded that programs incorporating more elements of the youth development framework (a framework that seemed very consistent with the assets and features of settings developed in this report) showed more positive outcomes—that is, programs that focused on increasing more different assets and included more different types of program characteristics and opportunities. However, the evidence for this conclusion is weak, and the number of assets and features included in specific programs has not been systematically manipulated in such a way that such a conclusion is warranted at this point based on experimental and quasi-experimental evaluations. Like the Catalano et al. review, Roth and colleagues also concluded that the most effective programs included both caring adult-adolescent relationships and life skills development. In addition, the authors concluded that longer-term programs were more effective than short-term programs with limited goals. Again, however, the evidence for this is minimal.

This review stands out because it included a framework to categorize youth development programs; it focused on community-based (rather than school-based) programs; and it insisted on rigorous standards of evaluation before concluding that a program was effective. Thus it provides quite comprehensive evidence that community programs focused on youth development can be effective.

Unfortunately these evaluations still did not reveal much about either the long-term effects or the generalizability of these programs. There was also no insight about which specific aspects of the programs were most effective for any particular outcome or population group. Nonetheless, they do provide useful information about promising programs that should be considered for replication and for more intensive evaluation.

Hattie and Colleagues

Hattie and colleagues (1997) performed a meta-analysis of the effects of adventure programs drawn from extensive database searches. These searches yielded 96 evaluations of adventure programs meeting the inclusion criteria for the review. The authors used sample size, the presence of control groups, methodological descriptions, and instrument quality to rate the evaluations as low, medium, or high in quality. Nine studies were excluded based on the four authors' agreement on their poor quality and because their means were so different from the other studies. School-based outdoor education program evaluations were also excluded because of a typically shorter duration, nonchallenging experiences (relative to other adventure programs), and evaluation results that differed from the more challenging programs.

Although adventure education programs do not usually take place in the communities from which the youth are being recruited and the evaluations of these programs suffer from the same methodological problems encountered in the previous reviews, we include the findings from this review because effective adventure programs can suggest potential program components important for healthy development. Adventure programs also typically include features of positive developmental settings outlined in Part I. Common features of adventure programs include wilderness or backcountry settings, groups of less than 16, mentally and physically challenging experiences, intense social interactions often relating to group problem solving and decision making, trained nondirective leaders, and an average duration of two to four weeks.

Hattie et al. concluded that short-term positive effects were maintained and sometimes even increased over time. More specifically, the authors concluded that adventure programs have significant effects on the kinds of psychological, emotional, and cognitive assets discussed in Chapter 3—such as self-control, confidence in one's abilities to be effective, good decision making, improved school achievement, leadership, independence, assertiveness, emotional stability, social comparison, time management, and flexibility.

General Conclusions

Positive Development Framework

- Two program components emerged as important across all reviews: service learning and mentoring. Service learning was a particularly crucial program component for youth ages 15 to 18.
- The vast majority of programs reviewed were school-based and included young people of all ages. Whether such programs can be successfully implemented in a more voluntary setting (e.g., during nonschool hours and in out-of-school settings) is not clear.
- There is little overlap between the measures collected in most of the evaluations summarized in these reports and the framework for positive adolescent development outlined in Part I. In part this reflects the fact that these studies were not designed to assess the features in this framework. But it might also suggest a scarcity of well-validated measures of personal and social assets and features of positive developmental settings (see Chapter 8 for more discussion of this issue). In part it also likely reflects the disconnection between research and practice traditions and points to the need for more collaborative efforts involving the research, practice, and policy communities in both designing and evaluating community programs for youth.
- Most evaluation studies show modest short-term effects; some show longer-term effects, but follow-up data are rare and, when collected, rarely cover a period of more than two years after the program end. In general, follow-up studies tend to show smaller effects over time.

The Quality of Evaluation

- Most of the evaluations conducted in school-based programs included in this review met high technical standards for assessing effectiveness for individual children. However, these programs focused more on preventing negative outcomes than on fostering positive development.
- Evaluations of more voluntary community-based programs are still less rigorous than the evaluations of school-based prevention programs. Possible reasons for this discrepancy are discussed in Chapter 7.

- Few evaluations are comprehensive. That is, they do not have: an analysis of program theory, quality information about implementation, quality information about effectiveness, quality analysis of why effects did or did not come about, an analysis of the replicability of the program, or an analysis of how important the program is and why.

THREE MODEL PROGRAM EVALUATIONS

Three programs—the Teen Outreach Program, Quantum Opportunities, and Big Brothers Big Sisters—stand out among the programs included in the meta-analyses and reviews just summarized for several reasons. First, these programs are consistent with the youth development framework laid out in Part I. Second, these programs illustrate that high-quality experimental evaluation can be done with community programs for youth. These three programs also reflect different program delivery mechanisms. Big Brothers Big Sisters and Quantum Opportunities Program are offered by community agencies, while the Teen Outreach Program has community components but is managed by schools. We now describe these in more detail because there is sufficient evidence that they can be used a promising models for the design of new youth programs.

Teen Outreach Program

Evaluators:	J.P. Allen et al. (1997)
Level of intervention:	Multilevel (community, school)
Target population:	9th-12th grade students
Evaluation research design:	Experimental with random assignment
Sample:	695 (342 experimental, 353 control)
Attrition analysis:	Dropped out of program prior to evaluation: 5.3 percent experimental; 8.4 percent control
Cost:	$500-700/student/academic year for class of 18-25 students

The Teen Outreach Program is a widely replicated program that involves both a school-based discussion curriculum focused on life skills, parent-adolescent communication, and future life planning and an intensive volunteer service experience. Although it was designed to prevent adolescent problem behaviors by promoting healthy social development in high school students, it focuses very little attention directly on sexual behavior and reproduction. The evaluation focused on three problem behaviors: teenage pregnancy, school suspension, and school failure. The program was designed to help adolescents understand and evaluate their future life options and develop life skills and autonomy in a setting that creates strong social ties to adult mentors. To accomplish these goals, three components were designed: supervised community service, classroom-based discussions of service experiences, and classroom-based discussion and activities related to social-developmental tasks of adolescence. The cost of offering the program to a class of 18 to 25 for an academic year is $500 to 700 per student, when both facilitator and site coordinator time is included in the cost. When staff time is provided as an in-kind contribution by a school and a community service organization, the direct costs of the program drop to under $100 per student.

Each adolescent participated in an intensive volunteer activity (drawn from a wide range of such opportunities) coordinated by trained staff working in cooperation with local community organizations. The activity was chosen by the participant with the help of trained staff who assisted by matching the individual's interests with community needs. Examples of activities included working as aides in hospitals and nursing homes, participating in walkathons, and peer tutoring. The program sites were required to provide a minimum of 20 hours per year of volunteer service for each participant. Participants averaged 45.8 hours of volunteer service during their 9 months of involvement.

Classroom discussions occurred at least once weekly throughout the academic year; trained facilitators, usually teachers or guidance personnel, led them. The Teen Outreach Curriculum created the framework for such activities as structured discussions, group exercises, role plays, guest speakers, and informational presentations. Discussions were designed to help students prepare for, and learn from, their service experiences by dealing with such topics as lack of self-confidence, social skills, assertiveness, and self-discipline. Discussions also focused on such developmental topics as values clarification, managing family relationships, and handling close relationships.

The program focused very little explicit attention on the three target problem behavior outcomes. For example, less than 15 percent of the "official" curriculum dealt with sexuality, and even these materials were often not used, either because they overlapped with similar information being offered in the school or were in conflict with community values.

Evaluation Design and Results

Because the program had showed promise in previous nonexperimental studies (Allen et al., 1990; Philliber and Allen, 1998) with high school students, program developers submitted the program to a rigorous evaluation. In this evaluation, 695 high school students in 25 schools nationwide were randomly assigned to either the intervention or a control group at either the student level or the classroom level. Student-level assignment was used when there were more students wanting the class than there were slots. In this case, students were randomly assigned to get the class or be assigned to a wait list for the following year. Classroom assignment was used when the school preferred to include the program in already existing courses. In this case, it was randomly decided which course would be involved in the program and which would not; students did not select the class knowing it was going to be involved in the program. Baseline data were gathered at the start of the program; posttest data were gathered nine months later at the end of the program. Data were collected during the 1991-1995 school years. (A subsequent additional evaluation has been completed but the results are not yet available). After controlling for initial experimental and control group nonequivalence on the outcome measures, fewer youth in the experimental group were suspended, failed courses, or became pregnant than students in the control groups.

Strengths and Limitations

Some aspects of the evaluation of Teen Outreach Program are exemplary. Initial nonexperimental evaluations of the program (Allen et al., 1990, 1994) indicated that it was very promising. The next logical step for a nationally distributed well-developed program showing promise was to evaluate it using the most rigorous evaluation method—an experimental design with random assignment. Great care was taken to assess dosage. Two indicators of dosage were included in the analysis: the number of classroom sessions attended and the number of hours of volunteer service. There were no significant dosage effects for either indicator on the prediction of pregnancy or academic suspension. However, a significant dosage effect was found for the relation between the number of volunteer hours and course failure: students who performed more volunteer service were at lower risk for course failure during the program. Consequently, the positive effects produced by the evaluation using 25 different sites gives a high degree of confidence that the program effects are generalizable.

However, neither the program design nor the evaluation was explicitly guided by an elaborated theory of change. In addition, only a limited range of outcomes was assessed, and little information was gathered about the quality of the implementation. Finally, no follow-up data were collected to assess how sustained the effects were.

In conclusion, the essentials of the program are well based in research, but the evaluation did not have a well-articulated theory of change. The evaluation research showed that the program reduced teenage pregnancies, school failure, and academic suspensions. It is especially effective with adolescents who need the program the most—at-risk youth. While no single study is beyond criticism, the technical quality of evaluation research on this program has steadily improved with each study, and no common bias runs throughout the entire program of studies. So replication and generalizability are not a problem. Dosage effects were included in the evaluation analyses. There is some evidence that more frequent participation in the program relates to outcomes, although there are selection issues. No fine-grained analyses were done to determine which program components were responsible for the effect.

Quantum Opportunities Program

Evaluators:	Hahn, Leavitt, and Aaron (1994)
Level of intervention:	Multi-level (community, school, work)
Target population:	9th-12th grade students receiving public assistance
Evaluation research design:	Experimental with random selection and assignment
Sample:	50 students (25 intervention, 25 control) at 5 sites
Attrition analysis:	88 of the 100 program participants; 82 of 100 control participants were interviewed in the follow-up evaluation.
Cost:	$10,600/student for 4 years; $2,650/student/year

The Quantum Opportunities Program was designed to serve very poor adolescents living in high-risk neighborhoods by providing education, community service, and development activities, as well as financial incentives, from 9th grade through high school graduation. Adolescents from families receiving public assistance entered the program in the 9th grade and continued for four years through high school.

It is a community-based, year-round, multiyear, and multilevel youth development program. Each participant was eligible to receive the following experiences each year:

- 250 hours of education activities, such as participating in computer-assisted instruction, peer tutoring, etc., with the goal of enhancing basic academic skills;
- 250 hours of developmental activities, including participating in cultural enrichment and personal development, acquiring life/family skills, planning for college or advanced technical/vocational training, and job preparation; and
- 250 hours of service activities, such as participating in community service projects, helping with public events, and working as a volunteer in various agencies.

Financial incentives were built into the project design. Staff and agencies received payments based on student participation numbers. Participants themselves received small hourly stipends ($1 increasing to $1.33) for participation, a $100 bonus, and $100 for college or training funds after completing 100 hours of programming.

Evaluation Design and Results

Participants were randomly selected from lists of 8th grade students from families receiving public assistance. The students were then recruited and randomly assigned to the experimental or control group. At the end of 9th grade, test scores declined for the intervention group and there were no significant differences in education expectations between the intervention and the control group. After two years—the end of 10th grade—academic and functional skill scores increased and exceeded control group participants in five areas. At the end of senior year, performance in all 11 academic and functional skill areas was greater for the intervention group than the control group. About 6 months after scheduled high school graduation, the intervention group showed benefits from the program in several areas.

Strengths and Limitations

Like the Teen Outreach Program evaluation, this evaluation was excellent in many ways. However, it also had limitations. First, a substantive theory of change was not explicitly stated and mediating causal processes were not investigated. Nonetheless, the program was designed with some attention to theory and explicit cause and effect relations: for example, it emphasized the importance of community through the service component; it taught responsibility through the program requirements; it provided opportunity through the rich set of offerings; it taught investment skills through earned stipends and college savings; it stressed the importance of meaningful adult relationships throughout the high school years; and finally, it recognized the importance of continuity across time by creating a four-year program. Each of these program design components is compatible with the committee's list of features of positive developmental settings.

The multiple components of the program produced multiple positive effects using a strong pre- and postexperimental design. Youth were not only randomly assigned to the program intervention and control groups, but they were also randomly selected prior to program recruitment. The positive effects of this study are particularly impressive considering the frequent difficulties in recruitment and retention of youth ages 15 to 18. The program was well implemented according to evidence of participation and retention rates, although there was no specific information regarding the quality of program activities. The theory behind the program was not well articulated in the evaluation design. Consequently, most of the goals proposed in the program design phase were not evaluated.

In summary, this program seems very promising and is grounded in research on the importance of service learning and mentoring. In general, the program effects look positive; however, there is no explicit theory of change. Consequently, we know little about why and for whom it worked. Like the Teen Outreach Program, the program offers a service-learning component for young people having difficulties in school. The program also has a mentoring component that the staff thinks is critical for positive results. The evaluation study was relatively small (100 youth from 4 cities in the intervention). Finally, the program is quite expensive. The extent to which the payments to the youth are essential has not been assessed.

Big Brothers Big Sisters

Evaluators:	Grossman and Tierney, 1998
Level of intervention:	Community and individual
Target population:	10- to 16-year-olds
Evaluation research design:	Experimental design with random selection and assignment
Sample:	1,138 (571treatment, 567 control)
Attrition analysis:	487 of the 571 treatment participants; 472 of the 567 control participants
Cost:	Average of $1,543/match/year

Big Brothers Big Sisters is a community-based mentoring program that matches an adult volunteer, known as a Big Brother or a Big Sister, to a child, known as a Little Brother or Little Sister, with the expectation that a caring and supportive relationship will develop. The match is well supported by mentor training and ongoing supervision and monitoring of the mentor relationship by a professional staff member. Ideally, the matched pair spends three to five hours per week together over the course of a year or longer. The activity goals are identified in the initial interview held with the parent or guardian and the child. The top priority is for the matched pair to develop a relationship that is mutually satisfying and provides contact on a regular basis. The goals established for a specific match are developed into an individualized case plan, which is updated by the case manager as progress is made and circumstances change over time. The case manager is responsible for maintaining contact with all parties in the match relationship.

In order to ensure effective matches between volunteers and youth and to monitor program quality, the professional staff screens all applicants, youth, and their families. Orientations are conducted with youth and volunteers, and training is provided for volunteers. Staff supervises matches between youth and volunteers by contacting all parties within two weeks of the initial match and then having monthly telephone contact with the volunteer for the first year of the program. The staff also contacts the youth directly at least four times in the first year.

Evaluation Design and Results

An experimental design using random assignment was used to evaluate the Big Brothers Big Sisters program at eight program sites: Phoenix,

Wichita, Minneapolis, Rochester, Columbus, Philadelphia, Houston, and San Antonio. Youth ages 10 to 16 who came to the agencies during the study period, October 1991 to February 1993, were randomly assigned to either the mentoring or the control group. Baseline data were collected, treatment subjects were matched with a mentor when possible, and control subjects were placed on a waiting list for 18 months. Pre- and posttreatment data consisted of self-assessment questionnaires on family background information and outcome variables. The evaluation sample consisted of 959 10- to 16-year-olds (487 treatment, 472 controls) from single-parent households. At pretest, 69 percent were between the ages of 11 and 13; 43.3 percent lived in households receiving public assistance; 27.1 percent were experiencing physical, emotional, or sexual abuse; 23 percent were minority girls, 15 percent were white girls, 34 percent were minority boys, and 28 percent were white boys.

Matches were found for 378 (78 percent) of the 487 members of the treatment group; 109 of the treatment group were not matched. The evaluators suggested three main reasons for the failure to match the 109 treatment youth: (1) 33 became ineligible for the program because their parent remarried, the youth became too old, or the residence of the youth changed; (2) 31 because the youth no longer wanted to participate; and (3) 21 because the staff couldn't find a suitable volunteer mentor. The other 24 were not matched for a variety of reasons such as parent or youth not following through on the intake process.

Youth in the treatment group (including both those who received a mentor and those who did not) were less likely to initiate drug and alcohol use than the waiting list youth; they also reported hitting others less often. Their grade point average was higher, and they attended school more often. Finally they also reported better parental relationships and more parental trust.

Strengths and Limitations

The Big Brothers Big Sisters program is a very promising program based on the multiple benefits to youth of being mentored by nonfamilial adults. The random assignment evaluation design meets high standards. One major weakness, however, is the total reliance on self-reporting by the youth for the outcome measures. Another is the failure to include implementation or process analysis. As a result, we really know little about why the average-level effects are obtained and why the program may have worked very well for some youth and not at all for others. A

good qualitative evaluation component would have provided preliminary answers to these questions, and such an evaluation is now under
way. A third weakness is the failure to gather follow-up data. Thus we
know nothing about the length of positive impact. Finally, because Big
Brothers Big Sisters does not have an explicit theory of change—the
analysis of implementation quality does not go beyond descriptions of
the number of contacts between mentor and young person and beyond
their reports of satisfaction with the relationship. And with regard to
this measure, many pairs did not meet as often as recommended by the
program. A much more detailed study of implementation is now under
way.

Three other aspects of the evaluation need to be noted. First, the
treatment group included some youth who were assigned to receive the
program intervention but were never matched; thus the analyses may
underestimate the effect size. Second, outcome effects were reported
using relative rather than absolute percentages, thereby possibly inflating
effect sizes.

In summary, Big Brothers Big Sisters is a very promising community
program for youth. The program is grounded in the research showing
that positive relationships with nonfamilial adults support positive development. The researchers included all youth assigned to the treatment
when they estimated the effects of the program. This procedure is likely
to underestimate the impact of the program on those who actually received the services. Nonetheless, the program yielded significant positive
benefits on multiple fronts. The evaluation was exemplary in some ways
and limited in others. A strong methodological design with random assignment was used to evaluate the program. However, one could be
more confident about the results if there were long-term follow-up data,
the analysis included site-level as well as individual-level information,
and more was known about the characteristics of each of the eight sites.

CONCLUSIONS ABOUT PROGRAM FEATURES

The committee was very interested in understanding why programs
are effective and particularly how and why they are effective in promoting adolescent development. The quality of information in most studies
about the particular features of effectiveness, however, was minimal.
Furthermore, these studies were not necessarily designed to collect information about those aspects of adolescent development outlined in this
report. However, we read the descriptions of these studies carefully for

clues as to why they might have worked and how they were related to the elements of the development framework we hypothesized as being important at the beginning of this report. Each program, in fact, included several components that were consistent with this framework. We learned that many programs can effectively promote healthy development, although we learned much less about why. Without such information, we cannot say very much about which particular components or combination of components were responsible for the programs' effectiveness. We therefore cannot draw firm conclusions about which and how many of the features of settings in Chapter 4 were critical for the success of these programs. Nevertheless, in this section we attempt to compare these programs with our framework.

It is important to keep in mind that we imposed our list of setting features onto programs that were not designed with this particular framework in mind; we therefore had to rely on our interpretation of the program descriptions and other information provided in the evaluation materials to infer whether a program offered a particular feature or not.

Supportive Relationships

Supportive relationships were a major component of most of the effective programs reviewed. Explicit mentoring activities are the most obvious examples of nurturing supportive relationships, but most of the programs provided youth with some form of regular supportive contact with nonfamilial adults. In many cases, mentoring was not explicitly stated as a program goal, but the adult-adolescent contact in these programs often took the form of mentoring. For example, Quantum Opportunities used an intensive case management approach to tailor their program to meet individual needs and circumstances. This approach required regular supportive interactions between the case manager and the adolescent. In addition, many of the programs officially designated mentoring as the central component of the program. The best example of this is Big Brothers Big Sisters. The positive effects of mentoring were clearly documented in the evaluation of this program. Follow-up was done to understand the factors contributing to supportive mentoring relationships. Through telephone interviews with 1,101 mentors in 98 mentoring programs and through youth focus groups and youth interview data (Herrera et al., 2000), the evaluators found that mentors with the closest and most supportive relationships reported more than 10 hours of contact per month, shared interests between the mentor and youth, and shared decision making about activities.

Opportunities to Belong

Healthy development is promoted by fostering a sense of belonging, an area which the Quantum Opportunities Program stressed. Instilling a sense of belonging was at the core of its mission as reflected in their motto, "Once in QOP, always in QOP." If participants stopped attending activities and disappeared from the program, program staff tracked them down to find out what was wrong, to assure them they were still part of their QOP "family," and to coax them back to the program. This attitude of refusing to give up on youth was considered by Hahn et al. (1994) to be a crucial component of the program. Although this outreach might have been seen as coercive, evidence from the student evaluations of the program suggest that this was not the case: for three of the four sites evaluated, 78-92 percent of the students thought the program was "very important" and 82-92 percent were "very satisfied" with the program. It is unlikely that students would give these responses if they felt coerced to attend or hassled by unwanted adult attention.

Positive Social Norms

Even when not explicitly stated as a program goal, all of these programs promoted positive social norms and discouraged norms related to the major problem behaviors of concern in these programs. Programs with a community service component— Quantum Opportunities and the Teen Outreach Program—best exemplify this feature. Youth participants were matched with an adult mentor and received classroom-based social problem-solving skills training and participated in community service activities with their mentors. The discussions in school were explicitly designed to support positive social norms among the students participating. In many cases, parents also participated in workshops, to enhance their ability to help their children maintain positive social norms and reject antisocial norms and pressures from peers to participate in problem behaviors. Programs that taught resistance skills also exemplify this feature.

Support for Efficacy and Mattering

Providing opportunities for autonomy, taking responsibility, and challenge are likely to be especially important for older adolescents as they approach the transition to adulthood. Most of the programs reviewed in this chapter did not address opportunities for developing a sense of efficacy. More such programs were reviewed in Chapter 5. However, programs with a focus on skill acquisition, such as the Penn Prevention Program, do exemplify this characteristic because such learning opportunities, if implemented as discussed in Chapter 4, are the best settings in which to acquire a strong sense of personal efficacy. We talk more about this in the next section. Support for mattering was more clearly evident in the effective programs reviewed in this chapter. This feature was most evident in programs that provided opportunities to participate in community service. Two of the model programs, Quantum Opportunities and the Teen Outreach Program, were successful in involving high school students in community service, life and family skills training, and support in planning for college and jobs.

Opportunities for Skill Building

Opportunities for skill building were plentiful in the programs reviewed. An emphasis on social skills was a frequent program goal. Building skills in resisting peer influences to engage in a wide range of problem behaviors (such as unprotected sex, drinking and drug use, and illegal behaviors) was common in programs primarily focused on preventing such problems as drug and alcohol use, teen pregnancy, and HIV/AIDS (see program descriptions in Table 6-1 for ENABL, Life Skills Training, Project ALERT, Positive Youth Development Program). Also, many of the programs focusing specifically on the parent-youth relationship include activities to teach youth and parents better communication skills (e.g., the Adolescent Transitions Project, Creating Lasting Connections, Functional Family Therapy, Improving Social Awareness–Social Problem Solving, the Midwestern Prevention Project, the Social Competence Program for Young Adolescents, the Teen Outreach Program).

Other programs focus on individual cognitive, social, and emotional skill development. Some focus on such social and emotional skills as coping and self-regulation (Coping with Stress Course, Functional Family Therapy, the Penn Prevention Project). Others provided employment or economic management skills through part-time employment with mentoring, encouragement for opening savings accounts, and financial incentives for participation (Quantum Opportunities, the Summer Training and Education Program, Louisiana State Youth Opportunities).

Integration of Family, School, and Community Efforts

Several programs excelled in integrating family, school, and community into their program design. The Midwestern Prevention Project includes a set of program activities to prevent adolescent drug use: (1) mass media programming with news clips, commercials, and talk show discussions on drug use incorporated with information on their program; (2) a school-based program teaching resistance and counteraction skills for drug use; and (3) parent education and organizing.

Project Northland also used a community-wide approach. Students received skills training to enhance their social competency in dealing with their parents, their peers, and the norms surrounding alcohol use. Parent education and involvement was also stressed through parent-student homework activities and through newsletters to parents containing educational information. Community-level changes in alcohol-related programs and policies were also targeted. Finally, the Valued Youth Partnership Program participants were given training in how to tutor and then engaged in tutoring of younger students for at least four hours per week. Parents were involved in school activities, and students were exposed to role models in the community through presentations and field trips.

Structure and Safety

These two characteristics of positive developmental settings from our list—appropriate structure and physical and psychological safety—received little mention in the program descriptions. Perhaps this omission reflects that fact that these characteristics are considered so basic that they are not worthy of explicit mention. One of the fundamental reasons for community programming for youth is to provide safe places for them to go. Wisdom would dictate then that programs must enable youth to feel and be psychologically and physically safe. To do this, programs need to have clear and consistent rules, expectations, and boundaries. Nevertheless, the absence of these features is likely to be a major reason why programs fail and why some programs produce negative results.

None of the programs included in this chapter dealt explicitly with the use of developmental appropriate levels of structure. Some of those reviewed in Chapter 5 did. These programs provided more opportunities for self-monitoring and active participation in rule making and enforcement as the youth matured.

SUMMARY

Our review of experimental and quasi-experimental evaluations of community programs for youth ages 10 to 18 leads to several general conclusions about these programs and the evaluation of these programs.

Community programs for youth, whether they are packaged in teen pregnancy prevention programs, mental health programs, or youth development programs, can facilitate positive outcomes for youth. This review of experimental and quasi-experimental evaluation of community programs for youth revealed that participation is associated with increases in such outcomes as motivation, academic performance, self-esteem, problem-solving abilities, positive health decisions, interpersonal skills, and parent-child relationships, as well as decreases in alcohol and tobacco use, depressive symptoms, weapon-carrying, and violent behavior. Although many of these studies were not designed around a positive youth development framework, many of the evaluations in fact included measures that reflected the personal and social assets and features of settings developed in this report.

Even with the most rigorous methods of evaluations, there is limited evidence that measures the impact of these experiences on the development of young people and therefore limited evidence on why program effects are or are not obtained from the evaluations reviewed. Some of these studies explicitly involved components consistent with the developmental framework outlined in Part I. However, without appropriate information, we cannot say very much about which particular components or combination of components were responsible for a specific program's effectiveness. Consequently, research is needed to sharpen the conceptualization of features of community programs and to explore whether other key features should be added to the list. This work should focus on how different populations are affected by different program components and features (e.g., age, gender, socioeconomic status, ethnicity, community environment, developmental readiness, personality, sexual orientation, skill levels). It should also focus on how to incorporate these features into community programs and on how to maintain them once they are in place. Finally, such research should identify program strategies, resource needs, and approaches to staff training and retention that can cultivate and support the features of positive developmental settings in community programs for youth.

Also, it is our view that evaluations designed with some of the principles outlined in the next chapter will tell us much more about why particular programs work and for whom they are likely to be most effective. And new programs can be designed with some of the principles outlined in earlier chapters. If such programs are designed from the beginning with a well-articulated theory of change grounded in solid developmental theory and research, we will learn a lot more about what programs might do to facilitate positive youth development and to prevent problems from emerging,

PART III

Evaluation and Social Indicator Data

As more funding becomes available for community programs designed to promote youth development, higher expectations are being placed on programs to demonstrate (and not just to proclaim) that they do indeed promote the healthy development of youth. Well-established programs that draw on public funds are being adopted in cities and communities throughout the United States. Increasingly, these programs are being expected to demonstrate that they actually do make a difference in young people's lives. It is precisely because these programs are being established in a wide variety of communities that it is important to know if they make a difference and, if so, under what conditions and for whom. Moreover, given the recent call for significant investments in public resources, it would betray public trust not to document the steps taken to implement these programs and to provide evidence of the effectiveness of programs.

How should one think about evaluation of community programs for youth in the future? What social indicators exist that help us understand community programs for youth? What else is needed in order to better understand and evaluate these programs?

Part III explores the various methods and tools available to evaluate these programs, including experimental, quasi-experimental, and non-experimental methods. Each method involves different data collection techniques, and each affords a different degree of causal inference—that is, whether a particular variable or treatment actually causes changes in outcomes. Findings from evaluations using these methods were incorporated into Part II. We turn now to exploring evaluation methodologies in more detail, looking specifically at the role for evaluation (Chapter 7) and data collection (Chapter 8) for the future of these programs.

There are particular challenges inherent to evaluating community programs for youth. Many of them tend to be relatively new and are continually changing in response to growing interest and investments on the part of foundations and federal, state, and local policy makers. In addition, the elements of community programs for youth rarely remain stable and consistent over time, given that program staff are always trying to improve the services and the manner in which they are delivered. Moreover, some programs struggle to overcome barriers during the implementation phase—for example, to receive a license or permits, to acquire appropriate space or renovate a facility, or to recruit appropriate staff and program participants. As a result, early implementation of programs may not follow the specific plan. Evaluation involves asking many questions and often requires an eclectic array of methods. Deciding what questions to ask and the methods to use for the development of a comprehensive evaluation is important to the wide range of stakeholders of community programs for youth.

CHAPTER 7

Generating New Information

This chapter explores the role of program evaluation in generating new information about community programs for youth. Evaluation and ongoing program study can provide important insights to inform program decisions. For example, evaluation can be used to ensure that programs are acceptable, assessable, developmentally appropriate, and culturally relevant according to the needs of the population being served. The desire to conduct high-quality evaluation can help program staff clarify their objectives and decide which types of evidence will be most useful in determining if these objectives have been met. Ongoing program study and evaluation can also be used by program staff, program users, and funders to track program objectives; this is typically done by establishing a system for ongoing data collection that measures the extent to which various aspects of the programs are being delivered, how are they delivered, who is providing these services, and who is receiving them. In some circles, this is referred to as reflective practice. Such information can provide very useful information to program staff to help them make changes to improve program effectiveness. And finally, program evaluation can test new or very well-developed program designs by assessing the immediate, observable results of the program outcomes and benefits associated with participation in the program. Such summative evaluation can be done in conjunction with strong theory-based evaluation (see later discussion) or as a more preliminary assessment of the potential usefulness of novel programs and quite complex social experiments in which there is no well-specified theory of change.[1] An example of the latter is the Move to Opportunity programs, in which poor families were randomly assigned to new housing in an entirely new neighborhood. In other words, program evaluation and study can help foster accountability, determine whether programs make a difference, and provide staff with the information they need to improve service delivery. They can generate new information about community programs for youth and the population these programs serve and help stakeholders know how to best support the growth and development of programs.

Different types of evaluation are used according to the specific questions to be addressed by evaluation. In general, there are two different types of evaluations relevant to this report:

1. Process evaluation (formative evaluation) describes and assesses how a program operates, the services it delivers, and the activities it carries out and
2. Outcome evaluation (summative evaluation) identifies the results of a program's efforts and considers what difference the program made to the young people after participating.

These two evaluative approaches can be thought of as a set of assessment options that build on one another, allowing program staff to increase their knowledge about the activities that they undertake as they incorpo-

---

[1]Summative evaluations can be used with such programs to assess impact and estimate its size. Such evaluations are often called for when the government has invested very large sums of money in a novel omnibus social experiment, such as those linked to recent welfare-to-work reform or large-scale school reform efforts. Often such evaluation focus only on outcome differences between the treatment and the control groups. However, without some theory of change and measures of the processes assumed to mediate the impact of the program, such evaluation leave many questions unanswered and do not provide good guidance for either modifying or replicating the program in the future. We do not discuss such evaluations in any detail in this report. Interested readers are encouraged to look at the more standard textbooks on program evaluation for additional information, such as Shadish et al. (2001).

Box 7-1
Process and Outcome Evaluation

Process evaluation helps explain how a program works and its strengths and weaknesses, often focusing on program implementation. It may, for example, document what actually transpires in a program and how closely it resembles the program's goals. Process evaluation is also used to document changes in the overall program and the manner in which services are delivered over time. For example, a program administrator might observe that attendance at a particular activity targeted to both youth and their parents is low. After sitting down and talking with staff, the program administrator discovers that the activity has not been sufficiently advertised to the parents of the youth participating in the program. Moreover, the project team realizes that the times in which the activity is scheduled are inconvenient for parents. Increased and targeted outreach to parents and a change in the day and time of the activity result in increased attendance. Thus, process evaluation is an important aspect of any evaluation, because it can be used to monitor program activities and help program staff to make decisions as needed.

Outcome evaluation facilitates asking if a program is actually producing changes on the outcomes believed to be associated with the program's design. For example, does participation in an after-school program designed to improve social and communication skills actual lead to increased engagement with peers and participation in program activities? Are the participants more likely to take on leadership roles and participate in planning program activities than they were before participating?

---

rate more options or activities into their evaluation (see Box 7-1 for elaboration). They can also serve as the foundation from which programs justify the allocation of public and private resources.

Process and outcome evaluations both rely on the collection of two types of data—qualitative and quantitative data (see Box 7-2 for elaboration). Quantitative data refer to numeric-based information, such as descriptive statistics that can be measured, compared, and analyzed. Qualitative data refer to attributes that have labels or names rather than numbers; they tend to rely on words and narrative and are commonly used to describe program services and characterize what people "say" about the programs.

Box 7-2
Quantitative and Qualitative Data

Quantitative data are commonly used to compare outcomes that may be associated with an intervention or service program for two different populations (i.e., those who received the service—or participated in the program—and those who did not) or from a single population but at multiple time points (e.g., before, during, and after participation in the program). For example, assume that an organization wants to compare two different types of tutoring programs. To accomplish this goal, they give a structured survey with numeric coded responses (such as a series of mathematical problems or a history or English knowledge test) to participants at the time they enter the program, and 3 and 6 months after the start of the program. The data collected by this survey (for example, scores on the tests of mathematical, historical, or English knowledge) are statistically analyzed to determine differences between the participants from each group.

Qualitative data are often derived from narratives and unstructured interviews or participant observations. A common misconception is that qualitative methods lack rigor and therefore are not scientific. In fact, qualitative methods can be just as scientific (meaning objective and empirical) as quantitative methods. They are the basis for much descriptive and classification work in both the social and natural sciences. They provide an opportunity to systematically examine organizations, groups, and individuals in an effort to extract meaning from situations; understand meaning ascribed to behaviors; clarify or further explore quantitative findings; understand how a service program operates; and determine whether a program or services can be adapted for use in other contexts and with other populations.

EVALUATING COMMUNITY PROGRAMS FOR YOUTH

In our review of studies and evaluations that have been conducted on community programs serving youth, we found that a wide range of evaluation methods and study designs are being used, including experimental, quasi-experimental, and nonexperimental methods (see Box 7-3). Part II provided examples of community programs for youth using both experimental or quasi-experimental methods, as well as a range of other nonexperimental methods of study, including interviews, focus

Box 7-3
Evaluation Design Methodologies

Experimental design involves the random assignment of individuals to either a treatment group (in this case participation in the program being assessed) or a control group (a group that is not given the treatment). Many believe that the experimental design provides some of the strongest, most clear evidence in research evaluation. This design also affords the highest degree of causal inference, since the randomized assignment of individuals to an intervention condition restricts the opportunity to bias estimates of the treatment effectiveness.

Quasi-experimental design has all the elements of an experiment, except that subjects are not randomly assigned to groups. In this case, the group being compared with the individuals receiving the treatment (participating in the program) is referred to as the comparison group rather than the control group, and this method relies on naturally occurring variations in exposure to treatment. Evaluations using this design cannot be relied on to yield unbiased estimates of the effects of interventions because the individuals are not assigned randomly. Although quasi-experimental study designs can provide evidence that a causal relationship exists between participation in the intervention and the outcome, the magnitude of the effect and the causation are more difficult to determine.

Nonexperimental design does not involve either random assignment or the use of control or comparison groups. Nonexperimental designs rely more heavily on qualitative data. These designs gather information through such methods as interviews, observations, and focus groups in an effort to learn more about the individuals receiving the treatment (participating in the program) or the effects of the treatment on these individuals. This type of research often consists of detailed histories of participant experiences with an intervention. Although they may contain a wealth of information, nonexperimental studies cannot provide a strong basis for estimating the size of an effect or for unequivocally testing causal hypotheses because they are unable to control for such factors as maturation, self-selection, attrition, or the interaction of such influences on program outcomes. They are, however, particularly useful for generating new hypotheses, for developing classification systems, and for gaining insight into people's understandings.

groups, ethnographic studies, and case studies. It also summarized some findings from studies using both nonexperimental and experimental methods.

There are differing opinions among service practitioners, researchers, policy makers, and funders about the most appropriate and useful methods for the evaluation of community programs for youth (Catalano et al., 1999; McLaughlin, 2000; Kirby, 2001; Connell et al., 1995; Gambone, 1998). Not surprising, there was even some disagreement among committee members about the standards for evaluation of community programs for youth. Through consideration of our review of various programs, the basic science of evaluation, and a set of experimental evaluations, quasi-experimental evaluations, and nonexperimental studies of community programs for youth, the committee agreed that no specific evaluation method is well suited to address every important question. Rather, comprehensive evaluation requires asking and answering many questions using a number of different evaluation models. What is most important is to agree to, and rely on, a set of standards that help determine the conditions under which different evaluation methods should be employed and to evaluate programs using the greatest rigor possible given the circumstances of the program being evaluated. At the end of this chapter, we present a set of important questions to be addressed in order to achieve comprehensive evaluation, whether it be by way of experiments or other methods.

QUESTIONS ASKED IN COMPREHENSIVE EVALUATION

To fully realize the overall effectiveness and impact of a program on its participants, a comprehensive evaluation should be conducted. A comprehensive evaluation addresses six fundamental questions:

1. Is the theory of the program that is being evaluated explicit and plausible?
2. How well has the program theory been implemented in the sites studied?
3. In general, is the program effective and, in particular, is it effective with specific subpopulations of young people?
4. Whether it is or is not effective, why is this the case?
5. What is the value of the program?
6. What recommendations about action should be made?

These questions have a logical ordering. For instance, answers to the middle questions depend on high-quality answers to the first two. To give an example, if one is not sure that a program has been well implemented, what good does it do to ask whether it is effective? The appropriate questions to answer in any specific evaluation depend in large part on the state of previous research on a program and hence often on the program's maturity. The more advanced these matters are, the more likely it is that one can go on to answer the later questions in the sequence above. While answering all six questions may be the ultimate goal, it is important to note that it is difficult to answer all questions well in any one study. Consequently, evaluations should not routinely be expected to do so. However, with multiple evaluation studies, one would hope and even expect that all of these questions will be addressed. Answers to all of these questions may also be obtained by synthesizing the findings from many evaluations conducted with the same organization, program, or element. They may also be answered by using various evaluation methods. We now take a brief look at these questions, realizing that they are interdependent.

Is the Theory of the Program Plausible and Explicit?

Good causal analysis is facilitated by a clear, substantive theory that explicitly states the processes by which change will occur. Ideally, this theory should be the driving force in program development and should guide the decision of what to measure and how. The theory should explicitly state the components that are thought to be necessary for the expected effects to occur (i.e., the specific aspects of the programs—such as good adult role models—that account for the programs' effects on such outcomes as increasing self-confidence). It should also detail the various characteristics of the program, the youth, and the community that are likely to influence just how effective the programs is with specific individuals (i.e., the moderators of the program's effectiveness, such as ethnicity or disability status). These components must then be measured to evaluate whether they are in place in the form and quantity expected.

At a more abstract level, the theory must also be plausible, taking into account current knowledge in the relevant basic sciences, the nature of the target population, and the setting in which the program intervention takes place. We provided an initial review of the existing literatures in Chapters 2, 3, and 4. Obviously, a program needs no further evaluation if this stage of the analysis shows that its most fundamental assumptions are at variance with well-supported current substantive theory or with the level of human and financial resources that can be made available to support it. Once specified, these causal models can be used for two purposes: (1) to design the assessment of the quality of program implementation and (2) when all the data are in, to judge how plausible it is to infer that the observed results are due to processes built into the program theory. Several of the evaluations we looked at provided good models of such an analysis. One is the evaluation of the Girls Inc.'s Preventing Adolescent Pregnancy Project (e.g., Postrado et al., 1997).

Finding a well-specified model underlying either program design or program evaluation is unusual. Few of the evaluations reviewed and discussed in this report had one (see Chapter 6 for examples). Development of such theoretically grounded program-specific models probably requires a prolonged and genuine collaboration between basic researchers, applied researchers, program developers, practitioners, and program evaluators. We highly recommend that more funds be directed to support such ongoing collaborations. Information in Chapters 2, 3, 4, and 5 provides a rudimentary basis for developing such theoretically grounded program models. Complex generic models are needed that involve theorizing at the community, program, cultural, and individual levels because these will help determine the classes of variables to be included in both program and outcome evaluations, and both ongoing reflective practice and program study. Gambone, Connell, and their colleagues developed one such model (Gambone, 1998; Connell et al., 2000). Another formed the basis for Public/Private Ventures' new project around community change for youth development (Sipe et al., 1998). Yet others were the basis of the Midwestern Prevention Project and the Communities that Care initiative (described in more detail in Chapter 5). But even these are quite general models. Models that are quite specific to the program under analysis are needed. Cook and his colleagues developed one such a model for their evaluation of the Comer School Intervention (Cook et al., 1999; Anson et al., 1991; Cook et al., 2000). This work is discussed in more detail later in the chapter.

How Well Was the Program Implemented?

Part of a program's operational theory deals with the treatment components and dosage necessary to achieve the expected outcomes. An empirical description and analysis of the implementation of the components of a program are therefore necessary to determine: (1) whether participants received the intended treatment and (2) how variation in the treatment actually received might be related to outcomes. However, too many outcome evaluations still contain sparse or nonexistent information about particular program elements. Without such a description, it is impossible to know, for instance, if lack of effectiveness might be due to poor program theory, poor implementation of what might otherwise be an effective treatment, or even poor evaluation that failed to detect true effects. If evaluators find that participants did not receive the planned treatment and the expected effects did not occur, then valuable information has been gained. It is obvious that the program is not likely to be effective in its current form, that a high priority of redesign is needed to improve implementation quality, and that the theory behind the program has not been tested in the evaluation since quality implementation is a precondition for a strong test of the theory. Without measures of implementation, the program can be evaluated in terms of its effectiveness, but the theory behind the program cannot be evaluated.

Obviously, it is impossible to achieve perfect implementation in the real world of social programming, but there is much to learn from empirical details about implementation, even when the expected effects do not occur. We found few examples of even systematic attempts at implementation assessment (one such example is the follow-up evaluations of Big Brothers, Sisters). Cook and colleagues' evaluations of the Comer School Intervention provide a good example of careful implementation assessment (Cook et al., 1999; Anson et al., 1991; Cook et al., 2000). We found a few good examples of attempts to measure exposure; these included ongoing evaluations of the Teen Outreach Program by Allan and colleagues (Allan and Philliber, 1998) and the ongoing evaluations of the Girls, Inc.'s Adolescent Pregnancy Prevention Project (Nicholson and Postrado, 1992; Postrado et al., 1997).

Programs in the early stages of development should focus their evaluation activities on implementation rather than outcome analysis. This is the period when the program itself is likely to change most rapidly as the original conception requires some accommodation to newly learned realities of place, time, and people. This process of growth should be carefully studied in its own right for the information it provides to a basic understanding of social systems and human development. Evaluation focused only on effectiveness is most appropriate when the program has matured, the theory of change has crystallized, and implementation has been studied enough to know that the program on the ground is not some distorted caricature of the program intended. In this case, one can reach reasonable conclusions about effectiveness since one has confidence that the program itself was well implemented and the outcome measures are indeed theoretically related to the "treatment." Both significant and null effects can inform conclusions about program effectiveness.

In determining how well a program was implemented, it is important not to forget that the comparison group is never a "no-treatment" group. It is essential to describe what happens in the comparison groups in terms of their opportunities, constraints, and exposure to positive developmental activities. Individuals not included in the experimental treatment may nonetheless gain access to, or be exposed to, similar (even if not identical) activities through other local organizations or through the influence of their friends who are in the treatment group. It is essential to describe these experiences, for few programs exist in a void, and many young people have potential access to more than one program with overlapping services. All experimental evaluations assess the consequences of exposure not of the experimental treatment in a void, but in terms of the contrast between the treatment and the comparison groups. When the comparison group experiences similar events to the treatment group, we can hardly expect to find treatment effects. Such would have to be due to the name of the organization rather than to the specific activities undertaken there. In this case, the finding of nonsignificant effects (null effects) should not be interpreted as an indication that the program is ineffective. Because such careful assessment of exposure to treatment and treatment-like conditions is rare and because some individuals in the treatment condition may not actually receive it, first-order estimates of treatment effects are conservative in that one is rarely sure of the true magnitude of differential exposure of the treatment and control group to the program. Nonetheless, these estimates do provide information to policy makers regarding the value-added of putting the treatment program into a community.[2]

The process evaluation to provide a description of implementation quality can be carried out using a wide variety of both qualitative and quantitative data collection techniques. Among the qualitative methods are ethnographic data collection using a time-sampling basis or open-ended interviews with young people and service practitioners and man-

---

[2]Individuals interested in this issue should consult references on the "intent-to-treat" debates (Shadish et al., 2001; Angrist and Imbrens, 1995).

agers. Ethnographic studies allow researchers to examine unexpected events in depth, to understand important mediating processes not part of the original theory, and to describe how the program evolves over time. Such methods require a substantial time and financial investment, but in our judgment, they are necessary for collecting rich descriptive data that allow the researchers to understand the program better and to communicate these understandings more graphically. Of course, the same kinds of data need to be collected with comparison group members whenever possible, adding to the time and dollar commitment involved.

Among the quantitative methods for describing implementation are closed-ended interviews or questionnaires administered to youth in the each group and to service practitioners. Good quantitative analysis requires a clear program theory and measures that can be used over time to determine the extent to which the program is moving toward sound implementation. When done well, these quantitative analyses can provide a good assessment of how well an intervention has been implemented in the way it was formulated at the time the data collection began. Some questionnaire items can also ask about changes in order to document the dynamic, changing nature of some programs.

It is important to remember that in experimental program evaluations, it is highly desirable—if not necessary in theory—that the assessment of implementation quality be identical for the treatment and control groups (the same is actually also true in other forms of evaluation). A difficulty here is that the control group members may be in a single alternative program or in none at all. Moreover, if implementation scores are to be attached to individual young people to describe the variation in treatment they actually receive, then the desirability of assessing implementation for all young people rather than a sample of them or for the setting in the aggregate increases. The greater the anticipated variability in individual exposure patterns, the greater the need for respondent-specific measures of implementation. These can be expensive and disruptive, although means do exist to deal with each of these concerns.

An important aspect of implementation is dropping out of a program. Dosage usually involves some form of length of program exposure. Indeed, program practitioners are reluctant for their program to be evaluated by criteria that include in the evaluation those who have had limited exposure to program activities. This is understandable; consequently, at a minimum, exposure lengths need documenting, since retaining young people in the program is something all programs strive for and success in this area speaks to the developmental appropriateness of the content and the skills of the staff. If it turns out that there are group differences in the length of exposure to program activities in a randomized experiment comparing two different programs, for example, then this information can be used to get an unbiased program effect. It is important that the information on differences in exposure is considered in relation to the variation in changes in important developmental outcomes. Since practitioners certainly want to see analyses that evaluate their program at its strongest (even if not in its most typical state), some subanalyses assessing impacts for the subset of young people that attends a program for a long period of time and is exposed to activities that meet the state of the art in youth programming are important.

Is the Program Effective?

Various evaluation methods can be used to answer this question, including randomized experiments, quasi-experiments, interrupted treatment designs, theory-based evaluation, and qualitative case studies

Randomized Experiments

This effectiveness question can be rephrased in the following way: Would any observed changes in the youth exposed to the activities under evaluation have occurred without the program? In other words, would the changes have occurred because of temporal maturation alone, because of selection differences between the kinds of young people exposed to two different sets of experiences that are being contrasted, due to statistical regression, or due to being tested on two different occasions and learning from the first one what to say or write on the second one? Although attributing change to the treatment by ruling out the effects of alternative change-inducing forces is central to science, funders, and most taxpayers, it seems to be a lower priority for many program practitioners. Documenting desired change during the course of program exposure is not the same as attributing the change to the program rather than to one of the many other forces that get people to change spontaneously.

The best way to answer the effectiveness question is through an evaluation that is experimental in design. However, despite the fact that experimental designs with random assignment allow the highest level of confidence in evaluating planned program effects (Shadish et al., 2001), true experimental designs with random assignment are not always the most appropriate design; these designs are most useful when a causal question is being asked and not all evaluations are designed to address a causal question. (Common noncausal questions include: How well was the program implemented? What is the cost-benefit ratio for the program?) Randomized experiments are also not always practical, although they have turned out to be feasible in far more contexts than was thought to be the case even a decade ago (Gueron, 2001).

Nonetheless, they are often difficult to implement and program staff are often reluctant to participate in experimental evaluations for a variety of reasons—ranging from the difficulty and inconvenience often imposed by this method to very serious concerns about the ethics of denying an opportunity or service to a large portion of the adolescents needing it. Even so, experiments are the method of choice for evaluating the effectiveness of programs in communities, and program staff need to be part of the ongoing debates about the feasibility of random assignment, raising their objections and carefully considering the responses made to these objections. What is not desirable is that some veto be pronounced without serious consideration having been given to a strong design. In this connection, it is important for those who fund evaluation to be explicit in favoring random assignment experimental evaluations when the question of cause and effect is being asked. Such favoring exists in most disciplines today, but there is mixed support for this method in the emerging area of community programs for youth. And although the ethics of denying service to needy adolescents is a very serious concern, there are often more applicants for the program than can be served. In this case, random selection either into the program or onto a wait list can be implemented in a manner that is fair to all potential participants.

Quasi-Experiments

Strong quasi-experimental designs are sometimes a more realistic approach to assessing effectiveness. Shadish, Cook, and Campbell (2001) discuss a wide number of quasi-experimental designs that vary in their strength for inferring a causal relationship between programs and change in young people. At a minimum, a strong quasi-experimental design entails two things: (1) extensive knowledge of young people's behavior and attitudes prior to or at the onset of treatment exposure, including pretest information on the very same measures that will be used for the posttest outcome assessment, and (2) comparison groups that are deliberately and carefully selected to be minimally different from the program groups. The latter is attained through careful matching procedures on reliable variables that are as highly correlated with the major outcomes as possible. Even stronger designs are outlined in Shadish, Cook, and Campbell (2001).

Done properly, both experimental and quasi-experimental methods provide quite valid information about program effectiveness. Internal validity is best addressed by the random assignment of subjects to control and experimental groups. But without it, pretest measures can be used to make sure the groups are similar on the highest and most distinct correlates of the major outcomes. Then statistical tests can be used to determine whether the two groups remain similar over time (that is, that those who drop out of the study from the two groups are similar to each other—leaving the remaining members of the two groups similar to each other on the pretest measures). Analyzing the experimental-control group contrast in order to assess whether there are differences between the groups on valid and theoretically appropriate outcome measures provides sound evidence of the effectiveness of the program.

However, as discussed earlier, doing rigorous experimental and quasi-experimental evaluation studies is very difficult for community programs for youth because such programs, by their very nature, make randomized trial designs very difficult to implement. Consequently, stakeholders should be sure they need this level of evaluation before asking for it. Also, as discussed previously, the best programs for youth are dynamic and evolving in nature. In other words, they are continually experimenting with ways to improve and are better characterized as learning systems than as a tightly specified program. Such programs are difficult to evaluate with a randomized trial design. Box (1958) has provided an alternative model of evaluation that is better suited to this type of situation—the "evolutionary evaluation method." Essentially, Box outlines a method for doing mini-randomized trials within an organization to test the effectiveness of new activities and program modifications. As far as we know, this method has not been used in community programs for youth, but it would a useful tool for organizations to use as they make changes in their array of programs.

Interrupted Time-Series Designs

Interrupted time-series is another methodology that can be used for evaluating programs aimed at youth in a community (Biglan et al., 2000). The method requires a series of observations prior to entering a program and then at least one observation afterward, although more are desirable. These observations can be of individual young people or on some collective, such as those attending the program at previous time points. But in the latter case, the object of evaluation has to be some change within a program rather than the program itself. Statisticians argue for about 100 time points, but that is usually not possible. This is why Cook and Campbell (1979) and Shadish et al. (2001) argue in favor of abbreviated time-series in which the deviation from a past trend can be observed even if the nature of the correlated error in the series has to be assumed rather than directly measured. At issue is noting whether there is a shift in the abbreviated series' mean or trend following entry into a program, or whether it is a program introducing some new practice that is being evaluated. The value of this approach is that it can rule out alternative interpretations to the program effect that are based on maturational changes in the young people or on statistical regression common in situations in which a program is begun or modified because the situation in a community has suddenly worsened. The major problem, though, is that events that occur simultaneously with the new program or practice may also be responsible for any changes observed. To counter this alternative explanation, it is often useful to introduce a control time-series from a location nearby, where the new practice under evaluation was not implemented. Shadish et al. (2001) provide a long list of variants on the abbreviated time-series analysis that can be used in specific kinds of circumstances.

Yet another evaluation possibility is offered by regression-discontinuity designs (Shadish et al., 2001). These have been repeatedly reinvented over the past 35 years in one social science discipline after another. Their key element is assignment to a program based on a quantitative score and nothing else. Thus, if young people can be assessed in terms of need or merit or their turn in the queue to enter a program, and if program participation depends on this score and nothing else, then an unbiased inference can be made about the program's effects. If there is a main effect of the treatment, then there will be a discontinuity in the intercept of the regression line at the score that determines treatment eligibility; and if there is an interaction with the assignment score (or some correlate thereof), then the regression slopes will differ on each side of the cutoff. It seems counterintuitive at first that this design should result in unbiased inference. After all, assignment to treatment depends on the very selection processes that the randomized experiment was designed to rule out. Yet both designs have a key characteristic in common—that the assignment to treatments is completely known. This is the key design characteristic necessary for producing an unbiased statistical inference. With the randomized experiment, assignment is known to depend only on some equivalent to the coin toss, while in the regression-discontinuity design, it depends only on the score on the quantitative assignment variable.

Neither of these evaluation possibilities has been used much for examining youth programs—and neither will be easy to implement. Yet there are circumstances in which there is a long previous time-series of information at either the individual or the community level. We recommend in the next chapter that communities gather information about the well-being of their youth on a much more regular basis. If such information were systematically available in more communities, using the interrupted time-series design to assess program effectiveness at the community level would become much easier. There are also likely to be other circumstances in which it is ethical and politically acceptable to assign to services only those most in need, those most meritorious, or those who most press for program entry. Often this occurs when there is more demand for the program than spaces available. Of course, having more demand for the program than supply also means that a randomized experiment is feasible, and a randomized experimental evaluation is superior to the regression-discontinuity design, even if only because its statistical power is greater. If evaluationary practice is to be improved in the youth development area, there will have to be greater concern for random assignment, regression-discontinuity, interrupted time-series, and quasi-experiments that have strong rather than weak designs. At a minimum, this means designs with pretest measures on the same variables as the outcomes, matched control groups, replications of the treatment, and statistical analyses that take account of modern developments in statistics, especially propensity score analyses (Rosenbaum, 1992) and recent versions of instrumental variables that emphasize local control groups, pretests, direct observation of the determinants of program participation and sensitivity analyses (Heckman et al., 1996).

Theory-Based Evaluation

Some evaluators have suggested an alternative method for inferring effectiveness—theory-based evaluation. These evaluation theorists believe that theory-based evaluation can answer the question of whether the program is effective.

Theory-based evaluation acknowledges the importance of substantive theory, quantitative assessment, and causal modeling, but it does not require experimental or even quasi-experimental design. Instead it focuses on causal modeling derived from a well-specified theory of the processes that take place between program inputs and individual change. If the causal modeling analyses suggest that the obtained data are consistent with what the program theory predicts, then it is presumed that the theory is valid and success of the program has been demonstrated. If time does not permit assessing all the postulated causal links, information on the quality of initial program implementation nonetheless will be gathered because implementation variables are usually the first constructs in the causal model of the program. If the first steps in the theory are proceeding as predicted, the evaluators can then recommend that further evaluations be conducted when sufficient time has passed for the proposed mediating mechanisms to have their full effect on the proposed outcomes. This should prevent any inclinations toward premature termination of programs, even though it does not demonstrate that the ultimate outcomes have been reached.

It is without question that the analysis of substantive theory is necessary for high-quality evaluation. Otherwise, analyses of implementation and causal processes cannot be carried out. However, the key question is whether a theory-based model can substitute for experiments rather than be built into them. It is not logical that long-term effects will come about just because the proposed mediators have been put into place. Without control groups and sophisticated controls for selection, it is impossible to conclude with any reasonable degree of confidence that the program is responsible for the changes observed rather than some co-occurring set of events or circumstances. Theory-based experimental approaches provide more confidence that it is the program itself that is accounting for the effects, and they also provide strong clues as to whether the program will continue to be effective in other sites and settings that can recreate the demonstrably effective causal processes. We support the use of program theory in evaluation, but as adjuncts to experiments rather than as substitutes.

Qualitative Case Studies

Some argue that qualitative case studies are sufficient for producing usable causal conclusions about a program's effects. These are studies that focus on gaining in-depth knowledge of a program through interviews with various individuals involved, on-site observation, analysis of program records, and knowledge of the literature on programs like the one under review. Such studies involve little or no quantitative data collection and hence little manipulation of the data. Moreover, although some case studies include multiple program sites both for purposes of generalization and for comparison of different kinds of programs, case studies often concentrate on only a few sites, sometimes only one, because resources are usually too limited to collect in-depth information on many sites. The result is therefore to gain in-depth knowledge of only a few sites.

Case studies, done singly or at a sample of sites, are useful for describing and analyzing a program's theory, for studying program implementation, for surfacing possible unintended side effects, and for helping explain why the program had the effects it did. They are also very useful at the stage of theory development. Some programs are thought to work: sometimes this conclusion is based on randomized treatment designs of omnibus programs; at other times, it is based on more subjective criteria, such as user satisfaction or continued evidence of high performance by its users on criteria valued in the community. High-quality case studies can help one understand more about these programs. In turn, this information can be used to design and then evaluate the effectiveness of these newly designed programs using the more quantitative experimental designs discussed earlier in this chapter.

Qualitative case studies can also help reduce some of the uncertainty about whether a program has had specific effects, since they often rule out some of the possible spurious reasons for any changes noted in an outcome. Finally, qualitative case studies often provide exactly the kinds of information that are useful to policy makers, journalists, and the public. These studies provide the kind of rich detail about what it means to youth and their families to participate in particular programs. Of course, such information can be misused, particularly if it is not gathered with rigorous methods; such misuse of information is also possible using quantitative experimental methods. But when done with scientific rigor, particularly if done in conjunction with rigorous experimental and quantitative quasi-experimental studies, qualitative information can provide very important insights into the effectiveness of youth programs.

A separate issue is whether such studies reduce enough uncertainty about cause to be useful. The answer is complex and depends in part on how this information is to be used. In the committee's view, such information can often be useful to program practitioners who want information that will help them improve what is going on at their site. Case studies are probably a better source of information than having no information about change and its causes, and program personnel want any edge they can get to improve what they do. Leavened by knowledge from the existing relevant literature, the data collected on site, and the staff's other sources of program knowledge, the results of a case study can help local staff improve what they do.

However, when the purpose of the evaluation is to estimate the effectiveness of a program in helping participants, we have doubts about the utility of case studies. There are three reasons for this. First, it is often difficult to assess how much each participant has changed from their entry into the program to later. Second, and perhaps most importantly, there is no counterfactual against which to assess how much the participants would have changed had they not been in the program. And third, conclusions about effectiveness always involve a high degree of generalization—e.g., across persons, service practitioners, program inputs—and many qualitative researchers are reluctant to make such generalizations. They prefer to detail many known factors that make some difference to an outcome, and this is not the same as noting what average effect the program has or how its effectiveness varies by just a few carefully chosen factors.

Identifying the Most Appropriate Method

Experimental evaluation methods are often considered the gold standard of program evaluation and are recommended by many social scientists as the best method for assessing whether a program influences developmental outcomes in young people. However, many question the feasibility, cost, and time intensiveness of such methods for evaluating community programs for youth. In order to generate new, important information about community programs for youth, the committee recommends that the kind of comprehensive experimental evaluation discussed in this chapter be used under certain circumstances (see also footnote 1):

1. The object of study is a program component that repeatedly occurs across many of the organizations currently providing community services to youth;
2. An established national organization provides the program being evaluated through a system of local affiliates; and

3. Theoretically sound ideas for a new demonstration program or project emerge, and pilot work indicates that these ideas can be implemented in other contexts.

Comprehensive experimental evaluation is useful when the focus of evaluation is on elements that can be found in many organization providing services to youth: how recruitment should be done and continued participation should be supported; how youth and parent involvement should be supported; how youth's maturity and growing expertise should be recognized and incorporated into programming; how staff members should be recruited and then trained; how coordination with schools should be structured; how recreational and instructional activities should be balanced; how mentoring should be carried out; how service learning should be structured and supported; and how doing homework should be supported. Typically, these are components in any single organization, but they are extremely important because they are common issues in organizations across the country. In our view, such elements are best examined by way of experimental research in which a sample of organizations is assigned to different ways of solving the problem identified. Although such work has the flavor of basic research on organizational development, it is central to an effectiveness-based practice of community youth programming.

Equally critical to an effectiveness-based practice approach is knowledge of the individual- and community-level factors that influence the effectiveness of these practices for different groups of individuals or communities. Consequently, it is also important that experimental methods be used to assess the replicability of such practices in different communities and with different populations of youth. Particular attention here needs to be paid to such individual and community differences as culture, age and maturity, sex, disability status, social class, educational needs, and other available community resources.

Comprehensive experimental evaluations are also called for in two other contexts. The first is when the target of evaluation is a national organization that has affiliates in many locations across the United States. The best model of this is the evaluation completed on Big Brothers Big Sisters to assess the effects of membership and of participation across the affiliates included in the sampling design. Many of these national organizations have been providing services to youth for many years and carry a disproportionate burden of current service provision. As a result, even when programs are still developing at the margins, many have mature program designs. Since the total effect of these organizations is amplified across its affiliates, experimental evaluation with random assignment helps illuminate how effective these programs are.

The final context for comprehensive experimental evaluation is when some bold new idea for a new kind of service surfaces and critical examination shows that the substantive theory behind the idea is reasonable and that it is indeed likely to be able to be implemented. This situation is often called a demonstration project. Such demonstrations provide the substantive new ideas out of which the next generation of superior services is likely to emerge. As such, they deserve to be taken very seriously and to be evaluated by rigorous experiments.

Programs that meet the following criteria should be studied on a regular, ongoing basis with a variety of either nonexperimental methods or more focused experimental, quasi-experimental and interrupted time-series designs, such as those advocated by Box (1958):

1. An organization, program, project, or program element has not sufficiently matured in terms of its philosophy and implementation;
2. The evaluation has to be conducted by the staff of the program under evaluation;
3. The major questions of interest pertain to the quality of the program theory, implementation of that theory, or the nature of its participants, staff, or surrounding context;
4. The program is quite broad, involving multiple agencies in the same community; and
5. The program or organization is interested in reflective practice and continuing improvement.

If Effective, Why?

An explanation of the reasons why a program is effective is important because it identifies the processes that are thought to be present for effectiveness to occur (Cook, 2000). This knowledge is crucial for replication of program effects at new sites because of the uniqueness inherent in delivering the program to new populations and in new settings. Causal or explanatory knowledge not only identifies the critical components of program effectiveness, but also specifies whether these components are moderator variables (variables that change the relation between an intervention and an outcome; common moderator variables include all types of individual difference constructs, such as sex, ethnic group, disability status, age, and social class) or mediator variables (variables that mediate the impact of an intervention on specific outcome variables; common mediators variables are the many personal and social assets discussed in Chapter 3—these are often hypothesized to mediate the impact of program features on adolescent outcomes, such as school achievement, avoidance of getting involved in problematic behaviors, and conditions such as very early pregnancy). Supported by a clear understanding of the causal processes underlying program effectiveness, practitioners at new sites can decide how the processes can best be implemented with their unique target population and their unique community characteristics.

Mixed methods are the most appropriate way to answer the question of why a program is effective. Theory-based evaluation is especially appropriate here and depends on the following steps (Cook, in press):

1. Clearly stating the theory a program is following in order to bring about change. This theory should explicitly detail the program constructs of both mediator and moderator relations that are supposed to occur if the intended program intervention is to impact major target outcomes. Chapters 2 and 3 can serve as an initial basis for developing elaborated theories of change.

2. Collecting both qualitative and quantitative data over time to measure all of the constructs specified in the program's theory of change.

3. Analyzing the data to assess the extent to which the predicted relations among the treatment and the outcome variables have actually occurred in the predicted time sequence. If the data collection is limited to only part of the postulated causal chain, then only part of the model can be tested. The goal, however, should be to test the complete program theory.

A qualitative approach to theory-based evaluation collects and synthesizes data on why an effect came about; through this process, this approach provides the basis to derive subsequent theories of why the change occurred. The qualitative data are used to rule out as many alternative theories as possible. The theory is revised until it explains as much of the phenomenon as possible.

Both quantitative and qualitative implementation data can also tell us a great deal about why programs fail. In addition, these studies make it clear how the programs are nested into larger social systems that need to be taken into account. When adequate supports are not available in these larger social systems, it is unlikely that specific programs will be able to be implemented well and sustained over time.

If Effective, How Valuable?

If a youth program is found effective, a comprehensive evaluation can then ask: Is it more valuable than other opportunities that could be pursued with the resources devoted to the program? Or, less comprehensively, is it more valuable than other programs that pursue the same objective? The techniques of benefit-cost analysis and cost-effectiveness analysis can offer partial but informative answers to these questions.

The fundamental idea of benefit-cost analysis is straightforward: comprehensively identify and measure the benefits and costs of a program, including those that arise in the longer term, after youth leave the program, as well as those occurring while they participate. If the benefits exceed the costs, the program improves economic efficiency—the value of the output exceeds the cost of producing it—and makes society better off. If the costs exceed the benefits, society would be better off devoting the scarce resources used to run the program to other programs with the same goal that do pass a benefit-cost test, or to other purposes.

Choices among competing uses of scarce public and nonprofit resources inherently embody judgments about relative benefits and costs. Benefit-cost analysis seeks to make the basis of such choices explicit so that difficult trade-offs can be better weighed. At the same time, benefit-cost analysis neither can nor should be the sole determinant of funding decisions. Aside from the limitations of any specific study, this technique cannot take into account moral, ethical, or political factors that are crucial in determining youth program policy and funding.

Any benefit-cost analysis must consider several key issues. What counts as a benefit? A cost? How can one measure their monetary value? If a benefit or cost is not measurable in monetary terms, how can it enter the analysis? How can one extrapolate benefits or costs after a youth leaves a program and any follow-up period when impact data are gathered? The costs of youth programs mostly occur at the outset, while the benefits may be realized many years later. How should benefits and costs at different times be valued to reflect the fact that a dollar of benefit received in the far future is worth less a dollar received in the near future, and that both are worth less than a dollar of cost incurred in the present? How can one assess benefits and costs to youth who participate in the program, to taxpayers or other program funders, and to society as a whole? Persons who bear the costs of a program may well differ from those who share in the benefits. How can one incorporate these distributional impacts into the analysis? An enormous literature has arisen to address these issues. There are several excellent texts on the subject (e.g., Boardman et al., 1996; Zerbe and Dively, 1997).

If the principal benefit expected from a youth program cannot be given monetary values, cost-effectiveness analysis can be an alternative to benefit-cost analysis (Boardman et al., 1996). Suppose, for example, that the primary goal is to increase volunteer activity in community groups and that other possible program impacts are of little import to decision makers. In such a case, programs might be compared in terms of the number of volunteer hours they inspire per dollar of cost. Decision makers will want to fund the program that produces the largest increase in hours per dollar spent.

Focusing on one goal is a strength in that it obviates the need to express the value of the outcome in monetary terms. Yet when interventions have multiple goals and no one has clear priority, cost-effectiveness data may not offer much guidance. If one youth program increases voluntary activity by 20 percent and reduces drug use by 15 percent and an alternative, equally costly program has an increase of 12 percent and a reduction of 20 percent, which is better? When there are multiple types of benefits, none of which dominates, and when some can be cast in monetary terms, a benefit-cost analysis that considers both monetary and nonmonetary benefits will usually provide more useful information than a cost-effectiveness analysis.

Systematic benefit-cost analysis has hardly been applied to youth programs, except for those likely to reduce juvenile crime (Aos et al., 2001). While application of this methodology to youth development programs is complex, it is no more so than in other areas of social policy, in which it has made significant contributions to research and policy analysis (e.g., health and mental health, early childhood education, job training, welfare-to-work programs). To advance youth program evaluation in this direction will require more rigorous evaluations with adequate follow-up periods and suitable data on a broad set of impacts.

Analysts and practitioners may be concerned that benefit-cost analysis will lead decision makers to focus too narrowly on financial values and downplay or ignore other important program impacts that cannot be translated into financial terms. However, a careful analysis will discuss nonmonetary benefits and emphasize that a complete assessment of programs when important social values are at stake, such as in the area of youth development, must weigh such benefits along with the monetary ones. Analyses that fail to do so can be criticized for presenting an incomplete picture.

As with other evaluation methods, any benefit-cost analysis has limitations. It can be questioned because its results rest on judgments about which impacts to quantify and various other assumptions needed to conduct an analysis. Time and resource constraints prevent investigation of all possible benefits and costs. Some effects may be inherently unquantifiable or impossible to assess in financial terms yet considered crucial to a program's success or political viability. Nonetheless, when carefully done with attention to the findings' sensitivity to different assumptions, benefit-cost analysis can improve the basis on which youth development policy decisions rest.

SUMMARY

In this chapter, we reviewed fundamentals of evaluation and important questions for the development of a comprehensive evaluation strategy. Several conclusions emerge from this discussion.

First, there are many different questions that can be asked about a program. A priority for program practitioners, policy makers, program evaluators, and other studying programs is to determine the most important questions and the most useful methods to evaluate each program. It is very difficult to understand every aspect of a program in a single evaluation study. Like other forms of research, evaluation is cumulative.

The committee identified six fundamental questions that should be considered in comprehensive evaluation:

- Is the theory of the program that is being evaluated explicit and plausible?
- How well has the program theory been implemented in the sites studied?
- In general, is the program effective and, in particular, is it effective with specific subpopulations of young people?
- Whether it is or is not effective, why is this the case?
- What is the value of the program?
- What recommendations about action should be made?

While it is difficult to answer all six questions well in one study, multiple studies and evaluations could be expected to address all of these questions. Comprehensive evaluation requires asking and answering many of these questions through various methods. Opinions differ opinions among program stakeholders (e.g., service practitioners, researchers, policy makers, and funders) about the most appropriate and useful methods for the evaluation of community programs for youth. No specific evaluation method is well suited to address every important question. And while there is tension between different approaches, the committee agrees that there are circumstances that are appropriate for the use of each of these methods. The method used depends primarily on the program's maturity and the question being asked. It is rare to find programs that involve comprehensive evaluations, and they are probably most warranted with really mature programs that many people are interested in.

The committee concluded that studying program effectiveness should be a regular part of all programs. Also, not all programs require the most extensive comprehensive experimental evaluation outlined in this chapter. In order to generate the kind of information about community programs for youth needed to justify large-scale expenditures on programs and to further fundamental understanding of role of community programs in youth development, comprehensive experimental program evaluations should be used when:

- the object of study is a program component that repeatedly occurs across many of the organizations currently providing community services to youth;
- an established national organization provides the program being evaluated through many local affiliates; and
- theoretically sound ideas for a new demonstration program or project emerge, and pilot work indicates that these ideas can be implemented in other contexts.

Such evaluations need to pay special attention to the individual- and community-level factors that influence the effectiveness of various practices and programs with particular individuals and particular communities.

The committee also discussed the need for more ongoing collaborative teams of practitioners, policy makers, and researchers/theoreticians in program design and evaluation. We conclude from case study materials on high-quality comprehensive evaluation efforts that the odds of putting together a successful high-quality comprehensive evaluation are increased if there is an ongoing collaboration between researchers, policy makers, and practitioners. Yet such collaborations are hard to create and maintain.

When experiments are not called for, a variety of nonexperimental methods and more focused experimental and quasi-experimental studies are ways to understand and assess these types of community programs for youth and help program planners and program staff build internal knowledge and skills and can highlight theoretical issues about the developmental qualities of programs. Such systematic program study should be a regular part of program operation.

Comprehensive evaluation is dependent on the availability, accessibility, and quality of both data about the population of young people who participate in these programs and instruments to track aspects of youth development at the community and program levels. The next chapter explores social indicators and data instruments to support these needs.

CHAPTER 8

Data and Technical Assistance Resources

o *Participates in volunteer activities*
o *Has a positive outlook*
o *Reads for pleasure*

o *Misses school regularly*
o *Has been arrested*
o *Participates in a gang*

Over the past decade, communities, cities, states, and nations have become increasingly interested in knowing what percentage of their youth population is doing well and what percentage is doing poorly (Brown and Corbett, forthcoming; Kingsley, 1998). To estimate these numbers, scientists and policy makers have generated both a growing list of social indicators of well-being and problem behaviors and set about gathering the data. As a result, there are now data and related technical assistance resources to support youth development work. This work, however, has also produced a keen awareness among practitioners of the limitations of these resources and the need to increase their quality, breadth, and availability in the coming decade (MacDonald and Valdivieso, 2000).

In this chapter we review these resources in light of the youth development framework developed in Part I and the variety of practical applications for which the data and resources are needed. Our review of data and resources includes: (1) relevant administrative and vital statistics data that are commonly available at the community level, (2) community surveys and topic-specific instruments that can be used to track aspects of youth development not well covered by administrative data, and (3) selected national surveys focusing on youth. We then discuss data collection to support implementation and reflective practice in individual community programs for youth. Finally, we review the efforts of key national intermediary organizations that have developed resources and technical assistance materials for use by local youth development efforts interested in social indicator data. The chapter concludes with suggestions regarding: (a) the need for enhanced access of community youth programs to social indicator data and to the training needed to use them effectively, (b) the development and fielding of new measures, and (c) an expanded role for national intermediaries to support these goals.

USES OF SOCIAL INDICATOR DATA

The uses of social indicator data for community programs for youth and youth initiatives include needs assessment, service targeting, goals tracking, program accountability, and reflective practice to improve program and policy effectiveness over time. Any assessment of available data resources to support this work needs to be understood in the context of their use.

Needs and Resource Assessment

Assessing the needs of youth in a community is a common starting point for many community youth initiatives. Whole communities may do a general assessment using available data to identify the areas of greatest need for their youth, which can then be addressed in a coordinated fashion by multiple programs and agencies. Organizations (e.g., the United Way, the YWCA, a local synagogue) can also use such data to shape their own programs, targeting their efforts in areas of greatest need (United Way of America, 1999). Strengths in the community (cultural, financial, etc.) that could be mobilized to meet the needs are often identified as part of the same process.

Most communities are limited to available administrative data sources, such as service program data, health surveillance, vital statistics, school performance data, decennial census, police reports, and so on. Because of the limited nature of these data, some communities are fielding their own surveys for a more complete assessment. In many cases, however, community programs for youth are started in response to needs that are obvious to those who work with the youth without consulting any data resources. Nonetheless, however, a more formal documenting of need can help even in these cases to elicit the cooperation and interest of other actors both inside and outside the community, including funders.

Tracking Progress Toward Goals

Virtually all youth initiatives have some goals that can be translated into social indicator language. Community-wide youth initiatives often set goals to improve selected dimensions of youth well-being in specific and measurable ways. These goals then serve to focus the activities of multiple organizations in the community. In Tillamook County, Oregon, for example, the community agreed to focus on lowering the teen birth rate, which was then one of the highest in the state. Many local organizations, some with very different ideas and strategies for addressing the issue, worked to reduce teen births in the county. Over a period of four years, the rate was cut by 70 percent, giving the county the lowest teen birth rate in the state (National Campaign to Prevent Teen Pregnancy, 1997).

The federal *Healthy People 2010* initiative is another useful example. Participating states and communities adopt specific goals across a host of health outcomes to be achieved by the year 2010.[1] Public and private health organizations focus their efforts on one or more of these goals so that, together, they can make measurable progress at the community or state level. Social indicator data are the primary source used to assess this progress. Individual programs can also use social indicator data as tools for setting and tracking progress toward their specific goals.

Accountability

Social indicator data are increasingly used by funders to hold programs and initiatives accountable for measurable results in many areas,

---

[1]For more information, visit <http://web.health.gov/healthypeople>

including youth well-being and development. Successful improvement in the targeted areas of development may be met with increased funding. Failure to meet specified goals may result in the provision of technical assistance to overcome problems or in the loss of funding or autonomy. Such accountability practices are becoming increasingly common in state and local educational assessment efforts, for example (Brown and Corbett, forthcoming). Community-level indicators are rarely used for this purpose, as individual programs are not generally expected to have a community-wide impact on youth well-being. Instead, they are held accountable for outcomes to program participants.

Reflective Practice

Community programs for youth can also use social indicator data to monitor their own success and to guide program refinement (i.e., they can use social indicator data as part of reflective practice). At its most formal level, programs can develop a detailed model relating program activities to interim and long-term project goals for participating youth (United Way of America, 1999; Gambone, 1998; Weiss, 1995). In the best case, such a model of the links between program activities and youth outcomes will be based on existing research (when it exists), theory, and the shared beliefs of those running the program. Both program activities and youth outcomes can then be measured and tracked over time. Failure to produce the expected results could indicate inadequate implementation of some part of the program, or it may call into question one or more of the underlying assumptions of the model. Practices, the model, or both can then be reevaluated as a result and the programs can be modified.

In many respects reflective practice functions like program evaluation, even though it lacks the methodological rigor required to draw firm causal inferences about the relations between program activities and youth outcomes (see Chapter 7 for discussion of evaluation methodologies). However, the level of certainty required to qualify results as scientific knowledge is not needed to produce good guides for responsible program management. And programs can sometimes incorporate some of the practices associated with experimental evaluations into their reflective practices. For example, they can compare the social indicator data from their catchment area with social indicator data being collected longitudinally in other comparable catchment areas (stimulating a quasi-experimental design, provided that the data are being collected over time beginning before the program change is put into place).

DATA SOURCES

Communities and youth programs interested in tracking indicators of youth development have two major sources of data to draw from: administrative and related data sources (e.g., school records, crime reports, social service receipt, vital statistics, decennial census) and surveys. Every community already has data relevant to youth development from its administrative data collection efforts, although there can be substantial differences across communities in the accessibility of those data to the public, even among the agencies that collect them. Few communities go to the added effort and expense of collecting survey data, although this is an excellent way to achieve a complete picture of the status of youth and the social factors affecting their development. Over the past decade, however, the number of communities conducting surveys has increased substantially.

In this section we review the data resources available to communities through the lens of the youth development framework developed in this report. This framework identified four outcome domains of development—described as personal and social assets—in Chapter 3 and eight social setting domains—described as features of positive developmental settings in Chapter 4. We also include "negative outcomes and behaviors" as a separate outcome domain.

We examine the types of indicator data available in each of the domains in our framework for commonly available administrative data, and for three of the more advanced survey instruments used for assessing youth development at the community and state levels. These are reviewed in terms of their coverage across the domains, data and measurement quality, and the extent to which their measures are grounded in the scientific literature. Topic-specific research instruments and national surveys are also discussed.[2] The section finishes by considering issues of public access to the data generated by these sources.

---

[2]Several major federal publications series, not reviewed here, provide regularly updated trend data on children and youth across a wide variety of domains. These include:

Trends in the Well-Being of America's Children and Youth (<http://aspe.hhs.gov/hsp/99trends>)

Administrative and Related Sources

Every community collects a substantial amount of data on their children and youth. Administrative sources include school records, educational assessments, vital statistics (birth and death records), police data on reports and arrests, child welfare and public assistance records, health surveillance systems, emergency room admissions data, and so on (Coulton and Hollister, 1998; Coulton, 1995). In addition, data from the decennial census provide detailed economic and demographic information on youth, their families, and their neighborhoods.

These data have a number of advantages in addition to their ubiquity. First, someone has already paid for their collection. If they are not already available to the public, they can often be made available at a relatively modest cost. Second, many of these sources are capable of generating indicator estimates down to the neighborhood level. This is particularly important for community programs for youth, many of which serve limited geographic areas within the larger community. Neighborhood-level data allow programs to make strategic location decisions to areas of greatest need, assess needs and strengths in neighborhoods they already serve, and track changes in these characteristics over time. The last is particularly important for community programs for youth when their goals extend beyond program participants to include changes at the neighborhood level (e.g., reductions in gang activity).

Third, administrative data provide information that cannot be gathered using existing community surveys on youth development. Standardized education assessments, for example, are important measures that are not covered by such surveys. Neighborhood characteristics (e.g., crime levels, teen birth rates) derived from administrative reporting systems provide indicators of social settings that are more objective in the sense that they are not dependent, as the surveys are, on youth perceptions.

Some potential problems with these data should be kept in mind. First, many of these sources can have problems with data quality and consistency (Coulton and Hollister, 1998; Coulton, 1998). For example,

Youth Indicators 1996: Trends in the Well-Being of American Youth (<http://nces.ed.gov/pubsearch/pubsinfo.asp?pubid=96027>)

America's Children: Key National Indicators of Well-Being: 2000 (<http://www.childstats.gov>)

changes in police policy for the disposition of juvenile offenses may result in dramatic increases or decreases in arrest rates without any change in the actual rate of juvenile crimes committed. Even census data, which are very reliable overall, have been shown to substantially underestimate the number of both black and white children in large urban settings (West and Robinson, 1999).

Second, data sources often use different and incompatible geographic units when they report (e.g., school catchment area, census tract, health district, or other specially defined service area). This can limit the ability to draw on multiple data sources to produce a picture or profile for particular neighborhoods.

Other problems can include a lack of separate estimates for important population subgroups (e.g., Hispanics), long time lags between data collection and release, and a lack of public accessibility. In many communities, estimates that could support planning efforts outside local government never make it beyond the walls of the agencies and departments that collect them.

Table 8-1 presents the types of indicator data available from administrative data and from the three community survey instruments we reviewed, sorted by the domains in our youth development framework. In the youth outcome domains, administrative data are quite strong in the areas of cognitive development, negative outcomes or behaviors, and physical health. They are weak sources of indicator data in the areas of psychological, emotional, and social development. And, with the exception of the cognitive development domain, the indicators are heavily weighted toward negative outcomes. This should not be surprising given the reliance on crime, vital statistics, health surveillance, and social service receipt data, all of which focus primarily on negative events.

Among the social setting domains that influence youth development, administrative data are strongest in the safety, social norms, and opportunities for skill building domains. They are weak to nonexistent in the structure, emotional and intellectual support, opportunities for efficacy, and integration domains.

Community-Level Surveys of Youth

For this review we have chosen three of the best known and most widely used surveys of youth at the state and community levels. All three surveys are based entirely on youth reports, are commonly administered in the classroom, are relatively inexpensive to administer and process, and take an hour or less to complete. These are:

- Profiles of Student Life: Attitudes and Behaviors;
- the Student Survey of Risk and Protective Factors, and Prevalence of Alcohol, Tobacco, and Other Drug Use; and
- the Youth Risk Behavior Survey.

Profiles of Student Life: Attitudes and Behaviors

The Profiles of Student Life: Attitudes and Behaviors (PSL-AB) survey, developed by the Search Institute, has been administered in over 1,000 communities since 1989. It is designed for youth in grades 6 through 12 and is based on a comprehensive framework grounded in the youth development literature (Scales and Leffert, 1999). The framework includes eight asset areas: four internal (commitment to learning, positive values, social competencies, and positive identity) and four external (support, empowerment, boundaries and expectations, and constructive use of time). There are 40 assets in all, as well as multiple measures of thriving and risk behaviors.

The questions used in the survey were culled primarily from national surveys. About half of the assets are measured as scales based on three or four items. A psychometric analysis of these scales revealed Cronbach's alpha coefficients ranging from to .31 to .82, with about two-thirds of the scales exceeding the .60 level, a common cutoff point used in research. The validity of the assets is primarily face validity based on their relationship in the research literature to the promotion of healthy behavior, the prevention of risk behaviors, or both. Analyses based on PSL-AB data revealed strong relationships between the number of assets a youth has and the prevalence of risk and thriving behaviors. These analyses are based on large but nonrepresentative and disproportionately white samples across multiple communities (see Leffert et al., 1998, for details).

Although the assets and their representative measures are grounded in existing academic research, the research base is, as its designers freely admit, rather thin or mixed for a number of the assets, such as empowerment, positive values, cultural competence, self-esteem, and sense of purpose (Leffert et al., 1998).

Clearly, some of the measures used in the PSL-AB race ahead of the underlying science, and a number of the constructed scales fall well be-

TABLE 8-1 Youth Development Outcomes and Social Settings Measures in Administrative Data and Community Surveys

	Community Administrative Data	Profiles of Student Life: Attitudes and Behaviors (PSL-AB)	Student Survey of Risk and Protective Factors, and Prevalence of Alcohol, Tobacco, & Other Drug Use (SSRP)	Youth Risk Behavior Survey (YRBS)
Youth Outcomes				
Cognitive development	School grades; standardized test scores/assessments; high school dropout or completion rates	Achievement motivation; school engagement; time doing homework; reads for pleasure	Academic achievement; school engagement	
Psychological development	Suicides	Moral character (caring, social justice, integrity, honesty); self-efficacy; self-esteem; mattering; positive outlook; depression; attempted suicide	Moral character (attitudes toward negative behaviors, drug use); honesty with parents; depression	Sad/depressed; attempted suicide, suicide ideation; vomit or take laxatives to keep from gaining weight
Emotional development		Takes personal responsibility; plans ahead; makes choices	Rebelliousness	
Social development	Participation rates in school clubs, organizations, and	Volunteer/service activities; participation in creative	Skills negotiating with parents; peer pressure	Hours watching TV

	other extracurricular activities	activities (music, theater, and other arts); participation in sports, clubs, or other organizations, in or out of school; empathy, sensitivity, and friendship skills; cultural diversity (knowledge of and respect for other groups); peer pressure resistance skills; hours watching TV	resistance skills regarding drinking	
Physical development	Participation rates in school sports and physical education; death rate by cause; violent youth crime victimizations; incidence of school violence; prenatal care receipt by teen mothers	Participation in sports activities; physical health behaviors; whether a victim of violence		Vigorous exercise; strengthening exercise; physical education classes; sports team activity; height, weight; safety (helmet, seat belt use); exercise-related injury; threatened or injured with a weapon; forced to have intercourse; tried to quit smoking; pregnancy prevention and condom use; nutrition (detailed); dieting; timing of last routine physical exam; pre-

Continued

TABLE 8-1 *Continued*

				vention of pregnancy, AIDS, or other sexually transmitted diseases discussed at exam; timing of last visit to dentist; use of sun screen/sun block of SPF15 or higher
Negative outcomes and behaviors	Teen birth rate (total and nonmarital); teen rate of STD; teen arrest rate, by type of arrest (violence, drugs, truancy); school suspension or expulsion; school dropout	Drug use; sexual activity; anti-social behaviors; violence; driving and alcohol; school problems; gambling; attitudes toward drug use, sexual activity	Drug use (detailed); school suspension, arrested, carried handgun, fighting; sold drugs; gang membership; perceived risk in using drugs; intention to use drugs as an adult; engaged in negative risk-taking activities	Drug use (detailed); driving and alcohol; carry weapon, gun; fighting; physical fighting with boyfriend/girlfriend; sexual activity (detailed); drugs and intercourse; pregnancy
Social Setting				
Appropriate structure		Clear rules and monitoring (family, school); neighbors monitor young people's behavior	Clear rules and monitoring (family); youth consulted in family decisions that affect him/her; youth perceives opportunities to shape school activities and rules	Ever asked to show proof of age when buying cigarettes?
Physical and	Reports of abuse/neglect	Feels safe in home, school,	Youth feels safe at school;	School or trip to school

239

psychological safety	of youth; youth injuries requiring hospitalization; violent crime rate; school violence reports	and neighborhood	community disorganization; perceived availability of drugs, hand guns; family conflict seen as unsafe
Supportive relationships		Positive parent/youth communication; family provides high levels of love and support; support from adults besides parents; community support (caring, value youth); school environment as caring, encouraging	Positive parent/youth relationships (closeness, activities); number of home and school moves; perceived community support for prosocial involvement
Belonging	Gang membership (police report)	Youth cares about the school; religious attendance; hanging out with friends	Religious attendance; community attachment; gang membership
Positive social norms	Neighborhood crime rates		
	High percentage of single-parent families in neighborhood; high rates of social service receipt in neighborhood	Parents and other adults provide positive role models; friends model positive behaviors	Friends' involvement in drug use, arrest, school suspension, school dropout, theft; peer attitudes on drug use, carrying handgun; friends in gang; neighborhood laws

Continued

TABLE 8-1 *Continued*

			and norms favorable to drug use; parents' attitudes about drug use, antisocial behavior; antisocial behavior by other family members (drug use, carry gun, suspended/expelled from school)	Taught about AIDS/HIV in school
Support for efficacy		Parents help youth to succeed in school; youth encouraged to do well (parents and teachers)	Youth perceives lots of chances to engage in class discussions and activities; teachers praise youth when they work hard and do well	
Opportunities for skill building	Proportion of youth required to perform community service; capacity of community-sponsored youth programs (centers, sports, etc.); students with Individual Education Plans; percent of students in gifted/talented	Youth given useful roles within community	Opportunities for prosocial involvement in community (sports, scouting, 4-H, service clubs); youth perceives many opportunities for involvement in school sports, clubs, etc.	
Integration of family, schools, and community	Proportion of parents who come to parent-teacher conferences	Whether parents come to school meetings/events	School lets parents know when youth performs well	

low accepted research minimums. However, the primary goal of the Search Institute in developing and promoting the use of this survey was to inform social action by providing communities with a common language, a unified and complete vision of positive youth development, and the means to identify and strengthen the developmental processes in their community. Science played and continues to play an important role in the development of this instrument, but there is a willingness to go beyond the science when it serves an important practical purpose.

The use of the assets framework to guide instrument construction has resulted in a very comprehensive survey that includes measures in every domain of our own youth development framework and multiple measures in most domains (see Table 8-1). It is the most well-rounded of the data sources included in this review. There are, however, no cognitive measures per se. Instead there are measures of academic motivation, school engagement, and related activities like time doing homework. Measures of psychological and emotional development include a host of measures related to moral character, as well as both positive and negative measures of mental health and measures of adolescents' capacities to take responsibility for their actions, plan ahead, and make their own choices. The survey is particularly strong in social development measures, including participation in sports, clubs, music, art, and theater activities both in and out of school; volunteering in the community; capacity for empathy and sensitivity; friendship skills; and respect for cultural diversity. Physical health measures include participation in sports activities, whether the student "takes care of their body," sexual activity, and whether the youth has been a victim of violence. The list of negative outcomes and behaviors is broad and includes questions about drug use (including alcohol and cigarettes), violence, drunk driving, gambling, and eating disorders.

The coverage in the social setting domains is nearly as impressive. Measures of structure include the presence of clear rules and monitoring of the youth's activities in the family, the school, and the neighborhood. Supportive relationships are explored in the family, with adults outside the family, in the school, and in the community. Measures of the opportunity to belong are weaker and rely only on whether the youth care about their school. Measures of social norms focus on the presence of positive role models among parents, friends, and other adults. Questions on safety focus on whether the youth feels safe at home, in school, and in the neighborhood. Support for efficacy and mattering questions focus on levels of encouragement and help to do well in school and on whether the youth feel that they are given useful roles in the community. There are questions on skill building per se, and information in the final domain (integration of family, school, and community) is limited to whether parents come to meetings or events at school.

Student Survey of Risk and Protective Factors, and Prevalence of Alcohol, Tobacco, and Other Drug Use

The Student Survey of Risk and Protective Factors, and Prevalence of Alcohol, Tobacco, and Other Drug Use (SSRP), developed by the Social Development Research Group at the University of Washington, focuses on the risk and protective factors influencing drug use, violence, and misbehavior in the lives of youth ages 12 to 18. The survey was specifically designed to inform the development of preventive interventions to reduce youth risk behaviors in schools and communities and to support outcome evaluations of such interventions (Pollard et al., 1999). Development was funded by the Center for Substance Abuse Prevention of the Substance Abuse and Mental Health Services Administration, U.S. Department of Health and Human Services. The survey is now being fielded with representative statewide samples in six states: Kansas, Maine, Oregon, South Carolina, Utah, and Washington.

Risk and protective factors were included in the survey only when they had been found to predict future drug use and criminal or delinquent behaviors in at least two longitudinal studies in the research literature. The final instrument resulted from a rigorous development process that included cognitive pretesting, and pilot tests, as well as validation of risk and protective factors based on statewide samples of 6th, 8th, and 11th grade students in Oregon. Risk and protective factors are measured using multi-item scales. All scales exhibit high reliability with alphas of .65 or higher, with most in the high .7 and .8 ranges. The factors have good predictive validity in their relation with the problem behaviors in the survey (Pollard et al., 1999a; Arthur et al., undated).

The survey's coverage of the domains in our youth development framework is broad in the sense that there is at least one measure in every outcome and social setting domain except one, physical health. However, a closer look reveals that the instrument is considerably more focused on negative outcomes than the PSL-AB. While the negative outcomes and behaviors domain is richly detailed, measures in the other outcome domains are a bit thin and tend to be defined in relation to risk behaviors. In the psychological and emotional development domain, for example, measures of moral character focus on attitudes toward negative behaviors and activities, and the measures of psychological health are limited to depression. One of the two social development measures asks about peer resistance skills against drinking.

The indicators of social settings are considerably more well rounded and positive, although even here measures in the social norms domain focus totally on risk behaviors on the part of friends and family, and attitudes about risk behaviors. The survey contains multiple positive measures for structure, supportive relationships, support for efficacy and mattering, and opportunities for skill building. There is overlap between the PSL-AB and the SSRP constructs in these domains, although each contains important constructs that are not present in the other. In the SSRP, for example, there are several constructs related to the youth's role in decision making in the family and the school.

Youth Risk Behavior Survey

The Youth Risk Behavior Survey (YRBS), developed by U.S. Centers for Disease Control and Prevention (CDC), was fielded in 42 states and 16 major metropolitan areas in 1999.[3] A national survey was also fielded. It is a school-based, self-report survey of students in grades 9 through 12. Several states, including Alaska, Montana, Nevada, Oregon, Utah, and Vermont, have in some years provided the additional funds needed to generate samples for all school districts in the state that wanted to participate. One of the great advantages to communities who field this survey, in addition to the intrinsic value of the data, is the availability of comparable estimates for their state as a whole, as well as for the nation. A significant limitation is that it does not provide information on out-of-school youth, a population of great interest to many community programs.

The survey was first conducted in 1990 and has been administered every two years since 1991. It was designed by national experts in the field of adolescent health, with substantial input from representatives from all 50 state and 16 metropolitan-area education agencies. A detailed rationale, grounded in adolescent health research literature, was developed for all of the measures included in the survey instrument.[4]

---

[3]2001 Youth Risk Behavior Survey: Item Rationale for the 2001 Questionnaire. <www.cdc.gov/nccdphp/dash/yrbs/2001rationale.htm>

[4]To download a copy of the 1999 report, go to <http://www.cdc.gov/nccdphp/dash/yrbs/index.htm>

The survey is composed entirely of single-item measures; there are no multi-item scales. States may add their own questions to the survey and may also choose not to field questions that they find problematic. It is not uncommon for states to omit certain sex-related questions, for example.

The CDC works with participating state and local education agencies, which administer the survey, to produce survey samples that are representative of their youth in-school populations. In 1999, 22 of the 42 participating states fielded representative samples. CDC staff receive raw data from participating agencies, process the data, and provide estimates back to the states. In addition, summary results that include estimates for participating states and metropolitan areas are published by the CDC (Centers for Disease Control and Prevention, 2000c).

In comparison with the other surveys in Table 8-1, this survey focuses rather narrowly on health-related conditions and behaviors. There are, for example, no questions related to cognitive or social development and only four questions refer to the social setting in which youth develop (including one focused on television watching). However, the questions in the domains of physical development and safety and negative outcomes and behaviors are very rich, covering important issues not touched on in the other surveys. Questions unique to the YRBS include: height and weight (from which one can develop an obesity measure); forced intercourse; pregnancy; the co-occurrence of drug use and intercourse; detailed nutrition information; use of sunscreen or sunblock at SPF15 or higher; timing of last routine physical exam; incidence of physical fighting with one's boyfriend or girlfriend; and incidence of vomiting or taking laxatives to prevent weight gain. In addition, the questions about physical exercise and sexual activity are more detailed than in the other surveys.

Topic-Specific Survey Instruments

In addition to the more general-purpose surveys just discussed, there are many more narrowly focused instruments that have been developed specifically for youth program monitoring and evaluation purposes. These instruments focus on individual constructs and commonly go into more depth on a topic than the more general surveys. They are most useful to community programs for youth trying to affect a particular outcome, like youth conflict resolution skills or teen pregnancy.

An effort led by the U.S. Department of Agriculture's Cooperative

Extension Service professionals working with the Children, Youth, and Families At-Risk Initiative and Evaluation Collaboration Project has resulted in the cataloguing of well over 100 such measurement instruments, with separate work groups focusing on outcomes for children, youth, the family, and the community. This information was created for use by those engaged in USDA-supported State Strengthening community projects, a major community development program.

As part of this project, the Youth National Outcome Work Group identified multiple available instruments for the following outcome areas:

- Risk behaviors: risk-taking, substance abuse, sexual activity, academic risk, delinquency, and violence.
- Social competencies: social competence, relationships, conflict resolution, decision making, social responsibility, communication, goal setting, problem solving, social and environmental navigation, and valuing diversity.

The workgroup produced a searchable database, available on-line,[5] which includes the following information for each instrument: name, author, basic description, scales and subscales in the instrument, psychometric information (reliability and validity), notable advantages and disadvantages, cost, contact information, and references. A separate work group focused on the family is producing a similar set of reviews for measures related to parent and family well-being. Some of the measures they have collected are directly applicable to the families of adolescents. These work groups are now disbanded, but their work continues to be a valuable resource.

National Survey Instruments

National surveys that focus on aspects of youth development have a number of strengths that make them good potential sources of measures that may be appropriated for use at the local level. First, these surveys are all well designed by some of the nation's top researchers. Second, they offer the possibility of a national benchmark against which localities can compare their own status. Third, and perhaps most important,

---

[5]The web site is located at <http://ag.arizona.edu/fcr/fs/nowg/index.html>/.

three of the national surveys we reviewed include parent and teacher as well as youth interviews. While parent interviews may be too expensive to undertake for community-wide surveys (in-school youth surveys are comparatively much less expensive), they may be appropriate at the program level, particularly if parents are actively involved in the youth program. Both parent and teacher surveys offer points of view that are different from those offered by youth, which can provide important additional information for those engaged in the development of youth policy and programs at the community level.

In addition, all of these surveys are longitudinal, meaning they collect information on the same youth at multiple points in time.[6] This means that the youth development measures in these surveys can be rigorously assessed in terms of their predictive validity for future development, including the transition to adulthood.

Tables 8-2 and 8-3 list the measures and constructs, organized according to the domains in our youth development framework, for the following major national youth surveys:[7]

- National Education Longitudinal Survey of Youth (NELS)
- National Longitudinal Survey of Adolescent Health (Add Health)
- National Longitudinal Survey of Youth, 1997 Cohort (NLSY97); and
- Monitoring the Future (MTF).

Overall, these surveys have taken a holistic approach, offering questions in most of the 14 domains in our youth development framework. While youth outcome measures are based almost exclusively on youth reports across all surveys, measures of social setting often include responses from parents, teachers, and schools. The NELS and Add Health surveys are particularly strong in this regard, the NELS gathering information in every social setting domain from someone other than, or in

---

[6] Monitoring the Future is primarily a cross-sectional survey, but a longitudinal sample has also been followed over time (see Purpose and Design, Monitoring the Future Survey, at <http://monitoringthefuture.org/purpose.html>)

[7] For additional information on NELS88, visit <http://www.nces.ed.gov/surveys/nels88>
For additional information on Add Health, visit <http://www.cpc.unc.edu/addhealth>
For additional information on NLSY97, visit <http://www.bls.gov/nlsy97.htm>
For additional information on MTF, visit <http://www.monitoringthefuture.org>

addition to, the youth as well as measures of cognitive skills in several subject areas. These multiple sources offer richer data for understanding social settings, providing measures of settings that are not directly affected by the well-being of the youth who inhabit those settings.

Gaining Access to Data

In order for community youth development efforts to take advantage of social indicators, they need ready access to the data. For many years, it was common for administrative data collected by one agency to stay within that agency, even though other government agencies and local private organizations could greatly benefit by using it. This is still true in many communities, although the situation has improved substantially over the past decade due to advances in computerization, the rise of the Internet, an increase in comprehensive statewide and community-wide planning efforts, such as the Oregon Benchmarks and Vermont's Framework for Collaboration, and the rise of private social indicator-focused projects such as the Annie E. Casey Foundation's Kids Count effort (Brown and Corbett, forthcoming; Kingsley, 1998).

It is increasingly common for agencies to make their indicator data available to all through regular publications and on-line searchable databases. There has also been an increase in the development of data warehouses, through which indicator data from many sources are made accessible to the public. A prime example of this sort of effort at the community level is the Cleveland Area Network for Data and Organizing (CAN DO). Data from the decennial census, vital statistics, crime, child welfare, and other sources are made available in an on-line database that users can access and display in tables or maps for neighborhoods throughout Cleveland, Ohio, and the surrounding suburban municipalities. The data are stored in a geographic information system (GIS), which allows users to create complex social profiles of local neighborhoods and to map need in relation to available resources (e.g., the location of licensed child care programs in relation to families with young children). The intended consumers of these data include nonprofit, community-based organizations and government agencies that can use them to aid in planning, as well as academics, students, and the public. CAN DO is a member of the National Neighborhood Indicators Project, whose members include organizations in a dozen cities across the country similarly engaged in the development of neighborhood information systems (Kingsley, 1996).

TABLE 8-2 National Youth Surveys: Youth Development Outcomes

Youth Outcomes	National Educational Longitudinal Survey (NELS)	National Longitudinal Survey of Adolescent Health (Add Health)	National Longitudunal Survey of Youth, 1997 Cohort (NLSY97)	Monitoring the Future (MTF)
Cognitive development	Academic achievement; standardized test scores; school engagement	Academic achievement; standardized test scores; good decision making	Academic achievement; standardized test scores	Academic achievement; school engagement; standardized test scores
Psychological development	Self-worth; locus of control; self-efficacy; religiosity; moral character	Mental health; self-worth; moral character; self-efficacy; religiosity; positive outlook	Optimism; positive outlook; mental health	Religiosity; self-worth
Emotional development	N/A	Emotion self-regulation; emotional coping skills	Emotion self-regulation	Emotion knowledge
Social development	Connectedness (peers, parents; siblings); commitment to prosocial institutions (service); civic engagement	Commitment to conventional institutions; connectedness (parents, peers); connectedness to neighborhood; life skills	Connectedness (parents, peers); work involvement	Connectedness to peers; civic engagement; multicultural caring/ understanding

Physical development	N/A	Sexual behaviors; physical activity; physical health; sleep habits; physical difficulties; health care use; diet/nutrition; healthy habits (helmet and seatbelt use, sun exposure, safe sex); healthy habits knowledge (nutrition; safety; sex); pregnancy	Physical activity; nutrition/ diet; health knowledge; has physical/emotional condition; trouble sleeping	Physical activity; sleep; nutrition; seatbelt wearing
Negative outcomes/ behavior	Cigarette/drug/alcohol use; skipping/late for/cut/s uspended from school; fighting; illegal activities/ arrested; gang involvement; performs below ability (emotionally, cognitively, socially); teen parent	Drunk driving; school suspension; sexual victimization; sexually transmitted diseases; unsafe sex; cigarette/ alcohol/drug use; fighting; illegal activity/arrested; violent weapon possession; suicidal behavior; unsafe adventurous activities	Sexual activity; cigarette/ alcohol/drug use; illegal activities/arrested	Fighting; stealing; trespassing; property damage; arrest; anger; drugs/alcohol/cigarette use; carrying/using weapons; drunk driving
Other	Time usage		Time usage	

TABLE 8-3 National Youth Surveys: Features of Social Settings Affecting Youth Development

Features of Settings	National Educational Longitudinal Survey** (NELS)	National Longitudinal Survey of Adolescent Health (Add Health)	National Longitudinal Survey of Youth, 1997 Cohort (NLSY97)	Monitoring the Future (MTF)[a]
Structure	Clear parental rules; parental monitoring; parental encouragement (P+Y for all)	Clear rules (Y); communication between environments (P); monitoring (P)	Parent: monitoring (Y); clear/fair rules (Y+P); teacher: clear/fair rules	Parent: clear/fair rules; monitoring; School: clear/fair rules
Supportive relationships	Positive parent-child interaction/relationships; positive child-other adult interaction; parental/other-adult encouragement (P+Y for all)	Positive parent-child interaction/relationship; closeness of parent-child relationship (P+Y for all)	Positive parent-child interaction/relationship; emotional support; parental encouragement (Y for all)	Positive parent-child interaction/relationship
Belonging	Gang membership (Y); opportunity for extra-curricular participation (Y+S); parental community involvement (Y+P)	Feel part of group; feel valued by others; opportunity for extra-curricular participation; opportunity for involvement with religious institution (Y for all)	Opportunity for extra-curricular participation; parental involvement in school/community (Y for all)	Civic involvement; opportunity for extracurricular participation; feeling a part of a group
Social norms	School policies (S); peer norms (positive and negative) (Y)	Peer norms (positive and negative); neighbor intervening (Y for all)	Peer norms (positive and negative) (Y for all)	Peer norms (positive and negative)

Physical and psychological safety	Perceptions of physical safety at school (Y +T)	Perceptions of physical safety; victimized; violence in home/school; presence of gun/alcohol/drugs in home (Y for all)	Perceptions of physical safety in neighborhood/school (Y)	Victimized
Support for efficacy	High parental/other-adults'/peer expectations (Y+P); positive youth programs (Y); youth participates in rule making (Y+P)	High parental expectations; youth participates in rule making (Y for all)	Positive youth programs (Y)	High parental expectations
Opportunities for positive development/skill building	Availability of positive extracurricular activities and sports teams (S); learning tools in the home (P)	Access to health services; availability of positive extracurricular activities (Y for all)	Learning tools in the home; availability of positive extracurricular activities (Y for all)	Availability of civic opportunities and positive extracurricular opportunities
Integration of family, school, and community	Parental involvement in community/school; parent knowledge of child's friends and friends' parents; English language competence (child and parent) (P+Y for all); communication between environments	Parent knowledge of child's friends and friends' parents (P)	Parental involvement in school/community (P); communication between environments (Y)	N/A

Note: Respondents are as follows: Y = Youth; P = Parent, T = Teacher, S = School

[a] Youth was respondent for all questions.

For social survey data for youth development, the access issues are a little different. Several states have provided funding and support to field community-level surveys that focus on youth. Oregon, Vermont, and several other states have done this in the past with the YRBS. Colorado and Vermont have done the same with the PSL-AB. The state of Minnesota fields its own Minnesota Student Survey every three years, asking questions on a voluntary basis to all public school youth in grades 6, 9, and 12. In addition, many individual communities have contracted with the Search Institute to field the PSL-AB, using the results for comprehensive youth development planning.

Most communities, however, do not have access to the unique and important information that can only be gathered using such surveys as the ones reviewed above. The costs of fielding such surveys are themselves a barrier, although clearly many communities have made the decision that the information gained is worth the expense. In 2000 the PSL-AB, for example, could be fielded for between $1.65 and $2.00 per youth, with additional charges of several hundred dollars each for the production of reports (Search Institute, 2000).

For individual community programs for youth seeking to use social indicator data to monitor the activities and the success of their own program, the items in these surveys may be too general. For many purposes, such programs need to monitor elements that are specific to their program, looking at issues of process and implementation as well as outcomes. For them, a more tailored approach is needed, one that usually requires professional technical assistance.

ASSESSING PROGRAM IMPLEMENTATION AND OPERATION

When a program has just been launched, program managers, staff, participating youth and their parents, funders, and other stakeholders need information on whether it has been implemented according to design and, if not, how services and operations differ from those envisioned in the program's underlying model. When a program has moved past implementation into the routine operating stage, information to determine whether it has continued to operate according to design and at the desired level of quality and efficiency will be similarly useful. Also useful will be data on total program costs and average cost per youth served.

Until enough time has passed to allow collection of any but the most short-term outcome indicators, all that stakeholders have for assessing program progress and the possible need for change is information on implementation, operation, and costs. Such information can be used to produce process evaluations and cost studies and to provide performance monitoring. Findings from these analyses can stimulate communication about program goals, progress, obstacles, and results among program managers, staff, participants, funders, and others.

The "developmental quality" of a youth program may be defined as the extent to which it provides a social setting and a set of activities that should facilitate positive youth development. Developmental quality is the key characteristic that a program can directly control via its internal activities. It must attend to the developmental quality of youth experiences, regardless of the specific activities (e.g., mentoring, peer tutoring, theater productions, team sports) it sponsors. Based on regular assessments of developmental quality, a program can engage in dynamic reflective practice to fine-tune its service delivery and management practices. If so indicated, it can take corrective steps to align activities with the model on which the program is premised. To produce useful process evaluations, performance monitoring, and self-assessment, youth development programs therefore need valid, reliable indicators of the developmental quality of the experiences they provide.

Indicators of developmental quality are important for a second reason. Because of their small size, informal nature, and limited resources, many youth development programs will never undergo a rigorous impact evaluation using control or comparison groups, nor will they obtain high-quality data on developmental or long-term outcomes of the youth they serve. For such programs, information about long-term outcomes over which they may exert influence but cannot directly or fully control (e.g., school completion, good character, civic involvement) does not provide a good standard for program accountability. Rather, indicators of the developmental quality of the program necessarily provide the key information for judging whether it is likely to have positive effects on youth development. If the program's model is valid and data on the developmental quality of its activities indicate that it provides a setting and a set of activities that facilitate positive youth development, one may reasonably conclude that the program contributes to positive youth development.

That is, when good impact data are not going to be available, indicators of the developmental quality of a program's activities provide a fair mechanism for holding it accountable for what it can best control. This is an important use of such indicators besides the short-term feedback they can provide about program operation. Hence, we focus discussion on indicators of developmental quality because of their essential and unique importance for youth development programs.

Although many community programs for youth recognize the value of data on developmental quality, most lack the staffing, knowledge, and other capacity to measure it. Even if programs had wanted to do so, until recently they would have searched in vain for good measurement tools applicable to youth development programs. The development of such tools has been a major challenge to the field. As a more common understanding of how community programs for youth need to be structured to promote positive development has emerged, there have been notable advances in meeting this challenge.

The work of Public/Private Ventures (P/PV), in conjunction with other partners in the youth development community, exemplifies recent progress in developing indicators of developmental quality for any youth activity, regardless of its specific goals. Building on Gambone and Arbreton (1997), P/PV has developed a sophisticated set of forms and scales to assess seven dimensions of developmental quality, each with subcategories. They are adult-youth relations, peer support, quality of staff presentation, behavior management, opportunities for decision making and leadership, youth engagement in the activity, and the quality of the space or location. These seven dimensions encompass the eight factors that facilitate youth development identified in this report.

Observers use the instrument first to record information on an activity, focusing on observations of positive and negative behaviors for each subcategory. They then use the observations to evaluate each dimension of the activity's quality. The instrument seeks both quantitative and qualitative observations and judgments. After using it to record three independent observations and assessments of the activity, observers prepare an overall assessment and recommendations for improvement. To foster uniform implementation of the evaluation instrument, observers receive a manual that provides detailed instructions on how to observe and assess activities and fill out the forms. The instrument does not produce a summary measure of an activity's overall developmental quality. Rather, it yields a rich picture of the degree of success a program is achieving along multiple dimensions that contribute to developmental quality.

Independent observers have used the instrument to evaluate activities in the San Francisco Beacons Program and will use it to evaluate Extended Service Schools, supported by the DeWitt Wallace Reader's Digest Fund. In the future, executive directors and other supervisors could use it to evaluate their organization's activities. If supervisors decide to share the evaluation forms with their activities' leaders and tell them that the criteria on the forms are what they were going to be evaluated on, the forms could help leaders see that an activity can mean much more to youth than just an opportunity to do whatever its specific goal happens to be—making pottery, playing basketball, learning computer skills, etc. Efforts are under way to more fully automate data collection and processing via hand-held computers. Although still a work in progress, this instrument represents cutting-edge practice.

Even if a program scores high on factors that promote developmental quality, it needs to know whether each participating youth experiences meaningful involvement with its positive development environment. Thus, programs also need indicators of participation over time by individual youth to measure the "dosage" of developmental factors. Yet the best that most programs currently do is collect daily attendance information.

Youth, of course, may simultaneously attend more than one program, switch programs over time, or mix program participation with involvement in other activities (e.g., extracurricular school activities, music lessons, religious training) that may also contribute to positive development. High-quality dosage data therefore cannot be based entirely on individual agency records but require tracking individual youth across programs and other activities.

The Community Network for Youth Development (CNYD), a local intermediary organization based in San Francisco, has advanced the use of data for reflective practice through its Youth Development Outcomes Project. CNYD grounds its work with agencies in a coherent, research-based youth development framework developed in conjunction with the Community Action for Youth Project (CAYP). CNYD brings together funders and youth-serving agencies to build consensus and agency capacity around issues of assessment, accountability, and best practice to promote healthy youth development.

The outcomes project led to the creation of two surveys—one for junior high and high school youth, the other for elementary school-children—that provide concrete measures of young people's program experiences. The questions seek to capture the extent to which participants experience the supports and opportunities that facilitate healthy youth development. The dimensions of developmental quality tapped in this survey overlap with those in the P/PV instrument but are not identical. The survey also gathers information on the duration and intensity of a youth's participation in the program. Findings that revealed program shortcomings helped engage funders and agencies in discussions of why programs were falling short in some areas and how resources might be more effectively deployed.

A complementary self-assessment form completed by agency staff examines organizational practices in areas viewed as critical to supporting a program's developmental quality. These include creating safe, reliable, and accessible activities and spaces; providing a range of diverse, interesting skill-building activities; ensuring continuity and consistency of care; high, clear and fair standards; and several others.

Taken together, the participant and agency instruments provide comprehensive data to help organizations create focused strategies for improving the developmental quality of their programs, given their resource constraints. If used skillfully in a process of quality improvement, such data can raise the cost-effectiveness of an agency's management and programming activities. The general capacity building process and the specific instruments show potential for replication, and the youth survey may be adapted for publication on the web.

The CNYD and P/PV approaches to assessing developmental quality share a common theoretical framework. They overlap in the constructs of developmental quality they examine and how they operationalize those constructs. But there is an important difference between the two. P/PV focuses on assessing the practices of specific activities (e.g., making pottery) in terms of their developmental quality, whereas CNYD aims at assessing how well the overall organization fosters positive youth development via specific activities as well as its general organizational environment. Both have value.

Evidence in Roth (2000) suggests that youth-serving organizations are likely to welcome assistance for building their capacity to assess the developmental quality of their programs and act on those assessments. Roth surveyed executive directors of youth-serving organizations about the goals and characteristics of their programs. Many of the program goals reported by directors match up well with the personal and social assets of positive youth development discussed in this report. She also found that many program characteristics reported by directors are closely related to our list of features of positive developmental settings.

Qualitative Data for Community Programs for Youth

Thus far this chapter has focused on quantitative social indicators and measures of program implementation, operation, and impact. This focus reflects the fact that most resources for data collection and program evaluation have been channeled in quantitative directions. Like experimental evaluation methods, quantitative data are often viewed as more objective, easier to understand, and more highly valued by funders and policy makers than qualitative data.

Nonetheless, as has been suggested in the last few chapters, qualitative data can also play important roles in the design, implementation, and evaluation of community programs for youth and aid in the understanding of the process of positive youth development. Methods to generate qualitative data on programs and the social and cultural context in which they operate include direct observation; open-ended interviews with key informants, staff, and participants; focus groups; ethnographic studies; the use of diaries kept by informants; and detailed case studies.

Correctly understood, qualitative data neither are inferior to nor substitute for quantitative data (Lin, 2000). Rather, by trading breadth for depth, qualitative data can complement statistical evidence in several respects (Sherwood and Doolittle, 2000). Data from field research can play an important role in planning the specific way services are provided. For example, qualitative research on the determinants of successful mentoring relationships is fairly consistent about what practices make for effective mentoring (Sipe, 1996). Such findings can be translated into guidelines for coaching and supervising mentors on an ongoing basis. Identifying better mentoring styles would be very difficult with standard quantitative survey methods. Focus groups can be used to help design services that more fully respond to the realities of the intended clients' lived experiences and motivations. Hence, such services are more likely to be used (see Furstenberg et al., 1992 as an example of this use of focus group data; see Branch et al., 1998 as an example in the youth program area).

Detailed interviews and observations of line staff and participants are essential to determine if actual program operations are, in fact, those intended by the program planners. Such information allows evaluators to decide whether the quality of program services was sufficient to produce a fair test of whether the services made a difference. It can offer insights about the reasonableness of the underlying model and about problems likely to arise during implementation and ongoing operation.

These insights would also provide lessons for replication. For example, Plain Talk, a community program aimed at improving adolescent knowledge of sexuality and use of methods to prevent pregnancy and sexually transmitted diseases, took a long time to implement. Field research showed that community lay trainers needed more time than initially envisioned to become sufficiently comfortable with sexuality issues before they were ready to engage other members of the community (Walker and Kotloff, 2000).

The P/PV instruments discussed earlier collect both qualitative and quantitative information for assessing the developmental quality of youth activities. The quantitative data provide a general view of which aspects of an activity are running satisfactorily and which may need improvement or intervention by senior management. But only the qualitative data can provide information on the specific behaviors of staff and youth and the details of daily activities that would allow the program managers to take concrete steps to improve operations.

Qualitative data may yield more complete, more nuanced, and context-specific understandings of the nature of correlations and causal relationships in the process of youth development that have been uncovered by quantitative data (e.g., by using some of the major datasets discussed in this chapter). Similarly, qualitative data can help explain subtle causal mechanisms through which a program works (or fails to work)—the "how," whereas quantitative analysis typically shows only "how much" the program affected an outcome of interest. Such data can play a key role in formal, extensive impact studies if gathered early in the project and used to develop hypotheses that are investigated further through subsequent quantitative work. If time permits, additional qualitative research can then elucidate the findings from the quantitative hypothesis testing and suggest yet newer hypotheses—and so on through an iterative process that may yield much richer understanding than reliance on only one kind of data. Even community programs for youth that do not undergo rigorous impact evaluation can supplement small-scale quantitative assessment of program quality with data from focus groups, individual interviews, and careful observation of program operations. The latter can aid in interpreting quantitative findings as well as suggest new questions for future quantitative assessment.

Qualitative data can allow exploration of how program services are understood and experienced both by participating youth and by those who choose not to participate. Neighborhood youth may have some idea of what motivates them, what they found stimulating in a program, what drew them to it, why they were prepared to give it time over a period of months or perhaps years, and whether they think that participating in it affected them in particular ways. Such data can also help program operators, funders, and policy makers understand what parents care about in programs their children may attend. They can clarify various stakeholders' expectations for a program and what would constitute success in their eyes.

Program research based on qualitative data has important limitations as well. Samples are often small and not necessarily representative, even if drawn from program participants. Verifying conclusions from qualitative data is difficult. So is generalizability. Qualitative research is costly to do well. Telling stories, however interesting or compelling they may be, is not a substitute for rigorous analysis of qualitative data. Despite these and other limitations (Lin, 2000), qualitative data can play important roles in the design and analysis of community programs for youth.

National Intermediary Organizations

A number of national groups have become important in assisting community programs to enhance their capacity to collect and use data in their design, planning, and evaluation efforts. A number of these are focused specifically on youth development programs. These groups are playing an increasingly important role in the education of youth program staff around youth development concepts, in organizing available data-related materials for use by such groups, and in consulting with individual programs to develop data collection and analysis strategies to support planning and reflective practice. They are providing essential information and services to the youth program community.

- The Youth National Outcome Work Groups, mentioned earlier, provides more than detailed information on measures relevant for youth development. They support work groups in the areas of child, youth, family, and community development. In addition to information on measures, they provide easy to understand primers for each domain of well-being covered by the work group and an extensive bibliography for those who are interested learning more about a particular domain.[8]

---

[8]For additional information, visit <http://ag.arizona.edu/fcr/fs/nowg/ythindexintro.html>

- National Youth Development Information Center is a web-based information center set up by the National Collaboration for Youth to provide comprehensive practice-related information to youth— serving organizations throughout the country at low or no cost. The site includes a section on outcome measures and program evaluation, which lists major guides on youth outcome measures and evaluation approaches. There is also a section that provides youth-related statistics and collections of statistical data.[9]

- The Youth Development Mobilization Initiative, Center for Youth Development and Policy Research, Academy for Educational Development has a goal to ensure long-term institutional support for youth development by creating a communication network between policy makers and practitioners at the local level. It is currently developing a project, Youth Development/Community Indicators: On the Plus Side, which seeks to maximize the development of community-level social indicators using existing administrative and related data resources to support positive youth development planning and policy. It intends to work with several localities (including their current partners in Albuquerque, New Mexico, Hampton, Massachusetts, and Milwaukee, Wisconsin), as well as a national advisory board of youth development experts in this effort, to develop best practices that can be followed by other communities.[10]

- The Aspen Roundtable on Comprehensive Community Initiatives is comprised of 33, substantive experts, policy officials, and program heads who examine and discuss issues surrounding the strengthening of Comprehensive Community Initiatives. The roundtable's web site features a catalogue of measurement instruments related to community research. This feature, called Measures for Community Research, is one of the first resources of its kind and will serve as a clearinghouse for the collection and distribution of instruments and other tools related to key community-level outcomes. This resource includes a separate section on youth-related measures.[11]

- National Neighborhood Indicators Project is working with local institutions in a dozen cities to develop neighborhood-level indi-

---

[9]For additional information, visit <http://www.nydic.org.>
[10]For additional information, visit <http://www.aed.org/us/cyd/ydmobilization.html>
[11]For additional information, visit <http://www.aspenroundtable.org>

cator data systems that can be used to support a variety of development activities throughout the community. Partners include groups in the cities of Atlanta, Baltimore, Boston, Chicago, Cleveland, Denver, Indianapolis, Miami, Milwaukee, Oakland, Philadelphia, Providence, and Washington, DC. In addition to facilitating a variety of peer support activities, the project is developing a National Neighborhood Data System, which will provide easily accessible data at the census tract or zip code level for major metropolitan areas, as well as a series of handbooks and other tools on the use of information in community capacity building.[12]

SUMMARY

Community programs for youth benefit from ready access to high-quality data that allows them to assess and monitor the well-being of youth in their community, the well-being of youth they directly serve, and the elements of their programs that are intended to benefit those youth. Programs may use social indicator data for needs assessments, service targeting, goals tracking, program accountability, and in support of reflective practice to improve program and policy effectiveness over time. They also benefit from information and training to help them use these data tools wisely and effectively. In this chapter we have reviewed surveys and other measurement instruments, the data generated from these tools, and related technical assistance resources that can be used by youth development programs; we were pleasantly surprised to find a relatively rich set of tools and information.

Every community already has a great deal of data collected through its social programs and educational systems, its vital statistics and health surveillance systems, and the decennial census. Some communities have been more active than others in developing these data resources to guide policy and program development for children and youth. A systematic review of the potential of these data sources to yield useful indicators could provide a guide for communities seeking to maximize the use of their own data resources at a reasonable cost.[13]

Even when exploited to their full potential, administrative, vital statistics, and related data sources can cover only limited geographic areas

---

[12]For additional information, visit <http://www.urban.org/nnip>

[13] The Center for Youth Development, through its proposed On the Plus Side initiative, intends to produce such a review.

and only some components of a youth development framework. Adding local survey data in diverse communities, as has been done in a number of states and individual communities, can help create a more complete picture.

A number of states and many individual communities have fielded youth surveys at the local level. Steps should be taken to expand opportunities so that more communities can benefit from such data. For example, the Centers for Disease Control and Prevention, which sponsors the Youth Risk Behavior Surveillance survey, could expand its use in additional metropolitan areas (it is currently fielded in 16 major metropolitan areas) and work with interested states to expand its use down to the school district level. Furthermore, in order to make it a more useful tool for positive youth development, the Centers for Disease Control and Prevention could work to develop optional modules that focus on the domains of development and social settings in which it is currently weak.

Research on many aspects of positive youth development is still in its early stages, with the result that many of the indicators used to represent youth development outcomes in existing surveys are not well tested. Areas in need of particular attention include life skills, social, emotional, and psychological development, as well as most of the domains of developmental settings. Most of the psychometric work that has been done on indicators used in the two most complete community surveys on youth development (the Profiles of Student Life: Attitudes and Behaviors and the Student Survey of Risk and Protective Factors, and Prevalence of Alcohol, Tobacco, and Other Drug Use) are based on cross-sectional data and, in the case of the PSL-AB, on nonrepresentative samples. Longitudinal surveys allow one to explore a crucial aspect of social indicators, namely their relationship to future development as one moves from adolescence into adulthood. The Values in Action initiative, led by psychologists Martin Seligman and Christopher Peterson, is attempting a rigorous classification of strengths and virtues that will include definitions, existing research and available measures, promotional and inhibiting factors, and other valuable information that should provide a useful information base to guide future research and measurement development in this area.

There is evidence that youth-serving organizations have an interest in building their capacity to assess the developmental quality of their programs. To produce useful process evaluations, performance monitoring, and self-assessment, however, community programs for youth need valid, reliable indicators of the developmental quality of the experiences they provide. The evaluation research community, working with practitioners, needs to build on recent progress made in improving the quality and scope of these indicators. Research is needed to determine whether appropriate indicators vary depending on the characteristics of the specific youth population served by a program. As understanding of the determinants of positive youth development improves, the indicators should be periodically revisited and, if necessary, revised. To this end, methods for collecting information on individual youth participation in one or more community programs also require development and implementation. At a minimum, youth-serving organizations should track individuals' attendance and their involvement in specific activities. Data on individuals' participation across programs and in informal activities that affect developmental assets can be gathered and incorporated into basic and evaluation research.

Geographic information system databases can greatly enhance the utility of social indicator data for community programs for youth by allowing users to draw on multiple data sources to pinpoint areas of need at the neighborhood level. This is particularly important to community programs for youth, which often serve particular neighborhoods within the larger community. An increasing number of communities are putting their data into GIS systems, and some, like those participating in the National Neighborhood Indicators Project, are making them available to all community organizations. Funding to optimize systems in communities with functioning GIS systems will support the needs of local community programs for youth by increasing the relevant data available through the system and the ease with which it can be accessed.

Many community programs also lack staff knowledge and the funds to take full advantage of social indicators as tools to aid in planning, monitoring, assessing, and improving program activities. Individual programs and communities would benefit from opportunities to increase their capacity to collect and use social indicator data. Greater access to professional knowledge and advice on data and measurement issues, via the Internet and through individual consultation, will allow community programs for youth to be more effective and efficient as they design their own monitoring and evaluation strategies. This will require support from funders to develop the internal expertise and external consultants needed. National and local intermediaries, like the Center for Youth Development, and state organizations, like the Indiana Youth Institute, also provide invaluable information, support, and professional advice to state and local youth programs. Efforts to move to Internet-based systems for documenting and disseminating successful assessment tools and protocols, administering assessment instruments, inputting the responses, and analyzing the data would also simplify, streamline, and lower the costs of collecting and inputting program data and also deserve support.

PART IV

The Intersection of Practice, Policy, and Research

Public interest in and funding for youth activities during nonschool hours increased dramatically during the second half of the 1990s. Concerns about children's performance on standardized tests, worries over supervision with increasing numbers of mothers working outside the home, and the sudden emergence of fiscal surpluses combined to create enthusiastic bipartisan support for after-school programs (National Research Council and Institute of Medicine, 2000a).

There are a number of policy and system-level supports and barriers that affect the future direction, growth, and funding of community programs for youth. This section highlights these supports and barriers and makes recommendations for future policy, practice, and research. Funding is probably the most critical issue. But political support, public interest, and professional networks are also critical to sustain interest and promote the growth of these programs.

As has been emphasized throughout this report, community programs for youth provide opportunities to facilitate their well-being and promote successful transitions to adulthood. Chapter 9 reviews public and private support for these kinds of opportunities. Chapter 10 summarizes a series of conclusions about adolescent well-being and development, program design, and implementation and presents the committee's recommendations in the areas of practice and policy and evaluation, research, and data collection.

Funding and Support for Programs

C ommunity programs for youth have been a national concern at least episodically since the New Deal, when the National Youth Administration was a significant star in the constellation of agencies formed to confront the ravages of the Great Depression. The New Frontier and the Great Society featured a renewed interest in the subject, as part of the 1960s War on Poverty, through such programs as the Neighborhood Youth Corps, Upward Bound, and VISTA.

"After-school programs" has become the current operative language among federal, state, and local policy makers and foundations. The new federally funded programs that began appearing about 1997 are based largely in schools, staffed by school-hired personnel, and dedicated heavily to helping improve children's academic performance. Most of the new funding is supporting programs in elementary schools, with some in middle schools. Almost none of the new focus is at the high school level, although there was also a new, smaller infusion of funding for community programs to assist lower-income youth in gaining entry to the labor market. The new government funding was accompanied by some increased support from foundations, both national and local, for infrastructure to assist with staff development, research, and evaluation, in addition to program activities. Some of the foundation initiatives reflected a more three-dimensional emphasis around the family, schools, and community on youth development that the latest government efforts have lacked.

Although the recent surge of interest in out-of-school activities is gratifying, it is still limited in scope. While a series of national policies on youth development, including get-tough criminal justice policies related to youthful offenders, exist in disjointed form, there is as yet no broad, positive national policy for youth development. Even the new funding, substantial as it is, is modest compared with the number of children who need assistance (National Research Council and Institute of Medicine, 2000a). If there is one barrier above all others to an ample supply of high-quality community programs for children whose parents cannot afford to pay for them, it is the lack of reliable, stable funding streams to support them. It seems that parents are still the major funders of after-school programs, which means that many children, particularly those in lower-income families, are not served. The lack of consistent and sufficient funding leads to other barriers: untrained staff, low pay, high turnover, and inadequate facilities.

Nevertheless, what was previously a nonsystem is now moving toward becoming a formal system, with increased attention to programs that support adolescent development and to the importance of supporting adolescents by supporting families, schools, and communities. The response is still riddled with gaps, especially along lines of income and race, but governments at all levels that previously resisted funding activities during out-of-school hours have become involved to an unprecedented degree. Stable institutional mechanisms to support and ensure quality are still not in place, but the number of young people being reached seems to have increased. We do not have an overarching national policy to promote positive youth development, but a youth development field is closer to reality than it was five years ago.

This chapter reviews the multiple and varied sources of funding available to community programs for youth and discuss other nonfinancial institutional support for these programs. It is by no means a comprehensive summary, but rather serves as evidence of the financial and political support that exists for the development and continuation of current and future program efforts.

FUNDING

Community programs for youth are funded in a variety of ways. The funding structure of a program often relates directly to the institution that administers it (for example, if it is administered by a public or private agency), but in most cases programs patch together funding from many sources. The nature of program funding affects its design and stability, which in turn affect the extent to which it can promote developmental outcomes. Is the program public, private, or quasi-public? Who funds it? What is the annual program budget? What are the primary sources of money? If these sources are public, how much is federal, state, and local? For public sources, what is the funding by sector (e.g., health—including mental health and physical health—education, labor, justice, and agriculture)? If privately funded, is the funding primarily from philanthropies (e.g., foundations, United Way, a local business/service organization), membership dues (e.g., Boy Scouts), or user fees? Is funding stable over time or is it short-term temporary funding that must be raised from new sources periodically?

Programs face a variety of challenges related to funding. YouthBuild, for example, has been involving young people in leadership development and job training through housing rehabilitation since 1978. The program has grown from 10 to 4,600 participants and has received funding from a variety of sources, including Congress, federal agencies, and foundations. Because funds can fluctuate dramatically, they have also initiated local fundraising in order to increase the sustainability of local programs (Dahlstrom, 1998).

Smaller autonomous organizations are particularly affected by the challenges of funding development and funding management, since the smaller the organization, the more likely it is that the program and administrative functions are inextricably linked. In interviews with 26 grassroots youth programs, service practitioners indicated that the time and resources devoted to fundraising represent their biggest administrative burden (Quern and Raider, 1998).

There is great variation from program to program in the kind of funding they are able to secure and maintain. The sources of funding affect a program's stability, as well as its ability to serve young people whose families cannot afford to pay fees.

The United Way of Southeastern Pennsylvania and the Philadelphia Citizens for Children and Youth (1998) reported that after-school programs cost from $600 to $1,000 per child per year in their region. They estimate that more than 300,000 children in the state and more than 50,000 in the city of Philadelphia need financial assistance in order to participate in these programs. In a review of two youth programs in the Philadelphia area, this report highlighted the disparate nature of the funding for these programs. A large, well-established agency with locations in low- and middle-income neighborhoods reaching 5,000 youth each year received funding from the following sources: corporations (2 percent); federal competitive grants (5 percent); federal child care and child care food programs (17 percent); foundations (13 percent); individuals/special events (9 percent); membership and child care fees (34 percent); state funding (3 percent); and the United Way (16 percent). A smaller, well-established program with several sites serving 1,000 youth each year received funding from the following sources: corporations (8 percent); federal competitive grants (25 percent); federal child care and child care food programs (none); foundations (32 percent); individuals/special events (10.5 percent); membership and child care fees (1 percent); state funding (none); and the United Way (23 percent). The smaller program was heavily dependent on the philanthropic community and special federal government grants, which offer less long-term support and require a greater focus on prevention activities than on broad youth development goals.

Federal Funding

21st Century Community Learning Centers

The biggest single funding development in recent years has been the rapid expansion of 21st Century Community Learning Centers (CCLCs), funded in fiscal year (FY) 2000 at $453 million, increasing to an $846 million appropriation in FY 2001 (U.S. Department of Education, 2000). The effort began with $750,000 in FY 1995 and grew to $200 million in FY 1999 (General Services Administration, 2001; McCallion, 2000). The CCLCs provide funds primarily to schools and school districts, in some cases working in partnership with community-based organizations, for after-school, weekend, and summer activities. As of FY 1999 the programs were serving 400,000 children and youth and 200,000 adults (McCallion, 2000). With the new grants awarded in 2001, this program has increased its support to 6,800 centers, serving 1.2 million children and 400,000 adults (U.S. Department of Education, 2000).

The legislation authorizing CCLCs stressed collaboration with non-profit organizations and businesses and focused on an array of activities much broader than academic supplementation. Relatively little collaboration exists in practice, however, and an academic focus predominated most of the first phase of funded programs. Most of the sites are quite new, since the program first received substantial funding in FY 1998. It appears that more enrichment and collaboration are occurring as the sites are gaining experience. The U.S. Department of Education, which administers the program, has contracted with Mathematica Policy Research to conduct a four-year evaluation; however, there is no outcome information as yet (McCallion, 2000).

The Clinton administration reauthorized the program in 1999 with the following new provisions: allowing grants for up to five years, requiring local matching grants, making nonprofit organizations eligible for up to 10 percent of the grants (with the concurrence of the local school district), and targeting grants explicitly to inner cities, small cities, and rural areas. Some in Congress have suggested that as the program gets larger, it will become unwieldy to require applications directly to Washington, D.C. Instead, they have suggested that the program should be converted to a formula mechanism, which would decentralize decisions about grantees to the state or the local level (McCallion, 2000).

Programs include a variety of approaches. Michigan State University, for example, received an $8.2 million CCLC grant to expand its Kids Learning in Computer Klubhouses (KLICK!) program from 9 to 20 middle schools around the state, and from 1,600 to 11,000 students. The program gives low-income students experience with computers, digital equipment, and robotics (Girod and Zhao, 2000). Good Shepherd Services, a respected youth-serving agency in Brooklyn, New York, received $865,015 to expand its work in four low-income elementary schools, enabling it to offer Saturday programming, to upgrade its computer training activities, and to add more activities and services for parents (Gonzalez, 2000).

A significant partnership with the Charles Stewart Mott Foundation has been critical to the implementation of the CCLC program. Mott has committed nearly $100 million over a seven-year period (began in 1997) to two entities that offer training and assistance to CCLC applicants and grantees and to the Afterschool Alliance, an alliance of government and private-sector partners that is dedicated to increasing public awareness of the need for such programs (Charles Stewart Mott Foundation, 2001).

Youth Opportunity Grants

A second, important new pool of relevant federal funding is the U.S. Department of Labor's Youth Opportunity Grants, added in FY 2000 at a level of $250 million. This new program was funded at $375 million for FY 2001 (Lordeman, 1998). Aimed at 14- to 21-year-olds, especially those who have not finished high school, the program has some dimensions of a youth development program. Each of the three dozen grants (some urban, some rural, and some involving American Indians) involves a partnership of employment and training and other public agencies, public schools and community colleges, community-based organizations, and private employers. Based on the experience of over three decades of youth employment programs, its activities are comprehensive, including participant outreach for skills and interpersonal training, job placement, commitments from employers to hire these young adults, and continuing support for them after they are at work (Brown, 1999).

The city of Los Angeles, for example, has received a grant for $11 million, renewable for a total of up to $44 million over five years, to provide services to youth in the high-poverty areas in Watts and the Eastside of the city, where there is a disproportionate number of public housing residents. The programs are based in existing youth centers and rely on participation of diverse public agencies, nonprofit organizations, and private employers focused on employment and training, education, housing, law enforcement, social services, and community development (U.S. Department of Labor, 2000).

Workforce Investment Act

As part of the repackaging of federal employment and training programs in 1998, the long-standing summer jobs program and the considerably smaller pot of funds for year-round youth job training were consolidated by the Workforce Investment Act. Funded at a total of $1 billion, the program offers the possibility of new strategies for at-risk youth to combine summer work experience with year-round activities in ways that introduce an academic component in the summer and year-round exposure to the world of work. The act was based on principles of youth development and involves mentoring, community service, leadership development, positive peer-centered activities, and long-term follow-up elements. The new local Workforce Investment Boards were created by the act to replace the previous Private Industry Councils as distributors of the funds. They are required to establish youth councils to advise on a youth strategy, and 30 percent of the funds must be spent on out-of-school youth (Institute for Youth Development, 2000; Brown, 1999). Where Youth Opportunity Grant funds have been awarded, Workforce Investment Act youth funding can be added to enrich programs and reach more young people.

Americorps

Building on long-standing programs like VISTA and Foster Grandparents and on initiatives begun during the George H.W. Bush administration (1988-1992), the Corporation for National and Community Service—which administers the Americorps Program— has grown to offer over $500 million annually in a series of programs that both involve and serve young people (General Services Administration, 2001; Institute for Youth Development, 2000). In many communities there are youth-serving programs funded by Americorps (and the VISTA components of the corporation's programs). Very often the staff members in these programs include young people (junior and senior high school students) from the low-income neighborhood or area being served. Sometimes they are youth who dropped out of school and are in Americorps as members of bridge programs to finish high school and move into the job market. For some, these bridge programs are an avenue out of welfare. A substantial proportion of these activities have roots in the kinds of positive youth development activities stressed throughout this report.

Temporary Assistance for Needy Families

Temporary Assistance for Needy Families (TANF) was created by the Personal Responsibility and Work Opportunity Reconciliation Act of 1996 and was the successor to Aid to Families with Dependent Children (AFDC), or welfare (Reder, 2000). As a block grant, the $16 billion is available annually to the states for a wide variety of purposes, including community programs for youth. Consequently, whether the precise purpose is child care for school-age children and youth or prevention of teen pregnancy or welfare receipt, TANF is an important source of funding for community programs for youth (Kaplan and Sachs, 1999). Expert groups like the Center on Law and Social Policy (Greenberg, 1998) and the Finance Project (Flynn, 1999) have authored and distributed handbooks explaining how TANF funds can be used for out-of-school-hours programs.

Although only a relatively small part of these funds are being used for community programs for youth, the fact that after-school child care currently is critical to successful welfare-to-work strategies opens the possibility for substantial funding for community programs for youth through this source. Some states and counties have used funds in this way. Los Angeles County allocated $74 million of combined TANF and state welfare funds for an after-school program that was slated to operate in 225 elementary schools and 40 middle schools by fall 2000. Los Angeles County is also using $35 million for a Community-Based Teen Services Program to reach youth in 35 high school areas with large percentages of TANF recipients, as well as $13.5 million to provide summer jobs to 9,000 young people from TANF families (Flynn, 1999). Similarly, Illinois is using TANF funds to pay for about a third of its $18.5 million Teen REACH program, a model youth development and pregnancy and substance abuse prevention program that includes academic help, recreation, mentoring, and life skills training. The program was in 75 sites at the end of 1999, including both schools and nonprofit organizations like the Boys and Girls Clubs, reaching an estimated 34,000 youth ages 10 to 17 (Flynn, 1999; Cohen and Greenberg, 2000). Florida, Georgia, Kentucky, Massachusetts, Michigan, New York, North Carolina, Pennsylvania, South Carolina, Texas, Vermont, and Wisconsin, as well as Mecklenburg County (Charlotte), Philadelphia, and Washington County, Ohio, all use TANF funds to help finance after-school and summer programs, teen pregnancy prevention programs (Flynn, 1999; Cohen and Greenberg, 2000), and Youth Corps and Conservation Corps programs (Cohen, 2000a).

Other Federal Programs

U.S. Department of Agriculture

The U.S. Department of Agriculture (USDA) has been a pioneer in community programs for youth, with its decades-old 4-H program. Begun as a way to involve farm and other rural youth in constructive community activities, 4-H now runs programs in urban areas, contributing to positive outcomes for millions of young people every year. A special appropriation through USDA for a national Children, Youth, and Families at Risk initiative enables 4-H to focus particular activities on at-risk youth and families (U.S. Department of Agriculture, 2001). The USDA is also an important source of funding for meals and snacks for children participating in a variety of community programs for youth, including schools (Langford, 2000a; Wilgoren, 2000). The 4-H program receives support from a combination of federal, state, and local public funding.

U.S. Department of Justice

The U.S. Department of Justice (DOJ) is a significant provider of community programs for youth. Most of what it offers for youth comes from either block or formula grants to states that can be used for community programs for youth or more specialized program grants administered from Washington, D.C., for such activities. In the former category are the Byrne Formula Grant Program ($508 million in FY 2000), the Juvenile Accountability Incentive Block Grants ($221 million in FY 2000), and the formula grant portion of the Juvenile Justice and Delinquency Prevention (JJDP) Program ($76.5 million in FY 2000) (General Services Administration, 2001). Among the 26 permissible purposes of Byrne grants is gang prevention, and about $12 million of the Byrne funds went to crime and gang prevention in FY 1998 (General Services Administration, 2001; Reder, 2000). Although the spirit of the legislation is targeted toward enforcement activities, the Juvenile Accountability Incentive Block Grants can be used for prevention programs. However, some states and localities are reluctant to use these funds because they are required to either enact or certify that they are considering prosecution of additional juveniles as adults, graduated sanctions, and the opening of juvenile records. The long-standing JJDP formula grant provides another source of funds for such community prevention programs.

The smaller specialized programs funded directly from Washington, D.C., include the Juvenile Mentoring Program (JUMP) ($12 million in FY 2000), the Weed and Seed Program ($32 million in FY 2000), the special emphasis portion of the JJDP program ($23.8 million in FY 2000), the Tribal Youth Program ($12.5 million in FY 2000), the Gang-Free Schools and Communities Program ($16.9 million in FY 2000), and a special appropriation of $50 million for the Boys and Girls Clubs of America (up from $40 million in FY 1999) (General Services Administration, 2001).

DOJ, especially through the Office of Juvenile Justice and Delinquency Prevention (OJJDP), has taken a special interest in recent years in stimulating the creation of community programs for youth. OJJDP sponsored SafeFutures demonstration projects in six sites that sought to link research findings about risk and protective factors for youth with the best current program knowledge about juvenile delinquency prevention. SafeFutures stressed collaboration among key local agency players in young people's lives (Office of Juvenile Justice and Delinquency Prevention, 1998). Children at Risk was another DOJ initiative developed in partnership with the Center for Substance Abuse at Columbia University. Begun at the end of the George H.W. Bush administration and expanded the following year, this program worked in five sites to create multiagency networks to serve 11- to 13-year-olds who met specified risk criteria. Both efforts involved colocation of staff, individualized case management with extra training for case managers, parental involvement, mentoring, and careful monitoring of day-to-day operations (Harrell et al., 1999).

U.S. Department of Housing and Urban Development

The U.S. Department of Housing and Urban Development (HUD) provides programs and services primarily to residents of public housing. Its HOPE VI program for revitalization and demolition of severely distressed public housing ($1.25 billion in FY 2000) allows up to 15 percent of each grant to be used for community and supportive services programs for youth. Other accounts for public housing include funding for services that include community programs for children who live in public housing. HUD's Community Development Block Grant ($4.2 billion in FY 2000, is used to support community programs for youth. HUD also administers dedicated appropriations for YouthBuild ($42.5 million in FY 2000, described earlier) and Communities in Schools ($5 million in FY 2000), which brings supportive services for low-income children and families into school settings (General Services Administration, 2001).

U.S. Department of Education

In addition to the CCLCs, the U.S. Department of Education offers a number of other funding opportunities relevant to community programs for youth. Up to 5 percent of the $7.9 billion Title I program of compensatory education for low-income children can be used for coordinated services (General Services Administration, 2001). Bilingual education and Individuals With Disabilities Education Act (IDEA) funds are occasionally used for programs provided outside the standard school day and year. The Safe and Drug-Free Schools and Communities Act distributes funds through a formula grant ($439 million in FY 2000) and a discretionary pool ($90 million in FY 2000) (General Services Administration, 2001; Fairman, 2000). This program has been widely criticized for failing to produce measurable outcomes. Nevertheless it has survived numerous attempts to cut its funding (Cooper, 2000; Frammolino, 1998) because it is highly popular with school administrators. This popularity stems from the fact that it provides flexible funding for schools to undertake a wide variety of activities in the name of drug and violence prevention. This flexibility makes it a useful source of funds for entrepreneurial local program operators. Another program experiencing growth in recent years is Gaining Early Awareness and Readiness for Undergraduate Programs (GEAR UP) ($200 million in FY 2000). This program provides college preparation activities for middle school students through parnerships between school and other community-based organizations (General Services Administration, 2001).

U.S. Department of Labor

Additional Department of Labor funding relevant to community programs for youth comes through the Job Corps and the School-to-Work Programs. The Job Corps ($1.3 billion in FY 2000) serves low-income youth ages 16 to 24 mainly in Job Corps centers often located outside the communities of its participants (Lordeman, 1998; Richardson and House, 1999). The school-to-work programs provide seed money to get new school-to-work systems into place. These programs typically involve community partnerships between community organizations schools, and employers. Its funding, conceived as an initial stimulus to the states, is about to end (Reder, 2000).

U.S. Department of Health and Human Services

The U.S. Department of Health and Human Services (DHHS) offers a number of block grants that can be used for community programs for youth. The Substance Abuse and Mental Health Services (SAMSHA) block grant ($1.5 billion in FY 2000), for example, requires a percentage of its funds to be spent on prevention; in many localities, community programs for youth have drawn on these funds for activities linked to substance abuse prevention grants. Many agencies funded by the Community Services Block Grant (CSBG) ($527.7 million in FY 2000) serve youth (General Services Administration, 2001). For example, community action agencies, originally created as part of the War on Poverty, receive a portion of their funding under the CSBG.

Entitlement programs administered by DHHS also offer possibilities to states for support of community programs for youth. For example, Oregon, Tennessee, and other states have reorganized their Medicaid programs to obtain "section 1115 waivers," which enable the states to fund prevention and health promotion efforts at the community level in such areas as teen pregnancy, violence, and drug and alcohol abuse (English, 1997).

States can also reorganize their child welfare protection systems and deploy federal Title IV-E (of the Social Security Act) funds from out-of-home care to community programs. The architects of the initial Beacons Schools in New York City discovered that they could use Title IV-E funds as a partial financing source because so many of the children projected to participate were at risk of being removed from their homes for neglect or abuse (Alliance for Redesigning Government, 2001). Similarly, because it was organizing and coordinating neighborhood and school-based services that were keeping children out of foster care, the Local Investment Commission of Greater Kansas City, Inc., in conjunction with its community-based partner organizations, used Title IV-E to recover some of its administrative costs (Center for the Study of Social Policy, 2001).

DHHS categorical programs are important, too. The Community Health Centers (CHC) program ($826.5 million in FY 2000) provides opportunities for youth programming. Many of the clinics funded by this program define their responsibility to youth to include broad-based public health activities. Consequently, they offer not only health care and reproductive health services, but also activities and services designed to support the positive development of their participants. The CHC program is widely regarded as very successful; one reason for the success is the continuity of funding it has provided to grantees. Another, smaller effort with similar funding continuity is the Runaway and Homeless Youth program ($43.6 million in FY 2000). Established in 1974, it has funded many of its grantees continuously since that time. Like the CHCs, these programs typically receive funding from multiple public and private sources, but the funding they receive from DHHS is a stable base that enables them to survive shifts in other fund sources. Finally, Title X of the Public Health Service Act, which supports family planning ($254 million in FY 2001), has been very important in supporting family planning services to young people (General Services Administration, 2001; Institute for Youth Development, 2000).

In 1995, the Centers for Disease Control and Prevention (CDC) established the Community Coalition Partnership Programs for the Prevention of Teen Pregnancy to demonstrate the communities can mobilize and organize resources in support of programs to prevent initial and repeat teen pregnancies. CDC awarded nearly $3.3 million multiyear cooperative agreements to 13 community programs, as well as provided technical assistance and training. These demonstration projects, administered by the CDC's Division of Reproductive Health, are in communities of at least 200,000 or more that have a teen birth rate of 1.5 times the national average for young females ages 15 to 19. The strategy of the partnership programs is based on the premise that young people who are experiencing success, are hopeful about their futures, and are supported by their communities will postpone pregnancy and childbearing.

Future Prospects

In September 2000, as the 106th Congress was drawing to a close, a bill was introduced that, if enacted, has promise of offering a stable source of federal funding to support the creation of a positive and coherent national youth policy. The Younger Americans Act, which was reintroduced in the 107th Congress, was developed by a broad coalition of national nonprofit organizations led by the member organizations of the National Collaboration for Youth, the United Way of America, and America's Promise. Introduced by Senator James Jeffords of Vermont, with the cosponsorship of Senators Max Cleland of Georgia, Christopher Dodd of Connecticut, Edward Kennedy of Massachusetts, and Ted Stevens of Alaska, when in full operation it would provide $2 billion annually for youth development programs chosen by a local community board that includes young people as one-third of its membership. The bill would also create a federal advisory committee to help coordinate youth policy on a national level (National Youth Development Information Center, 2000a). Former Senator Nancy Kassebaum promoted a similar idea in the early 1990s—the Youth Development Block Grant—as a part of the Young Americans Act, but could not gather enough momentum to get it funded (Kassebaum, 1995). The Younger Americans Act was enacted as part of the Human Services Reauthorization Act of 1990. This act called for a national youth policy that ensures the rights of young people and promotes development of a continuum of needed educational, health, and social services for young people whose families cannot ensure their well-being.

The current proposal is in effect a successor to Senator Kassebaum's bill, but it is more promising because a number of issues that blocked wide support of the earlier bill have been resolved and because more funds are available now. With a new Congress and a new administration, only time will tell whether this bill will be passed.

President George W. Bush included after-school programming as part of his presidential campaign agenda. He proposed opening up the funding for 21st Century Learning Centers to broad-based bidding so that faith-based organizations (Education Week, 2001), youth development groups, and local charities could compete equally with schools for the funds (Chaddock, 1999).

President Bush also proposed a $400 million add-on to the Child Care and Development Block Grant to fund certificates that would help an additional 500,000 low-income parents to pay for after-school programs. This funding is often an important support for many local community programs for youth, particularly those for children younger than 13. These grants are provided to states and tribes to assist low-income families with child care. This funding allows states maximum flexibility in developing child care programs and policies that best suit the needs of children and parents, and therefore after-school programs are eligible for this funding.

In fall 2000 a group of federal agencies and nonprofit youth-serving organizations, convened by the U.S. Department of Health and Human Services' Family and Youth Services Bureau, collaborated on the development of a framework to promote and support youth development (2001). This framework declared that the time is right to promote youth development principles through community-based organizations and schools. It included a definition of youth development that is consistent with the framework developed in this report and it provided examples of programs that promoted these principles.

State and Local Public Funding

Increased opportunities for community programs for youth have also emerged at the state and local level. In fact, there are many good examples of coordination around youth development policies at the state and local level. Support for such initiatives is being driven by federal funding, as well as state and local funding.

In 1998, the U.S. Department of Health and Human Services' Family Youth Services Bureau awarded state Youth Development Collaboration Projects grants to nine states (Arizona, Colorado, Connecticut, Iowa, Maryland, Massachusetts, Nebraska, New York, and Oregon) to develop and support innovative youth development strategies. These grants were designed to enable states to develop or strengthen youth development strategies and target all youth, including youth in at-risk situations, such as runaway and homeless youth, youth leaving the foster care system, abused and neglected children, and other youth served by the child welfare and juvenile justice systems. These states are making strides in promoting youth development policy. Although each state's plan is unique, each aims to:

- enhance relationships between state and local government to develop and implement youth development policies and programs;
- build on existing youth collaborations and organizations;
- articulate a statewide policy and understanding of youth development;
- develop and implement statewide training programs based on effective principles and best practices of youth development;
- involve youth in planning; and
- evaluate results.

These objectives are being achieved in various ways. State initiatives include activities such as developing statewide web sites to link agencies and programs involved in youth development activities; involving youth in state policy decision making; developing a state framework for a comprehensive youth development policy; and providing state training opportunities for both youth workers and youth leaders.

California has perhaps the most extensive network of activities driven by new state funds allowing expansion of local efforts already in place as well as the establishment of new initiatives. A $50 million state appropriation in 1998, the After School Learning and Safe Neighborhoods Partnership Program, was expanded to $85 million in 1999 (California Department of Education, 1999a, 199b; Foundation Consortium, 2000). In at least four cities, the new state funds are supporting inclusion of more children in programs already operating with local public and private dollars: LA's BEST in Los Angeles, Beacons Schools in San Francisco, the Critical Hours Program in San Diego, and START in Sacramento. The new state funds, with the new federal CCLC and TANF funds, combined with private sources, were projected to have added 1,200 new sites serving 95,000 additional children across the state by the 2000-2001 school year (Foundation Consortium, 2000). Almost none of the new funds, however, are being spent on high school age youth, and observers estimate the overall number of young people in need of services to be 1.2 to 1.5 million statewide (Dominguez-Arms, 2000). The new state legislation requires spending on youth development activities apart from academic enrichment, yet a substantial number of the new sites across the state are essentially homework centers. Also, priority for funding under the new state program is to be given to schools in which half or more of the students are eligible for free or reduced-price school lunches (California School Boards Association, 1999a).

California's experience exemplifies a fact that is ubiquitous across the nation—outside of the basic cost of paying for schooling, it spends far more on younger children than it does on youth. For example, as its after-school investment was ramping up to $85 million, it was undertaking implementation of its recent Proposition 10, which by popular vote created a 50-cent excise tax on tobacco products to be spent on early childhood supports and services, with revenues projected at $690 million for FY 2000 (California School Boards Association, 1999a).

Efforts in other states reflect a variety of approaches to after-school programming. Governor (now Senator) Thomas Carper of Delaware made what the National Governors' Association calls "extra learning opportunities," or ELOs, his Chairman's Initiative during his period as chair in 1998 and 1999 (National Governor's Association, 1999). In response to a survey he conducted, 26 states said they had increased or were planning to increase funding for ELOs (Olsen, 2000). Maryland recently enacted an After-School Opportunity Fund, which requires a $10 million allocation by 2001. Kentucky is spending $37 million to reach 150,000 students through its Extended School Services program, up $16 million since 1991-1992. New York raised funding for after-school programs from $500,000 to $10 million for the 1999-2000 school year and added $15.2 million for the Extended Day and School Violence Prevention program. Ohio Governor Bob Taft obtained $60 million, to be spent over two years, for his OhioReads program, which will engage community organizations, libraries, and 20,000 volunteers in seeking to have all children reading at grade level by the 4th grade. He also added another $31 million for a new summer remediation program. In addition to Teen REACH in Illinois, discussed earlier, the state is spending $8.5 million on Summer Bridge, which will provide summer learning and after-school opportunities for 19,000 students most at risk of not being promoted to the next grade. Delaware is adding $10.4 million for its Extra Time Program, which increases instructional time for low-achieving students (National Governor's Association, 2000).

At the local level, Boston is an example of a city devoting major attention to expanding the quantity and quality of community programs for youth, with its 2:00 to 6:00 After-School Initiative. In FY 2000 the city committed $10.5 million to the initiative and helped leverage $17 million over the previous two years from federal, state, and private sources. Partly due to advocacy emanating from Boston, total state funding for out-of-school-hours programs had gone up from $3.7 million in FY 1998 to $15.5 million in FY 2000, and funding for school-age child care had gone from $51 to $72 million over the same period. The United Way increased its funding for relevant programs in Boston by $2.4 million, or 19 percent, during that time (City of Boston, 2000a).

As a consequence of the increased funding, 57 elementary and middle schools are now being kept open until 6:00 p.m., 11 new after-school programs in school buildings are being run by the YMCA of Greater Boston, 40 new after-school programs operate in predominantly black churches, and other after-school care has been expanded (City of Boston, 2000a).

One impressive product of the city's 2:00 to 6:00 After-School Initiative is an extensive up-to-date, user-friendly finance guide listing possible sources of funding at all levels of government. Federal and state funds actually dispensed locally are identified as such, with the appropriate local official and office listed. When the state or federal government needs to be contacted directly, that is indicated, too. A section on web sites and publications is included as well (City of Boston, 2000a).

Relevant organizations from around the state have also developed a legislative advocacy coalition to work in the legislature for funding, an expanded age range of eligibility for child care, increased voucher reimbursement rates for agencies, and a larger state contribution to the vouchers available to families. Parents United for Child Care (PUCC), with support from the Finance Project of Washington, D.C., and the MOST Initiative (discussed in more detail below), convened a broad-based civic and governmental working group to recommend steps for advancing out-of-school programs in the city and the state. Over 60 organizations came together to create a professional advancement and development project for youth workers. A wide variety of educational, arts, museum, and other programs and institutions came forward to make technical assistance available to individual youth-serving organizations. The MOST Initiative and PUCC combined to create a pool of practitioners trained as Quality Advisers, to work with programs on improving their opportunities for youth. College-level course work is now offered for after-school providers. The United Way has also worked with youth-serving organizations to develop and put into use outcome measures to determine program quality (City of Boston, 2000b; Sachs, 1997).

All of these achievements, monetary and structural, are summarized together with thoughtful recommendations for future action in a comprehensive report of the Mayor's Task Force on After-School Time, *Schools Alone Are Not Enough: Why Out-of-School Time Is Crucial to the Success of Our Children* (City of Boston, 2000b).

A number of states and localities have adopted innovative forms of financing for community programs for youth. The Finance Project, through its Out-of-School Time Technical Assistance Project, has pulled together information on these approaches and disseminated it widely (Langford, 1999):

- Pinellas County, Florida, pioneered the idea of a special taxing district to support children's services in 1946. Six Florida counties now have authority to levy such special taxes, generating about $63 million in FY 1995. While child care is the main program expenditure, 19 percent of the funds collected in Palm Beach County were allocated to out-of-school-time activities for children ages 6 to 12.
- Seattle has a special Families and Education property tax levy of 23 cents per $1,000 of assessed valuation, which generates about $10 million annually for early childhood development, school-based child and family services, student health services, and out-of-school-hours programs.
- Proposition J, passed in 1991 by the voters of San Francisco, sets a budget floor and earmarks 2.5 percent of property tax revenue as a set-aside for children's services. In 1995 the budget floor was $44.7 million and the set-aside Children's Fund was $13.8 million, to be divided equally among child care, health and social services, job readiness, and a combination of delinquency prevention, education, libraries, and recreation.
- Oakland, California, voters approved Measure K, creating a Kids First Fund in 1996, which generated $5.2 million in 1998, $1 million of which was directed to special youth development grants.

- New Mexico used tobacco settlement funds to create a special trust fund for after-school programs.
- Kansas has created an Endowment for Youth Fund into which it has placed all of its tobacco settlement funds, the income from which will support a broad Children's Initiative Fund.
- Other innovative ideas continue to be developed: San Francisco uses fees from real estate developers, Massachusetts sells a special "Invest in Children" license plate, and Colorado offers a voluntary contribution check-off on income tax forms to finance improvements in child care.

The New York State Youth Bureau system has also developed a youth development framework for much of its cross-departmental funding. Founded in 1971, the Association of New York State Youth Bureaus has over 200 members representing youth bureaus and youth boards, not-for-profit youth service organizations, and municipalities throughout New York State. The mission of the association is to promote the physical, emotional, and social well-being of youth and families in New York State through a unified, statewide network of youth service programs and professionals. New York State has 109 county, town, city, and village youth bureaus. This network has grown steadily since 1945 and now encompasses all 62 counties, including New York City. Youth bureaus support youth development programs that address identified community needs. Community members, local businesses, human service professionals, educators, clergy, parents, and young people are all a part of the planning process.

In a publication commissioned by the Robert Wood Johnson Foundation to assist its Urban Health Initiative, the Finance Project listed other strategies to maximize the amounts of funds available and their efficient use. These include efficiencies from colocation of staff and purchasing pools, as well as state and county action to pool or decategorize funds from various sources so as to make them more user-friendly for community agencies. Pooling and decategorization have been used in Iowa; Missouri; and Monroe County (Rochester), New York (O'Brien, 1997).

Charter schools are another important new state and local source of financing. As discussed previously, there is increased interest in connecting activities during out-of-school time more closely to what children are doing in school (without losing a broader youth development focus). Charter schools enable a program that works with young people after school and during the summer to connect to them even more fully. The Center for Youth Development and Policy Research at the Academy for Educational Development in Washington, D.C., has been in the forefront of the movement urging community-based organizations to investigate the possibility of opening a charter school. Some long-standing youth programs, like El Puente in Brooklyn, have operated schools for years, because it was possible in New York City for alternative schools to receive designation as public schools long before the idea of charter schools caught hold. El Puente discovered some time ago the advantages of working with its young people throughout the day (Academy of Educational Development, 2000a). This opportunity is now available to others on a more widespread basis. The Mesa (Arizona) Arts Academy, a K-8 school located at the Grant Woods Branch of the Boys and Girls Clubs in Mesa, is a more recent example of a charter school. Charter schools are more than just a financing idea; they enable schools and the community programs to share the mission of adolescent development.

Foundations

Foundations, especially local foundations, have supported national youth-serving organizations and settlement houses for decades. In the late 1980s and early 1990s the Carnegie Council on Adolescent Development put the idea of positive youth development in the spotlight for foundation and public policy consideration. Local foundations followed with important efforts. For example, the Chicago Community Trust undertook a multineighborhood, multiyear initiative that created a number of new youth-serving organizations, which are still operating. The Fund for the City of New York established the Youth Development Institute, which provided technical support and evaluation for the Beacons Schools and other youth-serving organizations. It became the prototype for other local youth development intermediaries around the country (Fund for the City of New York, 1993).

In the mid-1990s the DeWitt Wallace-Reader's Digest Fund took an especially important step by starting the MOST Initiative (Making the Most of Out-of-School Time). It awarded grants to public and private collaborations in Boston, Chicago, and Seattle to pursue a comprehensive approach to school-age care for low-income children ages 5 to 14. Designed in conjunction with the National Institute on Out-of-School Time (NIOST) at the Wellesley College Center for Research on Women, MOST not only started new programs, but also paid attention to staff training and development, standards for worker competencies, program content, data collection, evaluation, and a host of other important issues. Its commitment was to develop an infrastructure and operate on a scale such that the effort in each community would be sustainable and systems change could occur. The foundation's grants leveraged multiple contributions from both public and private sources in each of the three cities and resulted in thousands of new school-age care spaces, hundreds of better-trained staff, and an array of new services and programs for families through partnerships with park districts, schools, youth-serving organizations, cultural institutions, and others. Since 1993 the foundation has spent about $10 million on the program. The Chapin Hall Center for Children has been engaged to conduct an evaluation (National Institute on Out-of-School Time, 2001b).

The DeWitt Wallace-Reader's Digest Fund also undertook an extended schools initiative that in the last half of the 1990s awarded over $13 million to support 20 communities–in each adopting one of three nationally recognized extended-service school models: Beacons Bridges to Success (originally undertaken by the United Way of Central Indiana), Community Schools (based on the work of the Children's Aid Society of New York City), and the West Philadelphia Improvement Corps (initially started at the University of Pennsylvania) (Olsen, 2000; National Institute on Out-of-School Time, 2001b). Each set of communities was assigned an intermediary organization to help with implementation issues and an evaluator. Sustainability was a major goal for each community, and the Finance Project was engaged to work with each community on a business plan to identify both cash and in-kind resources and assist in developing a strategy to pursue a broad base of support in the community with key champions in both the private and public sectors (Marchetti, 1999). The experience of this initiative, timed fortuitously to be available as the CCLC program began, contributed to the implementation of that effort.

The William T. Grant Foundation's mission is to promote research that will help the "nation value youth as a resource." The foundation directs funding to three programs that support this mission: a focus on youth development, systems that affect youth, and enhancing the public's view of youth. In order to focus on youth development, the foundation funds research on six key topics: civic development, diversity and intergroup relations, strengthening ties between youth and adults, diffusion of youth creativity and marketing to youth, the impact of new technologies, and the transition to adulthood. Grants associated with the focus on youth development made up 34 percent of 1999 appropriations and 48 percent of all awards.

The foundation's second program focuses on the systems that have an impact on youth development. This program funds policy analyses and evaluations of programs that promote youth development. Grants for this program comprised 41 percent of 1999 appropriations and 28 percent of all awards. The W.T. Grant Foundation's third program focuses on the public, both generally and by subgroups, including business leaders, policy makers, media professionals, youth program leaders, and scholars. This program supports research that tracks the perceptions of and attitudes toward young people. Grants for this program accounted for 13 percent of 1999 appropriations and 12 percent of all awards.

Two important foundation actors with a specific focus on the out-of-school hours at the present time are the Charles Stewart Mott Foundation and the Open Society Institute (OSI). As mentioned earlier, the Mott Foundation is playing a vital role in helping with the CCLCs. The Mott Foundation has a long history of supporting community schools that open their buildings to deliver human services beyond the traditional academic focus of the school for families and children. It was therefore natural that the CCLCs would pique the Mott Foundation's interest. Mott got involved in two big ways. One was to continue to fund the National Center for Community Education and the National Community Education Association to offer training and assistance to the CCLC grantees. This also included engaging the Finance Project to do the same kind of sustainability work that was already being done with the DeWitt Wallace-Reader's Digest grantees. The second was to create the Afterschool Alliance, which launched a public awareness campaign about the importance of after-school programs. The J.C. Penney Company, Inc. was an initial partner in the alliance, along with the U.S. Department of Education, the Entertainment Industry Foundation, *People* Magazine, the Creative Artists Agency Foundation, and the Advertising Council (Afterschool Alliance, 2000). The Mott Foundation will have invested $95 million in these two projects by 2003.

The Open Society Institute, started by philanthropist George Soros, started the After-School Corporation (TASC) and pledged up to $25 million a year for five years to stimulate new after-school programs in New York. He required a three-to-one match of public or other private funds for each dollar of his contribution, and in the first year and a half brought in more than $30 million in New York City and state funding and more than $10 million from a variety of private sources. Grantees are nonprofit organizations that work with the schools, and by spring 2000 there were 100 participating schools in New York City and nine other locations around the state (After-School Corporation, 2000). The programs are located primarily in elementary schools, with some in middle, junior, and senior high schools (Wilgoren, 2000). TASC programs operate only on school days and are heavily focused on homework assistance, complemented by various arts, sports, and other recreational activities. The program costs $1,000 per participant annually, plus start-up, facilities, and staff training costs (Wilgoren, 2000). This cost does not include the supplies and other in-kind contributions from the New York City Board of Education. The Mott Foundation and the Carnegie Corporation of New York have also funded an ongoing evaluation of this program, carried out by the Policy Studies Associates, Inc., of Washington, D.C. (Policy Studies Associates, Inc., 2000).

Adherents of community programs taking a youth development approach were heartened in the early 1990s by the enthusiasm in the foundation community for programs like the Beacons and by foundation investments like those made by DeWitt Wallace. However, the more narrow academic focus of much of the new wave of after-school programs and the changed emphasis of some of the key foundations have been disappointing.

Foundations like Annie E. Casey, which premises its new 22-city initiative on the fact that families and communities should have an interactive relationship, are pursuing an approach that is congruent with a youth development perspective. Casey staff examined past efforts of the foundation and concluded that its previous efforts at community building had not focused consciously enough on strengthening communities and neighborhoods, and previous family-supporting strategies had not focused sufficiently on helping females function more effectively in the communities around them. Casey's new priorities will support efforts to serve youth through a three-dimensional emphasis on schools, neighborhoods, and families (Annie E. Casey Foundation, 2001).

National Youth-Serving Organizations

National youth-serving organizations serve as an important support for community programs for young people because they are catalysts for a significant flow of funding to their local "franchisees." The Carnegie Council found that there were over 17,000 youth development organizations in the United States, only several thousand of which were independent of any national affiliation (Carnegie Corporation of New York, 1992). National organizations have created a "brand name" that enables their local affiliates to raise funds. And they function as an important funding source as well, with their funds being generated from government at all levels, foundations, corporations, private donations, and fees. At the same time, the local franchises may also support the national organization in part with their member dues. The combined totals add up to substantial sums.

The Carnegie Council on Adolescent Development summarized the funding that flows through or is accounted for by national youth-serving organizations. Although the figures are from the early 1990s, they are indicative of the large role of these organizations. Furthermore, the funding amounts mentioned here relate to the budgets of the national organizations and do not even take into account the aggregate budgets of their many local chapters.

- The Boy Scouts' annual budget was $75.5 million; the Girl Scouts' $32.7 million.
- The Boys and Girls Clubs were spending $16.1 million (they are much larger now).
- Junior Achievement had a budget of $8.4 million.
- Multipurpose organizations had youth components that were not accounted for separately, like the American Red Cross at $1.4 billion, the YMCA at $35.4 million, and the YWCA at $12.1 million.

Corporations

Many private-sector companies make contributions to community programs for youth based in the places where they do substantial business or have major activities. For example, City Year, a youth-service program originally based in Boston and now operating in over a dozen cities, is supported by over a hundred companies that have invested over $40 million in it since its founding in 1988. It was initially backed by Bain and Company, BankBoston, The Equitable, and General Cinema and now has national sponsors led by Timberland, which alone has invested over $10 million to help with City Year's national expansion. City Year emphasizes that its corporate sponsors go well beyond checkbook philanthropy in their support, participating extensively in service days with City Year teams (City Year, 2001).

Beyond its involvement with City Year, Timberland is deeply interested in community service, offering its employees 40 hours a year of paid time to do community service. This policy has resulted in the performance of over 78,000 hours of service since 1992. Recently, Timberland has teamed up with Community Impact!, a community youth organization in Washington, D.C., and a local entrepreneur to open a retail store in a low-income neighborhood that employs local youth, provides entrepreneurial training, and sets aside a third of its profits to pay for college scholarships for local youth (Timberland Company, 2000).

Best Buy is another company that has taken a particular interest in positive youth development. Its Children's Foundation makes grants to youth-serving (ages 5 to 18) organizations in communities in which the company has a strong presence, as well as to national youth-serving organizations. About 60 percent of the giving is to local organizations and about 40 percent to its national partners; it is currently giving away about $2 million annually (Best Buy, 2000).

FUNCTIONAL SUPPORTS

More assured funding is vital to deal with all of the limitations and structural problems that community programs for youth face, but money alone will not solve the problems. More money may provide higher wages and reduce turnover, but institutional mechanisms need to be created to achieve stability. This includes credentialing staff and continuing their training while they are on the job, developing career ladders, agreeing on desired outcomes for youth, developing curricula and methodology to pursue those outcomes, developing management assistance, creating apparatus for networking with peer organizations, enhancing research and evaluation, and increasing advocacy for the field and for individual programs. These needs are present whether the youth-serving organization is a local autonomous organization, an affiliate of a national organization, or a public agency.

The needs can be met in various ways. National technical assistance and policy organizations, like the Academy for Educational Development's Center for Youth Development and Policy Research, are important, too. More and more local or multicity organizations within states have developed a big enough network of program sites to be able to do their own inservice training, handle their own external relations, and use consultants for other needs. Local governments' youth program coordinating agencies in some cities help to meet some of the needs, playing a key role in moving their jurisdiction toward a real system of community programs for youth. Many national youth-serving organizations also provide technical support to their affiliates through national training programs and training materials that can be used at the local level.

National Technical Assistance and Policy Organizations

The Center for Youth Development and Policy Research has helped community programs for youth in multiple ways. One example is Community YouthMapping, which as of mid-2000 had youth "mapping" their communities' youth needs and programs in over 30 communities. The most sophisticated and long-standing of these efforts is in Pinellas County, Florida. This effort has spawned a continuing constructive dialogue between local young people and the larger community, with concrete results in terms of expansions in services, better information, and empowering of the young people. Denver's YouthMapping was specifically helpful in choosing activities for the three Beacons Schools that were being developed in Denver and in stimulating youth involvement in the governance of the Beacons. Detroit's YouthMapping created an inventory of resources in two neighborhoods and strengthened relations with the adult community in those neighborhoods (Academy of Educational Development, 2000b).

A second activity modeled by the Center for Youth Development is YouthBudgeting. Indianapolis and the surrounding Central Indiana region did a YouthBudget exercise to find out how much they were spending on youth development outside their expenditures on schooling. The process was instructive in showing concretely how difficult it is to get an accurate understanding of the full range of community programs and in demonstrating how little of the funding for activities comes from the United Way and private foundations. Two striking facts emerged: only 5 percent of the funding was from private sources, and 79 percent of the funding was from the federal government. Also, while much of the work can be carried out by nongovernmental organizations, public funding is essential to enable these organizations to fulfill their responsibilities (Newman et al., 1999).

Several other agencies provide a variety of services to help communities and organizations provide high-quality youth programs. The Search Institute, based in Minneapolis, is dedicated to an asset-based approach to youth development, providing publications and support for families, communities, businesses, and nonprofit organizations, especially in the faith community, to nurture children and adolescents in ways that build on the communities' strengths. Based on research involving over 100,000 children from 6th through 12th grade over a period of years, the Search Institute has identified 40 developmental assets that, when present in sufficient combination and strength, produce positive outcomes. Through its continuing research, resource materials, presentations, training, and networking, it works with people all over the country (Search Institute, 2000). The National School Age Child Care Alliance, headquartered in Boston, has state affiliate alliances in more than 40 states. It is primarily a professional organization for out-of-school-hours providers, focusing on both practitioner training and program accreditation (National School-Age Care Alliance, 1998). Finally, the National Youth Development Information Center, a project of the National Collaboration for Youth, provides practice-related information about youth development to national and local youth-serving organizations.

Another useful new resource is www.afterschool.gov, a government-sponsored web site that contains a database of federal grants and loans for after-school programs; links to government guides, reports, and research; links to recommendations on building strong programs; and other useful information on developing and providing after-school programs.

The Institute for Youth Development has developed some useful tools to assist organizations identify funding opportunities. *The Federal Grants Manual for Youth Programs: A Guide to Youth Risk Behavior Prevention Funding, Volume I* is a comprehensive listing of federal grants available from the Department of Health and Human Services to states, organizations, and individuals to help youth avoid unhealthy risk behaviors. *Volume II*, contains listings of federal grants available from other cabinet-level departments and agencies to states, organizations, and individuals to help youth avoid unhealthy risk behaviors

Training

Preservice and inservice education and training are important functional supports for youth workers to develop skills in working with adolescents, instill the values of youth development among staff, and to promote a professional career development. Organizations like the Child and Youth Care Learning Center, based at the University of Wisconsin-Milwaukee, have been doing youth worker training for many years (Boyle, 2000). Others are part of a growing proliferation of training programs occurring now. The Springfield (Massachusetts) College of Human Services now has eight campuses around the country that provide a youth worker training program. The BEST system, run by the National Training Institute for Community Youth Work, provides training opportunities at 15 sites (Academy for Educational Development and National Training Institute for Community Youth Work, 2000). The Child Welfare League of America is moving toward a regionalized training system. National organizations like Girls, Inc. and Boys Town have their own training programs. There are a few university-based youth work education programs, like the one at Nova University in Florida and the Child Development and Child Care Program at the University of Pittsburgh. The DeWitt Wallace-Readers Digest Fund has also been particularly active in supporting the development of youth worker training programs with a $55 million investment.

The National Institute on Out-of-School Time (NIOST), founded in 1978, is a leader in the area of youth worker training, offering training in a variety of forms and for a variety of audiences. It runs a series of multiday sessions to increase skills as workers gain experience. It offers help with program design and founded a 20-city network of program leaders to communicate and share problems and solutions. NIOST also disseminates information on out-of-school time research (National Institute on Out-of-School Time , 2001).

Local Intermediaries

An emerging participant in the dialogue about community programs for youth are local capacity-building intermediary organizations that assist individual local programs with program design, operations, fund development, networking, and evaluation. These were discussed in some detail in Chapter 5 and again in Chapter 8. Perhaps the earliest of these in the nonprofit sector, and a prototype for others, is the Youth Development Institute of the Fund for the City of New York, which was founded in the early 1990s to serve the Beacons Schools.

SUMMARY

Policy and instrumental support for community programs for youth improved considerably during the decade of the 1990s. Almost a billion dollars of new annual federal funds for these activities has been added over the past eight years. More state and local funding, foundation funding, and private-sector funding have also increased the resources targeted toward community programs for youth. In addition, a significant number of local intermediary organizations were formed to assist in reducing the barriers faced by these programs. National, state, and local policy, practice, and research organizations are involved in supporting programs in their efforts to promote adolescent development.

Despite all of this good news, barriers still exist to improving and increasing opportunities for all young people to benefit from community programs. Neither the new funding nor the presence of new intermediaries and other institutional supports are occurring on a scale that meets existing diverse needs of the young people, their families, and their communities. Youth-serving organizations, especially independent, local, multipurpose ones, often have to cobble together funding from as many as 40 or more sources.

The challenge goes beyond a stable supply of adequate funding. Stable institutional mechanisms in local areas are needed to manage these activities. A stable institutional framework includes three levels: the front-line organizations and personnel who deliver services and interact directly with young people, including the volunteers who are vital to the effort; the local support mechanisms for the front-line effort—those who manage the funding and the education and training and the other needed supports and those who do the technical assistance and the research and evaluation; and finally, the counterparts of those support mechanisms at state and national levels. To have a genuine youth development field, all are necessary.

Many argue that the increased funding support—particularly the 21st Century Learning Centers Program—is skewed toward public schools and does not adequately support the involvement of community-based organizations. In addition, the CCLP emphasis is tilted toward academic activities and does not pay as much attention to other developmental needs. Finally, there is concern that this funding is primarily directed at younger elementary and middle or junior high school children. Some believe this program should be redesigned with a more explicit youth development strategy. Others argue for increased flexibility to allow programs to be administered through community-based organizations, as well as schools. Some also argue for supporting programs and organizations already in place rather than redesigning the program from scratch.

Policy and instrumental support for these programs has improved considerably during the last couple of decades. However, there is still no overall positive youth development policy at the national level. There is no dedicated funding stream for community programs that promote youth development. None of the new annual funding for such community programs over the past eight years ensures a developmental focus. Furthermore, much of the funding of youth programs continues to be categorical funding—forcing programs to narrowly focus their agenda and cobble together funding from multiple sources. There has just begun to be consistent efforts to bring federal agencies together around a developmental perspective extending through adolescence, but it remains to be seen whether the new federal leadership will continue to support these efforts. The future success of community programs for youth in promoting adolescent development and well-being and the successful transition to adulthood is dependent on consistent, reliable, and broad-based support at the federal, state, and community levels.

CHAPTER 10

Conclusions and Recommendations

I n recent years, a number of social forces have changed both the landscape of family and community life and the expectations for young people. A combination of factors have weakened the informal community support once available to young people: high rates of family mobility; greater anonymity in neighborhoods, where more parents are at work and out of the home and neighborhood for long periods, and in schools, which have become larger and much more heterogeneous; extensive media exposure to themes of violence and heavy use and abuse of drugs and alcohol; and, in some cases, the deterioration and disorganization of neighborhoods and schools as a result of crime, drugs, and poverty. At the same time, today's world has become increasingly complex, technical, and multicultural, placing new and challenging demands on young people in terms of education, training, and the social and emotional skills needed in a highly competitive environment. Finally, the length of adolescence has extended to the mid- to late twenties, and the pathways to adulthood have become less clear and more numerous. In addition, many youth are entering the labor market with inadequate knowledge and such skills as the ability to communicate effectively, resolve conflicts, and prepare for and succeed in a job.

Concerns about youth are at the center of many policy debates. The future well-being of the country depends on raising a new generation of skilled, competent, and responsible adults. Yet at least 25 percent of adolescents in the United States are at serious risk of not achieving "productive adulthood" and face such risks as substance abuse, adolescent pregnancy, school failure, and involvement with the juvenile justice system. Depending on their circumstances and choices, they may carry those risks into their adult lives. Public investments in programs to counter such trends have grown significantly over the past decade or so. For the most part, these efforts have targeted specific problems and threats to young people. Substantial public health investments have been made to prevent teen smoking, sexually transmitted diseases, and other health risks. Major funding has been allocated to the prevention and control of juvenile delinquency and youth crime.

This report has explored the research and evaluation on adolescent development and community programs for youth. This chapter presents the committee's primary conclusions and recommendations. We had the task of considering various aspects related to community programs for youth—from developing a general understanding of adolescent development, the needs of youth, and the fundamental nature of these programs, to critically examining the research, evaluation, and data instruments they use. We have organized the conclusions and recommendations around two primary themes: (1) policy and practice and (2) research, evaluation, and data collection.

POLICY AND PRACTICE

The committee began its work by drawing up a set of core concepts about adolescents that serve as a foundation for this report.

Some youth are doing very well. The good news for many young people is that many measures of adolescent well-being have shown significant improvement since the late 1980s. Young people are increasingly graduating from high school and enrolling in higher education. Almost half of the high school seniors participate in community service. Most young people are participating in physical exercise. Serious violent crime committed by adolescents, some illicit drug use, and teen pregnancy are down.

Some youth are taking dangerous risks and doing poorly. Some social indicators suggest continuing problems, particularly for minority youth living in poor communities and youth living in poor, single-parent families. Youth from poor inner-city and rural areas are doing substantially worse on national achievement tests than youth from more affluent school districts. School dropout is particularly high among Hispanic youth and adolescents living in poor communities. Many young women and men are engaging in unsafe sex, exposing them to sexually transmitted infections. Smoking cigarettes, obesity, and gun violence on school campuses have all increased.

All young people need a variety of experiences to develop to their full potential. All youth need an array of experiences to reduce risk-taking and promote both current well-being and successful transition into adulthood. Such experiences include opportunities to learn skills, to make a difference in their community, to interact with youth from multicultural backgrounds, to have experiences in leadership and shared decision making, and to make strong connections with nonfamilial adults. These experiences are important to all young people, regardless of racial or ethnic group, socioeconomic status, or special needs.

Some young people have unmet needs and are particularly at risk of participating in problem behaviors. Young people who have the most severe unmet needs in their lives are particularly in jeopardy of participating in risk behaviors, such as dropping out of school, participating in violent behavior, or using drugs and alcohol. Young people with the most severe unmet needs often live in very poor and high-risk neighborhoods with few opportunities to get the critical experiences needed for positive development. They are often experience repeated racial and ethnic discrimination. Such youth have a substantial amount of free, unsupervised time during their nonschool hours. Other youth who are in special need of more programs include youth with disabilities of all kinds, youth from troubled family situations, and youth with special needs for places to find emotional support.

Promoting Adolescent Development at the Program Level

Understanding adolescent development and the factors contributing to the healthy development of all young people is critical to the design and implementation of community programs for youth. A priority of the committee's work was identifying what is necessary for adolescents to be happy, healthy, and productive at the present time, as well as successful, contributing adults in the future.

Adolescence is a time of great change: biological changes associated with puberty, major social changes associated with transitions between grade levels and changing roles and expectations, and major psychological changes linked to increasing social and cognitive maturity. With so many rapid changes comes a heightened potential for both positive and negative outcomes. Although most individuals pass through this developmental period without excessive problems, a substantial number experience difficulty.

The committee reviewed the basic tenets of human development, particularly during adolescence, and summarized the key characteristics of adolescent development. We focused on aspects of adolescent development and successful transitions to adulthood that have implications for program and policy design.

Beyond eliminating problems, the committee agreed that young people need skills, knowledge, and a variety of other personal and social assets to function well during adolescence and adulthood. But deciding what constitutes positive youth development is quite complex. Many characteristics were considered, and the committee recognized that selecting any particular set involved judgments regarding what is good. Nonetheless, longitudinal research does provide support for the links of some youth characteristics to subsequent positive adult outcomes. We were able to agree that there are some universal needs—such as the need to feel competent, to be socially connected, and to have one's physical needs taken care of—that provide a basis for suggesting a set of assets and experiences very likely to be important for well-being. We also agreed that the failure to have these needs met is very likely to have negative consequences for well-being. We also agreed that there is extensive cultural specificity in exactly how these needs are met, as well as in the exact nature of how the assets are manifested in particular individuals. This means that the local cultural context must be taken into account as programs are designed and evaluated.

Based on a review of theory, practical experiences, and empirical research in the fields of psychology, anthropology, sociology, and others, the committee identified a set of personal and social assets that both represent healthy development and well-being during adolescence and facilitate successful transitions from childhood, through adolescence, and into adulthood. We grouped these assets into four broad developmental domains: physical, intellectual, psychological and emotional, and social development. Box ES-1 summarizes the four domains and specifies the assets within each.

Conclusions

❏ Individuals do not necessarily need the entire range of assets to thrive; in fact, various combinations of assets across domains reflect equally positive adolescent development.

❏ Having more assets is better than having few. Although strong assets in one category can offset weak assets in another category, life is easier to manage if one has assets in all four domains.

❏ Continued exposure to positive experiences, settings, and people, as well as abundant opportunities to gain and refine life skills, supports young people in the acquirsition and growth of these assets.

The committee recognized that very little research directly specifies what programs can do to facilitate development, let alone how to tailor it to the needs of individual adolescents and diverse cultural groups. Few studies have applied the critical standards of science to evaluate which features of community programs influence development.

Despite these limitations, there is a broad base of knowledge about how development occurs that can and should be drawn on. Research demonstrates that certain features of the settings that adolescents experience make a tremendous difference, for good or for ill, in their lives. There is good evidence that personal and social assets develop in developmental settings that incorporate the features listed below and in Table ES-1. The exact implementation of these features, however, needs to vary across programs, with their diverse clientele and differing constraints and missions. Young people develop positive personal and social assets in settings that have the following features:

- Physical and psychological safety and security;
- Structure that is developmentally appropriate, with clear expectations for behavior as well as increasing opportunities to make decisions, to participate in governance and rule-making, and to take on leadership roles as one matures and gains more expertise;
- Emotional and moral support;
- Opportunities for adolescents to experience supportive adult relationships;
- Opportunities to learn how to form close, durable human relationships with peers that support and reinforce healthy behaviors;
- Opportunities to feel a sense of belonging and being valued;
- Opportunities to develop positive social values and norms;

- Opportunities for skill building and mastery;
- Opportunities to develop confidence in one's abilities to master one's environment (a sense of personal efficacy);
- Opportunities to make a contribution to one's community and to develop a sense of mattering; and
- Strong links between families, schools, and broader community resources.

❏ **Since these features typically work together in synergistic ways, programs with more features are likely to provide better supports for young people's positive development.**

Although all of these features are key to the success of children and adolescents at all ages, specific settings may focus their priorities differently to meet the developmental needs of particular participants—for example, younger children need more adult-directed structure and supervision than older youth and the skills that one needs to learn in childhood are different from those that need to be learned in adolescence. Supportive, developmental settings, as a result, must be designed to be appropriate over time for different ages and to allow the setting to change in developmentally appropriate ways as participants mature. Positive development is also best supported by a wide variety of these experiences and opportunities in all of the settings in which adolescents live—the family, the school, the peer group, and the community. Still, exposure to such opportunities in community programs can compensate for lack of such opportunities in other settings.

❏ **Community programs can expand the opportunities for youth to acquire personal and social assets and to experience the broad range of features of positive developmental settings.**

Programs can also fill gaps in the opportunities available in specific adolescents' lives. Among other things, these programs can incorporate opportunities for physical, cognitive, and social and emotional development; opportunities to deal with issues of ethnic identity, sexual identity, and intergroup relationships; opportunities for community involvement and service; and opportunities to interact with caring adults and a diversity of peers who hold positive social norms and have high life goals and expectations.

Recommendation 1—Community programs for youth should be based on a developmental framework that supports the acquisition of personal and social assets in an environment and through activities that promote both current adolescent well-being and future successful transitions to adulthood.

Serving Diverse Youth at the Community Level

Community programs are provided by many different individual organizations, each with their own unique approach and programmatic activities. They may be provided by local affiliates of large national youth-serving organizations or may be an independent organization that is affiliated with a public institution, such as a school or public library. They also may be small, autonomous grassroots organizations that exist independently in a community.

The focus of the activities may be sports and recreation, faith-based lessons, music and dance, academic enrichment, or workforce preparation. Programs may be targeted only to girls or only to boys; to a particular ethnic or religious group; or to young people with special interests. In addition, programs differ in their objectives, and some may choose to give more emphasis to particular program features.

Community-wide organizing of youth policies, as well as support for individual programs, also varies from community to community. Where there is a community infrastructure for support, the organizing body in a community might be the mayor's office, a local government agency, or a community foundation. It might be a private intermediary organization or an individual charismatic leader, such as a minister or a rabbi of a local religious institution. However, it is often the case that there is no single person or group that is responsible for either monitoring the range and quality of community programs for youth or making sure that information about community programs is easily accessible to members of the community.

Conclusion

❑ Adolescents in communities that are rich in developmental opportunities for them experience reduced risk and show evidence of higher rates of positive development. A diversity of program opportunities in each community is more likely to support broad adolescent development

and attract the interest of and meet the needs of a greater number of youth.

The complex characteristics of adolescent development and the increasing diversity of the country make the heterogeneity of young people in communities both a norm and a challenge. Therefore, effective programs must be flexible enough to adapt to this existing diversity among the young people they serve and the communities in which they operate. Even with the best staff and best funding, no single program can serve all young people or incorporate all of the features of positive developmental settings. A diversity of program opportunities in each community is more likely to support broad adolescent development and attract the interest of and meet the needs of a greater number of youth.

To provide for the most appropriate kinds of community programs for the diversity of youth in a community, communities should regularly assess the needs of adolescents and families and review available opportunities for their young people. While individual communities will invariably answer this challenge differently and make different judgments about the most appropriate ways to meet adolescent and community needs, there are several specific steps that the committee recommends be taken to support this kind of community mapping and monitoring.

Recommendation 2—Communities should provide an ample array of program opportunities that appeal to and meet the needs of diverse youth, and should do so through local entities that can coordinate such work across the entire community. Particular attention should be placed on programs for disadvantaged and underserved youth.

Recommendation 3 – To increase the likelihood that an ample array of program opportunities will be available, communities should put in place some locally appropriate mechanism for monitoring the availability, accessability, and quality of programs for youth in their community.

Recommendation 4—Private and public funders should provide the resources needed at the community level to develop and support community-wide programming that is orderly, coordinated, and evaluated in reasonable ways. In addition to support at the community level, this is likely to involve support for intermediary organizations and collaborative teams that include researchers, practitioners, funders, and policy makers.

RESEARCH, EVALUATION, AND DATA COLLECTION

The multiple groups concerned about community programs for youth—policy makers, families, program developers and practitioners, program staff, and young people themselves—have in common the fundamental desire to know whether programs make a difference in the lives of young people, their families, and their communities. Some are interested in learning about the effectiveness of specific details in a program; others about the effects of a given program; others about the overall effect of a set of programs together; and others about the effects of related kinds of programs. Research, program evaluation, and social indicator data can play a significant role in answering such questions, improving the design and delivery of programs, and thereby, improving the well-being and future success of young people.

Research

The committee first reviewed research on both adolescent development and the features of positive developmental settings that support it. In both cases, the research base is just becoming comprehensive enough to allow for tentative conclusions about the individual assets that characterize positive development and features of settings that support it. The committee used a variety of criteria to suggest the tentative lists of both important individual-level assets and features of settings that support positive development outlined in Box ES-1 and Table ES-1. These suggestions are based on scientific evidence from both short- and long-term experimental and observational studies, one-time large-scale survey studies, and longitudinal survey studies reviewed by the committee. However, much more comprehensive work is needed.

Conclusions

❑ More comprehensive longitudinal and experimental research, that either builds on current efforts or involves new efforts, is needed on a wider range of populations that follows children and adolescents well into adulthood in order to understand which assets are most important to adolescent development and which patterns of assets are linked to particular types of successful adult transitions in various cultural contexts.

The list of features of positive settings, as well as both personal and social assets, that the committee has developed is provisional, the boundaries between the features are fuzzy, and the specific names given to each feature and asset reflect the terminology of the scientific disciplines in which the research was done. Research on a diverse group of adolescents followed well into adulthood is needed to understand which patterns of assets best predict successful adult transitions in various cultural contexts and how these assets work together in supporting both current and future well-being and success. Longitudinal research meets these objectives by collecting extensive psychological, social, and contextual information on the same individuals at different points in time. More experimental research that focuses on changing specific assets and characteristics of settings assumed to affect other assets is also needed in order to test causal hypotheses more sensitively.

❑ **Despite its limitations, research in all settings in the lives of adolescents—families, schools, and communities—is yielding consistent evidence that there are specific features of settings that support positive youth development and that these features can be incorporated into community programs.**

Community programs have the potential to provide opportunities for youth to acquire personal and social assets and have important experiences that may be missing or are in short supply in the other settings of their lives. Whether they are packaged as teen pregnancy prevention programs, mental health programs, or youth development programs, such programs can lead to positive outcomes for youth. There is limited research, however, measuring the impact of these experiences on the development of young people and therefore limited evidence on why program effects are or are not obtained. Few researchers have applied the critical standards of science to evaluate which features of community programs influence development, which processes within each activity are related to these outcomes, and which combinations of features are best for which outcomes. Thus, there is very little research that will help organizations decide how they should tailor program activities to the needs of individual youth and diverse cultural groups.

Consequently, research is needed to sharpen the conceptualization of features of community programs and to explore whether other key features should be added to the list. This work should focus on how different populations are affected by different program components and features (e.g., age, gender, socioeconomic status, ethnicity, community environment, developmental readiness, personality, sexual orientation, skill levels). It should also focus on how to incorporate these features into community programs and on how to maintain them once they are in place. Finally, such research should identify program strategies, resource needs, and approaches to staff training and retention that can cultivate and support the features of positive developmental settings in community programs for youth.

❏ **In the committee's judgment, current evidence supports the replication of a few specific integrated programs for positive youth development: the Teen Outreach Program, Big Brothers Big Sisters, and Quantum Opportunities are three prime examples.**

Very few integrated programs have received the kind of comprehensive experimental evaluation necessary to make a firm recommendation about replicating the program in its entirety across the country. However, there is sufficient evidence from a variety of sources to make recommendations about some fundamental principles of supportive developmental settings and some specific aspects of programs that can be used to design community programs for youth. These are captured by the features of supportive settings outlined in Table ES-1.

Recommendation 5—Federal agencies that fund research on adolescent health, development, and well-being, such as the Department of Health and Human Services, the Department of Justice, and the Department of Education, should build into their portfolios new or more comprehensive longitudinal and experimental research on the personal and social assets needed to promote the healthy development and well-being of adolescents and to promote the successful transition from childhood through adolescence and into adulthood.

Recommendation 6—Public and private funders should support research on whether the features of positive developmental settings identified in this report are the most important features of community programs for youth. This research should encourage program design and implementation that meets the diverse needs of an increasingly heterogeneous population of youth.

Program Evaluation

Evaluation and ongoing program study can provide important insights to inform program design, selection, and modification. Program evaluation can also help funders and policy makers make informed choices about which programs to fund for which groups of youth. The desire to conduct high-quality evaluation can help program staff clarify their objectives and decide which types of evidence will be most useful in determining if these objectives have been met. Ongoing program study and evaluation can also be used by program staff, program participants, and funders to track program objectives; this is typically done by establishing a system for ongoing data collection that measures the extent to which various aspects of the programs are being delivered, how are they delivered, who is providing these services, and who is receiving them. Such information can provide useful information to program staff to help them make changes to improve program effectiveness. Finally, program evaluation can test both new and very well developed program designs by assessing the immediate, observable results of the program outcomes and benefits associated with participation in the program.

Such summative evaluation can be done in conjunction with strong theory-based evaluation or as a more preliminary assessment of the potential usefulness of novel programs and quite complex social experiments in which there is no well-specified theory of change. In other words, program evaluation and study can help foster accountability, determine whether programs make a difference, and provide staff with the information they need to improve service delivery.

Clearly there are many purposes for evaluation. Not surprisingly then, there are different opinions among service practitioners, researchers, policy makers, and funders about the most appropriate and useful methods for evaluating community programs for youth. In part, these disagreements reflect different goals and different questions about youth programs. In part, they reflect philosophical differences about the purposes of evaluation and nature of program development. Program practitioners, policy makers, program evaluators, and others studying programs should decide exactly which questions they want answered before deciding on the most appropriate methods. The most comprehensive experimental evaluation, which involves assessment of the quality of implementation as well as outcomes, is quite expensive and involves a variety of methods. It also provides the most comprehensive information regarding both the effectiveness of specific programs and the reasons for their effectiveness.

Conclusions

❏ Very few high-quality comprehensive experimental evaluations of community programs for youth have adequately assessed the impact of the programs on adolescents.

This is presumably due to many factors—including the low priority accorded to evaluation by organizations struggling to fund services; inadequate funding for such evaluations and overreliance on program staff to conduct such evaluation, despite the fact that they have limited training to conduct such evaluations and limited time and funds to devote to such an effort; ethical concerns among practitioners and policy makers about the random assignment of some youth to programs and others to a control group receiving no services; unrealistic demands by many program funders for quick answers about the impact of programs they fund; and scarcity of the type of collaborative teams involving the research, practice, and policy communities needed to design and implement high-quality, comprehensive experimentally based evaluations. Comprehensive experimental evaluation takes time, money, and technical knowledge—features not always plentiful within agencies providing services to youth.

❏ Some high-quality experimental and quasi-experimental evaluations show positive effects on a variety of outcomes, including both increases in the psychological and social assets of youth and decreases in the incidence of such problem behaviors as early pregnancy, drug use, and delinquent behavior.

Usually, as expected given the complexity of the behaviors being assessed and the wide range of influences on these behaviors, these effects are small for the population being studied. Nonetheless, at the individual level, the effects can be quite large and life-transforming. Such impacts are rarely reported in standard experimental evaluations, because their goal is to estimate the average effect size. Most of these evaluations also tell us little about which components of programs are the most important contributors to the positive results, the cost-effectiveness of the programs, or the reasons why programs fail.

Randomized trial experimental evaluation is often recommended as the best method for assessing whether a program influences youth development, but this design can be costly, and time-consuming and may not always be the most useful and most appropriate method of study. In addition, unless coupled with an evaluation of the implementation and with methods designed to assess the reasons for the experimental effects, experimental evaluations by themselves provide only limited information about a program's effectiveness.

❏ **Experimental designs are still the best method for estimating the impact of a program on its participants and should be used when this is the goal of the evaluation.**

Comprehensive program evaluation is an even better way to gather complete information about programs. It requires asking a number of questions through various methods. The committee identified six fundamental questions that should be considered in comprehensive evaluations:

- Is the theory of the program that is being evaluated explicit and plausible?
- How well has the program theory been implemented in the sites studied?
- In general, is the program effective and, in particular, is it effective with specific subpopulations of young people?
- Whether it is or is not effective, why is this the case?
- What is the value of the program?
- What recommendations about action should be made?

All six questions may not be answered well in one study; several evaluations may be needed to address these questions. Thus comprehensive experimental evaluation can be quite expensive and time-consuming—but it provides the most information about program design, as well as fundamental questions about human development. Thus, it is particularly useful to both the policy and research communities, as well as the practice community.

In order to generate the kind of information about community programs for youth needed to justify large-scale expenditures on programs and to further fundamental understanding of role of community programs in youth development, comprehensive experimental program evaluations should be used when:

- the object of study is a program component that repeatedly occurs across many of the organizations currently providing community services to youth;

- an established national organization provides the program being evaluated through many local affiliates; and
- theoretically sound ideas for a new demonstration program or project emerge, and pilot work indicates that these ideas can be implemented in other contexts.

Comprehensive experimental evaluations are usually not appropriate for newer, less established programs or programs that lack a well-articulated theory of change underlying the program design. A variety of nonexperimental methods, such as interviewing, case studies, and observational techniques, and more focused experimental and quasi-experimental studies are ways to understand and assess these types of community programs for youth. Although the nonexperimental methods tell us less about the effectiveness of particular community programs than experimental program evaluations, they can, when carefully implemented, provide information about the strengths and weakness in program implementation and can be used to identify patterns of effective practice. They are also quite helpful in generating hypotheses about why programs fail.

Programs that meet the following criteria should be studied through nonexperimental or more focused experimental and quasi-experimental methods, depending on the goals of the evaluation:

- An organization, program, project, or program element that has not matured sufficiently in terms of its philosophy and implementation;
- The evaluation has to be conducted by the staff of the program under evaluation;
- The major questions of interest pertain to the quality of the program theory, the implementation of that theory, or to the nature of its participants, staff, or surrounding context;
- The program is quite broad, involving multiple agencies in the same community; and
- The program or organization is interested in reflective practice and continuing improvement.

Whether experimental or nonexperimental methods are used, high-quality, comprehensive evaluation is important to the future development and success of community programs for youth and should be used by all programs and youth-serving organizations.

Recommendation 7—All community programs for youth should undergo evaluation—possibly multiple evaluations—to improve design and implementation, to create accountability, and to assess outcomes and impacts. For any given evaluation, the scope and the rigor should be appropriately calibrated to the attributes of the program, the available resources, and the goals of the evaluation.

Recommendation 8—Funders should provide the necessary funds for evaluation. In many cases, this will involve support for collaborative teams of researchers, evaluators, theoreticians, policy makers, and practitioners to ensure that programs are well designed initially and then evaluated in the most appropriate way.

Data Collection and Social Indicators

Over the past decade, social indicator data and technical assistance resources have become increasingly important tools that community programs can employ to support every aspect of their work—from initial planning and design, to tracking goals, program accountability, targeting services, reflection, and improvement. There are now significant data and related technical assistance resources to aid in understanding the young people involved in these programs. Community programs for youth benefit from ready access to high-quality data that allow them to assess and monitor the well-being of youth in their community, the well-being of youth they directly serve, and the elements of their programs that are intended to support those youth. They also benefit from information and training to help them use these data tools wisely and effectively.

Conclusions

❏ Even when exploited to their full potential, administrative, vital statistics, and related data sources can cover only limited geographic areas and only some components of a youth development framework. Adding local survey data in diverse communities, as has been done in a number of states and individual communities, can help create a more complete picture.

Community programs for youth are interested in building their capacity to assess the quality of their programs. To produce useful process evaluations, performance monitoring, and self-assessment, however, program practitioners need valid, reliable indicators of the developmental quality of the experiences they provide. Such information would also facilitate the ability of communities to monitor change over time as new program initiatives are introduced into the community. If communities know how their youth are doing on a variety of indicators for an extended period of time both before and after a new program is introduced, they can use this information as preliminary evidence that their program is effective. Such inferences are strengthened if information on the same indicators is available in comparable communities that did not introduce that program at the same time. Research is needed to determine whether appropriate indicators vary depending on the characteristics of the specific youth population served by a program and as understanding of the determinants of positive youth development improves, these indicators should be periodically revisited and, if necessary, revised.

Many community programs also lack staff knowledge and the funds to take full advantage of social indicators as tools to aid in planning, monitoring, assessing, and improving program activities. Individual programs and communities would benefit from opportunities to increase their capacity to collect and use social indicator data.

Recommendation 9—Public and private funders should support the fielding of youth development surveys in more states and communities around the country; the development, testing, and fielding of new youth development measures that work well across diverse population subgroups; and greater coordination between measures used in community surveys and national longitudinal surveys.

Recommendation 10—Public and private funders should support collaboration between researchers and the practice community to develop social indicator data that build understanding of how programs are implemented and improve the ability to monitor programs. Collaborative efforts would further the understanding of the relationship between program features and positive developmental outcomes among young people.

Recommendation 11—Public and private funders should provide opportunities for individual programs and communities to improve their capacity to collect and use social indicator data. This requires better training for program staff and more support for national and regional intermediaries that provide technical assistance in a variety of ways, including Internet-based systems.

CONCLUDING THOUGHTS

The desire among program practitioners, policy makers, scholars, scientists, parents, and society to make sure young people are healthy, happy, safe, and productive is not new. Offering formal and informal programs in the community for adolescents during nonschool hours is not new. These programs have a long history of providing positive opportunities to keep youth safe and to facilitate their development and well-being. Various individuals and professional organizations are committed to better understanding these programs and providing technical assistance to encourage their success.

The scientific evidence that elucidates the ways in which community programs for youth provide opportunities to promote adolescent development and well-being, however, is less well developed. This report has explored these programs from this perspective and presented a set of recommendations targeted at various stakeholders: practitioners (program developers, practitioners, managers, and staff); community leaders (staff and leaders in a mayor's office, local government agencies, community foundations, private intermediaries, as well as individual community leaders); and national leaders (public and private funders, policy makers, researchers, and evaluators). The recommendations in this report have the potential to enhance existing community programs for youth, promote adolescent development among diverse groups of youth and varied communities, and increase knowledge about the links between community programs for youth and adolescent development.

Fundamental Principles of Human Development

H uman development is a complex process involving many influences interacting with each other in a cumulative fashion over time. These influences range from individuals' unique genetic makeup and genetically scripted maturational sequences to the political, historical, and cultural forces that shape the settings in which they live and mature. Bronfenbrenner (Bronfenbrenner and Morris, 1998) and others (e.g., Baltes et al., 1998; Cairns, 1998; Elder, 1998; Damon and Lerner, 1998; Magnusson and Stattin, 1998; Rutter et al., 1998) have stressed the complexity of these interacting systems in development; these complexities are described in detail in Chapter 2. These complex characteristics of development make heterogeneity the norm at both individual and social levels. At any one point in time, individuals of the same age will vary greatly in their abilities, their values and interests, their needs, and their social and institutional relationships and connections. To be successful at promoting positive youth development, community programs must find ways to both accommodate and make use of these heterogeneities.

Two other properties of human development are critical to the design of community programs for youth. First,

315

there are regularities in the sequence of development across time (e.g., Erikson, 1968; Piaget, 1971; Vygotsky, 1962). These regularities are assumed to result from three primary sources: (1) the genetically scripted maturational processes linked to such physical changes as brain development, sensormotor and physical maturation, and sexual maturation; (2) the logical sequences inherent in acquiring new skills and knowledge, in moving from more external (adult driven) regulation to increasingly internal regulation of behaviors and emotions, and in moving from a primary location within intimate family settings to increasing engagement with the outside world; and (3) the regularities in the sequences of social experiences provided by social and cultural groups for children, adolescents, and adults as they mature.

Second, social clocks[1] (Neugarten and Datan, 1976) and socially scripted sequences of socialization experiences (Elder, 1998) reflect cultural group adaptation to, and use of, these developmental regularities. For example, most cultures begin formal schooling at age 6. It is possible that this is the age when children have matured cognitively and socially to the point that they are ready for the challenges imposed by formal schooling. Of course, these socially scripted sequences themselves are likely to contribute to the regularities observed in human development (Higgins et al., 1983).

The psychologist Erik Erikson has provided the most fully developed theoretical model of these developmental regularities, illustrated in Table A-1 from the perspective of community programs for youth development. Like other theorists, he proposed that there are developmental tasks that must be addressed at particular ages or stages of life. These tasks change in systematic ways as people mature. How these developmental tasks are handled by individuals in the social settings in which they live will influence subsequent development. This means two things: (1) previous learning and development are critical to individuals' current

---

[1]Social clocks refers to the socially shared norms regarding when particular events are likely to take place in people's lives—like the expected age of marriage, completion of schooling, birth of children, retirement, etc. Socially scripted socialization experiences refer to the normative sequence of experiences provided for people as they grow up—like the age at which children begin and end formal schooling, the grade structure in the K-16 schooling process (when do the major school transitions occur—when do children move into middle school or junior high school, into high school, and into postsecondary schools), the ages at which children are allowed to drink, to drive, to vote, and to join the military, etc.

TABLE A-1 Stages of Development According to Erik Erikson

Life-Cycle Tasks	Program Cycle for Adolescents
Trust versus Mistrust	
Birth to 1 year. Infant learns to expect maternal love and consistency or develops a sense of insecurity.	Learn to trust in the caring, competence, resourcefulness and fairness of the program staff and safety of the program environment.
Autonomy versus Shame and Doubt	
1 to 3 years. Balance develops between parental control and the child's own autonomy or the child develops a sense of shame and self-doubt if the balance is not established.	Negotiate an acceptable range of autonomy in behavior and decision-making, learning to respect program rules and to value guidance.
Initiative versus Guilt	
3 to 6 years. Child uses his or her increasing autonomy to be on the move, planning and initiating actions, but may develop feelings of guilt if actions violate standards of propriety.	Initiate an honest attempt to collaborate with staff and peers toward self-development goals, learning to cope with or overcome feelings of ambivalence, sometimes from survivor's guilt.
Industry versus Inferiority	
7 to 11 years. Child becomes focused on producing things, instead of simply doing things, but may develop a sense of inferiority if not generally successful.	Strive industriously to achieve program-related goals, including learning new strategies for living and mastering new skills.
Identity versus Identity Confusion	
Adolescence. In moving from childhood to adulthood, a person consciously crafts a multidimensional image of self, but may suffer confusion if that identity is not validated and approved by others.	Resolve any tensions between old and new beliefs about one's self. Assimilate a focused and positive identity that fosters a healthy life style, satisfaction with one's self and a sense of positive anticipation about one's future.
Intimacy versus Isolation	
Young adulthood. Young adults seek companionship and love with another person or become isolated from others.	Consolidate friendships with other trainees and some program staff, while drifting away from less constructive past associations.
Generativity versus Stagnation	
Adulthood. Middle-age adults are productive, performing meaningful work and raising a family, or become stagnant and inactive.	Help to improve the program and to leave it in good condition for later cohorts of trainees who will enter future cycles of the program.
Integrity versus Despair	
Maturity. Older adults try to make sense out of their lives, either seeing life as a meaningful whole or despairing at goals never reached and questions never answered.	Person leaves the program knowing that they have done their best and can look back with pride at performance and achievements.

Sources: For the life-cycle model, see Berger, K.S., 1988, p. 37, and Erikson, E., 1963, ch. 7. For the program-cycle model, see the study of *YouthBuild* by Ferguson, R. and J. Snipes, 1997.

capacities, values, attitudes, etc. and (2) current experiences set the stage for future capacities, values, attitudes, etc. Consequently, we need to think about development as occurring over time with experiences in the present being critical for both current well-being and preparation for the future.

Looking at development from this general perspective makes especially salient the need for families, schools, and communities to provide developmentally appropriate and enriching experiences throughout childhood and adolescence in order to both foster well-being and ensure adequate preparation for the transition to adulthood. Without such a guiding framework, programs will not necessarily be designed to provide the kinds of experiences necessary to ensure that adolescents will be fully prepared for becoming effective and fully functional adults. Many researchers, theoreticians, service practitioners, and policy makers see this as especially true in today's increasingly complex and technological society.

Several other aspects of this model are important to understand. First, although the model suggests that there is a natural sequence in which each individual handles these developmental tasks, the specific challenges listed as typical of the different stages are actually operative throughout the life span. People are always dealing with each of these tasks. Second, nevertheless, due to both biological changes at the individual level and social changes imposed by the larger groups in which individuals reside, particular tasks are likely to become more salient at specific periods of life. The exact sequence in which these tasks emerge will depend on characteristics of both the individual and the social setting in which the individual is developing.

For example, Erikson proposed that confronting the challenge of personal identity formation occurred during adolescence and young adulthood and prior to confronting the challenge of intimacy. This ordering of tasks is probably most true for white American males. Other groups may have a different normative ordering. The exact ordering of the relative salience of the tasks should differ across cultural groups. Such variations need to be taken into account in designing programs for youth from different cultural groups. But what is likely to be more universal is the proposal that individuals both acquire new skills and needs and are confronted with new roles and responsibilities over the course of their life histories. The interaction of both of these types of changes moves individuals through stages such as those depicted in Table A-1. Finally, as noted above, given the cumulative nature of development, resolution of these challenges at any one point in time influences subsequent development on all of these challenges.

Erikson's model has been criticized for its potential cultural specificity and its apparent rigid adherence to the perspective that maturation is based on developmental stages. Limited research supports both of these concerns: sequences are more fluid than depicted in the static framework such as summarized in Table A-1, and cultural groups do vary in the sequence of the particular tasks and challenges proposed (Berger, 1988). But in his more elaborated writings, Erikson himself repeatedly stressed the fluidity of his model, particularly in response to cultural variations in experience and norms. Despite these criticisms, the model is a useful way to think about the complexity of development.

Theoretical Frameworks for Conceptualizing Positive Developmental Processes

G arbarino and Abramowitz (1992) suggest that the role of theory in social science is that of an "imagination machine." Theory generates questions and steers attention to the wide range of factors and phenomena that should be considered. There are numerous theories in developmental psychology, sociology, public health, anthropology, and other fields that direct attention to a panorama of individual, community, and cultural processes that are related to positive development. In the next few pages we use Bronfenbrenner's framework to briefly review this theoretical panorama. Following Bronfenbrenner, we focus on the multiple systems that affect development: (a) the adolescent engaged in the settings of her or his daily life (what he calls micro-systems),(b) the web of relationships that compose the community in which the child resides (meso- and exo-systems), and (c) the culture and society that provide the frame for development (macro-systems).

ADOLESCENT IN THE MICRO-SYSTEM: PSYCHOLOGY THEORIES

The central unit of development for Bronfenbrenner is the child interacting with the different settings or micro-systems of daily life (Bronfenbrenner, 1994). Jean Piaget, the most influential theorist of *cognitive development*, elucidated how children and adolescents are active and creative agents in these interactions and, ultimately, of their own development (Piaget, 1964). Even when they give answers to questions that an adult perceives as wrong, answers typically come from intelligent deductions using previous knowledge. Thus, we need to always ask how an adolescent is thinking about and conceptualizing his or her current experience.

While Piaget focused almost exclusively on the solitary individual interacting with an inanimate environment, other specialists in cognitive development gave more attention to the interpersonal environment in which learning and development take place. Vygotsky showed how learning was typically not solitary, but collaborative (Vygotsky, 1978). Children often don't think in isolation: teachers, parents, and apeers provide support and scaffolding that contributes to their thinking and learning. Another very different school of developmental theory, *object relations* and *attachment theory,* emphasizes the emotional quality of the interpersonal environment in which development takes place, particularly children's relationships with their primary caretakers. Mahler, Winnicott, Bowlby, and others have shown how the warmth and responsiveness of a child's significant others facilitate development, particularly development of a sense of self and the capacity to engage in healthy relationships in the future. Hostility or lack of trust creates anxiety, which disrupts development (Mahler et al., 1975; Winnicott, 1975; Bowlby, 1969).

These theories suggest that people are extremely malleable, that given the right environment, children can remake themselves as they wish. Research and theory in *behavioral genetics,* however, suggests there may be limits on how much individuals can change—although the nature of these limits are beyond the range of current knowledge (Plomin, 2000). The development of some human traits, like extroversion and novelty seeking, appear to be significantly constrained by genes, although other traits, such as prosocial and antisocial behavior, are clearly not so constrained (Plomin, 1994). It must be emphasized that the state of knowledge about the role of genes in psychological and social development is very limited (Collins et al., 2000). Scientists have mapped the human genome, but they know little about how it influences the development of individual differences. Research suggests that the processes may be complex: development always occurs in interaction with environments; certain environments may be more likely to bring out specific traits; genes may partly shape development by influencing the choices children make regarding the environments in which they spend time. Given the lack of knowledge, extreme caution is required in applying the ideas of behavioral genetics to real-life situations. Nonetheless, it is important to realize, as any parent with two or more children knows, that individuals are not infinitely malleable; some (and only some!) of the emotional and cognitive dispositions that they bring into a community program may not be substantially alterable, even with the greatest staff in the world.

This fact and the other theories covered above lead to another important psychological perspective concerned with *person-environment fit*. If individuals are not infinitely malleable, then the design of optimal learning environments requires that environments be adaptable to individuals, or it requires that individuals be selectively placed into environments that suit their dispositions. Piaget's (1971) and especially Vygotsky's (1978) theories also suggest that youth learn best in environments that provide information and support at a level that is at or somewhat above their current level of cognitive development (in what Vygotsky calls the "zone of proximal development"). These issues of person-environment fit appear to be particularly salient in early adolescence, when young people's abilities and needs are changing rapidly. Eccles et al. (1993) show that junior high schools often fail to provide this fit to the developmental stage of young adolescents, resulting in diminished levels of interest, motivation, and learning among junior high students. They theorize that a similar lack of developmental fit often occurs in the family, accounting for the increased rates of conflict that many young adolescents experience with their parents. The message of this theory, indeed of psychological theories in general, is that positive development is most likely to occur in environments that are attentive to and matched with the dispositions and developmental level of the individual. To engage an adolescent in growth, one must engage that human being in an environment that makes sense to her or him.

In addition, to be successful programs must be developmentally appropriate and must have a developmental agenda. That is, they need to have provisions for the participants to grow and take on new roles as they mature as program members. The activities also need to relate to the developmental agendas of the participants. For example, as adolescents mature, they should become more concerned about moving into the labor market. Organizations that take these changing interests into account in their programming are likely to be more successful at retaining participation as their members mature than organizations that do not (see McLaughlin, 2000).

THE MESO- AND EXO-SYSTEMS: ROLE OF COMMUNITY RELATIONSHIPS IN DEVELOPMENT

Bronfenbrenner stressed the importance of the meso- and exo- systems. In general, Bronfenbrenner's approach makes the complex interactions between individuals and their social settings salient. Adolescents grow in families that, in turn, exist within a much larger social system. Adolescents also participate in a variety of settings and institutions, such as community based programs and schools, that are part of this larger social system. Finally, these institutions are part of the larger social system and consequently are influenced by a variety of forces beyond their direct control. Understanding adolescent development requires an understanding of such complexities. Both designing community programs for youth and understanding what distinguishes successful programs from unsuccessful programs also requires an understanding of such complexities.

Bronfenbrenner made an important contribution to developmental science by drawing attention to the critical role of intermediate institutions—families, schools, places of work, communities, and so forth—and particularly the interrelationships between these institutions. Bronfenbrenner introduced the concept of the meso-system, which is the interlinkages among the different settings or micro-systems in a child or adolescent's life. Development is facilitated when there are meaningful linkages between settings, when parents know a child's friends, teachers, and coaches, and good communication exists among them. Bronfenbrenner also introduced the concept of the exo-system, which is the larger community in which a child lives and the set of connections (outside the view of the child) that occur within the institutions of that community. Again, development is facilitated when these connections involve meaningful communications.

The work of James Comer (1988) provides a valuable illustration of the importance of these connections. He described how school outcomes for children were greatly improved if their school operated as a community of teachers, school administrators, and parents who were in touch with each other. He also showed the negative consequences when teachers, school administrators, and parents were out of touch with each other because of differing cultural backgrounds. This lack of cohesion resulted in poor school performance among the students. He also showed that a school intervention designed to build channels of communication could both increase community and the quality of students' work. Certainly the same interlinkages are important to the effective functioning of a community program.

The concept of *social capital* from sociology is one useful way of thinking about these interlinkages. Social capital refers to the resources, such as access to information and assistance, that arise from social relationships (Coleman, 1988; Portes and Landolt, 1996; Portes, 1998). For adolescents, the concept of social capital is particularly useful in evaluating the developmental resources that are gained through young people's (and their parents', teachers', etc.) network of ties within the community (Astone et al., 1999). Through these relationships, youth gain access to educational opportunities, life skills, jobs, and support that give them an advantage in the adult world. Youth also profit from social ties in the exo-sphere: connections among their families, schools, and communities. For instance, adolescents whose parents are active in the PTA benefit from exchanges between teachers and their parents that reinforce academic activities. Similarly, youth whose parents are active in faith-based or other political or community-based organizations benefit from the social connection their parents form (Furstenburg et al., 1999). A critical point is that access to social capital is not universal. Some of the disproportionate social and economic disadvantage born by urban or poor rural children can be related to limitations in social capital available in many inner-city neighborhoods or isolated rural communities (Loury, 1977; Wilson, 1987). As the resources of communities, schools, community programs, and families are depleted, it becomes increasingly more difficult for young people to secure the support they need to make a successful transition to adulthood. Furthermore, when youth have few relationships that promote positive development, adolescents may seek social capital from groups, such as gangs, that fill developmental needs for leadership, independence, self-esteem, and autonomy. Community-based programs are an ideal place to help adolescents form long-term positive social capital.

The management perspective is another theoretical approach that helps our understanding of the interlinkages within the community that facilitate positive development in adolescents (Furstenberg et al., 1999; Jarrett, 1997). This perspective recognizes that parents play a critical role in orchestrating their children's daily lives, both through their daily practices and the decisions they make concerning the types of information and resources the child receives. This management includes promotive strategies aimed at creating positive experiences and helping children develop skills and interests, such as assisting with the child's schoolwork, encouraging the development of talents and interests, enrolling the child in special classes and programs, or getting an older sibling or other relative to help the child with homework. It can also include preventive strategies aimed at minimizing behavioral risks and negative outcomes, such as careful monitoring of the child's location, enforcing strong curfew practices, involving the child in positive protective activities, and discussing negative models. Like effective business managers, effective parents anticipate the future and take a proactive stance toward preparing for it. As children mature, other people become more central players in the process of management. Teachers, religious figures, peers, leaders of community programs, and other significant people come to influence the informational flow and resources available to the child; with guidance, adolescents themselves come to gradually assume this role of managing their lives and their developmental opportunities. Community programs for youth can play a very important role in helping adolescents learn to manage their own lives effectively. These programs can both teach these skills and provide adolescents with the information they need to make wise decisions on their own behalf.

THE MACRO-SYSTEM: CULTURAL THEORIES

No account of human development is complete unless it considers the ways that the systems just discussed differ across cultures (Schweder et al., 1998). Bronfenbrenner defines the macro-system as "the overarching pattern of micro-, meso-, and exosystem characteristics of a given culture or subculture" (Bronfenbrenner, 1994: 1645). Culture provides the templates and tools for young people's interactions with each setting. As discussed in Chapter 2, they may also specify different goals for development. Margaret Mead (1935) described how blueprints provided by culture shape development, as well as the institutions that influence development (family, religion, rites of passage, community structures). Recognizing a more active role played by the individual, other theorists emphasize that adolescents also shape settings.

Anthropologists' definitions of culture include symbolic and behavioral components, both of which are crucial to one of the positive features of settings we identify below. First, cultures are symbolic systems of shared beliefs, doctrines, values, and, importantly, meaning. They provide underlying conceptions of "how to be" and of "the good life and how to live it" (LeVine et al., 1988; Shweder et al., 1998). Both anthropologists and sociologists (e.g. Durkheim, 1951) have shown that individuals' embeddedness in (and sense of belonging to) a coherent cultural system is crucial to their well-being and experience of meaning. Without it, adolescents and adults experience alienation. Second, and interdependently, cultures are systems of behavior. They include practices, behavioral scripts, language—normative ways of doing things—and these are often organized around institutions (Shweder et al., 1998). In most cases, these systems of behavior have evolved over hundreds of years and provide a well-honed framework for community life. Development involves being socialized into the norms of one's culture, learning to use the behavior repertoire to achieve culturally meaningful goals. Acquisition of this knowledge of a cultural system is sometimes described as acquisition of cultural capital: it is knowledge that allows them to function effectively within that culture.

A problem with the simplified account offered thus far is that it presents culture as singular and static. Yet even in traditional cultures there are competing cultural ideas (Turiel, 1999) and in the United States there is a noisy marketplace of multiple cultures, culture wars, and changing systems of meaning and behavior. Adolescents have to sort through and choose among numerous alternative frames of meaning and ways of acting. Furthermore, the differing institutions that deal with adolescents may operate with conflicting cultural values and norms—the relationships that constitute meso- and exo-systems can be impeded by incompatible world views (Comer, 1988). For example, LaFromboise and Graff Low (1998) illustrate how adolescent behavior that Euro-American counselors view as bad can be viewed as a sign of progress by Hopi adults.

For Erikson (1968), the developmental task of adolescents faced with this noisy marketplace is to draw on and wrestle with the issues and contradictions of his or her society and historical period. The adolescent needs to choose values, decide what cultural group to belong to, and figure out how he or she relates to other cultural groups. This process is often more difficult for individuals in disenfranchised minority groups, who may confront conflicting cultural definitions of who they are and how they should act (Phinney and Kohatsu, 1997). Even if they acquire the cultural capital of the dominant group, they may find that members of that group have greater power to define the values and norms that are operative within a setting (Bourdieu and Passeron, 1977). In other ways it may be easier, in that minority groups learn more than one culture. As society continues to become more culturally diverse, such multicultural knowledge can become an asset, provided that the individual has gained the social skills needed to flourish in the dominant culture or in multicultural niches where the ability to navigate more than one culture is critical (LaFromboise et al., 1993).

All of these issues manifest themselves in varying ways in the daily settings of adolescents' lives, including their participation in community programs. The cultural perspective suggests a need to expand the earlier notion of person-environment fit to include cultural fit. Given that youth may be walking in the door with widely differing cultural backgrounds, knowledge, and agendas, it is essential that community programs be sensitive to how they are experienced by different youth. Taking the positive side, community programs can have an important role in assisting youth with addressing developmental issues of cultural belonging, which can be particularly acute in a changing and multicultural society.

APPENDIX C

Biographical Sketches

Jacquelynne Eccles *(Chair)* is the Wilbert McKeachie collegiate professor of psychology, women's studies, and education, as well as a research scientist at the Institute for Social Research, University of Michigan, and the interim chair of psychology at the University of Michigan. She has served on the faculty at Smith College, the University of Colorado, and the University of Michigan. In addition, she is past chair of the Advisory Committee for the Social, Behavioral, and Economic Directorate at the National Science Foundation, a member of the MacArthur Foundation Network on Successful Adolescent Development, the chair of the MacArthur Foundation Network on Successful Pathways through Middle Childhood, and associate editor of *Child Development.* Over the past 30 years, she has conducted research on a wide variety of topics ranging from gender role socialization, teacher expectations, and classroom influences on student motivation, to social development in the family and school context. Much of this work has focused on middle childhood and adolescence when health-compromising behaviors such as smoking increase dramatically. Using longitudinal survey methods, she has explored the characteristics of family, community, school, and peer groups that either protect against or encourage such risky behaviors during these periods of life. She is coauthor of *Women and Sex-Roles* and of *Managing to Make It*. She has a Ph.D. in developmental psychology from the University of California, Los Angeles.

Cheryl Alexander is professor of population and family health sciences and director of the Center for Adolescent Health Promotion and Disease Prevention at the Johns Hopkins School of Hygiene and Public Health. The Center for Adolescent Health is one of 26 prevention research centers funded by the Centers for Disease Control and Prevention. Her research has focused on health-risking behaviors of young adolescents, with a particular focus on gender differences in patterns of risk-taking. She has explored how social contexts including schools, neighborhoods, and families influence adolescent health risking behaviors. Most recently, she and her colleagues have begun to examine the effectiveness of community-based interventions in reducing adolescent health risks, such as tobacco use, early sexual intercourse, and sedentary behaviors. She was recently appointed to the Governor's Council on Adolescent Pregnancy and is a member of the Committee on Adolescent Health and Development, formerly the Forum on Adolescence. She has a B.S.N. from the University of North Carolina and an M.P.H and Ph.D. from Johns Hopkins University School of Public Health.

Brett Brown is senior research associate and area director for social indicators research at Child Trends, a nonpartisan, nonprofit research firm. He oversaw the design and production of first four editions of *Trends in the Well-Being of America's Children and Youth*, a comprehensive annual report featuring national trends in over 90 indicators of well-being released by the U.S. Department of Health and Human Services. For the past several years, he has been a consultant to the Federal Interagency Forum on Child and Family Statistics, playing a key role in the design and production of the first edition of *America's Children: Key National Indicators of Well-Being*, an annual report to the President. He is a member of the core working group on adolescent health for the *Healthy People 2010* project of the Centers for Disease Control and Prevention and has been part of an international group of researchers that is attempting to develop comparable indicators of child and youth well-being for advanced industrial societies. For the past several years, he has also provided technical assistance to the national and state Kids Count organizations sponsored by the Annie E. Casey Foundation. He has a Ph.D. in sociology from the University of Wisconsin.

Sarah Brown is director of the National Campaign to Prevent Teen Pregnancy, a private and independent initiative organized in 1995 to stimulate actions nationwide to reduce adolescent pregnancy. Before this, she was a senior study director at the Institute of Medicine, where her last project before founding the Campaign was directing a major study on unintended pregnancy. She has published numerous scholarly and popular articles on a wide variety of topics in maternal and child health and in reproductive health and is also a frequent public speaker and media contact on these issues. She serves on numerous advisory committees of national organizations and on several boards as well, including that of the Alan Guttmacher Institute. She has an M.A. in public health from the University of North Carolina.

Kenyon S. Chan is dean of the Bellarmine College of Liberal Arts and professor of psychology at Loyola Marymount University. His research focuses on social science perspectives on ethnic studies, social policy, and interdisciplinary analyses of race in America. He is recognized as an expert on the effects of race on the emotional development of children and has written extensively on the sociocultural factors that influence motivation, learning, and schooling with particular attention to poor and immigrant children. He has a Ph.D. in educational psychology from the University of California, Los Angeles.

Elizabeth Colson is professor emeritus in the Department of Anthropology at the University of California, Berkeley. Her primary research interest lies in the longitudinal study of social and cultural change. She is interested in development, the role of development agencies, migration, the impact of large-scale disruptions, and the adjustment of refugees and other forced migrants. She is a member of the National Academy of Sciences. She has a Ph.D. from Radcliffe College.

Thomas Cook is professor of sociology, psychology, education and social policy and faculty fellow in the Institute for Policy Research at Northwestern University. His major research interest is examining routes out of poverty, especially for racial minorities in the inner city, with special emphasis on how material and social resources activate self-help behavior. He is also studying the management strategies parents use in different neighborhoods, the differing levels of resources available to youth and their families, and how these neighborhood differences impact on parental coping techniques and adolescent development. He is a member of the MacArthur Network on Successful Adolescence in High-Risk Settings. He has a Ph.D. in communications from Stanford University.

Peter Edelman is a professor of law at Georgetown University Law Center, where he has been on the faculty since 1982. He took leave from 1993 until 1996 to serve in the U.S. Department of Health and Human Services, first as counselor to Secretary Donna Shalala and then as assistant secretary for planning and evaluation. He was associate dean of the Law Center in the late 1980s, director of the New York State Division for Youth in the late 1970s, and vice president of the University of Massachusetts before that. He was a legislative assistant to Senator Robert F. Kennedy from 1965 to 1968 and was issues director for Senator Edward Kennedy's presidential campaign in 1980. He served as law clerk to Supreme Court Justice Arthur J. Goldberg in 1962-1963 and to Judge Henry J. Friendly on the U.S. Court of Appeals for the Second Circuit, and was special assistant to Assistant Attorney General John Douglas in the U.S. Department of Justice following his Supreme Court clerkship. He has a J.D. from Harvard School of Law.

Caswell Evans is executive editor and project director, Surgeon General's Report on Oral Health on an Inter-Agency Personnel Agreement with the U.S. Department of Health and Human Services. In this capacity he is located at the National Institute of Dental and Craniofacial Research at the National Institutes of Health. The charge of the surgeon general's report was "to define, describe, and evaluate the interaction between oral health, health, and well-being (quality of life), through the life span in the context of changes in society." The report was released by the surgeon general in May 2000. He also serves as adjunct professor at the School of Public Health and the School of Dentistry at the University of California, Los Angeles. A member of the Institute of Medicine, he has a D.D.S. from Columbia University.

Ronald Ferguson is lecturer in public policy and senior research associate at the Wiener Center for Social Policy in the John F. Kennedy School of Government, Harvard University. His teaching and research cover topics in social policy and economic development, including special attention to problems associated with the education and employment of populations that experience disproportionate levels of poverty in the United States. He has a Ph.D. in economics from the Massachusetts Institute of Technology.

Amy Gawad *(Research Associate)* is a staff member with the Board on Children, Youth, and Families of the National Research Council/Institutes of Medicine. Prior to her work on youth development at the National Academies, she had responsibility at the board for the dissemination of *From Neurons to Neighborhoods,* a report on the science of early childhood development, and for supporting members of the Forum on Adolescence. She has an M.P.H. from the George Washington University School of Public Health.

Jennifer Appleton Gootman *(Study Director)* is a staff member with the Board on Children, Youth, and Families of the National Research Council/Institutes of Medicine. She was previously a social science analyst for the Office of Planning and Evaluation in the U.S. Department of Health and Human Services. Her work has focused on child and family policy for low-income families, including welfare reform, child care, child health, youth development, and teen pregnancy prevention issues. She has directed a number of community youth programs in Los Angeles and New York City, involving young people in leadership development, job preparedness, and community service. She has an M.A. in public policy from the New School for Social Research.

Robert Granger served on the Committee on Community-Level Programs for Youth until March 2000, when he became the new senior vice president at the William T. Grant Foundation, one of the funders of this project. Prior to this he served as senior vice president for education, children, and youth at the Manpower Demonstration Research Corporation. He is an expert on programs and policies for low-income children and youth. Selected by the MacArthur Foundation as a core member of its research network on middle childhood, he has conducted numerous empirical studies; in recent years, he has focused particularly on public policies related to the effects of welfare policies on children and the evaluation of comprehensive school reforms. He has an Ed.D. in early childhood education from the University of Massachusetts at Amherst.

Teresa LaFromboise is associate professor of education at Stanford University. She is concerned with helping ethnic minority students survive the cultural adjustments, major life transitions, and other stresses that are typical and often neglected in children and adolescents. As a counseling psychologist with clinical and teaching experience in a wide variety of university and American Indian reservation settings, she is well equipped to guide new teachers in multicultural counseling and inventions. She has also developed a complete life skills development curriculum of problem-based lessons aimed at reducing the risk of suicide among American Indian adolescents, which has already been shown to be successful in high school students and is now being extended to younger students and their families. She has a Ph.D. in counseling psychology from the University of Oklahoma.

Reed Larson is professor of human development and family studies at the University of Illinois at Urbana-Champaign. His research focuses on adolescents' daily emotions and experience, especially in the context of families and after-school activities. He has a Ph.D. in human development from the University of Chicago.

Milbrey McLaughlin is professor of education and public policy at the Stanford Graduate School of Education. She has been studying youth programs and neighborhood organizations since 1987. The first phase of this research focused on inner-city youth, and the second phase expands to include youth and their community resources from mid-sized cities to rural areas. She has a Ph.D. in education and social policy from Harvard University.

Elena Nightingale *(Scholar-in-Residence)* is a volunteer with the National Research Council and the Institute of Medicine of the National Academies. She is an adjunct professor of pediatrics at both Georgetown University Medical Center and George Washington University Medical Center. For more than eleven years she was special advisor to the president and senior program officer at Carnegie Corporation of New York and lecturer in social medicine at Harvard University. She is a member of the Institute of Medicine of the National Academies and a fellow of the American Association for the Advancement of Sciences, the New York Academy of Sciences, and the Royal Society of Medicine. She has also authored numerous book chapters and articles on microbial genetics; health (particularly child and adolescent health and well-being and health promotion and disease prevention); health policy; and human rights. She is a member of the Committee on Adolescent Health and

Development, a member emerita of the IOM Board on Health Promotion and Disease Prevention, and serves as liaison or advisor to several IOM activities. She has a Ph.D. in microbial genetics from the Rockefeller University and an M.D. from New York University School of Medicine.

Robert Plotnick serves on the faculty of the University of Washington as professor of public affairs, director of the Center for Studies in Demography and Ecology, and adjunct professor of economics, sociology and social work. He is also a research affiliate with the Institute for Research on Poverty, University of Wisconsin-Madison. His research has addressed a wide range of topics concerned with poverty, income inequality, income support policy, teenage and nonmarital childbearing, the application of benefit-cost analysis to social services, and related social policy issues. He has a Ph.D. in economics from the University of California, Berkeley.

Rebekah Pinto *(Senior Project Assistant)* is a staff member with the Board on Children, Youth, and Families of the National Research Council/ Institutes of Medicine. She has helped the board organize workshops related to children and computer technology, family stresses in the 21st Century, and urban school reform. Before joining the board she worked as a communications associate at Catholics for a Free Choice. Before joining the National Academies her research focused on public health, women's issues, and international family planning. She has a B.A. in anthropology from Indiana University of Pennsylvania.

Zena Stein is professor of public health (epidemiology) and psychiatry emerita at Columbia University. She is an expert in the prevention of AIDS in women and on the prevention of mental retardation. She is co-director of the HIV Center at Columbia with a major commitment to work in Southern Africa. Recently, her principal research efforts at the Center have been to develop protective methods for women that will reduce their risks of sexually transmitted infections; to study the epidemiology of perinatal HIV infection, including risks for maternal-infant transmission including breast feeding; factors involved in survival; and neurodevelopmental effects on infected infants. She has an M.A. in history at the University of Cape Town and an M.B. and B.Ch. in medicine at the University of Witwatersrand in Johannesburg, South Africa.

Related Reports from the National Academies

Adolescent Decision Making: Implications for Prevention Programs: Summary of a Workshop (1999)
Board on Children, Youth, and Families

Helping young people realize their potential often turns on their ability to make good decisions. To that end, the Forum on Adolescence convened a workshop that examined research on risk-taking and decision theory and the implications for programs to support healthy adolescent development. This workshop report highlights some of the factors that may influence how adolescents make decisions, including the role that emotions may play, the level of emotional maturity they have gained, and the way in which they think about their social world. Participants also looked at broader influences, such as the effect of the larger society and the media, and at programs for adolescents.

Adolescent Development and the Biology of Puberty: Summary of a Workshop on New Research (1999)
Forum on Adolescence

In one of its first activities, the Forum on Adolescence convened a workshop to explore new research on puberty and adolescent development. This workshop summary report examines the discussion by participants representing diverse fields, from pediatric and adolescent medicine to neuroendocrinology to psychiatry and other disciplines. Reviewing breakthroughs in science and technology—especially brain imaging and neuroendocrinology—that have sparked an explosion of new knowledge, participants emphasized that available evidence underscores the dual influence of biological and social factors on development. The report emphasizes the importance of policies and programs that promote positive development, not just the absence of problems. Adolescents themselves need to be engaged as young adults who can learn to respond effectively to day-to-day challenges and serve as role models in encouraging positive behaviors.

After-School Programs to Promote Child and Adolescent Development: Summary of a Workshop (2000)
Committee on Community-Level Programs for Youth

This volume summarizes the presentations and discussion at a workshop entitled Opportunities to Promote Child and Adolescent Development During the After-School Hours. The workshop was an effort to take stock of the current knowledge base on after-school programs and highlight key findings from recent research. This workshop summary report examines research on the developmental needs of children and adolescents—ages 5 to 14 years—and the types of after-school programs designed to promote the health and development of these young people.

The Best Intentions: Unintended Pregnancy and the Well-Being of Children and Families (1995)
Committee on Unintended Pregnancy

The Best Intentions explores family planning issues shedding light on the questions and controversies surrounding unintended pregnancy. The book includes specific recommendations to put the United States on a par with other developed nations in terms of contraceptive attitudes and policies, and it considers the effectiveness of over 20 pregnancy prevention programs. *The Best Intentions* offers frank discussion, synthesis of data, and policy recommendations on one of today's most sensitive social topics.

Children of Immigrants: Health, Adjustment, and Public Assistance (1999)
Committee on the Health and Adjustment of Immigrant Children and Families

Children of Immigrants represents some of the very best and most extensive research efforts to date on the circumstances, health, and development of children in immigrant families and the delivery of health and social services to these children and their families. This book presents detailed analyses of more than a dozen existing datasets that constitute a large share of the national system for monitoring the health and well-being of the U.S. population. The analyses enormously expand the available knowledge about the physical and mental health status and risk behaviors, educational experiences and outcomes, and socioeconomic and demographic circumstances of first- and second-generation immigrant children, compared with children with U.S.-born parents.

From Generation to Generation: The Health and Well-Being of Children in Immigrant Families (1998)
Committee on the Health and Adjustment of Immigrant Children and Families

Immigrant children and youth are the fastest growing segment of the U.S. population, and so their prospects bear heavily on the well-being of the country. *From Generation to Generation* explores what is known about the development of white, black, Hispanic, and Asian children and youth from numerous countries of origin. Describing the status of immigrant children and youth as "severely understudied," the committee both draws on and supplements existing research characterizing the current status and outlook of immigrants. The book discusses the many factors that shape the outlook for the lives of these children and youth and makes recommendations for improved research and data collection designed to advance knowledge about these children and, as a result, enhance their visibility in current policy debates.

Growing Up Tobacco Free: Preventing Nicotine Addiction in Children and Youths (1994)
Committee on Preventing Nicotine Addiction in Children and Youths

Tobacco use kills more people than any other addiction and we know that addiction starts in childhood and youth. *Growing Up Tobacco Free* provides a readable explanation of nicotine's effects and the process of addiction, documenting the search for an effective approach to preventing the use of cigarettes, chewing and spitting tobacco, and snuff by children and youths. It covers the results of recent initiatives to limit young people's access to tobacco and discusses approaches to controls or bans on tobacco sales, price sensitivity among adolescents, and arguments for and against taxation as a prevention strategy for tobacco use. The controversial area of tobacco advertising is thoroughly examined.

How People Learn: Brain, Mind, Experience, and School: Expanded Edition (2000)
Committee on Developments in the Science of Learning and the Committee on Learning Research and Educational Practice

When do infants begin to learn? How do experts learn and how is this different from nonexperts? What can teachers and schools do—with curricula, classroom settings, and teaching methods—to help children learn most effectively? *How People Learn* examines new research about the mind and the brain that provides answers to these and other questions. New evidence from many branches of science has significantly added to the understanding of what it means to know, from the neural processes that occur during learning to the influence of culture on what people see and absorb. *How People Learn* examines these findings and their implications for what we teach, how we teach it, and how we assess what our children learn. The book uses exemplary teaching to illustrate how approaches based on what is now known result in in-depth learning. This new knowledge calls into question concepts and practices firmly entrenched in the current education system.

Improving Intergroup Relations Among Youth: Summary of a Research Workshop (2000)
Forum on Adolescence

The study of interethnic and interracial interactions and relationships among youth, also called intergroup relations, has become a critical, complex, and challenging field in recent years. The Forum on Adolescence held a workshop to consider the findings of 16 research projects funded by the Carnegie Corporation of New York that have focused on intergroup relations. The goal of this workshop summary is to provide an opportunity to learn about the work and preliminary findings of the 16 projects, as well as to review the knowledge base regarding the effectiveness of interventions designed to promote peaceful, respectful relations among youths of different ethnic groups.

Integrating Federal Statistics on Children: Report of a Workshop (1995)
Committee on National Statistics and Board on Children and Families

Those who make and implement policies for children and families are seriously hampered by several features of the federal statistical system: categorical fragmentation, sampling strategies that follow adults and families rather than children, and lack of longitudinal data on children. This volume examines the adequacy of federal statistics on children and families. It includes papers on the relevant aspects of health care reform, family and community resources, interpersonal violence, the transition to school, and educational attainment and the transition to work.

Longitudinal Surveys of Children (1998)
Committee on National Statistics and Board on Children, Youth, and Families

The Committee on National Statistics and the Board on Children, Youth, and Families convened a workshop to discuss ways to foster greater collaboration and sharing of information among principal investigators of several longitudinal surveys of children. Among many topics discussed were issues of coverage and balance of content, sampling design and weighting, measurement and analysis, field operations, legitimation and retention of cases, data disclosure and dissemination, and resources available for longitudinal studies.

Losing Generations: Adolescents in High-Risk Settings (1995)
Panel on High-Risk Youth

This book argues that the problems of troubled youth cannot be separated from the settings in which they live—settings that have deteriorated significantly in the past two decades. The book examines what works and what does not in the effort to support and nurture adolescents and offers models for successful programs. It turns the spotlight on institutions that serve youth—the health care system, schools, the juvenile and criminal justice systems, and the child welfare and foster home systems—and how they are functioning. A number of difficult issues are addressed with research results and insightful analyses: access of poor youth to health insurance coverage, inequities in school funding, how child welfare agencies provide for adolescents in their care, and the high percentage of young black men in the criminal justice system.

Protecting Youth at Work: Health, Safety, and Development of Working Children and Adolescents in the United States (1998)
Committee on the Health and Safety Implications of Child Labor

Protecting Youth at Work provides a historical perspective on working children and adolescents in America and explores the framework of child labor laws that govern that work. The report presents a wide range of data and analysis on the scope of youth employment, factors that put children and adolescents at risk in the workplace, and the positive and negative effects of employment, including data on educational attainment and lifestyle choices. It also includes discussions of special issues for minority and disadvantaged youth, young workers in agriculture, and children who work in family-owned businesses.

Risks and Opportunities: Synthesis of Studies on Adolescence (1999)
Forum on Adolescence

Over the past two decades, researchers have made substantial progress in describing the complexity of adolescence and in determining the common features of adolescent development. Research shows that adolescence is a time of both great turmoil and great opportunity for America's youth. As one of the first activities of the Forum on Adolescence, *Risks and Opportunities* reviews and synthesizes nearly 60 reports published by the National Research Council and the Institute of Medicine regarding adolescent issues and topics relevant to their health and development.

Understanding Child Abuse and Neglect (1993)
Panel on Research on Child Abuse and Neglect

Child abuse and neglect are in the forefront of public attention, yet without a conceptual framework, research in this area has been highly fragmented, and understanding the broad dimensions of this crisis has suffered as a result. This volume provides a comprehensive, integrated, child-oriented research agenda for the nation.

Violence in Families: Assessing Prevention and Treatment Programs (1998)
Committee on the Assessment of Family Violence Interventions

Violence in Families examines the successes and failures of family violence interventions and makes recommendations to guide services, programs, policy, and research on victim support and assistance, treatments and penalties for offenders, and law enforcement. Included is an analysis of more than 100 evaluation studies on the outcomes of different kinds of programs and services. It explores the scope and complexity of family violence, including identification of the multiple types of victims and offenders, who require different approaches to intervention. The book outlines new strategies that offer promising approaches for service providers and researchers and for improving the evaluation of prevention and treatment services.

Youth Development and Neighborhood Influences: Challenges and Opportunities (1996)
Committee on Youth Development

Today's youth live and develop in a society that offers tremendous choices and challenges during the formative period of adolescence. The adolescent's environment is shaped profoundly by the presence or absence of many different factors, including family resources, community services, and educational and employment opportunities. This book examines the strengths and limitations of research on social settings and adolescence and identifies important research questions that deserve further study in developing this field. Also, it explores alternative methods by which the findings of research on social settings could be better integrated into the development of youth programs and services. Specific themes include the impact of social settings on differences in developmental pathways, role expectations, and youth identity and decision-making skills, as well as factors that contribute to variations in community context.

References

Aber, J.L., J.L. Brown, N. Chaudry, S.M. Jones, and F. Samples
    1996   The Evaluation of the Resolving Conflict Creatively Program: An Overview. *American Journal of Preventative Medicine.* 12(5):82-89.

Aber, J.L., S.M. Jones, J.L. Brown, N. Chaudry, and F. Samples
    1998   Resolving Conflict Creatively: Evaluating the Developmental Effects of a School-Based Violence Prevention Program in Neighborhood and Classroom Context. *Development and Psychopathology.* 10:187-213.

Abramowitz, R.H., A.C. Petersen, and J.E. Schulenberg
    1984   Changes in self-image during early adolescence. Pp. 19-28 in *Patterns of Adolescent Self-Image*, D. Offer, E. Ostrov, and K. Howard, Eds. San Francisco: Jossey-Bass.

Academy for Educational Development and National Training Institute for Community Youth Work
    1999   Building Local Infrastructure for Youth Development: The Added Value of Capacity-Building Intermediary Organizations. Accessed 2001. Available online at: http://www.aed.org/pubs_youth.html
    2000a   CBS Schools: A History of High Standards For All, Issue Brief II, Fall 2000. Accessed 2000. Available online at: http://www.aed.org/publications/CBO_Schools/cboschools2.html
    2000b   Community Youthmapping, Center for Youth Development and Policy Research. Accessed 2000. Available online at: http://www.aed.org.
    2000c   *Best Initiative*. Accessed 2001. Available online at: www.aed.org.

Acosta, D.T., and B.A. Holt
    1991   Give Teens The Programs They Want and Need. *Journal of Extension.* 29:29-30.

342

Adams G.R., R. Montemayor, and T.P. Gullotta
    1989   *Biology of Adolescent Behavior and Development.* Newbury Park, CA: Sage.

Afterschool Alliance
    2000   *Afterschool Alliance: About Us.* Accessed 2001. Available online at: www.afterschoolalliance.org.

Akron Children's Hospital
    2000   *Overview of the PATHS (Promoting Adolescents Through Health Services) Program.* Accessed 2001. Available online at: www.akronchilrens.org.

Albert, D.J., M.L. Walsh, and R.H. Jonik
    1993   Aggression in Humans: What is its Biological Foundation? *Neuroscience and Biobehavioral Reviews.* 17:405-425.

Alexander, K.L., S.L. Dauber, and D.R. Entwisle
    1993   First-Grade Classroom Behavior: Its Short- and Long-Term Consequences for School Performance. *Child Development.* 64:801-803.

Alexander K.L., D.R. Entwisle, and S.L. Dauber
    1994   *On the Success of Failure: A Reassessment of the Effects of Retention in the Primary Grades.* Cambridge: Cambridge University Press.

Allen, J.P., G. Kuperminc, S. Philliber, and K. Herre
    1994   Programmatic Prevention of Adolescent Problem Behaviors: The Role of Autonomy, Relatedness, and Volunteer Service in the Teen Outreach Program. *American Journal of Community Psychology.* 22(5):617-638.

Allen, J.P., S. Philliber, S. Herrling, and G.P. Kuperminc
    1997   Preventing Teen Pregnancy and Academic Failure: Experimental Evaluation of a Developmentally Based Approach. *Child Development.* 68(4):729-742.

Allen, J.P., S. Philliber, and N. Hoggson
    1990   School-Based Prevention of Teen-Age Pregnancy and School Dropout: Process Evaluation of the National Replication of the Teen Outreach Program. *American Journal of Community Psychology.* 18(4):505-524.

Allen, J.P., and S.P. Philliber
    1998   Who Benefits Most From a Broadly Targeted Prevention Program? Differential Efficacy Across Populations in the Teen Outreach Program. Manuscript submitted for publication.

Alliance for Redesigning Government and National Academy of Public Administration
    2001   *New York City Beacons School-Based Community Centers.* Accessed 2001. Available online at: www.alliance.napawash.org.

American Bar Association
    2000   *Guns in Schools,* Accessed 2001. Available online at: http://www.abanet.org/gunviol/schools.html

American Heart Association
    1996   *Understanding Obesity in Youth.* Accessed 2000. Available online at: www.americanheart.org.

American Library Association
    2000   Recognizing Excellence in Afterschool Programs for Young Adults. Chicago, IL: American Library Association.

American Youth Policy Forum
    1997   *Some Things Do Make a Difference for Youth: A Compendium of Evaluations of Youth Programs and Practices.* Washington, DC: American Youth Policy Forum.
    1999   *More Things That Do Make a Difference for Youth: A Compendium of Evaluations of Youth Programs and Practices.* Washington, DC: American Youth Policy Forum.

Ames, C.
1992   Classrooms: Goals, structures, and student motivation. *Journal of Educational Psychology.* 84:261-271.
Andrews, D.A., I. Zinger, R.D. Hoge, J. Bonta, P. Gendreau, and F.T. Cullen
1990   Does Correctional Treatment Work? A Clinically Relevant and Psychologically Informed Meta-Analysis. *Criminology.* 28(3):369-405.
Angrist, J.D., and G.W. Imbrens
1995   Two-Stage Least Squares Estimation of Average Causal Effects in Models with Variable Treatment Intensity. *Journal of the American Statistical Association,* 90:431-442.
Annie E. Casey Foundation
2000   Kids Count Data Book 2000: State Profiles of Child Well-Being. Baltimore, MD: The Annie E. Casey Foundation.
2001   *Welcome to the Annie E. Casey Foundation: Website Overview.* Accessed 2001. Available online at: www.aecf.org.
Anson, A., T.D. Cook, F. Habib, M.K. Grady, N. Haynes, and J.P. Comer
1991   The Comer School Development Program: A Theoretical Analysis. *Journal of Urban Education.* 26:56-82.
Aos, S., P. Phipps, R. Barnoski, and R. Lieb
2001   *The Comparative Costs and Benefits of Programs to Reduce Crime.* Olympia, WA: Washington State Institute for Public Policy.
Armstrong, N., and B. Simon-Morton
1994   Physical Activity and Blood Lipids in Adolescents. *Pediatric Exercise Sciences.* 6:381-405.
Arnett, J.J.
1998   Learning to Stand Alone: The Contemporary American Transition to Adulthood in Cultural and Historical Context. *Human Development.* 41:295-315.
1999   Adolescent Storm and Stress, Reconsidered. *American Psychologist.* 54:317-326.
2000a High Hopes in a Grim World: Emerging Adults' Views of Their Futures and "Generation X". *Youth & Society.* 31(3):267-286.
2000b Emerging Adulthood: A Theory of Development From the Late Teens Through the Twenties. *American Psychologist.* 55(5):469-480.
Arthur M. W., J. D. Hawkins, R. F. Catalano, and J. A. Pollard
no   *Item Construct Dictionary for the Student Survey of Risk and Protective Factors*
date   *and Prevalence of Alcohol, Tobacco, and Other Drug Use.* Seattle, Washington: Social Development Research Group, University of Washington.
Ashton, P.
1985   Motivation and the Teacher's Sense of Efficacy. Pp. 141-171 in *Research on Motivation in Education,* C. Ames and R. Ames, Eds. Orlando, FL: Academic Press.
Association for the Study and Development of Community
2000   Evaluation and Capacity Building of Community Impact! Final Report. Gaithersburg, MD: Association for the Study and Development of Community.
Astone, N., C. Nathanson, R. Schoen, and Y. Kim
1999   Family Demography, Social Theory, and Investment in Social Capital. *Population and Developmental Review.* 21(1):1-13.
Baker, D.P., and D.L. Stevenson
1986   Mothers' Strategies for Children's School Achievement: Making the Transition to High School. *Sociology of Education.* 59:156-166.

Baltes, P.B., and K.W. Schaie, Eds.
  1973   *Life-Span Developmental Psychology: Personality and Socialization*. New York: Academic Press.
Baltes, P.B., U. Lindenberger, and U.M. Staudinger
  1998   Life Span Theory in Developmental Psychology. Pp. 1029-1144 in *Handbook of Child Psychology: Theoretical Models of Human Development*, W. Damon and R.M. Lerner, Eds. New York: Wiley Publishers.
Bandeau, S.
  2000   Promises, Promises: The President's Budget: What's in It for Kids? *Youth Today*.
Bandura A.
  1994   *Self-Efficacy: The Exercise of Control*. New York: W.H. Freeman Publishers.
Banks, J.A.
  1995   Multicultural education and the modification of students' racial attitudes. Pp. 315-339 in *Toward a Common Destiny: Improving Race and Ethnic Relations in America*, W.D. Hawley and A.W. Jackson, Eds. San Francisco, CA: Jossey-Bass.
Baranowski, T., C. Bouchard, O. Bar-Or, T. Bricker, G. Health, S. Kimm, et. al.
  1992   Assessment, Prevalence, and Cardiovascular Benefits of Physical Activity and Fitness in Youth. *Medicine and Science in Sports and Exercise*. 24:S237-247.
Barber, B.L., J.S. Eccles, and M.R. Stone
  in   Whatever Happened to the Jock, the Brain, and the Princess? *Journal of Adoles-*
  press   *cent Research*.
Barker R. and P. Gump
  1964   *Big School, Small School: High School Size and Student Behavior*. Stanford, CA: Stanford University Press.
Baumeister, R.F., and M.R. Leary
  1995   The Need to Belong: Desire for Interpersonal Attachments as a Fundamental Human Motivation. *Psychological Bulletin*. 117(3):497-529.
Baumeister, R.F. and C. Sedikides
  1998   *Psychological Inquiry: An International Journal of Peer Commentary and Review* 9(1). Mahwah, NJ: Lawrence Erlbaum Associates, Inc.
Baumrind, D.
  1971   Current Patterns of Paternal Authority. *Developmental Psychology Monograph*. 4(1, Pt. 2).
Beauvais, F.
  2000   Indian Adolescence: Opportunity and Challenge. Pp. 110-140 in *Adolescent Diversity in Ethnic, Economic, and Cultural Contexts*, R. Montemayor, G.R. Adams, and T.P. Gullotta, Eds. Thousand Oaks, CA: Sage Publications.
Begley, S.
  2000   Getting Inside a Teen Brain: Hormones Aren't the Only Reason Adolescents Act Crazy. Their gray Matter Differs from Children's and Adults'. *Newsweek*. Copyright 2000.
Behrman, R.
  1999   The Future of Children: When School Is Out. Vol. 9. Los Altos, CA: The David and Lucile Packard Foundation.
Benard, B.
  2000   *Adolescent Society: Overview of "The Search for Structure: A Report on American Youth Today" by Francis Ianni*. Accessed 2001. Available online at: www.ltgov.wa.gov.
Bender J., C.H. Flatter, and J.M. Sorrentino
  2000   *Half a Childhood: Quality Programs for Out-of-School Hours*. Nashville, TN: School Age Notes.

Benson, P.L.
   1996   Beyond the "Village" Rhetoric. *Assets.* 1(1):3-4.
   1997   *All Kids Are Our Kids: What Communities Must Do to Raise Caring and Responsible Children and Adolescents.* San Francisco, CA: Jossey-Bass.
Benson, P.L., Y. Butler, H. Libbey, and G. Walker
   1999   An Initial Look at America's Promise: Successes, Challenges, and Opportunities. Minneapolis, MN: Search Institute & Public/Private Ventures.
Benson, P.L., and M.J. Donahue
   1989   Ten-year trends in at-risk behaviors: A national study of black adolescents. *Journal of Adolescent Research.* 4:125-139.
Benson, P.L., N. Leffert, P.C. Scales, and D.A. Blyth
   1998   Beyond the "Village" Rhetoric: Creating Health Communities for Children and Adolescents. *Applied Developmental Science.* 2(3):138-159.
Benson, P.L., K.S. Masters, and D.B. Larson
   1997   Religious Influences on Child and Adolescent Development. Pp. 206-219 in *Handbook of Child and Adolescent Psychiatry: Varieties of Development Vol. 4,* J.D. Noshpitz and N.E. Alessi, Eds. New York, NY: Wiley & Sons.
Benson, P.L., and R.N. Saito
   2000   The Scientific Foundations of Youth Development. Pp. 125-148 in *Youth Development: Issues, Challenges and Directions,* Public/Private Ventures, Ed. Philadelphia, PA: Public/Private Ventures.
Berger, K.S.
   1988   *The Developing Person Through the Life Span.* New York: Worth Publishers.
Berger P., and T. Luckmann
   1966   *The Social Construction of Reality.* New York, NY: Anchor Books.
Berla, N., A. Henderson, and W. Kerewsky
   1989   The Middle School Years: A Parents' Handbook. Columbia, MD: National Committee for Citizens in Education.
Berndt, T.J., and T.B. Perry
   1990   Distinctive Features of Early Adolescent Friendships. Pp. 269-287 in *From Childhood to Adolescence: A Transitional Period?,* R. Montemayor, G.R. Adams, and T.P. Gullotta, Eds. Newbury Park, CA: Sage Publications.
Best Buy
   2000   *Best Buy Community Relations: Overview of the Community Service Grants Program.* Accessed 2001. Available online at: www.bestbuy.com.
Biglan, A., D.V. Ary, and A.C. Wagenaar
   2000   The value of interrupted time-series experiments for community intervention research. *Prevention Research.* 1(1):31-49.
Bjorklund, D.
   1989   *Children's Thinking: Developmental Function and Individual Differences.* Pacific Grove, CA: Brooks-Cole.
Blanchette, C.M.
   1997   Testimony Before the Subcommittee on Youth Violence. At-Risk and Delinquent Youth: Multiple Programs Lack Coordinated Federal Effort, U.S. General Accounting Office.
Blos, P.
   1979   *The Adolescent Passage.* New York: International Universities Press.
Blum, R.
   1998   Healthy Youth Development as a Model for Youth Health Promotion. *Journal of Adolescent Health.* 22:368-375.

Blum, R.W., T. Beuhring, and P.M. Rinehart
    2000   Protecting Teens: Beyond Race, Income and Family Structure. Minneapolis, MN: Center for Adolescent Health, University of Minnesota.

Blum, R.W., and P.M. Rinehart
    1997   *Reducing the Risk: Connections That Make a Difference In The Lives Of Youth.* Minneapolis, MN: Division of General Pediatrics and Adolescent Health, University of Minnesota.

Blyth, D., and Leffert, N.
    1995   Communities as Contexts for Adolescent Development: An Empirical Analysis. *Journal of Adolescent Research.* 10(1):64-87.

Boardman, A., D. Greenberg, A. Vinnig, and D. Weimer
    1996   *Cost-Benefit Analysis: Concepts and Practice.* Upper Saddle River, NJ: Prentice Hall.

Booth, A., and J. Dunn, Eds.
    1996   *Family-School Links: How Do They Affect Educational Outcomes.* Hillsdale, NJ: Lawrence Erlbaum Associates.

Borduin, C.M., L.T. Cone, B.J. Mann, S.W. Henggeler, B.R. Fucci, D.M. Blaske, and R.A. Williams
    1995   Multisystemic Treatment of Serious Juvenile Offenders: Long-Term Prevention of Criminality and Violence. *Journal of Consulting and Clinical Psychology.* 63(4):569-578.

Boruch, R.F.
    1997   *Randomized Experiments for Planning and Evaluation.* Thousand Oaks, CA: Sage Publications.

Bourdieu, P., and J. Paseron
    1977   *Reproduction in Education, Society and Culture.* London: Sage.

Bowlby, J.
    1969   *Attachment and Loss: Attachment.* London: Hogarth Publishers.
    1973   *Attachment and Loss: Separation.* London: Hogarth Publishers.
    1988   *A Secure Base: Clinical Applications of Attachment Theory.* London: Routledge Publishers.

Box, G.E.P.
    1958   Evolutionary Operation: A Method for Increasing Industrial Productivity. *Applied Statistics.* 6(2):81-101.

Boykin, A.W.
    1986   The Triple Quandary and the Schooling of Afro-American Children. *The School Achievement of Minority Children,* U. Neiser, Ed. Hillsdale, NJ: Erlbaum Publishers.

Boyle, P.
    2000   In Milwaukee, Youth Worker Training Pays Off. *Youth Today.* 9(3).

Boys and Girls Clubs of America
    1999   Boys and Girls Clubs of America Body Works Program: Progress Report. Atlanta, GA: Boys and Girls Clubs of America.
    2000   *Programs: Sports, Fitness & Recreation.* Accessed 2001. Available online at: www.bgca.org.

Bradley, R.H., B.M. Caldwell, and S.L. Rock
    1988   Home Environment and School Performance: A Ten-Year Follow-Up and Examination of Three Models of Environmental Action. *Child Development.* 59:852-867.

Branch A., V. Smith, and L. Taylor
    1998   *A Study of Youth Development Opportunities for Youth Who Reside in Low Income Communities in Philadelphia.* Philadelphia, PA: Branch Associates.

Briere, J., and M. Runtz
  1991 The Long-Term Effects of Sexual Abuse: A Review and Synthesis. Pp. 3-13 in *Treating Victims of Child Sexual Abuse*, J. Brier, Ed. San Francisco, CA: Jossey-Bass.
Brindis, C.D., C.E. Irwin, E.M. Handley, D.K. Knopf, and S.G. Millstein
  1997 Improving Adolescent Health: An Analysis and Synthesis of Health Policy Recommendations. San Francisco, CA: National Adolescent Health Information Center; University of California, San Francisco.
Briss, P.A., S. Zaza, M. Pappaioanou, J. Fielding, L. Wright-De Aguero, B.I. Truman, D.P. Hopkins, P. Dolan Mullen, R.S. Thompson, S.H. Woolf, V.G. Carande-Kulis, L.M. Anderson, A.R. Hinman, D.V. McQueen, S.M. Teutsch, and J.R. Harris
  2000 Developing an Evidence-Based Guide to Community Preventive Services—Methods, Task Force on Community Preventive Services. *American Journal of Preventive Medicine*. 18(1):Supplement:35-43.
Bronfenbrenner, U.
  1994 Ecological Model of Human Development. Pp. 3-27 in *International Encyclopedia of Education*, 2, T. Husten and T.N. Postlethwaite, Eds. Oxford, England: Pergamon Press.
Bronfenbrenner, U., and P. Morris
  1998 The Ecology of Developmental Process. *Handbook of Child Psychology*, 5th, W. Damon and R. Lerner, Eds. New York: John Wiley.
Brookover W., C. Beady, P. Flood, J. Schweitzer, and J. Wisenbaker
  1979 *School Social Systems and Student Achievement: Schools Can Make a Difference*. New York: Praeger.
Brooks-Gunn, J., J.A. Graber, and R.L. Paikoff
  1994 Studying the Links Between Hormones and Negative Affect: Models and Measures. *Journal of Research on Adolescence*. 4:469-486.
Brooks-Gunn, J., and R.L. Paikoff
  1993 Sex Is A Gamble, Kissing Is A Game: Adolescent Sexuality & Health Promotion. Pp. 180-208 in *Promoting the Health of Adolescents: New Directions for the Twenty-First Century*, S.G. Millstein, A.C. Peterson, and E.O. Nightingale, Eds. New York: Oxford University Press.
Brooks-Gunn, J., and E.O. Reiter
  1990 The Role of Pubertal Processes. Pp. 16-53 in *At the Threshold: The Developing Adolescent*, S.S. Feldman and G.R. Elliott, Eds. Cambridge, MA: Harvard University Press.
Brooks-Gunn, J., and M.P. Warren
  1988 The Psychological Significance of Secondary Sexual Characteristics in 9- to 11-Year Old Girls. *Child Development*. 59:161-169.
Brown, B.B.
  1990 Peer Groups and Peer Cultures. Pp. 171-196 in *At the Threshold: The Developing Adolescent*, S.S. Feldman and G.R. Elliott, Eds. Cambridge, MA: Harvard University Press.
Brown, B., and C. Thomas
  1997 Social Indicators and Public Policy in the Age of Devolution, Special Report No. 71 Madison, WI: Institute for Research on Poverty, School of Social Work, University of Wisconsin-Madison, Available online at: www.ssc.wisc.edu.
Brown, B.V., and T. Corbett
  Forth- Social Indicators and Public Policy in the Age of Devolution. In *Trends in the*
  coming *Well-Being of Children and Youth*, Weissberg, R., Reyes, O., and Walberg, H., eds. Washington, DC: Child Welfare League of America.

Brown, D.
1999   *Advancing Youth Development Under the Workforce Investment Act.* Accessed 2001. Available online at: www.nyec.org.
Brown, R.D., and J.M. Harrison
1986   The Effect of Strength Training Program on the Strength and Self-Concept of Two Female Age Groups. *Research Quarterly for Exercise and Sports.* 57:315-320.
Buchanan, C.M., J.S. Eccles, and J.B. Becker
1992   Are Adolescents the Victims of Raging Hormones: Evidence for Activational Effects of Hormones on Moods and Behaviors at Adolescence. *Psychological Bulletin.* 111:62-107.
Burke, T.
1998   Liverpool's Lesson: Training Has Impact. *Youth Today.* 32-33.
Burt, M.R.
1998   Why Should We Invest in Adolescents? Washington, DC: The Urban Institute.
Cahill, M., J. Perry, M. Wright, and A. Rice
1993   A Documentation Report on the New York City Beacons Initiative. New York, NY: The Youth Development Institute, Fund for the City of New York.
Cairns, R.B.
1998   The Making of Developmental Psychology. Pp. 25-106 in *Handbook of Child Psychology: Theoretical Models of Human Development*, 5th ed., W. Damon and R.M. Lerner, Eds. New York: Riley Publishers.
Cairns R.B., and B.D. Cairns
1994   *Lifelines and Risks: Pathways of Youth in Our Time.* Cambridge: Cambridge University Press.
California Department of Education
2000   *Afterschool Learning and Safe Neighborhoods Program: Factsheet.* Accessed 2001. Available online at: http://www.cde.ca.gov.
California Department of Education and Division of Children Youth and Family Services
1999a   *After School Learning and Safe Neighborhoods Partnerships Program: Finger Tip Facts.* Accessed 2000. Available online at: www.cde.ca.gov.
1999b   *After School Learning and Safe Neighborhoods Partnerships Program: Frequently Asked Questions.* Accessed 2000. Available online at: www. cde.ca.gov.
California School Boards Association
1999a   *Focus on Small School Districts: Funding Opportunities for Small School Districts—Afterschool Programs.* Accessed 2001. Available online at: www. csba.org.
1999b   *Proposition 10: Opportunities for School and County Collaboration to Improve Early Childhood Development Programs.* Accessed 2001. Available online at: www.csba.org.
Camino, L.A.
1998   Building Local Infrastructure for Youth Development: The Added Value of Capacity-Building Intermediary Organizations. Washington, DC: Center for Youth Development and Policy Research.
Camp Fire Boys and Girls
2000   *Homepage: Welcome to Camp Fire Boys and Girls.* Accessed 2001. Available online at: www.campfire.org.
Campbell, D.T., and J.C. Stanley
1963   *Experimental and Quasi-Experimental Designs for Research.* Boston, MA: Houghton Mifflin Company.

Campbell, J.R., C.M. Hombo, and J. Mazzeo
   2000   *NAEP 1999 Trends in Academic Progress: Three Decades of Student Perfor-mance.* Washington, D.C.: National Center for Educational Statistics.
Camphor United Methodist Church
   2000   *Outline of Project Spirit.* Accessed 2000. Available online at: www.camphorumc.org.
Carnegie Corporation of New York
   1989   Turning Points: Preparing American Youth for the 21st Century, Report of the Task Force on Education of Young Adolescents and Carnegie Council on Adolescent Development. New York: Carnegie Corporation.
   1992   A Matter Of Time: Risk And Opportunity In The Nonschool Hours, Task Force on Youth Development and Community Programs and Carnegie Council on Adolescent Development. New York: Carnegie Corporation.
   1994   Starting Points: Meeting the Needs of Our Youngest Children. Task Force on Meeting the Needs of Young Children. New York: Carnegie Corporation.
   1995   Great Transitions: Preparing Adolescents For a New Century, Concluding Report of the Carnegie Council on Adolescent Development New York: Carnegie Corporation.
   1996   Years of Promise: A Comprehensive Learning Strategy for America's Children, Carnegie Task Force on Learning in the Primary Grades. New York: Carnegie Corporation.
Caspi, A.
   2000   The Child Is Father of the Man: Personality Continuities From Childhood to Adulthood. *Journal of Personality and Social Psychology.* 78(1):158-172.
Caspi, A., D. Lynam, T.E. Moffitt, and P.A. Silva
   1993   Unraveling Girls' Delinquency: Biological, Dispositional, and Contextual Contributions to Adolescent Misbehavior. *Developmental Psychology.* 29:19-30.
Caspi, A., and T. Moffitt
   1991   Individual Differences and Personal Transitions: The Sample Case of Girls at Puberty. *Journal of Personal Social Psychology.* 61:157-168.
Castro, F.G., G.R. Boyer, and H.G. Balcazar
   2000   Healthy Adjustment in Mexican American and Other Hispanic Adolescents. Pp. 141-178 in *Adolescent Diversity in Ethnic, Economic, and Cultural Context,* R. Montemayor, G.R. Adams, and T.P. Gullotta, Eds. Thousand Oaks, CA: Sage Publications.
Catalano, R.F., M.L. Berglund, J.A. Ryan, H.S. Lonczak, and J.D. Hawkins
   1999   *Positive Youth Development in the United States: Research Findings on Evaluations of Positive Youth Development Programs.* Seattle, Washington: Social Development Research Group, University of Washington School of Social Work.
Catalano, R.F., J.D. Hawkins, L. Berglund, J. Pollard, and M. Arthur
   2000   Prevention Science and Positive Youth Development: Competitive or Cooperative Frameworks? University of Washington.
Catholic Charities USA
   2000   *Overview of the Catholic Charities USA Website.* Accessed 2001. Available online at: www.catholiccharitiesusa.org.
Center for the Study and Prevention of Violence
   2000   *Blueprints for Violence Prevention: Program Information.* Accessed 2001. Available online at: www.colorado.edu.
Center for the Study of Social Policy
   2001   *Current Projects: Financing Reform of Children and Family Services.* Accessed 2001. Available online at: http://www.cssp.org/current.html.

Center for Youth Development and Policy Research
   1999   CBO Schools: A Crucial Education—Youth Development Link Washington, DC: Academy for Educational Development.
Centers for Disease Control and Prevention
   1998   State-Specific Pregnancy Rates Among Adolescents. Atlanta, GA: Centers for Disease Control and Prevention.
   1999   *AIDS Surveillance in Adolescents: L265 Slide Series.* Accessed 2001. Available online at: http://www.cdc.gov.
   2000a *Safe Motherhood: Investing in the Health of Women.* Atlanta, GA: National Center for Chronic Disease and Prevention.
   2000b *School Health Programs: An Investment in Our Nation's Future.* Accessed 2000. Available online at: www.cdc.gov.
   2000c *Youth Risk Behavior Surveillance System.* Accessed 2001. Available online at: http://www.cdc.gov/nccdphp/dash/yrbs/index.htm.
Centers for Disease Control and Prevention, National Center for Chronic Disease Prevention and Health Promotion, and Tobacco Information and Prevention Source (TIPS)
   1999   *African Americans and Tobacco.* Accessed 2001. Available online at: www.cdc.gov.
Chaddock, G.R.
   1999   Churches and Charities Round Out Afterschool Help. Christian Science Monitor, Nov 16.
Charles Stewart Mott Foundation
   1998a Making After-School Programs Count—Communities and Schools Working Together to Create Quality After-School Programs Flint, MI: Charles Stewart Mott Foundation.
   1998b Press Release: Poll Finds Overwhelming Support for After-School Enrichment Programs to Keep Kids Safe and Smart. Flint, MI: Charles Stewart Mott Foundation.
   2000   *21st Century Community Learning Centers Overview: Overview of Mott's Involvement.* Accessed 2001. Available online at: www.mott.org.
Chaskin, R.J., and T. Hawley
   1994   Youth and Caring: Developing a Field of Inquiry and Practice. Chicago, IL: The Chapin Hall Center for Children, University of Chicago.
Children's Aid Society
   1997   Building A Community School. New York, NY: The Children's Aid Society.
Chou, C.P., S. Montgomery, M.A. Pentz, L.A. Rohrback, C.A. Johnson, B.R. Flay, and D.P. MacKinnon
   1998   Effects of a Community-Based Prevention Program in Decreasing Drug Use in High-Risk Adolescents. *American Journal of Public Health.* 88(6):944-948.
Cicchetti, D., and S.L. Toth
   1996   Adolescence: Opportunities and Challenges. Rochester Symposium on Developmental Psychopathology, Volume VIII. Rochester, NY: University of Rochester Press.
City of Boston
   2000a *Financing Our Children's Future.* Boston: 2:00-to-6:00 Initiative.
   2000b *Schools Alone Are Not Enough: Why Out-of-School Time Is Crucial to the Success of Our Children.* The Mayor's Task Force on After-School Time. Boston, MA.
City of Seattle MOST Initiative
   1999   *Seattle MOST Initiative Accomplishments.* Accessed 2000. Available online at: www.ci.seattle.wa.us.

City Year
  2001   *Overview of the City Year Website.* Accessed 2001. Available online at:
         www.cityyear.org.
Clark, D.
  1999 Pathways to Adult Success for All Youth, St. Petersburg, Florida, Washington,
         DC: The Aspen Institute.
Clark R.M.
  1983   *Family Life and School Achievement: Why Poor Black Children Succeed or Fail.*
         Chicago, IL: University of Chicago Press.
  1988   Critical Factors in Why Disadvantaged Students Succeed or Fail in School. New
         York: Academy for Educational Development.
Clausen J.A.
  1993   *American Lives: Looking Back at the Children of the Great Depression.* New
         York: The Free Press.
Clyde, A.R.
  1999   A Conversation with Cole Wilbur. *Foundation News & Commentary.* 40(2):1-6.
  2000   A Conversation with Stanley S. Litow. *Foundation News & Commentary.* 41(3).
Cohen, M.
  2000a *Making TANF Work for the Corps: When and How TANF Funds Can Support
         Youth Corps Initiatives.* Accessed 2000. Available online at: www.clasp.org.
  2000b TANF Funds: A New Resource for Youth Programs. *Youth Notes: The News-
         letter of the National Youth Employment Coalition.*
Cohen, M., and M.H. Greenberg
  2000   Tapping TANF for Youth: When and How Welfare Funds Can Support Youth
         Development, Education and Employment Initiatives. Washington, DC: Center
         for Law and Social Policy.
Coleman, J.
  1988   Social Capital in the Creation of Human Capital. *American Journal of Sociol-
         ogy.* 94:95-120.
Coleman, J., E. Campbell, C. Hobson, J. McPartland, A. Mood, F. Weinfeld, and R. York
  1966   *Equality of Educational Opportunity Report.* Washington, DC: United States
         Government Printing Office.
Coleman, J.S.
  1990   Social capital. Pp. 300-321 in *Foundations of Social Theory,* J.S. Coleman Ed.
         Cambridge, MA: Belknap Press of Harvard University.
Coleman, J.S., and T. Hoffer
  1987   *Public and Private High Schools: The Impact of Communities.* New York, NY:
         Basic Books.
Collins, W.A.
  1990   Parent-Child Relationships in the Transition to Adolescence: Continuity and
         Change in Interaction, Affect, and Cognition. Pp. 85-106 in *From Childhood to
         Adolescence: A Transitional Period.* R. Montemayor, G.R. Adams, and T.P.
         Gullotta, Eds. Beverly Hills, CA: Sage Publications.
Collins, W.A., E.E. Maccoby, L. Steinberg, E.M. Hetherington, and M.H. Bornstein
  2000   Contemporary research on parenting: The case for nature and nurture. *The
         American Psychologist* 55:218-237.
Comer, J.P.
  1980   *School Power: Implications of an Intervention Project.* New York, NY: The
         Free Press.
  1988   Educating Poor Minority Children. *Scientific American.* 259(5):42-48.

Comer, J.P., and N.M. Haynes
  1991 Parent Involvement in Schools: An Ecological Approach. *The Elementary School Journal*. 91:271-277.
Communities in Schools, Inc.
  2000 *Overview of the Communities In Schools Website*. Accessed 2001. Available online at: www.cisnet.org.
Community Youth Development
  2000 Youth 2000. *Community Youth Development Journal*. 1.
  2000 Teens in the Spotlight: Youth and Adults Working Together to Improve the Lives of Teens, Community Youth Development Project of Sarasota County. Sarasota, FL: Community Youth Development Project of Sarasota County.
Compas, B.E.
  1993 Promoting Positive Mental Health During Adolescence. Pp. 159-179 in *Promoting The Health of Adolescents: New Directions For The Twenty-First Century*, S.G. Millstein, A.C. Peterson, and E.O. Nightingale, Eds. New York: Oxford University Press.
Compas, B.E., B.M. Wagner, L.A. Slavin, and K. Vannatta
  1986 A Prospective Study of Life Events, Social Support, and Psychological Symptomatology During the Transition from High School to College. *American Journal of Community Psychology*. 14:241-257.
Congress of National Black Churches
  2001 Congress of National Black Churches: About Us. Accessed 2001. Available online at: www.cnbc.org/home.htm
Connell, J., M.A. Gambone, and T. Smith
  2000 Youth Development in Community Settings. Pp. 281-324 in *Youth Development: Issues, Challenges and Directions*. Philadelphia, PA: Public/Private Ventures.
Connell, J.P., B.L. Halpern-Felsher, E. Clifford, W. Crichlow, and P. Usinger
  1995 Hanging in There: Behavioral, Psychological, and Contextual Factors Affecting Whether African American Adolescents Stay in High School. *Journal of Adolescent Research*. 10:41-63.
Connell, J.P., and B.L. Halpern-Fisher
  1997 How Neighborhoods Affect Educational Outcomes in Middle Childhood and Adolescence: Conceptual Issues and an Empirical Example. Pp. 174-199 in *Neighborhood Poverty: Context and Consequences for Children*, J.B. Brooks-Gunn, G.J. Duncan, and J.L. Aber, Eds. New York: Russell Sage Foundation.
Connell, J.P., and J.G. Wellborn
  1991 Competence, Autonomy, and Relatedness: A Motivational Analysis of Self-System Processes. Pp. 43-77 in *The Minnesota Symposia on Child Psychology*, M.R. Gunnar and L.A. Sroufe, Eds. Hillsdale, NJ: Lawrence Erlbaum Associates.
Connell, J.P., and M.A. Gambone
  1998 *Community Action for Youth Development: Evidence, Measures and Practices*.
Connolly, C.
  2000 Gore Proposes $11 Billion Increase for After-School Programs. *The Washington Post* A5, May 26.
Cook, T.D.
  2000 The False Choice Between Theory-Based Evaluation and Experimentation. *New Directions In Evaluation: Challenges and Opportunities in Program Theory Evaluation*. 87.

Cook, T.D., A. Anson, and S. Walchli
  1993 From Causal Description to Causal Explanation: Improving Three Already Good Evaluations of Adolescent Health Programs. *Promoting the Health of Adolescents: New Directions for the Twenty-First Century* , S.G. Millstein, A.C. Petersen, and E.O. Nightingale, Eds. New York, NY: Oxford University Press.
Cook, T.D., and D.T. Campbell
  1979 *Quasi-Experimentation: Design and Analysis Issues for Field Settings.* Boston, MA: Houghton-Mifflin.
Cook, T.D., F. Habib, M. Phillips, R.A. Settersten, S.C. Shagle, and S.M. Degirmencioglu
  1999 Comer's School Development Program in Prince George's County: A Theory-Based Evaluation. *American Educational Research Journal.* December.
Cook, T.D., H.D. Hunt, and R.F. Murphy
  2000 Comer's School Development Program in Chicago: A Theory-Based Evaluation. *American Educational Research Journal.* 37(2):535-597.
Cooper, E.F.
  2000 CRS Report for Congress. The Safe and Drug-Free Schools and Communities Program: Background and Context. Washington, DC: Congressional Research Service, The Library of Congress.
Cornerstone Consulting Group
  1999 The Replication Challenge: Lessons Learned From the National Replication Project for the Teen Outreach Program. Houston, TX: Pen 1.
Coulton, C.
  1998 Using Community-Level Indicators of Children's Well-Being in Comprehensive Community Initiatives. *New Approaches to Evaluating Community Initiatives: Concepts, Methods, and Contexts*, J. Connell, A. Kubisch, L. Schorr, and C. Weiss, Eds. Washington, DC: The Aspen Institute.
Coulton, C., and R. Hollister
  1998 Measuring Comprehensive Community Initiative Outcomes Using Data Available for Small Areas. *New Approaches to Evaluating Community Initiatives: Volume 2, Theory, Measurement, and Analysis*, K. Fullbright-Anderson, A. Kubisch, and J.P. Connell, Eds. Washington, DC: The Aspen Institute.
Council of Economic Advisers
  2000 Teens and Their Parents in the 21st Century: An Examination of Trends in Teen Behavior and the Role of Parental Involvement. The Finance Project, and U.S. Department of Health & Human Services
  1999 The Child Welfare Partnership Project: A Handbook for Successful Public-Private Partnerships 1999 Supplement. Washington, DC: U.S. Department of Health & Human Services.
Cross, W.E.
  1991 *Shades of Black: Diversity in African-American Identity.* Philadelphia, PA: Temple University Press.
  1995 Oppositional Identity and African American Youth: Issues and Perspectives. Pp. 185-204 in *Toward a Common Destiny: Improving Race and Ethnic Relations in America*, W.D. Hawley and A.W. Jackson, Eds. San Francisco: Jossey-Bass.
Csikszentmihalyi, M.
  1975 *Beyond Boredom and Anxiety: The Experience of Play in Work and Games.* San Francisco, CA: Jossey-Bass.
  1990 *Flow: The Psychology of Optimal Experience.* New York, NY: Harper Collins Publishers.
  1999 If We Are So Rich, Why Aren't We Happy? *American Psychologist.* 54(10):821-827.

Csikszentmihalyi, M., and K. Rathunde
  1998   The Development of Person: An Experiential Perspective on the Ontogenesis of Psychological Complexity. Pp. 635-684 in *The Handbook of Child Psychology: Theoretical Models of Human Development*, Fifth, R.M. Lerner, Volume Ed. New York: John Wiley & Sons, Inc.
CSR Incorporated
  1997   Understanding Youth Development: Promoting Positive Pathways of Growth. Washington, DC: U.S. Department of Health and Human Services, Administration for Children and Families.
Cynader, M.S., and B.J. Frost
  1999   Mechanisms of Brain Development: Neuronal Sculpting by the Physical and Social Environment. Pp. 153-184 in *Development Health and the Wealth of Nations: Social, Biological, and Educational Dynamics*, D.P. Keating and C. Hertzman, Eds. New York: The Guilford Press.
Dahlstrom, K.
  1998   Replicating Youthbuild: Empowerment Program Grows from 10 to 4,600. *@Mott.Now.* 1(6):1-8.
Damon, W.
  1997   *The Youth Charter*. New York, NY: Free Press.
Damon, W., and N. Eisenberg, Eds.
  1997   *Handbook of Child Psychology*. Brown University, Rhode Island, USA: John Wiley & Sons.
Damon, W., and R.M. Lerner, Eds.
  1998   *Handbook of Child Psychology: Theoretical Models of Human Development*. New York: Wiley.
Darling, N., and Steinberg. L.
  1997   Community Influences on Adolescent Achievement and Deviance. Pp. 120-131 in *Neighborhood Poverty: Volume II Policy Implications in Studying Neighborhoods*, J. Brooks-Gunn, G.J. Duncan, and J.L. Aber, Eds. New York: Russell Sage Foundation.
Darling-Hammond, L.
  1997   *The Right to Learn: A Blueprint for Creating Schools That Work*. San Francisco: Jossey-Bass.
Daro, D.A., and K.A. Harding
  1999   Healthy Families America: Using Research to Enhance Practice. *The Future of Children*. 9(1):1-20.
Deci, E.L., and R.M. Ryan
  1985   *Intrinsic Motivation and Self-Determination in Human Behavior*. New York, NY: Plenum Press.
DeLoache, J.S., K.F. Miller, and S.L. Pierroutsakos
  1997   Reasoning and problem solving. Pp. 801-850 in *Handbook of Child Psychology: 5th Edition, Vol. 2: Cognition, Perception, and Language*. W. Damon, Series Ed., and D. Kuhn and R.S. Siegler, Vol. Eds. New York: Wiley.
Department of Children, Youth, and Their Families
  2001   San Francisco Youth Commission: What we do. Accessed 2001. Available online at: http://www.sfgov.org/youth_commission/wedo.htm
Development Research and Programs Inc.
  2000   *Communities that Care: Prevention Strategies, A Research Guide to What Works*.
Diamant, A., and H. Cooper
  1991   *Living a Jewish Life: Jewish Traditions, Customs and Values for Today's Families*. New York, NY: Harper Perennial.

Dishion, T.J., and D.W. Andrews
    1995   Preventing Escalation in Problem Behaviors With High-Risk Young Adolescents: Immediate and 1-Year Outcomes. *Journal of Consulting and Clinical Psychology.* 63(4):538-548.
Dishion, T.J., J. McCord, and F. Poulin
    1999a   When interventions harm: Peer groups and problem behavior. *American Psychologist.* 54:755-764.
    1999b   Iatrogenic Effects in Early Adolescent Interventions That Aggregate Peers. *American Psychologist.* 54(9):1-10.
Doi, T.
    1990   The Cultural Assumptions of Psychoanalysis. Pp. 446-353 in *Essays on Comparative Human Development*, J. Stigler, R. Shweder, and G. Herdt, Eds. Cambridge, MA: Cambridge University Press.
Donahue, M.J.
    1987   *Technical Report of the National Demonstration Project Field Test of "Human Sexuality: Values and Choices."* Minneapolis: Search Institute.
Dotson, C.O., and J.G. Ross
    1985   Relationships Between Activity Patterns and Fitness. *Journal of Physical Education Recreational Dance.* 56(1):86-90.
Dryfoos, J.G.
    1990   *Adolescents at Risk: Prevalence and Prevention.* New York: Oxford University Press.
    1998   *Safe Passage: Making It Through Adolescence in a Risky Society.* New York, NY: Oxford University Press, Inc.
    2000   *Coalition for Community Schools: Evaluation of Community Schools, findings to date.* Accessed 2001. Available online at: www.communityschools.org.
Dubas, J.S., and B.A. Snider
    1993   The Role of Community-Based Youth Groups in Enhancing Learning and Achievement Through Nonformal Education. Pp. 159-174 in *Early Adolescence: Perspectives on Research, Policy, and Intervention*, Lerner, R.M. Hillsdale, New Jersey: Lawrence Erlbaum Associates, Inc.
Dubay, L.C., and G.M. Kenney
    1996   The Effects of Medicaid Expansions on Insurance Coverage of Children. Pp. 152-161 in *The Future of Children: Special Education for Students With Disabilities.* Los Altos, CA: David and Lucile Packard Foundation.
Dubrow, N.F., and J. Garbarino
    1989   Living in the War Zone: Mothers and Young Children in a Public Housing Development. *American Psychologist.* 1(68):3-20.
Duggan, P.
    2000   Powell Visits Texas "Friend," Faces the Usual Questions. *The Washington Post,* May 26.
Duncan, G.J., and S.W. Raudenbush
    1998   Neighborhoods and Adolescent Development: How Can We Determine the Links? Chicago, IL: Joint Center for Poverty Research: Northwestern University and University of Chicago. www.jcpr.org.
DuRant, R.H., A. Getts, C. Cadenhead, S.J. Emans, and E. Woods
    1995   Exposure to Violence and Victimization and Depression, Hopelessness, and Purpose of Life Among Adolescents Living In and Around Public Housing. *Journal of Developmental and Behavioral Pediatrics.* 16:233-237.
Durkheim E.
    1951   *Suicide: A Study in Sociology.* New York: Free Press.

Durlak, J.A., and A.M. Wells
  1997 Primary Prevention Mental Health Programs for Children and Adolescents. *American Journal of Community Psychology: Special Issue: Meta-Analysis of Primary Prevention Programs.* 25(2):115-152.
  1998 Evaluation of Indicated Preventive Intervention (Secondary Prevention) Mental Health Programs for Children and Adolescents. *American Journal of Community Psychology.* 26(5):775-802.
Dweck, C.
  1999 *Self-Theories: Their Role in Motivation, Personality, and Development.* Philadelphia, PA: Psychology Press.
Eccles, J., and R. Harold
  1996 Family involvement in children's and adolescent's schooling. *Family-School Links: How Do They Affect Educational Outcomes*, A. Booth and J. Dunn, Eds. Hillsdale, NJ: Lawrence Erlbaum Associates.
Eccles, J., S. Lord, and R. Roeser
  1996a Round Holes, Square Pegs, Rocky Roads, and Sore Feet: The Impact of Stage/Environment Fit on Young Adolescents' Experiences in Schools and Families. Pp. 47-93 in *Adolescence: Opportunities and Challenges—Rochester Symposium on Developmental Psychopathology Volume VIII,* D. Cicchetti and S.L. Toth, Eds. Rochester, NY: University of Rochester Press.
Eccles, J., S.E. Lord, R.W. Roeser, B.L. Barber, and D.M.H. Jozefowicz
  1996b The Association of School Transitions in Early Adolescence With Developmental Trajectories Through High School. *Health Risks and Developmental Transitions During Adolescence,* J. Schulenberg, J. Maggs, and K. Hurrelmann, Eds. New York: Cambridge University Press.
Eccles, J.S., A. Arbreton, C.M. Buchanon, J. Jacobs, C. Flanagan, R. Harold, D. MacIver, C. Midgeley, D. Reuman, and A. Wigfield
  1992 School and Family Effects on the Ontogeny of Children's Interests, Self-Perceptions, and Activity Choices. Pp. 145-208 in *Developmental Perspectives on Motivation, Volume 40 of the Nebraska Symposium on Motivation,* J. Jacobs, Ed. Lincoln, NE: University of Nebraska Press.
Eccles, J.S., and B.L. Barber
  1999 Student Council, Volunteering, Basketball, or Marching Band: What Kind of Extracurricular Involvement Matters? *Journal of Adolescent Research.* 14:10-43.
Eccles, J.S., C. Midgeley, C.M. Buchanan, A. Wigfield, D. Reuman, and D. MacIver
  1993 Development During Adolescence: The Impact of Stage/Environment Fit. *American Psychologist.* 48:90-101.
Eccles, J.S., and C. Midgley
  1989 Stage-Environment Fit: Developmentally Appropriate Classrooms for Young Adolescents. Pp. 139-186 in *Research on Motivation in Education,* C. Ames and R. Ames, Eds.
Eccles, J.S., A. Wigfield, and U. Schiefele
  1998 Motivation to Succeed. Pp. 1017-1095 in *Handbook of Child Psychology: Social, Emotional, and Personality Development*, Fifth Edition, N. Eisenberg, Volume Ed. New York: John Wiley & Sons, Inc.
Eder, D., and S. Parker
  1987 The Cultural Production and Reproduction of Gender: The Effect of Extracurricular Activities on Peer-Group Culture. *Sociology of Education.* 60:200-213.
Eisenberg, N., G. Carlo, B. Murphy, and P. Van Court
  1995 Prosocial Development in Late Adolescence: A Longitudinal Study. *Child Development.* 66:1179-1197.

Eisenberg N., and R.A. Fabes
  1998   Prosocial Development. Pp. 701-778 in *Handbook of Child Psychology*, 5th, N. Eisenberg, Ed. New York.
Ekston, R., M. Goertz, J. Pollack, and D. Rock
  1987   *High School and Beyond and the National Education Longitudinal Study.* Washington, DC: U.S. Department of Education, National Center for Education Statistics.
Elder G.H.
  1974   *Children of the Great Depression.* Chicago, IL: University of Chicago Press.
  1998   The Life Course of Human Development. Pp. 939-992 in *Handbook of Child Psychology: Theoretical Models of Human Development*, 5th ed., W. Damon and R.M. Lerner, Eds. New York: Wiley Publishers.
Elder, G.H., and R. Conger
  2000   *Children of the Land.* Chicago: University of Chicago Press.
Ellickson, P.L., and R.D. Hays
  1990-1 Beliefs about resistance self-efficacy and drug prevalence: Do they really affect drug use? Special issue: Nonexperimental methods for studying addictions. *International Journal of Addictions.* 25:856-861.
Elliott, D.S., and P.H. Tolan
  1999   Youth Violence: Prevention, Intervention, and Social Policy: An Overview. *Youth Violence: Prevention, Intervention, and Social Policy*, 1, D.J. Flannery and C.R. Huff, eds. Washington, DC: American Psychiatric Press.
Elliott, D.S., W.J. Wilson, D. Huizinga, R.J. Sampson, A. Elliott, and B. Rankin
  1996   The Effects of Neighborhood Disadvantage on Adolescent Development. *Journal of Research in Crime and Delinquency.* 33(4):389-427.
Elster, A.B., and N.J. Kuznets
  1994   *AMA Guidelines for Adolescent Preventive Services (GAPS): Recommendations and Rationale.* Chicago, Illinois: American Medical Association Department of Adolescent Health.
English, A.
  1997   Expanding Health Insurance for Children and Adolescents: Medicaid or Block Grants. *Youth Law News.* 1-28.
Entwisle, D.R.
  1990   Schooling and the Adolescent. Pp. 197-224 in *At the Threshold: The Developing Adolescent*, S.S. Feldman and G.R. Elliott, Eds. Cambridge, MA: Harvard University Press.
Entwisle, D.R., and K.L. Alexander
  1992   Summer Setback: Race, Poverty, School Composition, and Mathematics Achievement in the First Two Years of School. *American Sociological Review.* 57(1):72-84.
  1993   Entry into School: The Beginning School Transition and Educational Stratification in the United States. *Annual Review of Sociology.* 19:401-423.
Entwisle, D.R., K.L. Alexander, A.M. Pallas, and D. Cadigan
  1987   The Emergent Academic Self-Image of First Graders: Its Response to Social Culture. *Child Development.* 58:1190-1206.
Epstein, J.L.
  1990   School and Family Connections: Theory, Research, and Implication for Integrating Sociologies of Education and Family. *in Families in Community Settings: Interdisciplinary Perspectives*, D.G. Unger and M.B. Sussman, Eds. New York, NY: Haworth Press.

Epstein, J.L., and S.L. Dauber
1991   School Programs and Teacher Practices of Parent Involvement in Inner-City El-
       ementary and Middle Schools. *The Elementary School Journal.* 91:289-305.

Epstein, J.L., and J.M. McPartland
1979   Authority Structures. *Educational Environments and Effects*, H. Walberg, Ed.
       Berkeley, CA: McCutcheon.

Erikson E.
1963   *Childhood and Society.* New York, NY: Norton.
1968   *Identity: Youth and Crisis.* New York, NY: Norton.

Esbensen, F.-A., and D.W. Osgood
1999   Gang Resistance Education and Training (GREAT): Results from the National
       Evaluation. *Journal of Research in Crime and Delinquency.* 36(2):194-225.

Evangelical Press News Service
1999   Faith-Based Anti-Crime Effort Spreads Across U.S. *Marantha Christian Journal*,
       November 26.

Fairbanks North Star Borough School District
1999   *Joyce Epstein's Six Types of Parent Involvement.* Accessed 2001. Available
       online at: www.northstar.k12.ak.us.

Falkner, B., and S. Michel
1999   Obesity and Other Risk Factors in Children. *Ethnicity Disease.* 9:284-289.

Farrell, A.D., and A.L. Meyer
1997   The Effectiveness of a School-Based Curriculum for Reducing Violence among
       Urban Sixth-Grade Students. *American Journal of Public Health.* 87(6):979-
       984.

Farrington, D.P., G. Gundy, and D.J. West
1985   The familial transmission of criminality. Pp. 193-206 in *Crime and the Family*,
       A.J. Lincoln and M.A. Straus, Eds. Springfield, IL: Charles C. Thomas.

Feagans, L.V., and K. Bartsch
1993   A Framework for Examining the Role of Schooling During Early Adolescence.
       Pp. 129-142 in *Early Adolescence: Perspectives on Research, Policy, and Inter-
       vention*, R.M. Lerner, Ed. Hilsdalye, New Jersey: Lawrence Erlbaum Associ-
       ates, Inc.

Federal Interagency Forum on Child and Family Statistics
2000   *America's Children: Key National Indicators of Well-Being, 2000.* Washington,
       DC: U.S. Government Printing Office.

Feldman, S.S., and G.R. Elliott, Eds.
1990   *At the Threshold: The Developing Adolescent.* Cambridge, MA: Harvard Uni-
       versity Press.

Felner, R., A. Jackson, D. Kasak, P. Mulhall, S. Brand, and N. Flowers
1997   The impact of school reform for the middle grades: A longitudinal study of a
       network engaged in Turning Points-based comprehensive school transformation.
       Pp. 38-69 in *Preparing Adolescents for the Twenty-First Century: Challenges
       Facing Europe and the United States*, R. Takanishi and D. Hamburg, Eds. Cam-
       bridge: Cambridge University Press.

Ferguson, R.
1994   How Professionals in Community-Based Programs Perceive And Respond To
       The Needs Of Black Male Youth. Pp. 59-89 in *Nurturing Young Black Males:
       Challenges to Agencies, Programs, and Social Policy*, R.B. Mincy, Editor. Wash-
       ington, DC: Urban Institute Press.
1998   Teacher perceptions and expectations and the black-white test score gap. Pp.
       273-317 in *The Black-White Test Score Gap*, C. Jencks and M. Phillips, Eds.
       Washington, DC: Brookings Institution Press.

Ferguson, R., and J. Snipes
1997 Adapting Erikson to understand stages of engagement and identity development in the YouthBuild program. Pp. 245-318 in *YouthBuild in Developmental Perspective*, R. Ferguson and P. Clay, Eds. Cambridge, MA: MIT Department of Urban Studies and Planning, Chapter 9.

Fine, G.
1987 *With the Boys: Little League Baseball and Preadolescent Culture.* Chicago: University of Chicago Press.

Fine, M.
1991 *Framing Dropouts: Notes on the Politics of an Urban High School.* Albany, NY: State University of New York Press.

Fine, M., L. Weis, and L.C. Powell
1997 Communities of difference: A critical look at desegregated spaces created for and by youth. *Harvard Educational Review.* 67:247-284.

Fink, D.B.
1997 Profiles of Inclusion in Recreational Settings: A Case Study of Youth Programs in a Small Midwestern Town. Urbana-Champaign, IL: University of Illinois.

Finkelhor, D.
1990 Early and Long-Term Effects of Child Sexual Abuse. *Professional Psychology.* 21:325-330.

Fisher, C.B., J.F. Jackson, and F.A. Villarruel
1998 The Study of African American and Latin American Children and Youth. Pp. 1145-1207 in *Handbook of Child Psychology: Theoretical Models of Human Development*, Fifth, R.M. Lerner, Volume Ed. New York: John Wiley & Sons, Inc.

Flannery, D.J., D.C. Rowe, and B.L. Gulley
1993 Impact of Pubertal Status, Timing, and Age on Adolescent Sexual Experience and Delinquency. *Journal of Adolescent Research.* 8:21-40.

Flynn, M.
1999 Using TANF to Finance Out-of-School Time and Community School Initiatives. *Strategy Brief.* 1(2):1-11.

Ford, D.Y., and J.J. Harris
1996 Perceptions and Attitudes of Black Students Toward School: School, Achievement, and Other Variables. *Child Development.* 67(3):1144-1152.

Fordham, S., and J.U. Ogbu
1986 Black Student's School Success: Coping with the Burden of Acting White. *The Urban Review.* 18:176-206.

Foundation Consortium
2000 After School Learning. Accessed 2000. Available online at: http://www. foundationconsortium.org/site/shortcut/what/asl.htm.

Fountain, D.L., and A. Arbreton
1999 The cost of mentoring. Pp. 49-65 in *Contemporary Issues in Mentoring*, J.G. Grossman, Ed. Philadelphia: Public/Private Ventures.

Frammolino, R.
1998 Failing Grade for Safe Schools Plan U.S. Has Given $6 Billion to Combat Drugs, Violence. With Little Oversight, Money Has Gone for Marginally Successful Programs, Investigation Finds. *Los Angeles Times* September 6:81-96.

Fuligni, A.J., and J.S. Eccles
1993 Perceived parent-child relationships and early adolescents' orientation toward peers. *Developmental Psychology* 29:622-632.

Fund for the City of New York
1993   *Strengths and Limitations of the Beacon Mode I Recommendations.* Accessed 2000. Available online at: www.fcny.org.

Furano, K., P.A. Roaf, M.B. Styles, and A.Y. Branch
1993   Big Brothers/Big Sisters: A Study of Program Practices. Philadelphia, PA: Public/Private Ventures.

Furstenberg, F.F., T.D. Cook, J. Eccles, G.H. Elder, and A. Sameroff
1999   *Managing to Make It: Urban Families and Adolescent Success.* Chicago, IL: University of Chicago Press.

Furstenberg F.F., Jr., K.E. Sherwood, and M.L. Sullivan
1992   *Caring and Paying: What Fathers and Mothers Say About Child Support.* New York: Manpower Demonstration Research Corporation.

Galassi, J.P., S.A. Gulledge, and N.D. Cox
1997   Middle School Advisories: Retrospect and Prospect. *Review of Educational Research.* 67:301-338.

Gambone, M.A.
1997   Launching a Resident-Driven Initiative: Community Change for Youth Development (CCYD) From Site-Selection to Early Implementation. Philadelphia, PA: Public/Private Ventures.

1998   Challenges of Measurement in Community Change Initiatives. *New Approaches to Evaluating Community Initiatives: Volume 2, Theory, Measurement, and Analysis*, K. Fulbright-Anderson, A. Kubisch, and J.P. Connell, Eds. Washington, DC: The Aspen Institute.

Gambone, M.A., and A.J.A. Arbreton
1997   Safe Havens: The Contributions of Youth Organizations to Healthy Adolescent Development. Philadelphia, PA: Public/Private Ventures.

Garbarino, J.A., and R.H. Abramowitz
1992   The Ecology of Human Development. Pp. 11-33 in *Children and Families in the Social Environment*, J. Garbarino, Ed. New York, NY: Aldine de Gruyter.

García Coll, C.T., and K. Magnuson
2000   Cultural differences as sources of developmental vulnerabilities and resources: A view from developmental research. Pp. 94-111 in *Handbook of Early Childhood Intervention*, S.J. Meisels and J.P. Shonkoff, Eds. Cambridge: Cambridge University Press.

Ge, X., R.D. Conger, R.J. Cadoret, J.M. Neiderhiser, and W. Yates
1996a   The Developmental Interface Between Nature and Nurture: A Mutual Influence Model of Child Antisocial Behavior and Parent Behaviors. *Developmental Psychology.* 32:574-589.

Ge, X., R.D. Conger, and G.H. Elder
1996b   Coming of Age Too Early: Pubertal Influences on Girls' Vulnerability to Psychological Distress. *Child Development.* 67:3386-3400.

General Services Administration
2001   Catalog of Federal Domestic Assistance. Accessed June 2001. Available online at: http://www.cfda.gov.

George W. Bush for President Official Site
2000   *Governor Bush Outlines "After-School Enrichment" Initiative.* Accessed 2000. Available online at: www.georgebush.com.

Gerbner, G.
1996   *Television Violence and Alcohol Use Declines, But Smoking Still Shown as Risk-Free.* Center for Substance Abuse Prevention, October News Release.

Gerbner, G., L. Gross, M. Morgan, and N. Signorielli
  1994   Growing Up With Television: The Cultivation Perspective. Pp. 17-41 in *Media Effects: Advances in Theory and Research*, J. Bryant and D. Zillmann, Eds. Hillsdale, NJ: Lawrence Erlbaum.
Giddens, A.
  1990   *The Consequences of Modernity*. Stanford, CA: Stanford University Press.
  1992   *The Transformation of Intimacy*. Stanford, CA: Stanford University Press.
Girls Inc.
  2000a *Girls Inc. Homepage: Learn About Us*. Accessed 2001. Available online at: www.girlsinc.org.
  2000b *Sporting Chance*. Accessed 2001. Available online at: www.girlsinc.org.
Girod, M., and Y. Zhao
  2000   The Kulture of KLICK! (Kids Learning in Computer Clubhouses! Project). *Technological Horizons in Education Journal*. 27(7).
Glanz and Johnson, Editors
  1999   *Factors and Processes Contributing to Resilience: The Resilience Framework, In Resilience and Development: Positive Life Adaptations*. New York: Kluwer Academic/Plenum Publishers.
Gleick, J.
  1999   *Faster: The Acceleration of Just About Everything*. New York: Pantheon.
Goldenberg, C.N., and R. Gallimore
  1995   Immigrant Latino parents' values and beliefs about their children's education: Continuities and discontinuities across cultures and generations. Pp. 183-227 in *Advances in Motivation and Achievement*, P. Pintrich and M. Maehr, Eds. JAI Press, Inc.
Gonzales, C.
  2000   District 15 Gets 800G ED Grant. *New York Daily News,* May 30.
Goodenow, C.
  1993   Classroom Belonging Among Early Adolescent Students: Relationships to Motivation and Achievement. *Journal of Early Adolescence.* 13(1):21-43.
Goodyer, I.M.
  1997   Life Events and Difficulties: Their Nature and Effects. Pp. 171-193 in *The Depressed Child and Adolescent Development: Developmental and Clinical Perspectives*, I.M. Goodyer, Ed. Cambridge: Cambridge University Press.
Gore/Leiberman 2000 Campaign Website
  2000   *Agenda for Children and Families*. Accessed 2000. Available online at: www.algore.com.
Gorman-Smith, D.
  2000   The Interaction of Neighborhood and Family in Delinquency. *Poverty Research News.* 4(3):7-10.
Gottfredson, D.C., G.D. Gottfredson, and S. Skroban
  1998   Can Prevention Work Where It Is Needed Most? *Evaluation Review.* 22(3):315-340.
Graber, J.A., and J. Brooks-Gunn
  in   Expectations for and Precursors of Leaving Home in Young Women. *New Directions for Child Development: Leaving Home*, J.A. Graber, J.S. Dubas, and W. Damon, Eds. San Francisco, CA: Jossey-Bass.
  in   Reproductive Transitions: The Experience of Mothers and Daughters. *The Parental Experience in Midlife*, C.D. Ryff and M.M. Seltzer, Eds. Chicago, IL: University of Chicago Press.

Graber, J.A., J. Brooks-Gunn, and M.P. Warren
1995 The Antecedents of Menarchal Age: Heredity, Family Environment, and Stressful Life Events. *Child Development.* 66:346-359.

Greenberg, M.
1998 Spend or Transfer, Federal or State? Considerations in Using TANF and TANF-Related Dollars for Child Care. Washington, DC: Center for Law and Social Policy. Available online at: www.clasp.org.
2000 *Looking Ahead to Reauthorization of TANF: Some Preliminary Thoughts. Presentation to Bi-Partisan Welfare Reform Seminar for Senior Congressional and Administration Staff.* Accessed 2000. Available online at: www.clasp.org.

Greenberg, M.T., C. Domitrovich, and B. Bumbarger
1999 *Preventing Mental Disorders in School-Age Children: A Review of the Effectiveness of Prevention Programs.* University Park: Pennsylvania State University, Prevention Research Center.

Greene, R.
1998 Work Replaces Neighborhood as School Site. *The Abilene Reporter-News*

Grolnick, W.S., and R.M. Ryan
1987 Autonomy in Children's Learning: An Experimental and Individual Difference Investigation. *Journal of Personality and Social Psychology.* 52:890-898.
1989 Parent Styles Associated with Children's Self-Regulation and Competence in Schools. *Journal of Educational Psychology.* 8:143-154.

Grossman, J., and J. Rhodes
in   The Test of Time: Predictors and Effects of Duration in Youth Mentoring Rela-
press   tionships. *American Journal of Community Psychology.*

Grossman, J.B., and J.P. Tierney
1998 Does Mentoring Work? An Impact Study of the Big Brothers Big Sisters Program. *Evaluation Review.* 22(3):403-426.

Grotevant, H.D.
1998 Adolescent Development in Family Context. Pp. 1097-1149 in *Handbook of Child Psychology: Social, Emotional, and Personality Development*, Fifth, N. Eisenberg, Volume Ed. New York: John Wiley & Sons, Inc.

Gubba, E.M., C.M. Netherton, and J. Herbert
2000 Endangerment of the Brain by Glucocorticoids: Experimental and Clinical Evidence. *Journal of Neurocytology.* 29:439-449.

Gueron, J.
2001 The politics of random assignment: Implementing studies and affecting policy. In *Evidence Matters: Randomized Trials in Education Research,* F. Mosteller and R. Boruch, Eds. Washington, DC: Brookings Institute Press.

Guerra, N., L.R. Huesmann, and L. Hanish
1994 The Role of Normative Beliefs in Children's Social Behavior. Pp. 140-159 in *Review of Personality and Social Psychology, Development and Social Psychology: The Interface,* N. Eisenberg, Ed. London: Sage.

Haggerty R.J., L.R. Sherrod, N. Garmezy, and M. Rutter
1994a *Stress, Risk, and Resilience in Children and Adolescents: Processes, Mechanisms, and Interventions.* New York, NY: Cambridge University Press.
1994b Evaluation of the Quantum Opportunities Program (QOP). Did the Program Work? A Report on the Post Secondary Outcomes and Cost-Effectiveness of the QOP Program (1989-1993), A. Hahn. Waltham, MA: Brandeis University.

Hahn, A.
1995 The Central Role of "Age" in Youth Development Policy. *Contract With America's Youth: Toward a National Youth Development Agenda,* S. Halperin, et al., Eds. Washington, DC: American Youth Policy Forum.

Hahn, A., T. Leavitt, and P. Aaron
    1994   Evaluation of the Quantum Opportunity Program (QOP): Did the program
            work? Waltham, MA: Brandeis University, Heller Graduate School.
Halpern-Fisher, B.L., J.P. Connell, M.B. Spencer, J.L. Aber, G.J. Duncan, E. Clifford, W.E.
Crichlow, P.A. Usinger, S.LP.A.L. Cole, and E. Seidman
    1997   Neighborhood and Family Factors Predicting Educational Risk and Attainment
            in African American and White Children and Adolescents. Pp. 146-173 in *Neigh-
            borhood Poverty: Context and Consequences for Children*, J.B. Brooks-Gunn,
            G.J. Duncan, and J.L. Aber, Eds. New York, NY: Russell Sage Foundation.
Halpern, R., G. Barker, and W. Mollard
    1998   Youth Programs as Alternative Spaces to Be: A Study of Neighborhood Youth
            Programs in Chicago's West Town. Chicago, IL.
Hanson, S.L., and A.L. Ginsburg
    1987   Gaining ground: Values and high school success. *American Educational Research
            Journal*. 25:334-365.
Harrell, A., S. Cavanagh, and S. Sridharan
    1999   Evaluation of the Children at Risk Program: Results 1 Year After the End of the
            Program. *National Institute of Justice: Research in Brief*. 1-9.
Harris, J.
    1995   *The Nurture Assumption*. The Free Press.
Harter, S.
    1990   Causes, Correlates and the Functional Role of Self-Worth: A Life-Span Perspec-
            tive. Pp. 67-97 in *Competence Considered*, R.J. Sternberg and J. Kolligian, Eds.
            New Haven, CT: Yale University Press.
    1998   The Development of Self-Representations. Pp. 553-618 in *Handbook of Child
            Psychology: Social, Emotional, and Personality Development*, 5th ed., W.
            Damon and N. Eisenberg, Eds. New York: Wiley.
Harvard Family Research Project
    2001   *After School Learning Initiative*. Accessed 2001. Available online at: www.gse.
            harvard.edu.
Hattie, J.M.H.W., J.T. Neill, and G.E. Richards
    1997   Adventure Education and Outward Bound: Out-of-Class Experiences That Make
            a Lasting Difference. *Review of Educational Research*. 67(1):43-87.
Hauser, S.T., S.I. Powers, and G.G. Noam
    1991   *Adolescents and Their Families: Paths of Ego Development*. New York: The
            Free Press.
Havinghurst, R.J.
    1972   *Developmental Tasks and Education*. New York: McKay Publishers.
Hawkins, J.D., M.W. Arthur, and J.J. Olsen
    1998   Community Interventions to Reduce Risks and Enhance Protection Against Anti-
            Social Behavior. Pp. 365-374 in *Handbook of Antisocial Behaviors*, D.W. Stoff,
            J. Breiling, and J.D. Masers, eds. Seattle, WA: NIMH/John Wiley & Sons, Inc.
Hawkins, J.D., R.F. Catalano, and Associates
    1992   *Communities That Care: Action for Drug Abuse Prevention*. San Francisco,
            CA: Jossey-Bass.
Hawkins, J.D., R.F. Catalano, R. Kosterman, R. Abbott, and K.G. Hill
    1999   Preventing Adolescent Health-Risk Behaviors by Strengthening Protection Dur-
            ing Childhood. *Archives of Pediatric Adolescent Medicine*. 153:226-234.
Hawley, W.D., and A.W. Jackson, Eds.
    1995   *Toward a Common Destiny: Improving Race and Ethnic Relations in America*.
            San Francisco, CA: Jossey-Bass.

Hayes, C.D., and M. Flynn
  2000   Financing Community Initiatives for Urban Children and Youth: An Overview of Financing Strategies and Funding Sources. Washington, DC: The Finance Project.
Heath, S.B.
  1994   The Project of Learning from the Inner-City Youth Perspective. *New Directions for Child Development.* 63:25-34.
  1999   Dimensions of Language Development: Lessons from Older Children. Pp. 59-75 in *Cultural Processes in Child Development: The Minnesota Symposium on Child Psychology,* A.S. Masten, Ed. Mahwah, NJ: Lawrence Erlbaum.
Henderson, A.T., and N. Berla, Eds.
  1994   *A New Generation of Evidence: The Family Is Critical to Academic Achievement.* Washington, DC: Center for Law and Education.
Henggeler, S.W., G.B. Melton, L.A. Smith, S.K. Schoenwald, and J.H. Hanely
  1993   Family Preservation Using Multisystemic Treatment: Long-Term Follow-Up to a Clinical Trial with Serious Juvenile Offenders. *Journal of Child and Family Studies.* 2(4):283-293.
Herbert, J., and M. Martinez
  2001   Neural Mechanisms Underlying Aggressive Behaviour. Pp. 67-102 in *Conduct Disorders in Childhood and Adolescence,* J. Hill and B. Maughan, Eds. Cambridge University Press.
Herdt, G., and A. Boxer
  1993   *Children of Horizons: How Gay and Lesbian Teens Are Leading a New Way Out of the Closet.* Boston, MA: Beacon Press.
Herman-Giddens, M.E., E.J. Slora, R.C. Wasserman, C.J. Bourdony, M.V. Bhapkar, G.G. Koch, and C.M. Hasemeier
  1997   Secondary Sexual Characteristics and Menses in Young Girls Seen in Office Practices: A Study from the Pediatric Research in Office Settings Network. *Pediatrics.* 99:505-512.
Herrara, J.D., C.L. Sipe, W.S. McClanahan, A. Arbreton, and S.K. Pepper
  2000   Mentoring school-age children: Relationship development in community-based and school-based programs. Philadelphia: Public/Private Ventures.
Higgins, E.T., and J. Parsons-Eccles
  1983   Social cognition and the social life of the child: Stages as subcultures. Pp. 15-62 in *Social Cognition and Social Development,* E.T. Higgins, D.N. Ruble, and W.W. Hartup, Eds. Cambridge, MA: Cambridge University Press.
Higgins, E.T., D.N. Ruble, and W.W. Hartup, Eds.
  1983   *Social Cognition and Social Development.* Cambridge, MA: Cambridge University Press.
High/Scope Educational Research Foundation
  2000   The High/Scope Adolescent Approach: Curriculum for Youth Workers, Participant Guide. Ypsilanti, MI: High/Scope Press.
Hill, M.S., and W.-J.J. Yeung
  2000   Behavior and Status of Children, Adolescents and Young Adults: Discussion Draft. Ann Arbor, MI: University of Michigan.
Honig, M.I., J. Kahne, and M.W. McLaughlin
  1999   School-Community Connections: Strengthening Opportunity to Learn and Opportunity to Teach: Handbook of Research on Teaching. Stanford University, University of Illinois.

Howell, J.C., B. Krisberg, J.D. Hawkins, and J.J. Wilson
    1995   A Sourcebook: Serious, Violent, and Chronic Juvenile Offenders. Pp. 61-141 in *Preventing Serious, Violent, and Chronic Juvenile Offending: A Review of Evaluations of Selected Strategies in Childhood, Adolescence, and the Community.*, D.D. Brewer, J.D. Hawkins, R.F. Catalano, and H.J. Neckerman, Eds. Thousand Oaks, CA: Sage.

Howell, J.C., and J.P. Lynch
    2000   Youth Gangs in Schools. Office of Juvenile Justice and Delinquency Prevention, Juvenile Justice Bulletin, August 2000.

Huesmann, L.R., and N. Guerra
    1997   Children's Normative Beliefs About Aggression and Aggressive Behavior. *Journal of Personality and Social Psychology.* 72:408-419.

Hughes, D., and L. Chen
    1999   The Nature of Parents' Race-Related Communications to Children: A Developmental Perspective. *Child Psychology: A Handbook of Contemporary Issues*, C. Tamis-LeMonda and L. Balter, Eds. Philadelphia, PA: Psychology Press.

Huston, A.C., E. Donnerstein, and H. Fairchild
    1992   *Big World, Small Screen: The Role of Television in American Society*, Lincoln: University of Nebraska Press.

Hyman, J.B.
    1999   Spheres of Influence: A Strategic Synthesis and Framework for Community Youth Development. Baltimore, MD: Annie E. Casey Foundation.

Institute for Social Research
    various Monitoring the Future. Ann Arbor, MI: Institute for Social Research, University
    years   of Michigan.

Institute for Youth Development
    2000   The Federal Grants Manual for Youth Programs: A Guide to Youth Risk Behavior Prevention Funding. Vol. 2. Washington, DC: Institute for Youth Development. www.youthdevelopment.org.

Institute of Medicine
    1994   Growing Up Tobacco Free: Preventing Nicotine Addiction in Children and Youths, Committee on Preventing Nicotine Addiction in Children and Youths, Division of Biobehavioral Sciences and Mental Disorders. Lynch, B., and Bonnie, R., Eds. Washington, DC: National Academy Press.

    1995   The Best Intentions: Unintended Pregnancy and the Well-Being of Children and Families, Committee on Unintended Pregnancy, Division of Health Promotion and Disease Prevention. Brown, S., and Eisenberg, L., Eds. Washington, DC: National Academy Press.

    1997a Improving Health in the Community: A Role for Performance Monitoring, Committee on Using Performance Monitoring to Improve Community Health. Durch, J., Bailey, L., and Stoto, M., Eds. Washington, DC: National Academy Press.

    1997b *Schools & Health: Our Nation's Investment*. Washington DC: National Academy Press.

Interagency Executive Oversight Committee, General Services Administration
    2000   *Overview of the Federal Support to Communities Initiative*. Accessed 2001. Available online at: www.afterschool.gov.

International Youth Foundation-US
    2000   Finding Common Ground: Toward a Common Vision, Analysis, and Accountability for Youth. Takoma Park, MD: IYF-US.

    1999   The Youth Tomorrow Initiative: A Proposal. Takoma Park, MD: International Youth Foundation.

Jackson A.W., and G.A. Davis
2000   *Turning Points 2000: Educating Adolescents in the 21st Century.* New York: Teacher's College Press.

Jaffee, L., and R. Manzer
1992   Girls' Perspectives: Physical Activity and Self-Esteem. *Melpomene Journal.* 11:14-23.

Jarrett, R.L.
1997   African American Family and Parenting Strategies in Impoverished Neighborhoods. *Qualitative Sociology.* 20:275-288.

Jeffords, J., E. Kennedy, M. Cleland, and P. Murray
2000   *Younger Americans Act.* #S.3085: Section 101-403. Available online at www.nydic.org.

Jencks, C., and M. Phillips, Eds.
1998   *The Black-White Test Score Gap.* Washington, DC: Brookings Institution Press.

Jessor, R.
1993   Successful Adolescent Development Among Youth in High-Risk Settings. *American Psychologist.* 48:117-126.

Jessor, R., Ed.
1998   *New Perspectives on Adolescent Risk Behavior.* New York: Cambridge University Press.

Jessor, R., J.E. Donovan, and F.M. Costa
1991   *Beyond Adolescence: Problem Behavior and Young Adult Development.* New York: Cambridge University Press.

Jessor, R., and S.L. Jessor
1977   *Problem Behavior and Psychosocial Development: A Longitudinal Study of Youth.* New York, NY: Academic Press.

JMT Associates
1998   *Work-Site Schools: Another Option for More Classrooms.* Accessed 2000. Available online at: www.jmt-fla.com.

Johnson, D.W., and R.T. Johnson
1996   Conflict resolution and peer mediation programs in elementary and secondary schools: A review of research. *Review of Educational Research.* 66:459-506.

Jordon, W., and S.M. Nettles
1999   How Students Invest Their Time Out of School: Effects on School Engagement, Perceptions of Life Chances, and Achievement. Baltimore, MD: Center for Research on the Education of Students Placed at Risk.

Kaplan, A., and H. Sachs
1999   *Financing School-Age Out-Of-School Time Programs with Welfare Related Funding.* Accessed 2000. Available online at: www.welfareinfo.org.

Kazdin, A.E.
1997   Parent Management Training: Evidence, Outcomes, and Issues. *Journal of the American Academy of Child and Adolescent Psychiatry.* 36(10):1349-1356.

Keating, D.P.
1990   Adolescent Thinking. Pp. 54-89 in *At the Threshold: The Developing Adolescent*, S.S. Feldman and G.R. Elliott, Eds. Cambridge, MA: Harvard University Press.

Keel, P.K., J.A. Fulkerson, and G.R. Leon
1997   Disordered Eating Precursors in Pre- and Early Adolescent Girls and Boys. *Journal of Youth and Adolescence.* 26:203-216.

Keldner, S.H., C.L. Perry, L.A. Lytle, and K.I. Klepp
  1993   Community-Wide Youth Exercise Promotion: Long Term Outcomes of the Min-
          nesota Health Program and the Class of 1989 Study. *Journal of School Health.*
          63:218-223.
Kellam, S.G., X. Ling, R. Merisca, C.H. Brown, and N. Ialongo
  1998   The Effect of the Level of Aggression in the First Grade Classroom on the Course
          and Malleability of Aggressive Behavior into Middle School. 10:165-185.
Kendler, K.S., and L. Karkowski-Shuman
  1997   Stressful Life Events and Genetic Liability to Major Depression: Genetic Control
          of Exposure to the Environment? *Psychological Medicine.* 27:549-564.
Kessler, R.C., K.A. McGonagle, M. Swartz, D.G. Blazer, and C.B. Nelson
  1993   Sex and Depression in the National Co morbidity Survey: Lifetime Prevalence,
          Chronicity, and Recurrence. *Journal of Affective Disorders.* 29:85-96.
Keterlinus, R.D.
  1997   A Project to Develop and Refine Performance Indicators and Outcome Measures
          for Youth Development Programs: Draft Literature Review. Washington, DC:
          CSR, Incorporated.
Killian, E., and R. Brown
  1999   *Promoting Positive Development in Your Youth Programs.* Accessed 2000.
          Available online at: www.nce.unr.edu.
Kingsley G.T.
  1998   *Neighborhood Indicators: Taking Advantage of the New Potential.* Washing-
          ton, DC: The Urban Institute.
Kirby, D.
  1997   No Easy Answers: Research Findings on Programs to Reduce Teen Pregnancy.
          Washington, DC: National Campaign to Prevent Teen Pregnancy.
  1998   HIV Prevention Among Adolescents. San Francisco, CA: University of CA, San
          Francisco, Center for AIDS Prevention Studies, AIDS Resource Institute.
  2001   *Emerging Answers: Research Findings on Programs to Reduce Teen Pregnancy.*
          Washington, DC: National Campaign to Prevent Teen Pregnancy.
Kirby, D., and K. Coyle
  1997   Youth Development Programs. *Children and Youth Services Review.* 19
          (5/6):437-454.
Kirby, D., L. Short, J. Collins, D. Rugg, L. Kolbe, M. Howard, B. Miller, F. Sonenstein,
and L.S. Zabin
  1994   School-based programs to reduce sexual risk behavior: A review of effectiveness.
          Public Health Reports. 109:339-360.
Kleiber, D., and G. Roberts
  1981   The Effects of Sport Experience in the Development of Social Character: An
          Exploratory Investigation. *Journal of Sport Psychology.* 3:114-122.
Konopka Institute
  1999   Best Bets: The Health and Well-Being of Adolescents-Looking to the Future.
          Minneapolis, MN.
Kotloff, L.J., P.A. Roaf, and M.A. Gambone
  1995   The Plain Talk Planning Year: Mobilizing Communities to Change. Philadel-
          phia, PA: Public/Private Ventures.
Kretchner, N., J.L. Beard, and S. Carlson
  1996   The Role of Nutrition in the Development of Normal Cognition. *American
          Journal of Clinical Nutrition.* 63:997S-1001S.

Kumpfer, K.L.
1999 Factors and Processes Contributing to Resilience: The Resilience Framework. Pp. 179-224 in *Resilience and Development: Positive Life Adaptations*, Glantz and Johnson, Editors. New York: Kluwer Academic/Plenum Publishers.

LaFromboise, T., L.K. Coleman, and J. Gerton
1993 Psychological Impact of Biculturalism: Evidence and Theory. *Psychological Bulletin.* 114(3):395-412.

LaFromboise, T., and K. Graff Low
1998 American Indian Children and Adolescents. *Children of Color: Psychological Interventions With Culturally Diverse Youth*, J. Gibbs and L. Huang, Eds. San Francisco, CA: Jossey-Bass.

LaFromboise, T.D., and B. Howard-Pitney
1993 The Zuni Life Skills Development Curriculum: A Collaborative Approach to Curriculum Development. American Indian and Alaska Native Mental Health Research. *Journal of the National Center.* 4 (monograph):98-121.
1995 The Zuni Life Skills Development Curriculum: Description and Evaluation of a Suicide Prevention Program. *Journal of Counseling Psychology.* 42(4):479-486.

Landrine, H., J.L. Richardson, E. Klonoff, and B.R. Flay
1994 Cultural Diversity in the Predictors of Adolescent Cigarette Smoking: The Relative Influence of Peers. *Journal of Behavioral Medicine.* 17(3):331-346.

Langford, B.H.
1999 Creating Dedicated Local Revenue Sources for Out-of-School Time Initiatives. *Strategy Brief.* 1(1):1-11.
2000a Maximizing Federal Food and Nutrition Funds for Out-of-School Time and Community School Initiatives. *Strategy Brief.* 1(3):1-19.
2000b Strategy Brief: Maximizing Federal Food and Nutrition Funds for Out-of-School Time and Community School Initiatives. Vol. 1. Washington, DC: The Finance Project.

Larson, R.
in press Adolescence in the 21st century: A worldwide perspective-Report the study group on adolescence in the 21st century. *Journal of Research on Adolescence.* Special Issue.

Larson, R., and M.H. Richards
1991 Daily Companionship in Late Childhood and Early Adolescence: Changing Developmental Contexts. *Child Development.* 62:284-300.

Larson, R.W.
1994 Youth Organizations, Hobbies, and Sports as Developmental Contexts. Pp. 46-65 in *Adolescence in Context: The Interplay of Family, School, Peers, and Work in Adjustment*, R.K. Silbereisen and E. Todt, Eds. New York, NY: Springer-Verlag.
2000 Toward a Psychology of Positive Youth Development. *American Psychologist.* 55:170-183.

Larson, R.W., and S. Verma
1999 How Children and Adolescents Spend Time Across the World: Work, Play, and Developmental Opportunities. *Psychological Bulletin.* 125(6):701-736.

Lawler, E.E.
1976 Control Systems in Organizations. *Handbook of Industrial and Organizational Psychology*, M.D. Dunnette, Ed. Chicago, IL: Rand McNally.

Lee, V.E., and J.B. Smith
1993 Effects of School Restructuring on the Achievement and Engagement of Middle-Grade Students. *Sociology of Education.* 66:164-187.

Leffert, N., P.L. Benson, P.C. Scales, A.R. Sharma, D.R. Drake, and D.A. Blyth
1998   Developmental Assets: Measurement and Prediction of Risk Behaviors Among
        Adolescents. *Applied Developmental Science.* 2(4):209-230.
Leong, F.T.L., R.K. Chao, and E.E. Hardin
2000   Asian American Adolescents: A Research Review to Dispel the Model Minority
        Myth. *Adolescent Diversity in Ethnic, Economic, and Cultural Contexts,* R.
        Montemayor, G.R. Adams, and T.P. Gullotta, Eds. Thousand Oaks, CA: Sage
        Publications.
Lerner, R.M.
1993   The Role of Community-Based Youth Groups in Enhancing Learning and
        Achievement Through Nonformal Education. Pp. 159-174 in *Early Adoles-
        cence: Perspectives on Research, Policy, and Intervention,* J.S. Dubas and B.A.
        Snider, Eds. Hillsdale, NJ: Lawrence Erlbaum Associates, Inc.
Lerner, R.M., C.B. Fisher, and R.A. Weinberg
2000   Toward a Science for and of the People: Promoting Civil Society Through the
        Application of Developmental Science. *Child Development.* 71:11-20.
Lerner, R.M., and N.L. Galambos
1998   Adolescent Development: Challenges and Opportunities for Research, Programs,
        and Policies. *Annual Review of Psychology.* 49:413-446.
LeVine, R., P. Miller, and M. West, Eds.
1988   *Parental Behavior in Diverse Societies.* San Francisco, CA: Jossey-Bass.
Libman, I., and S.A. Arslanian
1999   Type II Diabetes Mellitus: No Longer Just Adults. *Pediatric Annals.* 28:345-
        354.
Liebman, C.S.
1990   Ritual, Ceremony and the Reconstruction of Judaism in the United States. Pp.
        309 in *Jews in America: A Contemporary Reader,* R.R. Farber and C.I. Waxman,
        Eds. Hanover & London: Brandeis University Press.
Lindberg, L.D., S. Boggess, L. Porter, and S. Williams
2000   Teen Risk-Taking: A Statistical Portrait. Washington, DC: The Urban Institute.
Lipsey, M.W., and D.S. Cordray
in   Evaluation Methods for Social Intervention. *Annual Review of Psychology.*
press   51:345-375.
Lipsitz, J.
1980   *Growing Up Forgotten.* New Brunswick, NJ: Transaction Books.
Lipsitz, J., A.W. Jackson, and L.M. Austin
1997   What works in middle-grades school reform. *Phi Delta Kappan.* 78(3):517-519.
Litchfield, A.W., D.L. Thomas, and B.D. Li
1997   Dimensions of religiosity as mediators of the relations between parenting and
        adolescent deviant behavior. *Journal of Adolescent Research.* 12:199-226.
Littell, J., and J. Wynn
1989   The Availability and Use of Community Resources for Young Adolescents in an
        Inner-City and Suburban Community. Chicago, IL: Chapin Hall Center for
        Children at the University of Chicago.
Loose, C.
1999   From Dance, Lessons for Life. *The Washington Post* B7, December 27.
Lord, S.E., J.S. Eccles, and K.A. McCarthy
1994   Surviving the Junior High School Transition: Family Processes and Self-Percep-
        tions as Protective and Risk Factors. *Journal of Early Adolescence.* 14:162-199.

Lordeman, A.
1998   CRS Report for Congress. Job Training Reform—Legislation in the 105th Congress. Washington, DC: Congressional Research Service, The Library of Congress.

Loury, G.
1977   A dynamic theory of racial income differences. Pp. 153-186 in *Women, Minorities, and Employment Discrimination*, P.A. Wallace and A. Le Mund, Eds., Lexington, MA: Lexington Books

Luthar, S.S., and E. Zigler
1992   Intelligence and Social Competence Among High-Risk Adolescents. *Development and Psychopathology*. 4:287-299.

MacDonald, G.B., and R. Valdivieso
2000   Measuring deficits and assets: How we track youth development now, and how we should track it. Pp. 149-184 in *Youth Development: Issues, Challenges, and Directions*. Philadelphia, PA: Public/Private Ventures.

MacIver, D.J., D.A. Reuman, and S.R. Main
1995   Social structuring of school: Studying what is, illuminating what could be. *Annual Review of Psychology*, M.R. Rosenzweig and L.W. Porter, Eds.

MacIver, D.J., D.J. Stipek, and D.H. Daniels
1991   Explaining Within-Semester Changes in Student Effort in Junior High School and Senior High School Courses. *Journal of Educational Psychology*. 83:201-211.

MacKenzie, D.L.
1997   Criminal Justice and Crime Prevention. Pp. 9,1-9,76 in *Preventing Crime: What Works, What Doesn't , What's Promising*, L.W. Sherman, D. Gottfredson, D. MacKenzie, J. Eck, P. Reuter, S. Bushway, and University of Maryland Department of Criminology and Criminal Justice, Eds. Washington, DC: U.S. Department of Justice.

Maehr, M.L., and C. Midgley
1996   *Transforming School Cultures*. Boulder, CO: Westview Press.

Magnusson, D.
1988   *Individual Development from an International Perspective*. Hillsdale, NJ: Lawrence Erlbaum Associates.

Magnusson, D., and H. Stattin
1998   Person-context interaction theories. Pp. 685-759 in *Handbook of Child Psychology. Volume 1: Theoretical Models of Human Development*, W. Damon and R.M. Lerner, Eds. New York: Wiley

Mahler M., F. Pine, and A. Bergman
1975   *The Psychological Birth of the Human Infant*. New York: Basic Books.

Mahoney, J., H. Stattin, and D. Magnusson
in   Youth Recreation Center Participation and Criminal Offending: A 20-Year Lon-
press gitudinal Study of Swedish Boys. *International Journal of Behavioral Development*.

Mahoney, J.L.
2000   School Extracurricular Activity Participation as a Moderator in the Development of Antisocial Patterns. *Child Development*. 71(2):502-516.

Mahoney, J.L., and R.B. Cairns
1997   Do Extracurricular Activities Protect Against Early School Dropout? *Developmental Psychology*. 33(2):241-253.

Mahoney, J.L., and D. Magnusson
in   Running Head: Parent Participation in Community Activities and the Persistence
press of Criminality. *Development and Psychopathology*.

Mahoney, J.L., and H. Stattin
  2000   Leisure Activities and Adolescent Antisocial Behavior: The Role of Structure and Social Context. *Journal of Adolescence.* 23:113-127.
Marchetti, D.
  1999   New Focus on Minding the Kids. *The Chronicle of Philanthropy.* December 2:7-8.
Marcia, J.E.
  1980   Identity in adolescence. Pp. 149-173 in *Handbook of Adolescent Psychology,* J. Adelson, Ed. New York: Wiley.
Marjoribanks K.
  1979   *Families and Their Learning Environments: An Empirical Analysis.* London: Routledge and Kegan Paul.
Markstrom-Adams, C., and M.B. Spencer
  1994   A model for identity intervention with minority adolescents. Pp. 84-102 in *Interventions for Adolescent Identity Development,* S. Archer, Ed. Newbury Park, CA: Sage.
Marshall, N.L., C. Garcia Coll, F. Marx, K. McCartney, N. Keefe, and J. Ruh
  1997   After-School Time and Children's Behavioral Adjustment. *Merrill-Palmer Quarterly.* 43(3):497-514.
Martinez, P., and J. Richters
  1993   The NIMH Community Violence Project: II. Children's Distress Symptoms Associated with Violent Exposure. *Psychiatry.* 56:22-35.
Masten, A.S.
  1994   Resilience in Individual Development: Successful Adaptation Despite Risk and Adversity. Pp. 3-25 in *Educational Resilience in Inner City America: Challenges and Prospects,* M.C. Wang and E.W. Gordon, Eds. Hillsdale, NJ: Lawrence Erlbaum Associates.
McCallion, G.
  2000   CRS Report for Congress. 21st Century Community Learning Centers: An Overview of the Program and Analysis of Reauthorization Issues. Washington, DC: Congressional Research Service, The Library of Congress.
McClanahan, W.S.
  1998   Relationships in a Career Mentoring Program: Lessons Learned From the Hospital Youth Mentoring Program. Philadephia, PA: Public/Private Ventures.
McLaughlin, M.
  2000   Community Counts: How Youth Organizations Matter for Youth Development. Washington, DC: Public Education Network.
McLaughlin, M., M. McDonald, and S. Deschenes
  2001   Mapping Opportunities to Learn: Youth Development Programming in the Bay Area. Stanford, CA: Stanford University: The John Gardner Center for Youth and Their Communities.
McLaughlin, M.W., M.A. Irby, and J. Langman
  1994   *Urban Sanctuaries: Neighborhood Organizations in the Lives and Futures of Inner-City Youth.* San Francisco, CA: Jossey-Bass Publishers.
McLearn, K.L., D. Colasanto, and C. Schoen
  1998   Mentoring Makes A Difference: Findings From The Commonwealth Fund 1998 Survey Of Adults Mentoring Young People. New York: The Commonwealth Fund.
Mead, M.
  1935   *Sex and Temperament in Three Primitive Societies.* New York: Dell.

Meece, J.L.
   1994   The Role of Motivation in Self-Regulated Learning. Pp. 25-44 in *Self-Regulation of Learning and Performance*, D.H. Schunk and B.J. Zimmerman, Eds. Hillsdale, N.J.: Lawrence Erlbaum Associates.

Merry, S.
   2000   Beyond Home and School: The Role of Primary Supports in Youth Development. Chapin Hall Center for Children.

Metropolitan Life
   1994   Metropolitan Life Survey of the American Teacher. Violence in America's Public Schools: A Survey of Students, Teachers, and Law Enforcement Officers. Alexandria, VA: National Association of Elementary School Principals.

Meyers, A.F., A.E. Sampson, and M. Weitsman
   1991   Nutrition and Academic Performance in School Children. *Clinical Applied Nutrition*. 1:13-25.

Midgley, C.M., H. Feldlaufer, and J.S. Eccles
   1989   Changes in Teacher Efficacy and Student Self-and Task-Related Beliefs During the Transition to Junior High School. *Journal of Educational Psychology*. 81:247-258.

Miller, B.C., M.C. Norton, X. Fan, and C.R. Christopherson
   1998   Pubertal development, parental communication, and sexual values in relation to adolescent sexual behaviors. *Journal of Early Adolescence*. 18:27-52.

Miller, B.M.
   1995   Out-Of-School Time: Effects On Learning in the Primary Grades. Wellsley, MA: School-Age Child Care Project, Center for Research on Women, Wellesley College.
   2000   Power of the Hours: The Changing Context of After School. *School Age Review*. (2).

Miller, B.M., and F. Marx
   1990   Afterschool Arrangements in Middle Childhood: A Review of the Literature. Wellesley, MA: School-Age Child Care Project, Center for Research on Women, Wellesley College.

Miller, G., M. Roukema, B. Gilman, J. Quinn, and B. Clement
   2001   *Younger Americans Act*. #H.R. 17: Section 101-403. Available online at www.nydic.org.

Mincy, R.
   1994a   A Model "Request for Proposals", in Nurturing Young Black Males. United Urban Press.
   1994b   Who Is Contributing? Breakdown by Type of Funding Source. Pp. 208-211 in *Nurturing Young Black Males: Challenges to Agencies, Programs, and Social Policy*, R.B. Mincy, Editor. Washington, DC: Urban Institute Press.

Moffitt, T.E.
   1993   Adolescence-Limited and Life-Course-Persistent Antisocial Behavior: A Developmental Taxonomy. *Psychology Review*. 100:674-701.

Moore, K.A., and D. Glei
           Taking the Plunge: An Examination of Positive Youth Development. *Journal of Adolescent Research*. 10(1):15-40.

Morley, E., and S.B. Rossman
   1997   Helping At-Risk Youth: Lessons From Community-Based Initiatives. Washington, DC: The Urban Institute.

Morrow, K.V., and M.B. Styles
   1995   Building Relationships With Youth in Program Settings: A Study of Big Brothers/Big Sisters. Philadelphia, PA: Public/Private Ventures.

Mortimer, J., C. Harley, and P. Aronson
  1999 How Do Prior Experiences in the Workplace Set the Stage for Transitions to Adulthood? Pp. 131-159 in *Transitions to Adulthood in a Changing Economy: No Work, No Family, No Future?*, A. Booth, A.C. Crouter, and M.J. Shanahan, Eds. Westport, CT: Praeger Publishers.
Mortimer, J., and R. Larson, Eds.
  2002 *The Changing Adolescent Experience: Societal Trends and the Transition to Adulthood.* New York: Cambridge University Press.
Mundy, L.
  2000 Closer to Home. *Washington Post Magazine* 7-11, 19-23.
Murnane, R.J., and F. Levy
  1996 *Teaching the New Basic Skills: Principles for Education Children to Thrive in a Changing Economy.* New York, NY: The Free Press.
National 4-H Council
  2000 *Who We Are: Mission and Departments.* Accessed 2001. Available online at: www.fourhcouncil.edu.
National Campaign to Prevent Teen Pregnancy
  1997 *Snapshots from the Front Line: Lessons About Teen Pregnancy Prevention from States and Communities.* Washington, DC: National Campaign to Prevent Teen Pregnancy.
  2000 *Recent Trends in Teen Pregnancy, Sexual Activity and Contraceptive Use.* Accessed 2001. Available online at: http://www.teenpregnancy.org.
  2001 Fact Sheet: Recent trends in teen pregnancy, sexual activity, and contraceptive use. Accessed 2001. Available online at: http://www.teenpregnancy.org/rectrend.htm
National Center for Chronic Disease Prevention & Health Promotion
  1999 *Youth Risk Behavior Surveillance System.* Accessed 2001. Available online at: www.cdc.gov.
National Center for Education Statistics
  1995 *Overview of TIMSS Project.* Accessed 2001. Available online at: http://nces.ed.gov.
National Center for Health Statistics
  1999 *Prevalence of Overweight Among Children and Adolescents: United States, 1999.* Accessed 2001. Available online at: http://www.cdc.gov.
  2000 Health, United States, 2000 With Adolescent Health Chartbook. Hyattsville, MD: Centers for Disease Control & Prevention, National Center for Health Statistics.
National Center for Injury Prevention & Control
  1999 *Youth Violence in the United States.* Accessed 2000. Available online at: www.cdc.gov.
  2000 *Fact Book For he Year 2000: Working To Prevent and Control Injury In The United States.* Accessed 2000. Available online at: http://www.cdc.gov.
National Clearinghouse on Families and Youth
  1991 Beyond Rhetoric: A New American Agenda for Children and Families. Final Report of the National Commission on Children. Washington, DC: U.S. Government Printing Office.
  1996 Reconnecting Youth and Community: A Youth Development Approach, U.S. Department of Health and Human Services and Administration for Children and Families.
  1996 Reconnecting Youth and Community: A Youth Development Approach. Washington, DC: U.S. Department of Health and Human Services.

National Collaboration for Youth
    1997   Compendium of Information Sources on Youth, Affinity Group of The National Assembly of National Voluntary Health and Social Welfare Organizations.

National Governor's Association
    1999   *Results of a 1999 Survey by the National Governors' Association Center for Best Practices.* Accessed 2000. Available online at: www.nga.org.

National Institute on Drug Abuse (NIDA)
    1996   National Survey Results on Drug Use from *The Monitoring the Future Study,* 1975-1998: Volume 1: Secondary School Students. Rockville, MD: NIDA.

National Institute on Out-of-School Time
    2000   *The MOST Initiative: Making the Most of Out-of-School Time.* Accessed 2001. Available online at: www.wellesley.edu.
    2001a Fact Sheet on School-Age Children's Out-of-School Time. Wellesley, MA. www.niost.org.
    2001b *Welcome to the National Institute on Out-of-School Time (NIOST).* Accessed 2001. Available online at: www.wellesley.edu.

National Research Council
    1999   *How People Learn: Brain, Mind, Experience, and School.* Bransford, J.D., Brown, A.L., and Cocking, R.R., Eds. Washington, DC: National Academy Press.

National Research Council and Institute of Medicine
    1995   *Integrating Federal Statistics on Children: Report of a Workshop,* Board on Children, Youth and Families and Committee on National Statistics. Washington, DC: National Academy Press.
    1996   *Youth Development and Neighborhood Influences: Challenges and Opportunities. Summary of a Workshop,* Committee on Youth Development, Chalk, R., and Phillips, D., Eds. Washington, DC: National Academy Press.
    1998a *From Generation to Generation: The Health and Well-Being of Children in Immigrant Families,* Committee on the Health and Adjustment of Immigrant Children and Families. Hernandez, D., and Charney, E., Eds. Washington, DC: National Academy Press.
    1998b *Longitudinal Surveys of Children,* Committee on National Statistics, Board on Children, Youth, and Families. West, K., Hauser, R., and Scanlan, T., Eds. Washington, DC: National Academy Press.
    1998c *New Findings on Poverty and Child Health and Nutrition,* Bridgman, A., and Phillips, D., Eds. Washington, DC: National Academy Press.
    1998d *Protecting Youth at Work: Health, Safety, and Development of Working Children and Adolescents in the United States,* Committee on the Health and Safety Implications of Child Labor, Board on Children, Youth, and Families, and National Research Council. Washington, DC: National Academy Press.
    1998e *Violence in Families: Assessing Prevention and Treatment Programs,* Committee on the Assessment of Family Violence Interventions, Board on Children, Youth, and Families, National Research Council. Chalk, R., and King, P., Eds. Washington, DC: National Academy Press.
    1999a *Adolescent Development and the Biology of Puberty: Summary of a Workshop on New Research,* Forum on Adolescence and M. Kipke, Ed. Washington, DC: National Academy Press.
    1999b *Revisiting Home Visiting: Summary of a Workshop,* Committee on Early Childhood Development, Board on Children, Youth, and Families. Margie, N., and Phillips, D., Eds. Washington, DC: National Academy Press.
    1999c *Risks and Opportunities: Synthesis of Studies on Adolescence.* Washington, DC: National Academy Press.

2000a *After-School Programs to Promote Child and Adolescent Development,* Committee on Community-Level Programs for Youth and Gootman, Jennifer Appleton, Ed. Washington, D.C.: National Academy Press.

2000b *Improving Intergroup Relations Among Youth: Summary of a Research Workshop,* Board on Children, Youth and Families, Forum on Adolescence, and Kipke, Michele, Ed. Washington, DC: National Academy Press.

National School-Age Care Alliance

1998 About NSACA. Accessed 2001. Available online at: http://www.nsaca.org.

2000 *NSACA Public Policy Goals for February 2000.* Accessed 2000. Available online at: http://www.nsaca.org.

National Youth Development Information Center

2000a *Homepage: National Youth Development Information Center.* Accessed 2001. Available online at: www.nydic.org.

2000b *National Foundations That Support Youth Development Programs.* Accessed 2000. Available online at: www.nydic.org.

Neugarten, B.L., and N. Datan

1973 Sociological Perspectives on the Life Cycle. Pp. 53-69 in *Life-Span Developmental Psychology: Personality and Socialization,* P.B. Baltes and K.W. Schaie, Eds. New York: Academic Press.

Neuser J.

1994 *Fortress Introduction to American Judaism: What the Books Say, What the People Do.* Minneapolis, MN: Fortress Press.

Newman, F.M., and Associates

1996 *Authentic Achievement: Restructuring Schools for Intellectual Quality.* San Francisco, CA: Jossey-Bass.

Newman, R., S. Smith, and R. Murphy

1999 The Cost of Youth Development. A Matter of Money: The Cost and Financing of Youth Development. Washington, DC: Academy for Educational Development.

Newman, S., J.A. Fox, E. Flynn, and W. Christeson

2000 America's After-School Choice: The Prime Time for Juvenile Crime, Or Youth Enrichment and Achievement. Washington, DC: Fight Crime: Invest in Kids. www.fightcrime.org.

Nicholson, H.J., and L.T. Postrado

1991 *Girls, Incorporated, Preventing Adolescent Pregnancy: A Program Development And Research Project.* New York: Girls, Incorporated.

1992 A comprehensive age-phased approach: Girls, Incorporated. In *Preventing Adolescent Pregnancy,* B.C. Miller, J.J. Card, R.L. Paikoff, et al., Eds. Newbury Park, CA: Sage Publications.

Noller, P., and V.J. Callan

1986 Adolescent and Parent Perceptions of Family Cohesion and Adaptability. *Journal of Adolescence.* 9:97-106.

O'Brien, M.M.

1997 Financing Strategies to Support Comprehensive, Community-based Services for Children and Families. National Child Welfare Resource Center for Organizational Improvement, The Finance Project.

Oden, S.

1995 Studying Youth Programs to Assess Influences on Youth Development: New Roles for Researchers. *Journal of Adolescent Research.* 10(1):173-186.

Office of Educational Research and Improvement.

1988 Youth Indicators 1988. Washington, DC: U.S. Government Printing Office.

Office of Juvenile Justice and Delinquency Prevention
1999   *OJJDP Factsheet on Juvenile Arrest Statistics: 1999.* Accessed 2001. Available online at: http://ojjdp.ncjrs.org.
Office of Juvenile Justice & Delinquency Prevention
1998   *Overview of the SafeFutures Program.* Accessed 2001. Available online at: ojjdp.ncjrs.org.
Ogbu, J.U.
1991   Immigrant and involuntary minorities in comparative perspective. Pp. 3-33 in *Minority Status and Schooling,* M.G. Gibson and J.U. Ogbu, Eds. New York: Garland.
1994   Understanding cultural diversity and learning. *Journal for the Education of the Gifted.* 17:355-383.
Olsen, D.
2000   12-Hour School Days? Why Government Should Leave Afterschool Arrangements to Parents. Vol. No. 372. Washington, DC: The Cato Institute.
Olweus, D., A. Mattssoon, D. Schalling, and H. Low
1988   Circulating Testosterone Levels and Aggression in Adolescent Males: A Causal Analysis. *Psychosomatic Medicine.* 50:261-272.
Osgood, D.W.
Having the Time of Their Lives: All Work and No Play? Pp. 176-186 in *Transitions to Adulthood in a Changing Economy: No Work, No Family, No Future?,* A. Booth, A.C. Crouter, and M.J. Shanahan, Eds. Westport, CT: Praeger Publishers.
Osgood, D.W., J.K. Wilson, P.M. O'Malley, J.G. Bachman, and L.D. Johnston
1996   Routine Activities and Individual Deviant Behavior. *American Sociological Review.* 61:635-655.
Ouellette, M.
2000   *Extra Learning Opportunities That Encourage Healthy Lifestyles.* Accessed 2000. Available online at: www.nga.org.
Paikoff, R.L., and J. Brooks-Gunn
1991   Do Parent-Child Relationships Change During Puberty. *Psychological Bulletin.* 110:47-66.
Partnership for Family Involvement in Education
2000   Working for Children and Families: Safe and Smart After-School Programs. Washington, DC: U.S. Department of Education & U.S. Department of Justice.
Pate, R.R., S.G. Trost, R. Mullis, J.F. Sallis, H. Wechsler, and D.R. Brown
2000   Community Intervention to Promote Proper Nutrition and Physical Activity Among Youth. *Preventative Medicine.* 31:S138-149.
Pate, R.R., D.S. Ward, G. Felton, R. Saunders, S.G. Trost, and M. Dowda
1997   Effects of a Community-Based Intervention to Promote Proper Nutrition and Physical Activity Among Youth. *Medicine and Science in Sports and Exercise.* 29(supplement):S157.
Pentz, M.A., D.P. MacKinnon, J.H. Dwyer, E.Y. Wang, W.B. Hansen, B.R. Flay, and C.A. Johnson
1989   Longitudinal Effects of the Midwestern Prevention Project on Regular and Experimental Smoking in Adolescents. *Preventative Medicine.* 18:304-321.
Pentz, M.A., J.H. Dwyer, D.P. MacKinnon, B.R. Flay, W.B. Hansen, Y.I. Wang, and A. Johnson
1989   A Multicommunity Trial for Primary Prevention of Adolescent Drug Abuse. *Journal of the American Medical Association.* 261(22):3259-3266.

Perry, C.L., S.H. Kelder, and K.-I. Klepp
  1994   Community-Wide Cardiovascular Disease Prevention in Young People. *European Journal of Public Health.* 4:188-194.
Perry, C.L., C.L. Williams, S. Veblen-Mortenson, T.L. Toomey, K.A. Komro, P.S. Anstine, P.G. McGovern, J.R. Finnegan, J.L. Forster, A.C. Wagenaar, and M. Wolfson
  1996   Project Northland: Outcomes of a Community wide Alcohol Use Prevention Program during Early Adolescence. *American Journal of Public Health.* 86(7):956-965.
Peshkin, A.
  1997   *Places of Memory: Whiteman's Schools and Native American Communities.* Mahwah, NJ: Lawrence Erlbaum Associates.
Peterson, A.
  1988   Adolescent Development. *Annual Review of Psychology.* 39:583-607.
Petersen, A., and B. Taylor
  1980   The Biological Approach to Adolescence: Biological Change and Psychosocial Adaptation. Pp. 117-155 in *Handbook of the Psychology of Adolescence,* J. Adelson, Ed. New York: Wiley.
Petersen, A.C., P.A. Sarigiani, and R.E. Kennedy
  1991   Adolescent Depression: Why More Girls? *Journal of Youth and Adolescence.* 20:247-271.
Petoskey, E.L., K.R. VanStelle, and J.A. DeJong
  1998   Prevention Through Empowerment in a Native American Community. *Drugs and Society.* 12(1/2):147-162.
Pettit, G.S., J.E. Bates, K.A. Dodge, and D.W. Meece
  1999   The Impact of After-School Peer Contact on Early Adolescent Externalizing Problems is Moderated by Parental Monitoring, Perceived Neighborhood Safety, and Prior Adjustment. *Child Development.* 70:768-778.
Phelan, P., and A.L. Davidson, Eds.
  1993   *Renegotiating Cultural Diversity in American Schools.* New York: Teachers College Press.
Phelan, P., A.L. Davison, and H.T. Cao
  1992   Speaking Up: Student's Perspectives on School. *Phi Delta Kappan.* 73(9):695-704.
Phillips, V.
  2000   Giving a Jump Start into Young Adulthood: After-School Mentoring Program Targets Girls from High-Crime Areas. *The Takoma Park Gazette* January 12: A1, A10.
Phinney J., I. Romero, M. Nava, and D. Huang
  in   *Influences on Ethnic Identity.* Los Angeles, CA: California State University.
press
Phinney, J.S.
  1990   Ethnic Identity in Adolescents and Adults: Review of Research. *Psychological Bulletin.* 108(3):499-514.
Phinney, J.S., C.L. Cantu, and D.A. Kurtz
  1997   Ethnic and American Identity as Predictors of Self-Esteem Among African American, Latino, and While Adolescents. *Journal of Youth and Adolescents.* 26:165-185.
Phinney, J.S., and E.L. Kohatsu
  1997   Ethnic and Racial Identity Development and Mental Health. Pp. 420-443 in *Health Crisis and Developmental Transitions in Adolescence,* J.J. Schulenberg, J. Maggs, and K. Hurrelman, Eds. New York: Cambridge University Press.

Piaget, J.
1964 Cognitive Development in Children. *Journal of Research in Science.* 2:176-186.
1971 *Biology and Knowledge.* Chicago, IL: University of Chicago Press.
Piaget J., and B. Inhelder
1973 *Memory and Intelligence.* London: Routledge and Kegan Paul.
Pintrich, P.R., R.W. Marx, and R.A. Boyle
1993 Beyond Cold Conceptual Change: The Role of Motivational Beliefs and Classroom Contextual Factors in the Process of Conceptual Change. *Review of Educational Research.* 63:167-199.
Pintrich, P.R., and D.H. Schunk
1996 *Motivation in Education: Theory, Research, and Applications.* Englewood Cliffs, N.J.: Merrill-Prentice Hall.
Pittman K.
1991 *Promoting Youth Development: Strengthening the Role of Youth Serving and Community Organizations.* Washington, D.C.: Center for Youth Development and Policy Research, Academy for Educational Development.
Pittman, K., T. Ferber, and M. Irby
1999 Developing and Deploying Young Leaders, Pittman, K., Irby, M., and Ferber, T. Takoma Park, MD: IYF-US, International Youth Foundation.
2000a Youth As Effective Citizens. Takoma Park, MD: International Youth Foundation.
2000b Unfinished Business: Further Reflections on a Decade of Promoting Youth Development. Takoma Park, MD: International Youth Foundation.
2000c What Fills the Empty Space? A Tool for Mapping Youth Investment, Pittman, K., Tolman, J., Ferber, T., and Irby, M. Takoma Park, MD: IYF-US, International Youth Foundation.
Pittman, K.J., and M. Irby
1996 Preventing Problems or Promoting Development: Competing Priorities or Inseparable Goals? Takoma Park, Maryland.
Plomin, R.
1994 Nature, Nurture, and Social Development. *Social Development.* 3:37-53.
2000 Behavioral Genetics in the 21st Century. *International Journal of Behavioral Development.* 24:30-34.
Policy Studies Associates
2000 Increasing and Improving After-School Opportunities: Evaluation Results From the TASC After-School Program's First Year: Executive Summary. Washington, DC: Policy Studies Associates, Inc.
Pollard, J.A., R.F. Catalano, J.D. Hawkins, M.W. Arthur, and A.J. Baglioni, Jr.
1999a *Measuring Risk and Protective Factors for Substance Abuse, Delinquency, and Other Problem Behaviors in Adolescent Populations. Technical Report SDRG #198.* Seattle, WA: Social Development Research Group.
1999b Running Head: Measuring Risk and Protective Factors. Seattle, Washington: Developmental Research and Programs, Inc.
Pollard, J.A., J.D. Hawkins, and M.W. Arthur
1999 Risk and Protection: Are Both Necessary to Understand Diverse Behavioral Outcomes in Adolescence? *Social Work Research.* 23(3):145-158.
Portes, A.
1998 Social Capital: Its Origins and Applications in Modern Sociology. *Annual Review of Sociology.* 24:1-24.
Portes, A., and P. Landolt
1996 The Downside of Social Capital. *The American Prospect.* 26:18-21.

Postrado, L.T., F.L. Weiss, and H.J. Nicholson
   1997   Prevention of sexual intercourse for teen women aged 12 to 14. *Prevention Researcher.* 4(1):10-12.
Prothrow-Stith, D., and M. Weissman
   1991   *Deadly Consequences.* New York: Harper Collins Publishers.
Quern, S., and D.M. Rauner
   1998   Working Paper on Administrative Resources and Supports for Grassroots Youth Programs: The Challenges to Providers and Ideas for Targeted Support. Chicago, IL: University of Chicago.
Quinn, J.
   1999   Where Need Meets Opportunity: Youth Development Programs for Early Teens. Pp. 96-116 in *The Future of Children: When School Is Out,* R. Behrman M.D., Editor. Washington, DC: The David and Lucile Packard Foundation.
Reder, N.D.
   2000   Finding Funding: A Guide to Federal Sources for Out-of-School Time and Community School Initiatives. Washington, DC: The Finance Project.
Resnick, M.D., P.S. Bearman, R.W. Blum, K.E. Bauman, K.M. Harris, J. Jones, J. Tabor, T. Beuhring, R.E. Sieving, M. Shew, M. Ireland, L.H. Bearinger, and J.R. Udry
   1997   Protecting Adolescents From Harm: Findings From the National Longitudinal Study on Adolescent Health. *The Journal of the American Medical Association.* 278(10):823-832.
Resnicow, K., T.N. Robinson, and E. Frank
   1996   Advances and Future Directions for School-Based Health Promotion Research: Commentary on CATCH Intervention Trial. *Preventative Medicine.* 25(4):378-383.
Richardson, J., and S. House
   1999   CRS Report for Congress. Children and Their Families: Federal Programs and Tax Provisions. Washington, DC: Congressional Research Service, The Library of Congress.
Richardson, J.L., K. Dwyer, K. McGuigan, W.B. Hansen, C.W. Dent, C.A. Johnson, S.Y. Sussman, B. Brannon, and B. Flay
   1989   Substance use among adolescents who take care of themselves after school. *Pediatrics.* 84:556-566.
Roaf, P.A., J.P. Tierney, and D.E.I. Hunte
   1994   Big Brothers/Big Sisters: A Study of Volunteer Recruitment and Screening. Philadelphia, PA: Public/Private Ventures.
Roberts, D.F., L. Henrikson, and P.G. Christenson
   1999   *Substance Use in Popular Movies and Music.* Rockville, MD: Office of National Drug Control Policy, Substance Abuse and Mental Health Services Administration.
Roberts, G.C., and D.C. Treasure
   1992   Children in Sport. *Sport Science Review.* 1(2):46-64.
Roberts, R., J. Phinney, L. Masse, Y. Chen, and I. Romero
   1999   The Structure of Ethnic Identity of Young Adolescents from Diverse Ethnocultural Groups. *Journal of Early Adolescence.* 19(3):301-322.
Robins, L.N., and J. Robertson
   1998   Exposure to 'Fateful' Events: A Confounder in Assigning Causal Roles to Life Events. Pp. 331-340 in *Adversity, Stress, and Psychopathology,* B.P. Dohrenwend, Ed. New York, NY: Oxford University Press.

Roderick, M.
1991   *The Path to Dropping Out: Evidence for Intervention.* Research Bulletin: Malcolm Wiener Center for Social Policy. Cambridge, MA: Harvard University, John F. Kennedy School of Government.
1993   *The Path to Dropping Out: Evidence for Intervention.* Westport, CT: Auburn House, Greenwood Publishing Group.
Roessel, M.
1993   *Kinaalda.* Minneapolis, MN: Lerner Publications.
Rogoff, B., J. Baker-Sennett, P. Lacasa, and D. Goldsmith
1995   Development Through Participation in Sociocultural Activity. Pp. 45-65 in *Cultural Practices As Contexts for Development*, J. Goodnow, P. Miller, and F. Kessel, Eds. San Francisco, CA: Jossey-Bass.
Romo, H.D., and T. Falbo
1996   *Latino High School Graduation.* Austin, TX: University of Texas Press.
Rook, A., and B. Alexander
1999   Youth Advocates Say Poor Kids Lose; Education Gets Boost. *Youth Today.* 24, 26-27.
Rosenbaum, J.E., D. Stern, M.A. Hamilton, S.F. Hamilton, S.E. Berryman, and R. Kazis
1992   *Youth Apprenticeship in America: Guidelines For Building an Effective System.* Washington, DC: William T. Grant Foundation Commission on Youth and America's Future.
Rosenberg, P.S., R.J. Biggar, and J.J. Goedert
1994   Declining Age at HIV Infection in the U.S. *New England Journal of Medicine.* 330(11):789-790.
Rosenbloom, A.L., J.R. Joe, B.S. Young, and W.E. Winter
1999   Emerging Epidemic of Type II Diabetes in Youth. *Diabetic Care.* 22:345-354.
Rosenholtz, S.J., and C. Simpson
1984   The Formation of Ability Conceptions: Developmental Trend or Social Construction? *Review of Educational Research.* 54:301-325.
Rosenthal R. and L. Jacobson
1968   *Pygmalion in the Classroom.* New York, NY: Rinehart & Winston.
Rossi A. S. and P. H. Rossi
1990   *Of Human Bonding.* New York: Aldine de Gruyter.
Roth, J.
2000   What We Know and What We Need to Know About Youth Development Programs. Paper presented as part of a symposium entitled Evaluations of Youth Development Programs at the biannual meeting of the Society for Research on Adolescence, Chicago, March 30, 2000.
Roth, J., and J. Brooks-Gunn
1999   How Research on Adolescence Can Inform Youth Development Programs in the Twenty-First Century. New York: Teachers College, Columbia University.
2000a What Do Adolescents Need for Healthy Development? Implications for Youth Policy. *Social Policy Report.* 14(2).
2000b *Running Head: Influences on Healthy Adolescent Development: From the Family to the Community.* New York: Center for Children and Families, Teachers College, Columbia University.
Roth J., J. Brooks-Gunn, B. Galen, L. Murray, P. Silverman, H. Liu, D. Man, and W. Foster
1997   *Promoting Healthy Adolescence: Youth Development Frameworks and Programs.* New York, NY: Columbia University, Teachers College.

Roth, J., J. Brooks-Gunn, L. Murray, and W. Foster
1998a Promoting Healthy Adolescents: Synthesis of Youth Development Program Evaluations. *Journal of Research on Adolescence.* 8(4):423-459.
Roth, J., J. Brooks-Gunn, T. Woods, L. Murray, W. Foster, and B. Galen
1998b Adolescents Out Of The Mainstream: The Potential of Youth Development Programs. *America's Disconnected Youth: Toward a Preventive Strategy,* D.J. Besharov and K.N. Gardiner, Eds. Washington, DC: Child Welfare League of America.
Ruben, K.H., W. Bukowski, and J.G. Parker
1998 Peer Interactions, Relationships, and Groups. Pp. 619-700 in *Handbook of Child Psychology,* 5th ed., W. Damon and N. Eisenberg, Eds. New York: Wiley.
Rutter, M.
2000 Psychosocial Influences: Critiques, Findings, and Research Needs. *Development and Psychopathology.* 12:375-405.
Rutter, M., J. Dunn, and R. Plomin
1997 Integrating Nature and Nurture: Implications of Person-Environment Correlations and Interactions for Developmental Psychopathology. *Development and Psychopathology.* 9:335-364.
Rutter, M., and N. Garmezy
1983 Developmental Psychopathology. Pp. 775-911 in *Handbook of Child Psychology: Socialization, Personality, and Social Development,* P.H. Mussen and E.M. Hetherington, Eds. New York: Wiley.
Rutter M., H. Giller, and A. Hagell
1998 *Antisocial Behavior by Young People.* Cambridge, UK: Cambridge University Press.
Rutter, M., and D. Smith
1995 Towards Causal Explanations of Time Trend in Psychological Disorders in Young People. Pp. 782-808 in *Psychological Disorders in Young People: Time Trends and Their Causes,* M. Rutter and D. Smith, Eds. New York: John Wiley.
Ryan, D.B.
1998 Kinaalda: The Pathway to Navajo Womanhood. *Native Peoples: The Journal of the Heard Museum.* Winter Edition.
Sabo, D., K. Miller, M. Farrell, G. Barnes, and M. Merrill
1998 *The Women's Sports Foundation Report: Sport and Teen Pregnancy.* East Meadow, NY: Women's Sports Foundation.
Sachs, J.
1997 The Boston Inventory: Putting Child Care Quality on the Map. *Child Care Bulletin.* (13).
Saito, R.N., and D.A. Blyth
1992 *Understanding Mentoring Relationships.* Minneapolis: Search Institute.
Sallis, J.F.
1993 Promoting Healthful Diet and Physical Activity. Pp. 209-241 in *Promoting the Health of Adolescents: New Directions for the Twenty-First Century,* S.G. Millstein, A.C. Peterson, and E.O. Nightingale, Eds. New York: Oxford University Press.
Sallis, J.F., T.L. McKenzie, and J.E. Alcaraz
1993 Habitual Physical Activity and Health-Related Physical Fitness in Fourth-Grade Children. *American Journal of Diseases of Children.* 147:890-896.
Sampson R. J. and J. H. Laub
1993 *Crime in the Making: Pathways and Turning Points Through Life.* Cambridge, MA: Harvard University Press.

1995 Understanding Variability in Lives Through Time. *Studies in Crime and Crime Prevention.* 4:143-158.

Sampson, R.J., and J. Morenoff
1997 Ecological Perspectives on the Neighborhood Context of Urban Poverty: Past and Present. Pp. 1-22 in *Neighborhood Poverty: Policy Implications in Studying Neighborhoods*, J. Brooks-Gunn, G.J. Duncan, and J.L. Aber, Eds. New York: Russell Sage Foundation Press.

Sampson, R.J.
2000 A Neighborhood-Level Perspective on Social Change and the Social Control of Adolescent Delinquency. Pp. 178-190 in *Negotiating Adolescence in Times of Social Change*, L. Crockett and R. Silbereisen, Eds. New York, NY: Cambridge University Press.

Sampson, R.J., S.W. Raudenbush, and F. Earls
1997 Neighborhoods and Violent Crime: A Multilevel Study of Collective Efficacy. *Science.* 277:918-924.

Scales, P.C.
1999 Increasing service-learning's impact on middle school students. *Middle School Journal.* 30(5):40-44.

Scales, P.C., and N. Leffert
1999 *Developmental Assets: A Synthesis of Scientific Research on Adolescent Development.* Minneapolis, MN: Search Institute.

Scales, P., P.L. Benson, N. Leffert, and D. Blyth
2000 Contribution of Developmental Assets to the Prediction of Thriving Among Adolescents. *Applied Developmental Science.* 4(1):27-46.

Schinke, S.P., M.A. Orlandi, and K.C. Cole
1993 Boys and girls clubs in public housing developments: Prevention services for youth at risk. *Journal of Community Psychology*, OSAP Special Issue, 28:118-128.

Schorr, L.B., and D. Yankelovich
2000 Perspective on Social Policy: What Works to Better Society Cannot Easily Be Measured. *Los Angeles Times.*

Schulte, B.
2000 In Kindergarten, A New Play on Academics: Some in Montgomery Question Bookish Approach. *The Washington Post* February 5: A1, A10.

Schunk, D.H.
1994 Self-regulation of self-efficacy and attributions in academic settings. In *Self-Regulation of Learning and Performance*, D. H. Schunk and B. J. Zimmerman, Eds. Hillsdale, NJ: Lawrence Erlbaum Associates.

Schunk, D.H., and B.J. Zimmerman
1994 *Self-Regulation of Learning and Performance.* Hillsdale, NJ: Lawrence Erlbaum Associates.

Schweinhart, L., H. Barnes, D. Weikart, W.S. Barnett, and A.S. Epstein
1993 Significant benefits: The High/Scope Perry Preschool study through age 27. *Monographs of the High/Scope Educational Research Foundation Number 10.* Ypsilanti, MI: High/Scope Press.

Schweinhart, L.J., and D.P. Weikart
1997 The High/Scope Preschool Curriculum Comparison Study through Age 23. *Early Childhood Research Quarterly.* 12(2):117-143.

Search Institute
2000a *Profiles of Student Life: Attitudes and Behaviors. General Information.* Minneapolis, MN: Search Institute.

2000b *Youth Development in Congregations: Applicability of Asset Buliding to the Faith Community.* Accessed 2000. Available online at: www.search-institute.org/congregations/assetbuilding.htm.

Seefeldt, V., M. Ewing, and S. Walk
1995   Overview of Youth Sports Programs in the United States. East Lansing, MI: Youth Sports Institute, Michigan State University.

Selman, R.L.
1980   *The Growth of Interpersonal Understanding.* New York: Academic Press.

Serbin, L.A., J.M. Cooperman, P.L. Peters, P.M. Lehoux, D.M. Stack, and A.E. Schwartzman
1998   Intergenerational Transfer of Psychosocial Risk in Women with Childhood Histories of Aggression, Withdrawal, or Aggression and Withdrawal. *Developmental Psychology.* 34(6):1246-1262.

Shadish, W.R., T.D. Cook, and D. Campbell
2001   *Experimental and Quasi-Experimental Designs for Generalized Causal Inference.* New York, NY: Houghton-Mifflin.

Shatté, A., and K. Reivich
no date Executive Summary: The Penn Resiliency Project. Philadelphia, PA: University of Pennsylvania.

Sherwood, K.E., and F. Doolittle
2000   What's Behind the Impacts: Doing Implementation Research in the Context of Program Impact Studies. Prepared for the Institute for Research on Poverty.

Shweder, R.A., J. Goodnow, G. Hatano, R.A. Levine, H. Markus, and P. Miller
1998   The Cultural Psychology of Human Development: One Mind, Many Mentalities. Pp. 865-938 in *Handbook of Child Psychology: Theoretical Models of Human Development*, 5th ed., W. Damon and R.M. Lerner, Eds. New York: Wiley.

Siegler, R.S.
1986   *Children's Thinking.* Englewood Cliffs, NJ: Prentice Hall.

Silbereisen, R.K., A.C. Petersen, H.T. Albrecht, and B. Kracke
1989   Maturational timing and the development of problem behavior. *Journal of Early Adolescence.* 9:247-268.

Silberg, J., M. Rutter, M. Neale, and L. Eaves
in   Genetic Moderation of Environmental Risk for Depression and Anxiety in Ado-
press   lescent Girls. *British Journal of Psychiatry.* Special Issue.

Simmons, R.G., and D.A. Blyth
1987   *Moving into Adolescence: The Impact of Pubertal Change and School Context.* Hawthorn, NY: Aldine de Gruyler.

Sipe, C.A.
1996   Mentoring: A Synthesis of Public/Private Venture's Research: 1988-1995. Philadelphia, PA: Public/Private Ventures.

Sipe, C.L., P. Ma, and M.A. Gambone
1998   *Support for Youth: A Profile of Three Communities.* Community Change for Youth Development. Philadelphia, PA: Public/Private Ventures.

Skinner, E.A.
1995   *Perceived Control, Motivation, and Coping.* Thousand Oaks, CA: Sage Publications.

Slavin, R.E.
1995   Enhancing intergroup relations in schools: Cooperative learning and other strategies. Pp. 291-314 in *Toward a Common Destiny: Improving Race and Ethnic Relations in America*, W.D. Hawley and A.W. Jackson, Eds. San Francisco, CA: Jossey-Bass.

Small, S., and B. Hug
  1991 *Teen Assessment Project*. Accessed 2001. Available online at: www.joe.org.
Small, S.A., and P.M. Day
  2000 *What Teenagers Need from Parents, Teachers and Other Adults*. Accessed 2001.
         Available online at: www.gibraltar.k12.wi.us.
Smetana, J.G.
  1995 Parenting styles and conceptions of parental authority during adolescence. *Child
         Development*. 66:299-316.
Smetana, J.G., J. Yau, and S. Hanson
  1991 Conflict resolution in families with adolescents. *Journal of Research on Adoles-
         cence*. 1:189-206.
Smith, S.
  1999 America's Youth: Measuring the Risk. Washington, DC: The Institute for Youth
         Development.
Smoll, F.L., R.E. Smith, N.P. Barnett, and J.J. Everett
  1993 Enhancement of Children's Self-Esteem Through Social Support Training for
         Youth Sport Coaches. *Journal of Applied Psychology*. 78(4):603-610.
Spencer, M.B.
  1995 Old Issues and New Theorizing about African-American Youth: A Phenomeno-
         logical Variant of the Ecological Systems Theories. Pp. 37-70 in *Black Youth:
         Perspectives on Their Status in the United States*, R.L. Taylor, Ed. New York:
         Praeger.
Spencer, M.B., D. Dupree, D.P. Swanson, and M. Cunningham
  1998 The Influence of Physical Maturation with Family Hassles in African American
         Adolescent Males. *Journal of Comparative Family Studies*. 29.
Spencer, M.B., J.L. Aber, S.P. Cole, S.M. Jones, and D.P. Swanson
  1997 Neighborhood and Family Influences on Young Urban Adolescents' Behavior
         Problems: A Multisample, Multisite Analysis. Pp. 212-336 in *Neighborhood
         Poverty: Context and Consequences for Children*, J. Brooks-Gunn, G. Duncan,
         and J.L. Aber, Eds. New York, NY: Russell Sage Foundation Press.
Spencer, M.B., and C. Markstrom-Adams
  1990 Identity processes among racial and ethnic minority children. *Child Develop-
         ment*. 61:290-310.
Spencer, M.B., P.A. McDermott, L. Burton, and T.J. Kochman
  1997 An Alternative Approach to Assessing Neighborhood Effects on Early Adoles-
         cent Achievement and Problem Behavior. Pp. 157-240 in *Neighborhood Pov-
         erty: Context and Consequences for Children*, J. Brooks-Gunn, G. Duncan, and
         J.L. Aber, Eds. New York, NY: Russell Sage Foundation Press.
Stattin, H., and D. Magnusson
  1990 *Pubertal Maturation in Female Development*. Hillsdale, NJ: Lawrence Erlbaum
         Associates.
Steele, C.M.
  1992 Race and the Schooling of Black Americans. *The Atlantic Monthly*. 269(4):67-
         78.
Steele, C.M., and J. Aronson
  1995 Stereotype Threat and the Intellectual Test Performance of African-Americans.
         Journal of Personality and Social Psychology.
Steinberg, L.
  1990 Autonomy, conflict, and harmony in the family relationship. Pp. 54-89 in *At the
         Threshold: The Developing Adolescent*, S.S. Feldman and G.R. Elliott, Eds.
         Cambridge, MA: Harvard University Press.

1997   *Beyond the Classroom: Why School Reform Has Failed and What Parents Need to Do.* Touchstone Books.

1999   *Adolescence.* Boston, MA: McGraw-Hill.

2000   We know some things: Parent-adolescent relations in retrospect and prospect. *Journal of Research in Adolescence.*

Steinberg, L., S.M. Dornbush, and B.B. Brown
1992   Ethnic Differences in Adolescent Achievement: An Ecological Perspective. *American Psychologist.* 47:723-729.

Steinberg, L., S. Fegley, and S.M. Dornbusch
1993   Negative impact of part-time work on adolescent adjustment: Evidence from a longitudinal study. *Developmental Psychology.* 29:171-180.

Steinberg, L., and A.S. Morris
2001   Adolescent development. *Annual Review of Psychology.*

Steinberg, L., N.S. Mounts, S.D. Lamborn, and S.M. Dornbusch
1991   Authoritative parenting and adolescent adjustment across varied ecological niches. *Journal of Research on Adolescence.* 1:19-36.

Stepp, L.S.
2000   Teenagers, Rising to the Challenge. *The Washington Post* March 9: C4.

Stevenson, D.L., and D.P. Baker
1987   The family-school relation and the child's school performance. *Child Development.* 58:1348-1357.

Stevenson, H.C.
1995   Relationship of Adolescent Perceptions of Racial Socialization to Racial Identity. *Journal of Black Psychology.* 21:49-70.

Strauss, V.
2000   Who Needs Homework? Parents and Professionals Alike Disagree on the Purpose of After-Hours Lessons. *The Washington Post* February 8: A11.

Strazzullo, P., F.P. Cappuccio, M. Tregvisan, A. DeLeo, V. Krogh, N. Giorgione, and M. Mancini
1988   Leisure Time Physical Activity and Blood Pressure in School Children. *American Journal of Epidemiology.* 127:726-733.

Stukas, A., G. Clary, and M. Snyder
1999   Service Learning: Who Benefits and Why. *Social Policy Report.* 13(4):1-19.

Sullivan, H.S.
1953   *The Interpersonal Theory of Psychiatry.* New York: Norton.

Suplee, C.
2000   Key Brain Growth Goes On Into Teens: Study Disputes Old Assumptions. *The Washington Post* March 9: A1, A14.

Susman, E.J., G. Inoff-Germain, E.D. Nottelmann, D.L. Loriaux, C.B. Cutler, and G.P. Chrousos
1987   Hormones, Emotional Dispositions, and Aggressive Attributes in Young Adolescents. *Child Development.* 58:1114-1134.

Task Force on Community Preventive Services
2000   Introducing the Guide to Community Preventive Services: Methods, First Recommendations and Expert Commentary. *American Journal of Preventive Medicine.* 18(1S).

Tatum, B.D.
1997   *Why Are All the Black Kids Sitting Together in the Cafeteria? And Other Conversations About Race.* New York, NY: Basic Books.

Templeton, J.
2000   Transitions in Youth Development: From Deficiency to Resiliency.

Terao, K., L. Morell, and C. Stevenson
2000   Save the Children, Inc U.S. Programs: 1998-99 Web of Support Initiative Wide Evaluation—Summary. San Mateo, CA: The Aguirre Group.

Thompson, R.
2000   The Edge of Innocence. *Washington Post Magazine* March 19: 9-15, 25-27.

Tierney, J.P., J.B. Grossman, and N.L. Resch
1995   Making a Difference: An Impact Study of Big Brothers Big Sisters. Philadelphia, PA: Public/Private Ventures.

Timberland Company
2000   Community Investment Guidelines. Accessed 2000. Available online at: http://www.timberland.com/belief/believe/investment.html.

Timmer, S.G., J. Eccles, and K. O'Brien
1985   How Children Use Time. Pp. 353-381 in *Time, Goods, and Well-Being*, F.T. Juster and F.P. Stafford, Eds. Ann Arbor, MI: Institute for Social Research.

Tong, S., I.D. Frasier, S. Ingenito, A.L. Sica, N. Gootman, and P.M. Gootman
1997   Age-related effects of cardiac sympathetic denervation on the responses to cardiopulmonary receptor stimulation in piglets. *Pediatric Research*. 41(1):72-77.

Traub, J.
2000   Schools Are Not the Answer. *The New York Times Magazine* January 16: 52-57, 68,83, 90-91.

Treuth, M.S., G.R. Hunter, R. Figueroa-Colon, and M.I. Goran
1998   Effects of Strength Training on Intra-Abdominal Adipose Tissue in Obese Prepubertal Girls. *Medicine and Science in Sports and Exercise*. 30:1738-1743.

Trioiano, R.P., K.M. Flegal, R.J. Kuczmarski, S.M. Campbell, and C.L. Johnson
1995   Overweight Prevalence and Trends for Children and Adolescents: The National Health and Nutrition Examination Surveys, 1963-1991. *Archives of Pediatrics and Adolescent Medicine*. 149:1085-1091.

Truman, B.I., C.K. Smith-Akin, A.R. Hinman, K.M. Gebbie, R. Brownson, L. Novick, R.S. Lawrence, M. Pappaioanou, J. Fielding, C.A. Evans, F. Guerra, M. Vogel-Taylor, C. Mahan, M. Fullilove, and S. Zaza
1989   Developing the Guide to Community Preventive Services-Overview and Rationale, U.S. Task Force on Community Preventive Services. Washington, DC: U.S. Department of Health and Human Services.

Turiel E.
1983   *The Development of Social Knowledge: Morality and Convention*. Cambridge: Cambridge University Press.
1999   Conflict, Social Development, and Cultural Change. *New Directions for Child and Adolescent Development*. 83:77-92.

U.S. Bureau of the Census
1997   Current Population Reports. Pp. 60-197 in *Money Income in the U.S.: 1996*. Washington, DC: U.S. Government Printing Office, U.S. Department of Education.

U.S. Department of Agriculture
2001   *CYFAR Program Overview*. U.S. Department of Agriculture: Children, Youth and Families at Risk. Accessed 2001. Available online at: www.reeusda.gov.

U.S. Department of Education
1998   *Communities Meeting the Need for After-School Activities*. Accessed 2001. Available online at: www.ed.gov.
1998   *Communities Meeting the Need for After-School Activities: Overview of LA's BEST Program*. Accessed 2000. Available online at: www.ed.gov.
1998   *Communities Meeting the Need for After-School Activities: Overview of the Beacon School Based Community Centers*. Accessed 2000. Available online at: www.ed.gov.

2000   *General Listing of All 21st Century Community Learning Centers.* Accessed 2000. Available online at: www.ed.gov/CFAPPS/CCLC.

U.S. Department of Health and Human Services

2001   *Toward a Blueprint for Youth: Making Positive Youth Development a National Priority.* Accessed 2001. Available online at: www.acf.dhhs.gov.

U.S. Department of Health and Human Services, and Office of the Assistant Secretary for Planning and Evaluation

1999a   Trends in the Well-Being of America's Children and Youth. Washington, DC: U.S. Department of Health and Human Services.

U.S. Department of Health and Human Services, and Substance Abuse and Mental Health Services Administration

1999b   National Household Survey on Drug Abuse. Washington, DC: U.S. Department of Health and Human Services.

U.S. Department of Labor

1997   *National Longitudinal Survey of Youth.* Accessed 2001. Available online at: www.bls.gov.

2000   *U.S. Department of Labor: Employment and Training Administration (Los Angeles, CA Community Development Department).* Accessed 2001. Available online at: www.doleta.gov.

U.S. General Accounting Office

1997   Welfare Reform: Implications of Increased Work Participation for Child Care. Washington, DC: U.S. General Accounting Office.

1998   Abstracts of GAO Reports & Testimony, FY 97. Washington, DC: U.S. General Accounting Office. Available online at: www.gao.gov.

Udry, J.R., L. Talbert, and N.M. Morris

        Biosocial foundations of adolescent female sexuality. Paper presented at the annual meeting of the American Sociological Association, Washington, DC.

United Way of America

1999   Achieving and Measuring Community Outcomes: Challenges, Issues, Some Approaches. Alexandria, VA: United Way of America.

1998   Watching Out for Children In Changing Times: Safe, Stimulated and Supervised in the Non-School Hours: A Report on Youth Programs, United Way of Southeastern Pennsylvania and Philadelphia Citizens for Children and Youth. Philadelphia, PA: United Way of Southeastern Pennsylvania/Philadelphia Citizens for Children and Youth.

University of California, Berkeley

2001   *Lawrence Hall of Science.* Accessed 2001. Available online at: www.lhs.berkeley.edu.

Vandell, D.L., and J.K. Posner

1999   Conceptualization and Measurement of Children's After-School Environments. Pp. 167-198 in *Measuring Environment Across the Life Span*, S.L. Friedman and T.D. Wachs, Eds. Washington, DC: American Psychological Association Press.

Voors, A.W., D.W. Hasha, L.S. Webber, B. Radhakrishamurthy, S.R. Srinivasan, and G.S. Berenson

1982   Clustering of Anthropometric Parameters, Glucose Tolerance, and Serum Lipids in Children With High and Low B and Pre B Lipoproteins: Bogalusa Heart Study. *Arteriosclerosis.* 2:346-355.

Vygotsky, L.S.

1962   *Language and Thought.* Cambridge, MA: MIT Press.

1978   *Interaction Between Learning and Development.* Cambridge, MA: Harvard Press.

W.K. Kellogg Foundation
  1998   Safe Passages Though Adolescence: Communities Protecting the Health and Hopes of Youth. Battle Creek, MI: W.K. Kellogg Foundation.
Walker, J.D., Jurich S., and American Youth Policy Forum
  1999   More Things That Do Make a Difference for Youth: A Compendium of Evaluations of Youth and Practices. Washington, DC: American Youth Policy Forum.
Walker, K., and L. Kotloff
  2000   Plain Talk: Addressing Adolescent Sexuality Through a Community Initiative. Philadelphia, PA: Public/Private Ventures.
Walker, K.E., B.H. Watson, and L.Z. Jucovy
  1999   Resident Involvement in Community Change: The Experiences of Two Initiatives. Philadelphia, PA: Public/Private Ventures.
Walsh, M.
  2001   Bush Eyes After-School Role for Faith Groups. *Education Week*. Copyright 2001.
Ward, B.A., J.R. Mergendoller, W.J. Tikunoff, T.S. Rounds, G.J. Dadey, and A.L. Mitman
  1982   *Junior High School Transition Study: Executive Summary.* San Francisco, CA: Far West Laboratory.
Waterman, A.L.
  1982   Identity Development from Adolescence to Adulthood: An Extension of Theory and a Review of Research. *Developmental Psychology.* 18:341-358.
Wehlage, G., F.M. Newmann, and W. Secada
  1996   Pp. 21-48 in *Authentic Achievement: Restructuring Schools for Intellectual Quality*, F.M. Newmann and Associates, Eds. San Francisco: Jossey-Bass.
Weiss, C.H.
  1995   Nothing As Practical As Good Theory: Exploring Theory-Based Evaluation for Comprehensive Community Initiatives for Children and Families. *New Approaches to Evaluating Community Initiatives: Concepts, Methods, and Contexts*, J. Connell, A. Kubisch, L. Schorr, and C. Weiss, Eds. Washington, DC: The Aspen Institute.
  1998   *Evaluation.* Upper Saddle River, NJ: Prentice Hall.
Weiss, H.
  2000   Reinventing Evaluation to Build High Performance Child and Family Interventions. Washington, DC: Institute for Law and Justice.
Weiss, H., and W. Morrill
  1999   Useful Learning for Public Action. *The Evaluation Exchange.* 2-4,14.
Weiss, H.B., and M.E. Lopez
  1999   New Strategies In Foundation Grantmaking For Children and Youth. Cambridge, MA: Harvard Family Research Project. http://hugse1.harvard.edu/~hfrp.
Wentzel, K.R.
  1991   Relations between social competence and academic achievement in early adolescence. *Child Development.* 62:1066-1078.
Werner, E.E., and R.S. Smith
  1982   *Vulnerable but Invincible: A Study of Resilient Children.* New York: McGraw-Hill.
  1992   *Overcoming the Odds.* Ithaca, NY: Cornell University Press.
West, K.K., and J.G. Robinson
  1999   *What Do We Know About the Undercount of Children? Population Division Working Paper No. 39.* Washington, DC: U.S. Bureau of the Census.
Wichstrom, L.
  1999   The emergence of gender difference in depressed mood during adolescence: The role of intensified gender socialization. *Developmental Psychology.* 35:232-245.

Wigfield, A., J. Eccles, D. MacIver, D. Reuman, and C. Midgley
  1991   Transitions at Early Adolescence: Changes in Children's Domain-Specific Self-Perceptions and General Self-Esteem Across the Transition to Junior High School. *Developmental Psychology.* 27:552-565.

Wigfield, A., and J.S. Eccles
  1992   The Development of Achievement Task Values: A Theoretical Analysis. *Developmental Review.* 12:265-310.

Wiggins, G., and J. McTighe
  1998   *Understanding by Design.* Alexandria, VA: Association for Supervision and Curriculum Development.

Wilgoren, J.
  2000   The Bell Rings but the Students Stay, and Stay. *The New York Times* January 24: A1, A18.

William T. Grant Commission on Work Family and Citizenship
  2000   The Forgotten Half: Pathways to Success for America's Youth and Young Families. Philadelphia, PA: Public/Private Ventures.

Wilson W.J.
  1987   *The Truly Disadvantaged: The Inner City, the Underclass and Public Policy.* Chicago, IL: University of Chicago Press.

Winkleby, M.A.
  1994   The Future of Community-Based Cardiovascular Disease Intervention Studies. *American Journal of Public Health.* 84:1369-1372.

Winnicott, D.W.
  1975   *Through Pediatrics to Psychoanalysis.* New York: Basic Books.

Winters, R.
  1999   A Portrait of Adolescence: A Focus Group Report. Washington, DC: Institute for Youth Development.

Wittgenstein L.
  1953   *Philosophical Investigations.* New York: Macmillan USA.

Wong, C., J.S. Eccles, and A.S. Sameroff
  no date Ethnic Identity as a Buffer Against Racial Discrimination. Unpublished Manuscript.

Wong, C.A., and E.D. Taylor
  1998   The Context of Peers in the Lives of African-American and White Adolescents. Paper presented at the 7th Biennial Meeting of the Society for Research on Adolescence, San Diego.

Wynn, J.R.
  2000   The Role of Local Intermediary Organizations in the Youth Development Field. Chicago, IL: The Chapin Hall Center for Children at the University of Chicago.

Yates, M., and J. Youniss
  1998   Community Service and Political Identity Development in Adolescence. *Journal of Social Issues.* 54:495-512.

Yates, M., and J. Youniss, Eds.
  1999   *Roots of Civic Identity.* Cambridge: Cambridge University Press.

YMCA of the USA
  2001   After School for America's Teens: A National Survey of Teen Attitudes and Behaviors in the Hours After School [Executive Summary] YMCA of the USA.

Youniss, J.
  1980   *Parents and Peers in Social Development.* Chicago, IL: University of Chicago Press.

  1997   *Community Service and Social Responsibility in Youth.* Chicago, IL: University of Chicago Press.

Youniss, J., J.A. McLellan, and M. Yates
  1997   What We Know About Engendering Civic Identity. *American Behavioral Scientist.* 40:620-631.

Youth Policy Forum
  2001   *Is the Concept of Full Service Community Schools Ready For Federal Support?* Accessed 2001. Available online at: www.aypf.org.

Yu, H.C., S. Soukamneuth, and M. Lazarin
  1999   Navigating the Ethnic and Racial Borders of Multiple Peer Worlds. Oakland, CA: Social Policy Research Associates.

Zahn-Waxler, C., B. Klimes-Dougan, and M. Slattery
  in   Internalizing problems of childhood and adolescence: Prospects, pitfalls, and
  press   progress in understanding the development of anxiety and depression. *Developmental Psychopathology.*

Zeldin, R.S., and L.A. Prince
  1995   Creating Supportive Communities for Adolescent Development: Challenges to Scholars. *Journal of Adolescent Research.* 10(1):1-14.

Zeldin, S.
  1995   Opportunities and Supports for Youth Development: Lessons From Research and Implications for Community Leaders and Scholars. Washington, DC: Center for Youth Development and Policy Research, Academy for Educational Development.

  1995   An Introduction to Youth Development Concepts: Questions for Community Collaborations. Washington, DC: Center for Youth Development and Policy Research, Academy for Educational Development.

  2000   Integrating Research and Practice to Understand and Strengthen Communities for Adolescent Development: An Introduction to the Special Issue and Current Issues. *Applied Developmental Science.* 4(1):2-10.

Zeldin, S., M. Kimball, and L. Price
  1995   What Are the Day-to-Day Experiences That Promote Youth Development? An Annotated Bibliography of Research on Adolescents and Their Families. Washington, DC: Center for Youth Development and Policy Research, Academy for Educational Development.

Zemelman, S., H. Daniels, and A. Hyde
  1998   *Best Practice: New Standards for Teaching and Learning in America's Schools.* Portsmouth, NH: Heinemann.

Zerbe, R., and D. Dively
  1997   *Benefit Cost Analysis: In Theory and Practice.* New York, NY: Addison-Wesley Educational Publishers.

Zill, N., C.W. Nord, and L.S. Loomis
  1995   Adolescent Time Use, Risky Behavior, and Outcomes: An Analysis of National Data. Rockville, MD: Westat, Inc.

Zimmerman, B.J.
  1989   A Social Cognitive View of Self-Regulated Learning. *Journal of Educational Psychology.* 81:329-339.

  2000   Attaining Self-Regulation: A Social-Cognitive Perspective. Pp. 13-39 in *Handbook of Self-Regulation*, M. Boekaerts, P.R. Pintrich, and M.H. Zeidner, Eds. San Diego: Academic Press.

Zimmerman, B.J., A. Bandura, and M. Martinez-Pons
  1992   Self-Motivation for Academic Attainment: The Role of Self-Efficacy Beliefs and Personal Goal Setting. *American Educational Research Journal.* 29:663-676.

Index